Jews and Judaism in World History

This book is a survey of the history of the Jewish people from biblical antiquity to the present, spanning nearly 2,500 years and traversing five continents.

Opening with a broad introduction that addresses key questions of terminology and definition, the book's ten chapters then go on to explore Jewish history in both its religious and non-religious dimensions. The book explores the social, political, and cultural aspects of Jewish history, and examines the changes and continuities across the whole of the Jewish world throughout its long and varied history. Topics covered include:

- the emergence of Judaism as a religion and way of life, from the world of the ancient Israelites as recounted in the Hebrew Bible through to encounters with the Greco-Roman civilization, and with Roman, Byzantine, Persian, Islamic and Christian rule
- the development during the Middle Ages of Judaism as an all-encompassing identity
- the effect on Jewish life and identity of major changes in Europe and the Islamic world from the mid-sixteenth through the end of the nineteenth century
- the complexity of Jewish life in the twentieth century, the challenge of anti-Semitism and the impact of the Holocaust, and the emergence of the current centers of world Jewry in the State of Israel and the New World.

Exploring the overarching themes that bind this complex history, while also taking care to note the broad diversity of the Jewish experience, this book will be a vital tool to all students of world history.

Howard N. Lupovitch is the Waks Family Associate Professor of Jewish History at the University of Western Ontario. He is the author of *Jews at the Crossroads: Tradition and Accommodation during the Golden Age of the Hungarian Nobility* (2007).

Themes in World History
Series editor: Peter N. Stearns

The Themes in World History series offers focused treatment of a range of human experiences and institutions in the world history context. The purpose is to provide serious, if brief, discussions of important topics as additions to textbook coverage and document collections. The treatments will allow students to probe particular facets of the human story in greater depth than textbook coverage allows, and to gain a fuller sense of historians' analytical methods and debates in the process. Each topic is handled over time – allowing discussions of changes and continuities. Each topic is assessed in terms of a range of different societies and religions – allowing comparisons of relevant similarities and differences. Each book in the series helps readers deal with world history in action, evaluating global contexts as they work through some of the key components of human society and human life.

Jews and Judaism in World History

Howard N. Lupovitch

Routledge
Taylor & Francis Group

LONDON AND NEW YORK

First published 2010
by Routledge
2 Park Square, Milton Park, Abingdon, Oxon OX14 4RN

Simultaneously published in the USA and Canada
by Routledge
270 Madison Ave, New York, NY 10016

Routledge is an imprint of the Taylor & Francis Group, an informa business

Typeset in Garamond by GreenGate Publishing Services, Tonbridge, Kent
Printed and bound in Great Britain by CPI Antony Rowe, Chippenham, Wiltshire

British Library Cataloguing in Publication Data
A catalogue record for this book is available
from the British Library

Library of Congress Cataloguing in Publication Data
Lupovitch, Howard N.
Jews and Judaism in world history /
Howard N. Lupovitch. – 1st ed.
p. cm. – (Themes in world history)
Includes bibliographical references.
1. Jews–History. 2. Judaism–History. I. Title.
DS117.L87 2009
909'.04924–dc22
2009026704

ISBN10: 0-415-46204-5 (hbk)
         0-415-46205-3 (pbk)
         0-203-86197-3 (ebk)

ISBN13: 978-0-415-46204-4 (hbk)
         978-0-415-46205-1 (pbk)
         978-0-203-86197-4 (ebk)

Contents

For Dahvi and Hanna

The aim of this book is to provide students of Jewish History with a compact, one-volume history of the Jews from antiquity to the present. As such, this book has benefitted from my exchanges with dozens of colleagues who specialize in various areas of Jewish History. Throughout I have tried to appose a straightforward narrative with more in-depth analysis and discussion of recent scholarly debates on various aspects of this narrative. In order to allow readers to encounter the historical experiences of Jews through the words of those who lived through or observed these events, I have included numerous direct quotations. Limitations on length precluded the use of footnotes or endnotes, so most of these direct quotations were drawn from one of the primary sources included in the list of further reading. In the end, I hope that readers will come to discover and embrace, as I have, the notion that a greater familiarity with the whole of Jewish History facilitates and enhances one's understanding of any part of that history.

Introduction: dimensions of Jewish history

Jewish history is more than the history of a religion called Judaism. Although Judaism is a central component, Jewish history also recounts the development of a civilization with a complex social order and political culture, and generations of social relations between Jews, and between Jews and non-Jews. Jewish civilization has been around in one form or another for more than three millennia, and has traversed five continents, from central Asia to the New World. Jews have come within the perception of intellectuals and statesmen from Aristotle to Zola, and have lived in a wide variety of contexts, including the ancient Near East, the Hellenistic world, Rome, Byzantium, Islam, Christendom, Europe, Russia, and the New World.

Given this diverse array of situations and vast time span, it is essential to begin by defining what is meant by Jew, Jewish, and Judaism. The term Jew or *Yehudi* is derived from the ancient Israelite kingdom of Judah or *Yehuda*. It was first used as a descriptor in reference to Mordechai ha-Yehudi, Mordechai the Jew, the uncle of Queen Esther and one of the protagonists in the biblical story of Esther. Mordechai the Jew is described as being among those "who were exiled from Jerusalem by Nebuchadnezzar, king of Babylonia, in 597 B.C.E." Strictly speaking, therefore, there were no Jews before the Babylonian exile. Biblical figures such as Abraham, Moses, David, Solomon, and the prophets are more aptly referred to as Hebrews or Israelites than as Jews.

The question remains, are the Jews best defined as a people, as the members of a religious faith, as a nation, or as an ethnicity? All of these designations have been tried in the past and all remain valid definitions of at least some facets of Jewish life. At some point, Jews were most easily recognizable and definable as one or more of these descriptions. Though ostensibly a matter of taxonomy and semantics, the problem of defining the Jews as a group points to the larger problem of encapsulating the diversity of the Jewish experience within a single narrative. Yet is it possible to encompass this diversity and multiplicity within a single historical narrative?

In answer to that question, historian Michael Meyer has suggested the metaphor of a rope. A rope is made up of strands none of which extends from one end to the other, yet the strands, still hold the rope together as a single coherent entity. So, too, the history of the Jews. Jews in the twentieth century are so vastly different from their ancient counterparts that there may be no common thread that runs the gamut of Jewish history from antiquity to the present. Thus, the challenge for the present-day reader and writer of Jewish history is to flesh out the strands of this rope and the connections between them without disregarding how different the strands are from one another.

Three aspects of Jewish history, in particular, are sufficiently broad to encompass the diversity of Jewish experience, but together add up to a distinct history. First, the history of the Jews is the history of a small people surrounded by larger, more powerful peoples. Whether a small independent kingdom amid neighboring empires or a small religious or ethnic minority living under foreign rule, Jews were faced with the challenge of preserving their culture in the face of alluring alternatives that were often culturally more sophisticated. In every age, there were Jews who chose these alternatives over their Jewish identity. Yet there were also Jews who struck a workable balance, living with one foot in the world of Jewish tradition and culture, and the other in the world of the mainstream. Every period and episode in Jewish history bears the imprint of a larger world in which Jews lived. Jewish identity, individual and communal, developed as a series of amalgams between an existing Jewish heritage and aspects of the surrounding non-Jewish world that were emulated and recast in an acceptable Jewish light.

Second, the complexity of Jewish history means that there has been a recurring or chronic tension between a search for uniformity and a search for diversity in Judaism and Jewish life. Recently, there has been a tendency to avoid referring to a single, monolithic Jewish experience. Instead, historians now speak of "Judaisms" instead of Judaism, and "cultures of the Jews" instead of Jewish culture. Indeed, the diversity of Jewish history and the multiplicity of Jewish experiences are undeniable. At the same time, though, twenty-first-century Jews still feel somehow connected to their ancient predecessors

Third, the tension between uniformity and diversity was at once complicated and facilitated by a series of migrations by Jews from one part of the world to another. It was complicated because migration meant dislocation and was often the result of some form of adversity: military defeat, religious persecution, or economic hardship. Migrating to a new home meant setting down new roots, rebuilding a life, and coming to terms with a new society and state and the accompanying array of new challenges and expectations. It was facilitated because Jews never arrived into a new homeland empty-handed; rather, they brought with them the cultural and communal baggage of their former home, and transplanted them into their new home. Starting over almost never meant starting entirely from scratch. Each new center of Jewish life built on the successes and learned from the difficulties of its predecessors. The seemingly endemic nature of Jewish migration gives an image of an overriding sense of Jewish homelessness and rootlessness in the diaspora.

This may have been true from time to time, but as often as not, Jews felt very much at home in the places where they lived, especially in those places where they lived for centuries.

This sense of rootedness may seem odd, especially for those who approach Jewish history from what Salo Baron called a "lachrymose view." Baron correctly noted a prevailing yet erroneous view that contends that Jewish history is a history of endless suffering and persecution. This view was validated in retrospect by the fact that every center of Jewish life eventually came to an end, and more recently by the Holocaust.

The notion of perpetual Jewish adversity in the diaspora is at the heart of several different approaches to Jewish history. The traditional rabbinic approach regards the worship or acknowledgment of God, the observance of Jewish laws, and the study of the Torah as the common thread of the Jewish experience. This approach equates good for and bad for Jews with good for Judaism and bad for Judaism ("Jewish history is Rashi and the Rambam [Maimonides]"). Jewish suffering and the persecution of Jews were seen as divine retribution for religious laxity and indifference. Zionist historians, though downplaying the role of religious observance and divine providence, embraced the lachrymose view of Jewish history to underline the futility of Jewish life in the diaspora and the overriding need to move to Israel.

Those who have sustained this lachrymose point of view have had to resort to connecting the dots between a series of adverse situations: the Crusades, the Black Death, the Age of Expulsions, the Italian ghettos, the Chmielnicki massacres, pogroms in Russia, and the destruction of European Jewry by Hitler. Yet these events were separated by centuries and by hundreds of miles. Between these events were less dramatic moments when Jews lived comfortably in the diaspora for extended periods of time. This point should not be overstated, yet while persecution is an undeniable feature of Jewish history, it was not the only feature. The situation for Jews in the diaspora was neither perfect nor perfectly awful.

The book is divided as follows: Chapter 1 will explore the world of the ancient Israelites as recounted in the Hebrew Bible, one of the pillars of western civilization, and how Judaism was forged from the matrix of ancient Israelite traditions and institutions. Chapter 2 will then consider how this society was challenged by the experience of exile and by its encounter with the Greco-Roman world – the other pillar of western civilization – and transformed from a territorial, cultic religion into a melange of Jewish sects vying to be the authentic heir of ancient Israel. Chapters 3, 4, and 5 will explore the tortuous crystallization of Rabbinic Judaism into the dominant and definitely authentic form of Judaism under Roman, Byzantine, Persian, and finally Islamic and Christian rule. They will show how it expanded into an all-compassing way of life by the end of the Middle Ages, regulating and governing all facets of Jewish life, and how it managed the growing complexity of Jewish identity under the rubric of a system of religious beliefs, practices, symbols, and institutions. Chapters 6 and 7 will consider how a series of changes in the polity, culture, and society of Europe and the Islamic world from the mid-sixteenth through the end of the nineteenth century transformed this all-encompassing Jewish identity – at times gradually, at times abruptly – into an increasingly compartmentalized way of life, forcing Jews to accommodate the new opportunities presented by cultural enlightenment and the desacralization of life, political emancipation, and the possibility of entering mainstream society. This transformation culminated in the emergence of new religious definitions of Judaism during the nineteenth century – notably Reform Judaism and Orthodoxy. Chapters 8, 9, and 10 will then turn to the emergence of secular definitions of Judaism at the beginning of the twentieth century, most famously Zionism and Bundism, and how these identities, alongside the preexisting religious identities, confronted the challenges of anti-Semitism and the radically new possibilities presented by the creation of the State of Israel and the openness of post-Second World War America. In all, this book will traverse a contiguous, albeit tortuous, series of steps, beginning with the world of the Hebrew Bible.

Chapter 1

The world of the Hebrew Bible

Studying the Hebrew Bible (Tanakh) as history poses a problem to the modern history reader: a scarcity of evidence, particularly with respect to the earlier books. There is virtually no extrabiblical corroboration whatsoever of events in the Pentateuch and the books of Joshua and Judges, and limited evidence for subsequent narratives. To be sure, there is circumstantial evidence: the Egyptian Twenty-second Dynasty imported slaves from Phoenicia via the Land of Canaan around the same time that the Israelites were purportedly enslaved in Egypt; a nomadic tribe called the Habiru wandered in the vicinity of Canaan around the same time as the Hebrews wandered in the desert; and the existence of the Banu Yamina, a warlike tribe that recalled the militaristic behavior of the Benjaminites in Judges 23. All three of these examples suggest a possible attestation of the biblical narratives, but none conclusively.

For the past two centuries, some scholars have concluded from this lack of corroboration that these stories were fictional accounts. This claim began with Julius Wellhausen, a nineteenth-century Protestant theologian who posited that there were four distinct authors of biblical narrative: the Jahwist, the Elohist, the Priestly author, and the Deuteronomist. This conceptualization has generally been known as the Documentary Hypothesis on, more colloquially, as JEPD. Despite considerable efforts by biblical scholars to add nuance to Wellhausen's seminal though crude claim, however, it is still not known whether these narratives were fictional or historical. The proposed authors of the text remained shrouded in speculation: a scribe in the court of King David or King Josiah, a northern anti-Davidic scribe, or a priest in exile.

The upshot is that these stories are best understood neither as history nor as fiction, but rather as myth; and the distinct literary voices as editors and redactors rather than authors. These stories were part of an oral/aural traditional of folklore that was retold in less formal settings such as around a military campfire between battles, or recited on formal occasions, such as the recitation rituals described in Deuteronomy 26: 1–9 and Joshua 24: 1–16. Eventually the stories were transcribed, collected, and canonized as the Hebrew Bible.

The availability of at least some evidence to corroborate the period from the United Monarchy on has led biblical scholars to follow two distinct approaches in determining the historicity of this later period. Some, mainly philologists, have followed a more minimalist approach. Noting the stylistic similarities between biblical texts and Persian and Babylonian writings from the sixth century B.C.E., these scholars have concluded that most of the biblical corpus is a literary invention of Jews living in the Persian diaspora.

Other scholars, mainly archeologists, have taken a more maximalist approach. Fortified with a variety of artifacts and records, these scholars have reconstructed enough of the biblical world to accept more of the biblical narrative as historical. The truth undoubtedly lies somewhere between these two approaches. What follows, therefore, is an attempt to separate the historical aspects of these stories from the literary attempts of later generations to fashion a more idealized picture of ancient Israel. Whether or not these stories concern real events, therefore, is less important than the certainty with which subsequent generations of Israelites and, later, Jews, believed that they do.

The biblical narrative that precedes the rise of the United Monarchy, in particular, reveals at least as much about the collective memory and world-view of later generations of Israelites and Jews as it does about pre-tenth-century B.C.E. Israelite society. Six elements of biblical narrative underscore the distinction between their historical and their mythical dimensions. First, the narratives of the Books of Joshua, Judges, I and II Samuel and I Kings are set during a period in ancient Near Eastern history known as the Assyrian Interregnum, the intermezzo between the collapse of the first Assyrian Empire during the mid-thirteenth century and the return of Assyria as a major imperial power in the region during the ninth century. Coupled with the declining Egyptian presence in Canaan owing to a series of battles with the peoples of the sea along the southern border of Egypt, the interregnum explains how smaller peoples like the Israelites and their neighbors aspired to – and, according to these narratives, attained – a measure of sovereignty. The possibility for sovereignty is at the heart of God's covenant with Abraham, Isaac, and Jacob. In addition to a multitude of descendants – a highly resonant promise to a numerically small people – their descendants are guaranteed possession of the Land of Canaan. The stories of Joshua's conquest of the land presaged the rise of the United Monarchy by describing the hill-dwelling clans that made up the Israelite tribal confederation overcoming and defeating the technologically superior Canaanites and Philistines. The eventual expansion of the United Monarchy to the promised borders described the promise coming to fruition.

Second, the ancient Israelites are more accurately characterized as monolatrous than as monotheistic. The Israelites worshiped Yahweh as the supreme deity, and regarded the shrine of Yahweh – the Tabernacle, referred to alternatively as Mishkan and Ohel Mo'ed – as the center of religious worship. Israelite devotion to Yahweh was idealized in the form of a two-dimensional covenant. Initially, the covenant revolved around a promise by

Yahweh to Abraham, the grandfather of Jacob. In exchange for untrammeled fidelity and obedience, Abraham and his heretofore childless wife were promised a multitude of descendants and possession of the Land of Canaan. As a guarantee, Abraham and his male descendants and followers bore the mark of the covenant – the basis of ritual circumcision. Alongside this unconditional promissory covenant was a conditional arrangement between Yahweh and the Israelites, delivered to Moses at Mount Sinai. According to the terms of this covenant, the Israelites agreed to follow a series of commandments (*Mitzvot*) for which they would be rewarded by God with the basic elements of a felicitous life, and suffer divine retribution if they violated these commandments.

Yet the covenant with Yahweh did not prevent the Israelites from frequently worshiping other local deities, notably Ba'al, the Canaanite god of rain. This was not surprising, given the absence of a reliable source of water in this region. Unlike the Egyptians and the peoples of Mesopotamia, for whom the Nile and the Tigris and Euphrates rivers overflowed annually and provided a more than adequate source of water, the peoples who lived in the Land of Canaan depended heavily on rainfall. The chronic concern for water is an underlying theme in the covenental relationship between God and Israel, particularly in the obligatory covenant in Deuteronomy. At the heart of the litany of blessings and curses enumerated in Leviticus and Deuteronomy, an abundance of seasonal rain to assure good crops is the ultimate reward; drought and the ensuing crop failure is the ultimate punishment for violating the terms of the covenant.

The worship of Ba'al and other local deities, reviled in biblical narrative, is nonetheless as prevalent as the worship of the God of Israel, and was the fatal flaw of the tribal confederation described in Judges and I Samuel. The solidarity and kinship of a covenantal community sustained the tribal confederation for nearly two centuries. In the end, however, the internal and external weaknesses of the confederation led to its collapse. The common belief in Yahweh or the covenant was unable to forge more than a limited sense of unity between the tribes. At times, when individual tribes were beset by a foreign adversary, the other tribes remained neutral. The Song of Deborah in Judges 5 is a literary condemnation of this lack of tribal solidarity. There were even instances when the tribes fought against one another. Only in exile is the Israelites' monolatrous relationship with Yahweh transformed into a monotheistic relationship.

The monolatrous worship of Jahweh was, in retrospect, a symptom of the presence of foreign elements in Israelite culture. God's commanding tone in Genesis and Exodus is reminiscent of an Egyptian style of rulership. Like an Egyptian Pharaoh, God speaks in absolutes. Divine injunctions to Abraham and Moses are not given conditionally, or even simply as commands, but rather as statements of fact. And the Israelites accept these commands in equally absolute terms: "We shall abide." The Deuteronomic Code, whose conditional tone differed starkly from the earlier divine commands, reflects the style of an Assyrian vassal treaty. On a more mundane level, foreign influence is reflected in the names of biblical figures. Gideon the judge is known also by a Canaanite name, Yeruba'al. Samson is linked to Delilah, a Philistine woman.

Third, the subjugation of the Israelites by more powerful empires implicitly cast the Israelites as physically and militarily inferior to their stronger neighbors. Once the larger powers returned to prominence, Israelite independence waned and eventually disappeared. Thus emerged the foundational notion of Israelite and later Jewish servitude to a temporal sovereign, mitigated by a belief in Yahweh, an omnipotent sovereign of the universe, and a manifest destiny that promised the ultimate conquest and inheritance of the Land of Israel.

Biblical narratives counterbalanced this undeniable fact. The heroes of biblical stories are often portrayed as conventionally lesser types defeating those presumed to be their betters. Guile and ingenuity, for example, typically defeated brute force, reminiscent of Odysseus being chosen over Ajax. The more sedate Jacob repeatedly outwits his stronger brother Esau. Similarly, two of the judges, Ehud and Gideon, outwit seemingly invincible opponents. Ehud executes Eglon, the king of Moab, by smuggling a knife into his royal chamber. Gideon misleads the Midianites into thinking that his army is far larger than three-hundred men. Contrary to the entrenched notion of primogeniture, moreover, younger sons frequently overshadow their elder brothers. Isaac, Jacob, Judah, Joseph, Ephraim, David, and Solomon were younger brothers who wound up outshining their older siblings. In contrast, Jacob's eldest son, Reuben, is mentioned only as failing to rescue Joseph.

Most poignantly, perhaps, in an age when women were rarely active players, women in the Bible are periodically the agent through which divine will is realized. Rebecca redeems Isaac's failure to recognize and choose Jacob as his successor. By helping Jacob trick Esau out of his birthright, Rebecca ensures that the covenant continues through Jacob and not through Esau. Judah's daughter-in-law Tamar has a child by her father-in-law after his sons fail to fulfill this responsibility. Though the product of a seemingly illicit relationship, the child ultimately becomes the ancestor of King David. In the Book of Judges, Ya'el the Kenite uses feminine guile to entrap and kill Sisera, the commander of the Canaanite army. An unnamed woman kills Abimelech, ending his illicit attempt to install himself as king over the tribal confederation.

Fourth, biblical narratives reveal a tension between centralized and localized worship of Yahweh. The Tabernacle and then Solomon's Temple are designated as the center and, eventually, as the only legitimate place to offer a sacrifice. At the same time, each Israelite household is instructed to offer the Passover sacrifice. Biblical narratives speak out periodically against local altars and shrines as vehicles for foreign worship, and outlaw them entirely during the reign of Hezekiah at the end of the eighth century and Josiah toward the end of the seventh.

Fifth, the relations between the Israelites and other tribes varied. Thus, neighboring tribes have mixed images in biblical narratives. For example, in the Book of Genesis the mythic ancestor of the Moabites is described as the offspring of an incestuous relationship between Lot and his daughter; this tale undoubtedly originated at a time of hostility between the Israelites and the Moabites. In sharp contrast, the title character in the Book of Ruth is a Moabite women who joins the Israelite faith out of intense devotion to her Israelite mother-in-law, and then goes on to become the ancestor of King David; this tale reflects a more amicable or even filial relationship with Moab. Similarly, the ebb and flow of the relations between the Israelites and the Edomites is reflected in the tempestuous relationship between Jacob and Esau, the two peoples' respective ancestors. Initially, Jacob and Esau are twin brothers, but at odds with one another even in the womb. Jacob steals his brother's birthright; Esau threatens to kill Jacob. By the reign of King David, Edom is an ally and vassal state; Jacob and Esau eventually make peace.

Finally, there is a recurring ambivalence toward temporal kingship; divine rule is often seen as a preferred alternative. Being God's chosen people compensated for holding a lowly position in the hierarchy of the nations of the region. For example, the victorious Gideon, fresh from his military triumph over the Midianites, rebuffs his followers' request that he be crowned king of Israel: "I will not rule over you, neither will my progeny – God will rule over you" (Judges 8:23). Such resistance to temporal kingship soon acceded to the practical need for a king, yet the notion that kingship somehow betrayed the covenantal relationship between Yahweh and Israel would fester to the very end of the First Commonwealth – and even beyond in the conceptualization of the Messiah as a scion of the Davidic monarchy. For this reason, Israelite kings would face the challenges often associated with a constitutional monarchy: negotiating between the demands of royal administration and the rigorous constitutional expectations and limitations imposed by the laws of Moses and the covenant with Yahweh.

The pro-Davidic, pro-monarchic voice underscored the need for monarchy by underlining three fatal flaws of the tribal confederation. First was its lack of strong and continuous leadership. The priesthood, while commanding some measure of financial support and loyalty from the tribes, was never able to manage day-to-day political and military affairs; this is illustrated in I Samuel by the story of Eli the high priest and his sons, who allowed the Ark of the Covenant to be captured in battle. The judges – a series of strong, charismatic military leaders – scored a series of military victories against neighboring tribes – and, in the case of Samson, even against the Philistines. However, the judges were unable to transfer their leadership and authority to their children, thus rendering their leadership limited and ephemeral.

Second, the tribal confederation was unable to prevent a rupture in the fabric of Israelite society, exemplified by the concluding line of the Book of Judges: "In those days, each man did that which was right in his eyes." This verse follows the story of a horrifying rape and murder that resulted from a lack of hospitality. The political and moral vacuum created by a lack of effective leadership under the tribal confederation set in motion a transition to two new, ultimately more effective forms of leadership: the king and the prophet.

In this regard, prophets played a key role in the success or failure of Israelite kings. Although ostensibly providing a religious liaison between God and Israel, prophets doubled as important political figures. They defended the commitments to the covenant by scrutinizing royal policies or actions in terms of divine law or instruction, and thus were an integral part of the checks and balances of ancient Israelite politics. At times, this meant affirming royal policy with divine sanction. More often, though, prophets provided a check on royal authority by exposing its unacceptability. In the most extreme cases, such as transition from the Omri to the Jehu Dynasty, prophets aided in the overthrow of one Israelite dynasty by another.

The complexities of Israelite kingship, and the often tempestuous relationship between king and prophet, were present already in the story of the rise and reign of Saul, the first Israelite king, and in his relationship with the prophet-judge Samuel. While anointing Saul according to divine instruction, Samuel echoed and elaborated Gideon's reservation about a temporal king displacing Yahweh as king. Thus, Saul found Samuel to be critic more than supporter. When Saul's military campaign against the Philistines faltered after some initial victories, he made two key blunders that incurred the wrath of Samuel and ultimately led to the end of Saul's short-lived dynasty. The first mistake occurred during a key battle with the Philistines. Saul, awaiting for Samuel to arrive and offer the required pre-battle sacrifice, opted to offer the sacrifice himself in violation of biblical law in order not to lose a tactical advantage by waiting too long to attack. Dramatically, Samuel arrived just as Saul finished performing the ritual sacrifice, and chastised him for his lack of faith in God. As Samuel stormed off, Saul grabbed at and tore his coat, an incident that Samuel then interpreted as a divine decision to tear kingship away from Saul.

In another incident, Samuel had commanded Saul to destroy King Agag along with his followers and livestock according to the biblical instruction to annihilate the tribe of Amalek — the biblical injunction of holy war. When Saul balked and spared Agag and the livestock, Samuel, after uttering one of the most chilling lines in the Hebrew Bible ("What is this sound of sheep that sounds in my ears?"), hacked Agag to pieces, and then reiterated the demise of Saul's dynasty. In retrospect, Saul's failure as king reflected the difficulty of navigating between the demands of kingship and the regulations of the Torah. Circumstances would mitigate this difficulty for Saul's successor, David.

The United Monarchy

The rise and reign of King David inaugurated the period of the United Monarchy is the central narrative in the Nevi'im section of the Tanakh. From that point in the Tanakh on, some aspects of biblical narrative have been attested to by archeological evidence. The population of the United Monarchy was most likely between 15,000 and 20,000 people, suggesting that the kingdom of David and Solomon did not extend very far beyond the limited expanse of a city-state and the territory immediately adjacent to it. This suggests that the borders of the kingdom described in II Kings, which are conveniently congruent with the promised borders delineated in Numbers and Deuteronomy, were more an element of a Jewish manifest destiny than a territorial reality.

The glorious rise of the United Monarchy, a golden age in the history of ancient Israel, reflected the outspoken view of the pro-monarchic editor of the Tanakh, though the voice of the anti-Davidic editor recurs periodically. David's "golden boy" biography combined the most appealing elements of preceding stories, including a Moses-esque rise from relative obscurity to kingship with the complex Nietzschean passion of a warrior-poet. Moreover, typical of the heroes of biblical narrative, David was the youngest of seven sons. Like Jacob, he tended sheep while his brother, like Esau, found fame and fortune through physical and military exploits, in his case fighting the Philistines under the command of King Saul. David's first encounter with battle occurred by happenstance as he delivered provisions from his father to his embattled brothers. A heroic defeat of Goliath paved the way for his emergence as the leader of a mercenary band that fought for Saul against the Philistines' army. His relationship with Saul, seemingly sealed by his marriage to Saul's daughter Michal and his epic friendship with Jonathan, unraveled when his military exploits exceeded Saul's ("Saul has killed his thousands, but David has killed tens of thousands"), and Saul declared him an outlaw. At this point, David became vassal to the king of the Philistines against Saul. As Saul's dynastic aspirations collapsed, Samuel passed the mantle of kingship to David. When Saul and his sons were killed in battle, the ensuing dynastic crisis brought David to the throne. It is noteworthy that David was crowned twice: in 1,000 B.C.E. in Hebron as the king of Judah, and seven years later in Shechem as the king of the remaining ten tribes. This dual ascension was the weak link of the United Monarchy ruled by David and Solomon. Theirs was a dual monarchy whose constituency parts were united by dynastic allegiance.

II Samuel and I Kings attributed four accomplishments to David as king of the United Monarchy, and these defined the ideal Israelite king. All subsequent Israelite kings, and even the Hasmonean dynasty several centuries later, would be measured according to the accomplishments of David. David established the Israelites as a local power. He defeated the neighboring tribes, including the Philistine city-states, reducing them to vassals and forcing them to pay tribute. Second, he extended the borders of his kingdom in all directions, thus creating a contiguous kingdom that contrasted the patch-work territory of the tribal confederation.

Third, David captured the heretofore impenetrable city of Jerusalem from the Jebusites. The military genius that this task required was matched by the political acumen David displayed by making Jerusalem the new capital of the United Monarchy. Situated neither in Judea nor within the land of any other Israelite tribe, Jerusalem could be claimed equally by all the tribes. Protected by the topography of the Judean Hills, Jerusalem would be easy to defend. David reinforced the centrality of Jerusalem by relocating the Tabernacle and the Ark of the Covenant to Jerusalem. From this point on, Jerusalem would remain the religious center of the Israelite and, later, of the Jewish world.

Fourth, David attained religious legitimacy for his dynastic reign as king of Israel, thus avoiding the sorts of problems confronted by Saul as he lost the endorsement of Samuel. David not only extended the borders, but reached those borders promised by biblical tradition – the Euphrates River to the north, the Mediterranean Sea to the west, the Egyptian border to the south, and the eastern desert. Thus, David transformed himself and his reign into the agent through which the biblical promise of the land was fulfilled. This, along with Samuel's endorsement, added a component of religious legitimacy that granted him wide latitude in the political and military endeavors under-taken by his dynastic successors.

David further enhanced this religious legitimacy through a series of diplo-matic moves. He subordinated the priesthood without alienating it. He won the support of the Aaronite priesthood, and then incorporated the indigenous Jerusalem priesthood as a second line of priests, the Zadokites, that was beholden to the dynasty. In contrast to Saul's alienation of Samuel by the end of his reign, David won the support of a leading prophet, Nathan. The crowning achievement in David's legitimacy was delivered by Nathan, who conveyed to David a corollary to the promissory covenant with the patriarchs: an eternal royal-grant covenant in the form of a divine promise that David's dynastic rule would never end. By accomplishing these tasks, David was able to unite the tribes, transforming a loose confederation into a more unified monarchy with a strong allegiance to the dynasty, to the Tabernacle, and to the city of Jerusalem.

In a sense, the passionate nature that had fueled David's successes as a war-rior, king, and poet surfaced in other ways periodically during his rise to power. While a vassal of King Saul, David sang to Saul to ease the latter's bouts of what appear to have been depression and schizophrenia. Once king, while transporting the Ark of the Covenant to Jerusalem, David sang and danced half-naked in the street, prompting censure from his wife Michal (now identified disparagingly as Eglah, or Cow).

The antimonarchic editorial voice of I Kings presented a darker side of this passionate nature, epitomized by his passion for married women, which periodically led him morally astray. When he was smitten by Abigail, he intimidated her husband until the latter suffered a fatal stroke, at which point David married her. More infamous was his illicit affair with Bath Sheba, a married women whom David seduced and impregnated while her husband, Uriah the Hittite, was fighting at the front. When Uriah returned from the front, David hoped that husband and wife would copulate, thus covering up the illicit affair and pregnancy. When Uriah refused to lie with Bath Sheba – either because he was suspicious or because the dictates of holy war inhibited embattled husbands from cohabiting with their wives – David sent Uriah back to the front with a bellerephonic letter in hand to be delivered to Uriah's commanding officer. In accordance with the instructions of the letter, Uriah was sent to the heaviest fighting, where he died in combat. At this point, David and Bath Sheba married. Soon after, he was censured by Nathan the prophet, and the child born to Bath Sheba died within a few days.

Similarly, the antimonarchic editor contrasted the unity that David imposed on the monarchy with the dysfunction of a royal family that was torn to shreds by conflict and vengeance. The rape of David's daughter Tamar by her stepbrother Amnon, described in I Kings, set in motion a series of avenging acts that left several of David's sons dead. The conflicts within the royal family led to two revolts by David's sons against him. Twice David was forced to flee. More significant perhaps was the fact that his rebellious sons found support among disgruntled constituencies from within what had been the leadership of the tribal confederation. This dissent would remain muted for another generation, but resurface after the death of Solomon.

The narratives regarding David and Solomon, whose successive reigns comprised the period of the United Monarchy, are an amalgam of pro- and anti-monarchic editorial voices. In tandem, David and Solomon represent both the strengths and ideals of Israelite heroism, and the principal shortcomings and failures of Israelite kingship. Both were younger sons who overcame their elder sibling's pride of place, Solomon through direct confrontation with Adoniah. David's military successes and prowess, more reminiscent of Esau than of Jacob, were balanced by his accomplishments as a poet-minstrel whose music soothed even the mania of King Saul. Solomon's diplomacy and wisdom were held by later generations in as high esteem as David's military conquests. By the same token, David's familial squabbles and Solomon's accommodating attitude toward foreign influence anticipated the two weaknesses of the Hasmoneans.

As a king, Solomon built on the successes of his father. He extended the regional influence of the United Monarchy by marrying the daughters of the king of Egypt and of every other important leader in the region. Among other things, this stabilized all four borders, particularly the southern border with Egypt.

Stable borders facilitated the expansion of commerce and trade. The alliance with Egypt expanded trade in horses and chariots. An alliance with the king of Tyre gave Solomon access to a lucrative coastal trade along the Mediterranean. Israelite merchants traded along the Red Sea all the way to Africa, and expanded the caravan trade into Arabia, including profitable trade in spices and other luxury goods. Finally, Solomon acquired a large quantity of copper and built an industry around it – although no one knows where exactly the copper came from.

Although there were no major wars during his reign, Solomon expanded the military to maintain stable borders. He fortified border cities. He transformed some cities into military bases, and erected a chain of military installations from the Sea of Galilee to the Dead Sea. The horse trade with Egypt allowed him to maintain a large standing army, complete with cavalry and chariots.

Yet perhaps Solomon's most memorable achievements were his construction projects in the city of Jerusalem. According to I Kings, he transformed the recently conquered Jebusite city into the largest and most impressive Israelite city. He built the City of David and a series of royal palaces for himself and for many of his three hundred wives. And, of course, he built the Temple of Solomon (alas, there are no archeological remains of this temple). The Temple embodied the Deuteronomic impulse toward centralization. It was the center of the cult of Yahweh, and also the commercial and cultural center of the United Monarchy. As a dynastic shrine, its preeminence insured that the priesthood would remain under the jurisdiction of the royal crown. From this point, the high priest was the highest royal official, and was chosen by the king. Under Solomon, moreover, Jerusalem became a more cosmopolitan city, epitomized by the appearance of a Wisdom School disseminating Wisdom Literature. The latter, recorded primarily in the biblical Book of Proverbs but also in scattered passages elsewhere in the Hebrew Bible such as Psalms 1, reflected the cultural assimilation of ideas from parallel schools in Egypt and Mesopotamia.

These achievements, though impressive, provided fodder for the antimonarchic voice of I Kings, who implicitly pointed to parallels between the reign of Solomon and servitude in Egypt and recalled the antimonarchic warnings of Samuel. The reign of Solomon was a time when the rich became richer and lived ever more comfortable lives – the good life described in Proverbs; while the lower classes became poorer and had to devote more of their time and energy to serving the needs of the state. The emergence of a wealthy commercial class accentuated the divisions between the wealthy and the lower classes. Undertaking massive construction projects and expanding the military required large sums of money and labor, leading to ever-increasing taxes and corvee obligations to the crown.

I Kings also contains murmurs of religious discontent. The large presence of foreign wives and their entourages, many of which operated a temple to a foreign deity, did not resonate well with the image of Jerusalem as the center of the Israelite religion. Later, rabbinic tradition would echo this dissent, noting that, despite having hundreds of wives, Solomon was blessed with only a single child (this claim ignores the obvious biological difficulty of trying to impregnate several hundred wives concurrently), a divine punishment for marrying outside the faith.

Yet perhaps the most lethal source of discontent was the political implications of Solomon's policies. In order to tax the populace more efficiently, Solomon reorganized his kingdoms along newly defined administrative lines that cut across tribal divisions, thus blurring the premonarchic identity and autonomy of the tribes. This gave the impression of refashioning the confederation into a Greater Judah. This dissent was couched in religious terms – that is, blurring the tribal lines violated the divinely ordained allotment of land to each tribe described at the end of the Book of Joshua. This would prove fatally divisive after Solomon's death.

During his reign, however, his personal charisma, like that of his father, held discontent and tensions in check. Indeed, if one measures a golden age as a combination of political strength, economic prosperity, and cultural flourishing, one could see the eighty-year tenure of the United Monarchy as a golden age. The territorial expansion of the kingdom through the subjugation of every neighboring tribe under David, coupled with the expansion of trade and the emergence of the Wisdom School under Solomon, warrant such a description.

The United Monarchy's fundamental weakness was its underlying organization. Judah, the other tribes, and the other territories of the monarchy were held together by a common allegiance to David and Solomon. In the mid-920s, Damascus revolted against Solomon, though he was able to suppress the revolt. The growing tensions between Judah and the rest of the tribes came to a head when Jeroboam, a royal official from one of the northern tribes, attempted to revolt against Solomon and was exiled to Egypt. The willingness of Egypt to grant Jeroboam asylum was a blow against Solomon and signaled the return of Egypt to a preeminent position in the region. These tensions remained latent under Solomon, owing largely to his divinely sanctioned and proverbially wise leadership and charismatic personality. The question remained after Solomon's death: what happens to such a monarchy when the king lacks the prestige of David or Solomon?

The Divided Monarchy

The period of the Divided Monarchy spanned the division of Solomon's kingdom into Israel and Judah in 922 to the destruction of Israel in 722. Divided politically, Israel and Judah remained largely undivided religiously and culturally. Israelites in both kingdoms worshiped the same deity (with the same synchretic and monolatrous posture), and continued to make pilgrimages to the temple in Jerusalem.

The Divided Monarchy is also marked by the emergence of two rival political parties. One scholar recently dubbed these an accommodationist-cosmopolitan party, which was willing to compromise the primacy of the Israelite religion for the sake of political gain; and a nationalist-reform party that, buttressed by the covenantal tradition, advocated limiting foreign influence regardless of the political or diplomatic consequences. The tensions between these two political outlooks would remain in play until the end of Israelite independence in the sixth century B.C.E.

When Solomon died, his son and successor Rehoboam inherited the divine sanction but lacked his father's wisdom and charisma. The succession from Solomon to Rehoboam was the exact inverse of the succession from David to Solomon. The latter succession had been complicated by family intrigue, but once Solomon ascended the throne, there was no further resistance. Rehoboam ascended with no family intrigue but encountered resistance from virtually every other direction. As with David and Solomon, Rehoboam's ascension to the throne required him to be crowned in Shechem by the northern tribes, as well as in Judah. In Judah, he was crowned without incident. In Shechem, however, he was greeted with a host of petitions and grievances against his father that the northern tribes asked him to address, especially the matter of excessively high taxes. As recounted in I Kings, Rehoboam was first counseled by an older cadre of advisers who had served Solomon that he address at least some of these grievances. A younger, more arrogant cadre consisting of his own contemporaries advised him to defy this resistance. Some scholars have suggested that the story of the sons of heaven in Genesis referred to Rehoboam and his entourage. The new king followed the latter group, at which point his emissary to the northern tribes was hanged, forcing Rehoboam and his entourage to flee back to Judah.

At this point, Jeroboam returned from Egypt and led a secession by the northern ten tribes. Neither Judah nor the northern tribes were strong enough to force the other party into some sort of union, and the United Monarchy split into two kingdoms: Judah in the south, and Israel in the north. Neither kingdom was able to hold on to the other parts of the United Monarchy – Moab, Transjordan, and Philistia – which broke away, leaving Judah and Israel as two rump kingdoms.

The inability of either side to restore a united monarchy resulted from four factors. First, proponents of a confederation had opposed any kind of monarchy even while the United Monarchy had existed. Second, neither side had the military capability to restore a union. Third, both kingdoms were too busy defending their own newly established borders; five years after the secession of the northern tribes, Shishak and the lionized Twenty-second Egyptian dynasty formed an alliance with Libya and attacked Judah and Israel. Finally, prophetic sanction for secession of the northern tribes precluded any religiously motivated initiative to restore a united kingdom. Loss of territory also meant loss of tribute and revenue and a truncating of trade, bringing an end to decades of economic expansion and prosperity, especially in Judah. Israel, a more fertile region, was able to sustain the level of trade and prosperity longer.

The secession of the tribes, ostensibly a political event, had religious ramifications. The kingdom of David, after all, was believed to be a fulfillment of covenantal promise. To justify secession, the northern tribes had to find a way to reject the Davidic dynasty without rejecting the notion of kingship, which they retained. In a sense, justification was found by combining elements of the promissory covenant with Abraham and the Siniaitic covenant with Moses. Jacob's son Joseph and grandson Ephraim were presented as an alternative line of succession to the biblical patriarchs. Joshua, from the tribe of Ephraim, was seen as the successor to Moses and the Sinaitic covenant. Ephraim became a metonym for the Northern Kingdom.

The fall of the United Monarchy did not lead to the end of Israelite independence. Remarkably, given the resurgence of Egypt during the tenth century and Assyria during the ninth, the Northern Kingdom lasted until 722, while the Southern Kingdom lasted until 586. In retrospect, it is not surprising that Northern Kingdom was conquered first. It was larger, more fertile, and wealthier, and therefore more of a prize for a foreign invader. In addition, the Northern Kingdom had no established dynasty, resulting in a series of bloody royal successions. It also housed more foreigners and, without an established religious center, encouraged more idolatry. The Southern Kingdom, though smaller, was easier to defend. Its ruling Davidic dynasty, coupled with the towering presence of the Temple in Jerusalem, created a much more stable government.

The rulers of both kingdoms had to straddle the often competing interests and demands of nationalists and accommodationists. In both kingdoms, the relative influence of the two parties ebbed and flowed. In Judah, Rehoboam continued his father's policy of allowing a foreign presence in Jerusalem; Rehoboam's mother, after all, was an Ammonite princess. Subsequent kings of Judah such as Asa (Rehoboam's grandson or great-nephew who ruled from 913 to 873) and his son Jehosephat (873–849) purged Jerusalem of pagan shrines and worship. Ultimately, though, nationalists and accommodationists in Judah were cowed by the strength of the dynasty, regardless of which party it favored.

The situation in Israel was more tumultuous. Jeroboam I, the dynamic and charismatic hero who had defeated the Davidic dynasty, attempted to stabilize his rule by establishing a rival Yahwist religious center that could replace the Temple in Jerusalem. He set up a temple in Bethel, harking back to the story of the mythical Jacob's encounter with God and the angels there. This was, at best, a limited success. Israelites from the Northern Kingdom continued to regard the Temple in Jerusalem as their religious center, and even make pilgrimage. After the death of Jeroboam in 901, a period of instability set in that lasted until 879.

At that point, the reign of the Omri Dynasty, which ruled from 879 to 843, reinvigorated the Northern Kingdom. The strength of this dynasty is attested to by the fact that Assyrian documents referred to the Northern Kingdom as "House of Omri" long after the fall of this dynasty. The political stability achieved by this dynasty resulted from a decidedly accommodationist policy. Omri married his son Ahab to Jezebel, daughter of Ittobaal, king of Tyre, allowing the Northern Kingdom to form a strong alliance against its principal threat, the Kingdom of Damascus. Ahab, after defeating Damascus, made an alliance with its king.

This alliance, however, came at a price: his consort Jezebel's campaign against Yahwism. While there had always been Israelite constituencies who had worshiped Ba'al, Jezebel carried this trend a step further by actively persecuting anyone who worshiped Yahweh. The struggle between Ba'alism and Jahwism spilled over into Judah. Jehosephat's daughter in-law Athaliah, who usurped throne when Jehosephat's son was killed, introduced Ba'al worship into Jerusalem.

The spread of Ba'al worship is the background for the prophetic careers of Elijah and Elisha. Like the prophet Nathan, Elijah and Elisha provided a check on royal authority and policy. Elijah, after predicting the death of Ahab and Jezebel at the hands of his enemies, challenged the primacy of Ba'alist priests in a dramatic ritual duel on the top of Mount Carmel in the presence of a large Israelite mob. After defeating the Ba'alist priests, Elijah incited the crowd to stone them to death, thus dealing a major blow to the royal support of Ba'al worship. Several years later, Elisha incited Jehu's bloody coup d'état that ended the reign of the Omri Dynasty.

Following Jehu's ascension in 843, the political-religious situation inverted. By ridding the Northern Kingdom of the Tyrian Ba'al, Jehu effectively ended the kingdom's alliances with its neighbors. The purge of the Omri Dynasty also eliminated most of the capable leadership. Thus, the latter half of the ninth dynasty was a period of religious reform but international decline from which the Northern Kingdom would never fully recover. Despite a brief period of resurgence under Jehoash after 800, the Northern Kingdom was significantly weakened when it encountered the threat of Assyria during the eighth century.

This was the background to the classical period in biblical prophecy, which lasted from the mid-eighth through the mid-sixth century. Biblical prophets, it should be noted, were not fortune-tellers, but purveyors of what were believed to be messages of divine origin. Prophets were the most intuitive social critics of their age, recognizing before anyone else, among other things, the growing threat of Assyria in the eighth century and, in the case of Jeremiah, Babylonia at the end of the seventh century. Since they often laid bare the popular misapprehensions of the present – predicting impending doom in times of prosperity, and redemption and hope in times of adversity –

they were often believed only posthumously. The "classical" or "literary" prophets (Isaiah, Jeremiah, Ezekiel, and the twelve "minor" prophets) differed from their earlier "pre-classical" predecessors in their more elaborate and widely preserved orations and in their ostensibly less frequent involvement in political conflicts. In fact, the literary prophets of the eighth century often entered the fray of political life.

More than anything else, the prophets railed against three types of crimes. First, they condemned acts of treason or heresy, in which they included not only the worship of foreign deities but also treaties with foreign governments as acts of faithlessness. Such condemnations were delivered succinctly by Isaiah ("How the faithful community has become a harlot") and Amos ("Assyria will not save you ... ") and more elaborately in the prophetic career of Hosea. Second, the prophets accused the priesthood of corrupting the Temple service, rendering the sacrificial cult an increasingly anemic form of prayer. Echoing Samuel's early criticism of rote sacrificial worship, Isaiah reported that Yahweh had tired of meaningless sacrifices ("What do I need with all of these sacrifices?"). Finally, the prophets spoke out against acts of immorality, specifically the ways in which the wealthy and powerful mistreated the powerless elements of Israelite society: the widow, the orphan, the poor, and the stranger.

The earliest of the classical prophets, Hosea and Amos, directed their criticism primarily at the Northern Kingdom during its final decades. The death of Jeroboam II, last great leader of the Northern Kingdom, in 746-745 coincided with the ascendancy of Tiglath Pileser III to the throne of Assyria. This posed a dilemma for Israelite kings: submit to the Assyrians or resist and fight. Amos and Hosea, for the most part, demanded faith in God, which meant no alliances with any neighboring kingdoms. Instead, the Northern Kingdom attempted to ally with smaller neighbors, ending tragically with defeat at the hands of Assyria in 722. At this point, the Assyrians, consistent with their method of dealing with conquered peoples, exiled much of the population of the Northern Kingdom to other parts of the Assyrian Empire. Thus, the ten tribes became the lost ten tribes.

The Assyrian conquest of the Land of Israel continued after the defeat of the Northern Kingdom. By 701, Assyria had conquered and destroyed all of the Southern Kingdom except Jerusalem, and had laid siege to the Israelite capital. This was the background to the emergence of Isaiah of Jerusalem to prophetic greatness. Although his call to prophecy, as described in Isaiah 6, had taken place nearly two decades earlier, his role during the siege of Jerusalem was his crowning moment.

This episode, described in Isaiah 36–38, and in II Kings 19, represented the ultimate test of God's unconditional promise of the Land of Israel. The conquest of Jerusalem, the last remaining piece of the Promised Land still in Israelite hands, would mark the nullification of this divine promise.

Thus, when an emissary from the besieging Assyrian army offered Hezekiah, the king of Judah, the opportunity to surrender and spare his people, Hezekiah was caught between the pragmatic choice in the face of a seemingly insurmountable Assyrian force, and faith in a divine promise. The situation recalled Saul's predicament several centuries earlier. Unlike Saul, who acted without prophetic sanction, Hezekiah consulted the prophet Isaiah, who instructed him not to surrender ("The City of Jerusalem will not be delivered into the hands of the king of Assyria" – Isaiah 37:10). Hezekiah accordingly refused to surrender, consistent with his overall religious outlook. More than a decade before the siege, he had implemented a series of pro–Yahwist reforms. He had suppressed the worship of Ba'al and other foreign gods, attempted to centralize the cult of Yahweh and discourage syncretic religious practices by suppressing local Israelite altars, and generally tried to enforce the laws of the covenant.

At this point, the biblical accounts diverge. According to the Book of Isaiah, the 185,000 Assyrian soldiers laying siege to the city were struck down by an angel. More plausible is the account from Chronicles, which claims that Hezekiah, while refusing to allow the Assyrians to enter, bought the survival of the city with a promise of tribute. Interestingly, the outcome of this episode was affirmed, implicitly at least, by the diary of the besieging general. In recounting the defeat of other cities, the general uniformly noted, "I came, I surrounded, I besieged, I conquered, I burn." With respect to Jerusalem, the diary noted, "I came, I surrounded, I besieged, I held the king in my hand like a bird in a cage." While not attesting to the divine intervention of an angel, the diary affirms that Jerusalem was one of the few towns that survived an Assyrian siege.

The failure of the Assyrians to take Jerusalem coincided with the beginning of the decline of Assyria itself during the seventh century, which allowed for the subsequent resurgence of Israelite independence. Coupled with the seemingly miraculous survival of Jerusalem in the face of impossible odds, this strengthened the Israelite belief in the promissory covenant to the point of overconfidence. From this point on, there would be an increasingly bold mood in the face of foreign threats. If Jerusalem could survive the Assyrians – the strongest army that had existed in the ancient Near East to that point – it could survive any threat. This growing overconfidence was noted by Isaiah in the last of his oracles in Isaiah 39 (Isaiah 40–65 are the oracles of a different prophet of the same name). When Hezekiah is greeted by an emissary from a little-known, faraway kingdom named Babylon who asks to see the royal treasury and armory, Hezekiah assents over the protests and warnings of Isaiah. Prophets, the first to identity a threat, were often ignored. Nearly a century later, the prophet Jeremiah would spend considerable energy trying to combat this lack of caution.

The period that followed the failed siege of Jerusalem was marked by the last gasp and then final decline of Assyria, and the subsequent rise of Babylonia; and by the continuing ebb and flow between nationalist and accommodationist impulses. Hezekiah's successor, Menasseh, was forced by the Assyrian kings Esarhaddon and Ashurbanipal I to pay homage in the form of tribute and to erect altars to Assyrian deities, even in the Temple. He also reinstituted local worship of Yahweh. This marked a complete reversal of his father's program of religious reform, and it continued during the reign of Menasseh's successor, Amon.

During the reign of Josiah, the situation inverted again. In 627, the death of Ashurbanipal, the last strong king of Assyria, marked the final decline of Assyria, which would collapse for good in 610. The power vacuum that followed the death of Ashurbanipal allowed Josiah to reassert the independence and authority of Judah in the region. Beginning in 627, Josiah reconquered much of northern Israel, including Samaria and the Galilee.

Emboldened by military victory, he undertook a series of internal reforms that reinstated and expanded those of Hezekiah. The precise background to these reforms is recorded in II Kings 22. Josiah sent a team of craftsmen to refurbish the Temple under the leadership of Hilkiyahu the priest, who discovered a scroll, Sefer ha-Torah (literally, the Book of Laws). At this point, Josiah undertook a series of religious and social reforms: a purge of foreign cults and practices; execution of foreign priests and eunuchs; suppression of magic and divination; desecration of local altars and cultic centers in Northern Israel, including the temple at Bethel; and the centralization of all public worship in the City of Jerusalem.

The parallels between these reforms and the law code found in the book of Deuteronomy has led historians to conclude that the scroll discovered in the Temple was part of the book of Deuteronomy, and to attribute this book and its inclusion in the Pentateuch to a scribe of Josiah. Other historians have suggested that these reforms were not prompted by the discovery of Deuteronomy, but reflected three broader trends: the resurgent Israelite nationalism in the wake of the Assyrian collapse; a general return to ancient tradition in the Near East that combined anxiety regarding the future with a nostalgic longing for the past; and the resurgence of Israelite prophecy, which had been relatively quiet since Isaiah – in particular, the appearance of the prophet Jeremiah.

In some ways, Jeremiah's prophetic mission had aims similar to those of Josiah's reforms: both aimed at reviving a commitment to the obligations articulated by the Sinaitic covenant in order to insure the survival of the Israelite people. At the same time, Jeremiah criticized the popular overconfidence that Josiah's military victories had reinforced. In one of his most profound oracles, Jeremiah derided the exaggerated faith in the inviolability of Jerusalem ("Do not believe those who falsely claim that ... this is the sanctuary of God").

True to form, Jeremiah's warning anticipated the events of the late seventh century. In 610, the Babylonians conquered Nineveh, the Assyrian capital. A year later, when the Egyptians marched against the Babylonians, Josiah attacked Egypt at Megiddo, where he was killed in battle. Soon after, as the Babylonians continued their conquest of the Near East, Jeremiah began to preach accommodation to Babylonian rule, a reversal of a prophetic tendency to oppose alliances with foreign governments. His repeated warnings not to challenge the Babylonian juggernaut went unheeded. In 598, King Jehoyakim joined an alliance of small states against Babylonia. Following the defeat of this alliance, the upper class of Judah was sent into exile, and Zedekiah, a quisling vassal, was installed as king of Judah. A decade later, unable to quiet the surging nationalist sentiments, Zedekiah joined a revolt against Babylonian rule. The revolt was defeated in 586, resulting in the destruction of the Temple and the wholesale expulsion of the Israelite population to other parts of the Babylonian Empire.

Exile and the return to Zion

There is relatively little historical evidence as to the precise nature of this exile. Historically, we know relatively little other than what the Tanakh tells us. There were no mass executions. Jews not from Judea left unharmed. Jews fared reasonably well in Babylonia, some even becoming part of the Babylonian Court. The priestly lineage remained intact. More important, perhaps, was the theological crisis set in motion by destruction of Judah and the Temple: How could Jerusalem be destroyed? What about the covenant? In addition, the exile raised an even larger problem: could the Israelite religion exist outside of the Land of Israel, or was Yahweh a territorial deity?

Subsequent Jewish responses addressed these questions in very different ways. Some Jews responded with utter despair, such as the anonymous author of Psalm 130: "Out of the depths I called to you, oh God," or Psalm 137: "By the waters of Babylon, we lay down and wept as we remembered Zion. ... If I forget thee, O Jerusalem, let my right hand wither." Others despaired, but attempted to explain theologically how such a tragedy could have happened. Two such individuals were the authors of the wisdom texts Ecclesiastes and Job. The former attributed these events to the emptiness of existence ("Vanity, vanity, all is vanity") or to a fatalistic circularity of life ("There is nothing new under the sun"). The author of the Book of Job, after trying at great length to explain the suffering of the righteous, concludes with God appearing to Job out of the whirlwind and explaining that the nature of theodicy is ultimately beyond human comprehension.

In sharp contrast to these responses was that of Jeremiah. Already in 597, Jeremiah, in a letter to the recent exiles, had defined the possibility of maintaining their religion outside the Land of Israel, thus laying the theological basis for Jewish life in the diaspora. In addition, Jeremiah predicted a return to Zion within seventy years, thus laying one of the cornerstones of the Jewish belief in the Messianic Age.

Once the possibility of Jewish life in the diaspora was sanctioned by Jeremiah, the Israelite religion was transformed to suit these radically new circumstances. This marked the birth of what eventually matured into Judaism. This transformation consisted primarily of four elements. First, the God of Israel was redefined from a national deity into the sovereign God of history, thus explaining world events, exile, and suffering as part of God's divine plan. Second, the centrality of the laws of the Torah now overshadowed the promise of the Land of Israel. Third, there was a concomitant reprioritizing of the nature of holiness, with holiness of time superseding holiness of place. The Sabbath, for example, became a temporal temple, in lieu of the destroyed Temple in Jerusalem. Finally, the people of Israel were now understood to be God's servants. This new understanding of the religion solved three problems at once: it allowed religion to continue in exile, it provided a theological explanation for the destruction of Jerusalem, and it provided hope for the future, with a notion of ultimate redemption and restoration.

One of the first applications of the notion of a universal God came in 538, when Babylonia was conquered quickly and effortlessly by Persia. The prophet Deutero-Isaiah described the Persian king Cyrus as the agent of God's vengeance on Babylonia. The ease with which Babylon fell affirmed the omnipotence of the God of Israel. Soon afterward, Cyrus issued his Edict of Restoration, which allowed for a restoration of a Jewish community in the Land of Israel and for the Temple to be rebuilt at Persian expense. His reasons for doing so were twofold: First, he wanted to create a stable community of loyal subjects on the Egyptian border, in light of the fact that Egypt was always a potential source of resistance. Second, such edicts were typical of Persian policy, which, as a rule, allowed indigenous cultures to run their own affairs as long as they were loyal and not disruptive.

Despite Cyrus's edict, no mass of Jews returned to Israel during the 530s. The Land of Israel was far from Babylonia, and the journey very dangerous. Also, Jews were well established in Babylon. That Jews were comfortable under Persian rule is attested to by the story of Esther. In this tale, the title character rises to the rank of queen, and her uncle Mordechai becomes the royal vizier after defeating his predecessor. At the end of the story, the Jews, faced with mortal danger, kill scores of the would-be assailants, many of whom are frightened by the imposing nature of the newly appointed Jewish vizier.

Those who did return, therefore, were the boldest and the most dedicated to rebuilding the Temple and the land. They arrived to find Jerusalem in ruins, without walls, and were vulnerable to attacks and raids by the local population, particularly the especially hostile Samarians. Not surprisingly, the Jewish population did not exceed 20,000 people. Owing to a lack of funds, manpower, and interest, the Temple project ground to a halt.

The accession of Darius I to the Persian throne in 522 altered the situation. Under Darius, stability and growth in Israel continued under the leadership of the priests. The Jewish population increased to 50,000. The Temple project recommenced in earnest around 520. By 515, the Temple was rebuilt, though a far cry from Solomon's temple.

The ensuing half-century, though, was a time of decline and hardship caused primarily by heavy taxation, and strained relations with the local populace. Religious laxity became a problem as well. The priests offered sick and diseased animals as sacrifices in the temple. The observance of the laws of Sabbath-day rest was largely ignored. Many Jews neglected to pay the requisite tithes to the Temple. In addition, many of the Jewish poor were reduced to servitude, and marriage between Jews and non-Jews became more frequent.

These difficulties prompted two reform initiatives: a short-lived, ad hoc, and largely ineffective effort by Nehemiah, a Jewish courtier and the cupbearer to the king of Persia, aimed at administrative organization; and a more effective effort by Ezra the Scribe, regarded by Jewish tradition as nearly on a par with Moses. Ezra's mandate was exclusively religious. He came to Judah on behalf of the Persian crown, armed with the laws of the Torah and the power to enforce them. With this power in hand, Ezra enacted a series of religious reforms through a public ceremony in which he invited Jews to reaffirm their commitment to the covenant. These reforms included a taboo on marriages between Jews and gentiles, and a ban on carrying out work on the Sabbath. It became obligatory to observe the Sabbatical year (a year of rest for the land every seventh year), to pay taxes for the upkeep of the Temple, and to bring wood and the first fruits to the Temple.

In addition, Ezra introduced a new way of understanding and interpreting the Torah. Previously, Jews had understood the Torah literally. Ezra pioneered an interpretive technique that came to be known as Midrash: deriving laws from the words of Scripture. Of particular importance was Ezra's redefinition of who was to be considered a Jew. Only those who could show the proper pedigree could be considered Jews. This new attitude toward foreigners was applied to two cases. Regarding the Samarians, even those who wanted to join were excluded, since they lacked the proper lineage. Of greater long-term impact was Ezra's injunction against intermarriage. He persuaded Jewish men to banish their foreign wives, resulting in the expulsion of 113 foreign wives.

In light of the new emphasis on law, Ezra instituted weekly public reading of the Law of Moses, a practice that continues to this day. He also oversaw the final editing of the Hebrew Bible (with the exception of the Book of Daniel, which was added several centuries later). Not surprisingly, the canonized Hebrew Bible ended with the narrative of the Chronicler, which ends with the reforms of Ezra. Though little is known about the period between the reforms of Ezra and the arrival of Alexander the Great in the Land of Israel in 332, it can be said that much of what Alexander found in 332 B.C.E. was similar to the Jewish society and religion forged by Ezra.

Chapter 2

The challenge of Hellenism

The arrival of Alexander the Great in the Land of Israel in 332 B.C.E. at the head of a large conquering army launched the encounter between Judaism and Hellenism. For Jews, this encounter would challenge a way of life that heretofore had been defined by the laws of the Torah as interpreted by the prophets and, since the time of Ezra, by the scribes. To be sure, Judaism and its antecedent Israelite traditions already reflected some influence of foreign cultures. Amid the varied Jewish responses to Hellenism would emerge for the first time several distinct conceptions of Judaism, each reflecting Hellenistic influence in its own way. For more than a century, these Jewish sects would vie to be the true expression of Judaism and to be sole heir of the ancient Israelite tradition. In retrospect, the destruction of the Temple would eventually render the final decision in this contest, allowing the Judaism of the Pharisees to win by default.

Hellenism affected neither Judaism nor Jews evenly. As a rule, the most developed aspects of Jewish life – specifically, its powerful religious component – were least affected. The religious dimension of Hellenism – that is, worshiping the pantheon of Greek gods in various cultic rituals – made the narrowest inroads into Jewish society. The non-religious dimensions of Jewish culture – language, philosophy, poetry, dress and other aspects of material culture, and the celebration of the body – were most visibly affected.

The material cost of immersing oneself in Hellenistic culture, moreover, was substantial; thus, Hellenism was more widespread among the more affluent elements within Jewish society: the Jewish aristocracy and the upper echelon of the priesthood. The impact of Hellenism also varied geographically. Jews in diasporic centers such as Alexandria tended to be more Hellenized, as did Jews in urban centers in the Land of Israel, including Jerusalem. Jews in the small towns and villages in the Galilee, southern Judah, and the Golan tended to be the least Hellenized. Geographic and economic factors affected both men and women. Affluent Jewish women in the diaspora were no less drawn to Hellenistic culture than their male counterparts. The upshot was a tapestry of Hellenism and Judaism blended together, sometimes seamlessly, at other times awkwardly, that formed a continuum of Jewish identities from the most Hellenized to the most ardently anti-Hellenistic.

Upon his arrival in the Land of Israel, Alexander found a country with a stable polity and economy, governed by three rival elites in Jerusalem: a coterie of affluent Jewish patricians, the priesthood, and a group of scribes known as the gerousia (council of elders). Alexander, self-modeled in the image of the Persian emperors, emulated the Persian policy regarding conquered indigenous people: he allowed the Jews to govern themselves largely undisturbed, as long as they paid tribute and swore loyalty. Thus, the Temple and priesthood remained intact, and the patricians and gerousia continued to share in local administration. Upon his death in 323, Alexander instructed that his empire be given to the strongest of his entourage. This led to a brief but decisive struggle between his leading generals, and the division of his empire into three parts. The eastern regions, including Egypt and the Land of Israel, were grabbed by Ptolemy, or Ptolemaeus; the central regions by Seleucus. The Land of Israel, situated on the border of the newly created Ptolemaic and Seleucid empires, became a point of contention between them. By 301, Ptolomaeus had conquered the Land of Israel, and would hold on to it until 198.

Ptolemaeus, like Alexander, ruled as an eastern-style sovereign and maintained Alexander's policy of allowing indigenous peoples to govern themselves. He stationed military garrisons in the Land of Israel, and began construction on a few Greek *poleis*, but otherwise left Jewish life alone. Nonetheless, Hellenism made its way in, partly via the garrisons and Greek cities; but also as Jews, without the need for coercion, voluntarily embraced the new and alluring culture. By the end of the third century B.C.E., there was a conspicuous presence of Hellenized Jews in the Land of Israel.

The Jewish attitude toward Hellenism remained unchanged as Judea and the other parts of the Land of Israel came under the rule of the Seleucid Kingdom in 198. After King Antiochus III conquered the Land of Israel in 198 with the help of a supportive Jewish constituency, he expressed his gratitude by recognizing the existing policy of minimal outside interference. He also exempted the priests and gerousia from paying taxes, protected the people from the excesses of his soldiers, and declared the Temple in Jerusalem to be sacred space – off limits to foreigners and unclean animals.

The hands-off policy of Ptolemaeus and Antiochus III coincided with a growing internal dispute within the priesthood between two rival families, the Oniads and the Tobiads. In retrospect, this was a struggle not only between two families for priestly hegemony, but also between two attitudes toward the boundary between religious and non-religious dimensions of Hellenistic civilization. The high priest in 198 was an Oniad priest, Simon II, whose father, Onias II, had been vanquished by Joseph ben Tobias. As high priest from 220 to 190, Simon II regained some of the family influence that had been taken by the Tobiads. He was minimally affected by Hellenistic culture. In 200, several of the Tobiads had allied with the Seleucids, breaking away from the family's alliance with the Ptolemies. Hyrcanus, a leading member of the Tobiads, remained allied with the Ptolemies; after the Seleucid conquest of Judea, he relocated to neighboring Ammon, where he established an independent princedom.

The feud between the Oniads and the Tobiads heated up during the 190s, when the high priest Onias III fought with the Tobiad captain of the temple, Simon. The latter, more Hellenized than his rival, wanted to eliminate certain ritual restrictions. When Onias refused, Simon appealed to the governor of Syria, who sided with him. He forced Onias to flee to Egypt and gave the high priesthood to the Tobiads. Tensions within the priesthood were still running high when, in 175, Antiochus IV Epiphanes came to the Seleucid throne.

Antiochus IV, commonly known for his role in the story of Hanukkah, spent much of his childhood in Rome as a prisoner of war. This was one factor that led him to abandon the Seleucid policy of minimal interference toward a policy of forced Hellenization. The more Hellenized elements within Jewish society, and especially within the Tobiad and Oniad families, looked to capitalize from this shift in policy. In 172, the deposed Onias III's brother Jason appeared before Antiochus IV, ostensibly to appeal on behalf of his brother; instead he cut a deal for himself. He offered the king more tax revenue and a substantial personal bribe, and offered to increase his bribe if the king would build a gymnasium and ephebia (military training college) in Jerusalem, thereby transforming Jerusalem into a Greek *polis*. Jason was appointed high priest and served until 172. In 171, the deposed Simon's brother Menelaus gave the king a tribute that was 300 gold coins larger than Jason's, leading the king to appoint Menelaus high priest and force Jason to flee. In 169, Jason returned with an army and forced Menelaus to flee temporarily; soon after, Meneleus returned and defeated Jason. Altogether Menelaus would serve as high priest for nine years, from 171 to 162.

By appointing Menelaus as high priest, Antiochus undermined the integrity of the high priesthood, and fundamentally altered the Seleucid policy of non-interference in internal Jewish affairs. Menelaus's Oniad and Tobiad predecessors had been culturally Hellenized but had the proper lineage for the office of high priest. Jason, though appointed illicitly by a foreign king, was at least of priestly lineage. Menelaus had no legitimate claim to the high priesthood. In retrospect, this blatant disregard for priestly lineage anticipated the beginning of the end of the priesthood as a legitimate form of religious leadership. The priesthood would survive for more than a century, but, from this point on, its legitimacy was steadily on the wane.

The corruption of the priesthood galvanized Jewish opposition to Hellenism with the emergence of a group of Jewish pietists, the Hasideans. These Jews strenuously opposed what they regarded as the excessive Hellenistic influence in the Land of Israel, especially in Jerusalem and among the ranks of the priesthood. As the Hellenistic presence increased under Antiochus IV, the Hasideans grew ever more restless.

Tensions in Judea peaked in 168 when Antiochus occupied the city of Jerusalem. Initially, his intention appeared to be to defeat Jason and defend his quisling high priest, Menelaus. As it turned out, Antiochus was in desperate need of money to fund his wars against the Romans, and was looking for an excuse to plunder the wealth of the Temple. To this end, he dismantled the walls of the City of David, built a citadel, and began to transform Jerusalem into a *polis*. He also issued a series of decrees covering all of Judea that outlawed the observance of the Sabbath and the dietary laws, the performance of circumcision, and the teaching of the Torah. In addition, he entered the Temple, plundered the treasury, and offered sacrifices to Zeus. Thus, Antiochus completed the transition to a policy of forced Hellenization in the broadest sense – that is, including the imposition of its religious dimension at the expense of the primacy of Judaism.

This policy, and in particular the violation of the Temple, elicited a violent protest from two groups within Jewish society: the Hasideans and the Hasmoneans. The Hasideans, refusing to comply with forced Hellenization, fled to the hills and conducted a series of guerrilla attacks. When confronted by Antiochus's troops, they fought back. When they refused to desecrate the Sabbath by fighting, many among them were killed, thus becoming the original Jewish martyrs.

The resistance of the Hasideans was joined by that of the Hasmoneans, a non-Jerusalemite priestly family from the small town of Modi'in. Led by Mattathias and his sons, the Hasmoneans incited a broad popular revolt against Antiochus and his policy. Owing to the "street name" of one member of the family, the Maccabees (literally, "the hammers"; later tradition associated the name with a biblical acronym, *"Mi kamocha ba-elim adonai"* – who is like thee, oh God), this conflict came to be known as the Maccabean Revolt.

By the end of 167, therefore, there were two armed conflicts taking place in and around Jerusalem: a civil war in Jerusalem between the Oniad and Tobiad families, and a guerrilla war led by Hasmoneans and the Hasideans against Antiochus. These two conflicts were superimposed on a cultural war between proponents and opponents of Hellenism. As the conflict continued, though, the aims of the Hasmoneans and Hasideans diverged, the Hasmoneans fighting for national liberation and political independence, and the Hasideans waging a cultural war against any and all intrusions of Hellenistic culture. Hellenized Jews remained largely neutral, or in some cases supported the forces of Antiochus.

The revolt took place in two stages. During the first stage, the rebels drove the Assyrian Greeks out of Jerusalem, liberating Jerusalem in 164. When Judah Maccabee, the leader of the rebel forces, and his followers arrived in the Temple, they found it defiled and devoid of usable oil. At this point, according to the Book of Maccabees, Judah and his followers purified and rededicated the Temple. The dedication ceremony took place on the twenty-fifth day of the Hebrew month of Kislev. In commemoration of the dedication of Solomon's

Temple, the rededication ceremony lasted eight days. (The story of the lights miraculously burning for eight days was added later, for reasons that will be discussed in the next chapter.)

During the second stage of the revolt, the Seleucid Greeks were driven out of the Land of Israel. In 163, Judah Maccabee laid siege to the city of Acra. The siege was unsuccessful, and at this point, non-Jewish residents of Greek cities in the Land of Israel rioted against Hasmonean forces. The Hasmoneans appeared to be on the verge of defeat. However, they received a reprieve when Seleucid soldiers were withdrawn and sent to fight the Romans. With a renewed advantage, Judah Maccabee soundly crushed the Greek rioters. Following this victory, he assumed the title of *nagid* (ethnarch). In 162, Menelaus was put to death and replaced with Alcimus, an Aaronite priest – thus restoring the legitimacy of the temple priesthood. Many Jews, especially the Hasideans, stopped fighting at this point, thus weakening the rebel forces. The Hasmoneans' conquest of the land and quest for full political independence continued. In 161, Judah made an alliance with the Romans. Soon after, he was killed in battle and succeeded by his brother, Jonathan. After Judah's death, the Seleucids and their Hellenized Jewish supporters regained control of Judea and rebuilt several of their strongholds, including Jericho and Jerusalem. Although Jonathan and the Hasmoneans were unable to make any gains, the decline of the Seleucid Empire after 153 gave the advantage back to the Hasmoneans. In 152, Jonathan defeated the much-weakened Seleucid army and retook the city of Jerusalem. As part of the settlement, Jonathan asked for, and was awarded, the high priesthood, thus rendering moot the struggle between Oniads and Tobiads. The Oniads and Tobiads would be supplanted by the Hasmonean dynasty; both families soon came to terms with new ruling dynasty. During the ensuing decade, more-over, Jonathan conquered additional territory, extending the borders of Judea even beyond the borders of the United Monarchy. In 143, Judean independence was recognized by the Seleucids, thus bringing the revolt to a fully successful conclusion.

The success of the revolt resulted from a combination of factors. The first-rate military and political leadership provided by the Hasmoneans was indispensable. In addition, the popularity of the Hasmoneans fostered a sense of national unity, especially when they were defending the purity of the Temple and Judaism against Hellenism and foreign intrusion. Yet although these considerations were important, the overarching reason for the success of the revolt was the decline and weakness of the Seleucid army. It was, after all, fighting the Romans at the same time. In retrospect, a strong, undistracted Seleucid army would have crushed the revolt.

The consequences of the revolt became clearer during the subsequent decades. At first glance, the victory of the Hasmoneans seemed to undo the hitherto subversion of the priesthood through simony and the appointment of illegitimate candidates such as Menelaus. However, the assumption of the high priesthood by the Hasmoneans, though not an outright disregard of priestly lineage, was nonetheless problematic. The Hasmoneans, though priests, lacked high priestly lineage. In contrast, by assuming the title of *nagid* and not king, Judah and his successors paid proper homage to the notion that only a descendant of David could restore the throne. In this regard, expanding the borders toward the promised borders further enhanced their legitimacy. From a cultural perspective, the war against Hellenism was successful in terms of religion: foreign worship was curtailed, and the foreign presence in the Temple eliminated entirely. Non-religious forms of Hellenism, though, continued to find adherents, even within the ruling Hasmonean dynasty.

The Hasmonean Dynasty reigned for eighty years from the Seleucid recognition of Judean independence in 143 until the arrival of the Romans in 63 B.C.E. This was in some ways a period of glorious triumph. National independence had been regained for the first time in 400 years, and further territorial expansion would follow. This was also a time of economic prosperity and growth, and an age of cultural explosion as multiple forms of Judaism emerged that embraced varying degrees of Hellenistic culture.

At the same time, a cloud of ambivalence hung over the Hasmonean dynasty. The legitimacy of the dynasty was never clear, particularly when the Hasmoneans assumed the title of king. In addition, the Hasmoneans themselves increasingly embraced Hellenistic culture at court, minting Greek coins, using Greek dress and language, and employing foreign mercenaries. For some, the Hellenistic character of the dynasty echoed an earlier prophetic warning against being deceived by appearances, and the prophetic injunction to reflect on biblical law and not foreign wisdom to determine right and wrong.

The Hasmonean Dynasty, also known as the Second Commonwealth, was marked by four developments. First, the Hasmoneans conducted an effective foreign policy that expanded the border steadily. John Hyrcanus, who ruled from 134 to 104, conquered Idumea, Samaria, and part of Transjordan, and forced the Idumeans to convert to Judaism. His son Alexander Jannai (103–86) annexed the entire Mediterranean coast from Egypt to Mount Carmel, except Ashkelon. He also extended his rule over many of the Greek city-states of Transjordan, marking the zenith of Hasmonean expansion and power, and exceeding the borders of the United Monarchy. By extending Judea to the biblically promised borders, the Hasmoneans acquired some of the legitimacy that David and Solomon had benefited from centuries earlier.

The quasi-legitimacy that the Hasmoneans gained from territorial expansion, however, was counterbalanced by their expanding dynastic claims. As long as they solicited at least nominal approval from a representative of Torah law, the Hasmoneans' rule was minimally problematic. Thus, in 140 B.C.E. the legislative assembly recognized Jonathan's brother Simon as high priest, ethnarch, and military commander, and made these titles hereditary. Several decades later, though, Aristobulus I (104–103) assumed the title of king.

When his brother and successor Alexander Jannai tried to make the authority of king and high priest absolute, and not subject to the approval of the legislative assembly, a crisis of legitimacy ensued. Traditional elements within the population questioned the legitimacy of ruling without Davidic ancestry and recognition of the authority of the Torah.

The growing ambivalence toward Hasmonean dynastic claims was aggravated by the emergence of two political parties or sectarian movements during the second century B.C.E.: the Pharisees and the Sadducees. The Pharisees (literally, separatists) first appeared around 150 B.C.E. during the reign of Jonathan Maccabee. Some have conjectured that they were the intellectual descendants of the scribes and gerousia, others that they were an offshoot of the Sadducees.

Pharisees were generally farmers and artisans drawn from the middle and lower classes, hailing from small towns and the countryside. Thus, they tended to be less Hellenized. Pharisees were distinguishable above all by their belief in an oral tradition of Jewish laws that existed alongside the written laws of the Torah. From this oral tradition, the Pharisees had evolved a more meticulous observance of Sabbath rest, ritual purity, dietary restrictions, and a ritual of personal prayer. Politically, some Pharisees were willing to accommodate the illegitimate Hasmonean rule, and even foreign rule, as long as religious toleration was guaranteed. Others, believing the Hasmoneans were illegitimate, called for revolt.

In contrast, the Sadducees regarded themselves as the heirs of the Zadokite priesthood. Most were priests; others were members of wealthy families that had married into priestly families. Sadducees were generally upper-class, Hellenized Jerusalemites. They rejected the oral tradition of the Pharisees. Instead, they interpreted the Torah in their own way.

The power and influence of each sect depended on winning the favor of the current monarch and controlling key institutions, notably older institutions such as the Temple and the Sanhedrin and newer ones such as the synagogue. The Temple remained firmly in the hands of the Sadducees. The Sanhedrin, a legislative assembly that dated back to the time of the gerousia, was easier to gain control over. The high priest presided over the Sanhedrin, giving the Sadducees a constant voice; the Pharisees gained control through numerical supremacy. Most confrontations between the sects took place in the Sanhedrin.

As an institution, the synagogue – an early epithet for a house of prayer – emerged during the late second and early first centuries B.C.E. as an important new focal point of Jewish communal life. Scholars have labored to pinpoint key aspects of this nascent institution. Opinions as to when it first emerged vary from the sixth through the first century B.C.E. In addition, some scholars claim that the first synagogues were established in the Land of Israel; others say in a diaspora Jewish community. Furthermore, some claim that the origins of the synagogue were external – that is, Hellenistic. Others root the synagogue in biblical and post-biblical stories of personal prayer, such as

Hezekiah's prayer on behalf of the city of Jerusalem described in II Kings and Isaiah 37. These scholars claim that the synagogue succeeded the city gate (*shaar ha'ir*) as the focal point of communal prayer. Finally, scholars disagree as to whether the primary function of the synagogue was communal prayer and study, or more literally as a place where Jews assembled for a much wider array of reasons: communal administration, commerce, socializing, in addition to praying and studying. Whatever the case, by the first century B.C.E. the synagogue was the principal place where communal prayers were recited; and synagogues were located in virtually every major Jewish community in the diaspora and in many communities in the Land of Israel.

The liturgy of the synagogue service took shape gradually, and it is not entirely clear what exactly comprised the liturgy. Clearly, the heart of the service was a public recitation of passages of the Pentateuch. Originally this meant reciting on each festival the biblical origins of the festival and the biblical instructions on how to observe it. The story of the Exodus from Egypt and the laws of Passover, for example, were read on Passover. The annual completion of the Torah reading came much later. As with the observance of Judaism in general, the canonization of the liturgy and the homogenization of the synagogue service would not crystallize for another thousand years.

As a new institution, moreover, the synagogue at times blurred the boundary between men and women, and provided greater opportunity for women. Women such as Rufina of Smyrna figured among the principal donors, officers, and leaders of the synagogue service. In the Temple, by sharp contrast, no women were ever allowed to offer a sacrifice or perform any other priestly duty. As a new focal point of a new form of worship and communal assembly, the synagogue was a spiritual frontier that opened possibilities that a male-dominated Jewish hierarchy would have to engage with and define for the next millennium. As the synagogue became a more established institution, it also became an increasingly male-dominated institution, however. The women's gallery and the male-led service, apparently absent from the synagogue at the time of its inception, became hallmarks of synagogue life by the time of the Talmud.

The centrality of personal prayer in the Pharisaic outlook, coupled with its non-Jerusalemite, extra-Temple orientation, made the synagogue into a natural Pharisaic institution. It also cemented and perpetuated the connection between the Pharisaic elite that spent time in Jerusalem and in the Sanhedrin, and the sect's grassroots following. As a rule, Hasmonean rulers needed support from either the Pharisees or the Sadducees. It was difficult, if not impossible, to win support from both sects simultaneously. John Hyrcanus, Aristobulus I, and Alexander Jannai favored the Sadducees, thus alienating the Pharisees. Salome Alexandra favored the Pharisees. At times, sectarian tensions grew violent. In one case, the conflict led to a popular uprising against the king–high priest, leading to royal troops killing thousands of protestors.

Yet the biggest threat to the survival of the dynasty was the infighting within the royal family. Each succession was accompanied by a dynastic crisis, and often bloodshed. The worst came at the end of the reign of Salome Alexandra, as the shadow of Rome loomed larger. In 67, her son, Hyrcanus and grandson Aristobulus, both claimed the right to succeed her, bringing Judea to the verge of civil war for the next four years. Finally, the two claimants agreed to submit to arbitration by a neutral third party, the Roman general Pompey. In 63 B.C.E., Pompey arrived at the head of an armed legion. Instead of arbitrating, he conquered Jerusalem, the first step toward reducing Judea from an independent kingdom to a province of the Roman Empire. Most of the territories that had been conquered under John Hyncanus and Alexander Yannai became separate provinces.

Pompeii imprisoned Aristobulus in Rome (which some have argued was the beginning of the Jewish community there) and named Hyncanus high priest. Hyrcanus, though, was a Roman puppet, whose authority was truncated to presiding over the Temple service and levying a Temple tax. Real power in Judea was now in the hands of Gubinius, the governor of Syria. In 57, Gubinius divided Judea into five administrative districts, replacing a centuries-old system that some claimed had been in effect in Judea since the time of Solomon. From this point, Judea was affected by larger events in the Roman Empire.

The reign of Herod

In 55, Gubinius was replaced as governor by Antipater, whose father had served under Alexander Yannai as *strategos* of Idumea. Antipater had two sons, Herod and Phasael, whom he repeatedly attempted to place in the limelight of Roman politics. To this end, he appointed Herod to govern Galilee and Phasael to govern Jerusalem. For Herod, this was to be the first step toward becoming king of Judea.

From 50 to 47, Herod – ruthless, ambitious, impetuous, and paranoid – began hunting down and executing cells of Jewish resistance to Roman rule in Galilee. In 47, he was summoned to appear before the Sanhedrin in Jerusalem to stand trial for murder and other criminal acts. Instead, he arrived at the trial with a legion of soldiers. The Sanhedrin was on the verge of convicting him, possibly incurring a major reprisal from Rome, when Hyrcanus intervened on orders of the governor and disbanded the Sanhedrin, thus avoiding a major confrontation. Herod wanted to attack Jerusalem at this point, but his brother and father dissuaded him, pointing out that civil wars would not look good on the résumé of an aspiring Roman statesman.

In 42, Herod and Phasael were promoted to tetrarchs of Judea. Two years later, the Parthians invaded the Near East. Antigonus, the son of imprisoned Aristobulus II, offered the Parthians Judean support if they restored him to the throne of Judea. After defeating the Romans, the Parthians restored

Antigonus, who had Hyrcanus's ears cut off, maiming him and thus rendering him ineligible to be High Priest. Antigonus, though, lasted only as long as the Parthians.

In response to the Parthian restoration of Antigonus, the Roman senate nominated Herod king of Judea, stipulating that he had to conquer Judea in order to rule. Herod invaded Judea. After the Parthians were defeated by the Romans in 38, Herod completed his conquest of the entire Land of Israel, including Judea and Galilee, within a year. Following Herod's conquest, Antigonus was beheaded by orders of Antony at the request of Herod. Herod then solidified his hold on new kingdom by marrying Mariamne, granddaughter of Hyrcanus II. He ruled for the next 41 years.

Herod was well liked by the Roman imperial court, thus relations between Judea and Rome improved. He was required to send troops to fight in Roman campaigns, allowed to mint coins and raise a small army, and was given unlimited authority over the life and death of his subjects. For a brief moment in 32 B.C.E., his position was uncertain when Antony was defeated by Octavian. Herod won over the latter, who gave him Cleopatra's possessions in the Land of Israel, including Samaria and part of Transjordan. This expanded Judea under Herod to the size it had been under Alexander Jannai. His relations with the Hasmonean royal family were far less cordial. He regarded the Hasmoneans as a constant threat, and murdered almost the entire royal family, including his wife Mariamne, his mother-in-law, and the children he had through Mariamne. The royal family was virtually extinct by 4 C.E.

Herod is perhaps best known for his extensive construction projects. He built twenty-two new cities, including Caesarea and Antipatris. He renovated older cities such as Jericho, and erected fortresses all over his kingdom. These included Masada, near the oasis Ein Gedi in the Dead Sea region. He also erected temples in honor of the Roman emperor in Samaria and Caesarea. Most notably, he began extensive renovations of the Temple in Jerusalem, a massive project that was completed only in 64 C.E. Later, rabbinic tradition would laud this project: "Whoever has not seen the Temple of Herod has never truly seen a beautiful edifice."

To pay for these costly renovations, Herod expanded the tax apparatus of the Hasmoneans. His economic policies favored the wealthy elite. Indeed, the unprecedented wealth of the elite during Herod's rule is attested to by archeological remains of houses with reservoirs and elaborate mosaic floors. His policies favored Jerusalem over the countryside. Not surprisingly, the Galilee region became the main source of tension and discontent. Yet he kept such tensions in check, maintaining the peace for more than forty years.

More complex, perhaps, were his policies regarding religion. To the Jews, he presented himself as a Jew – the scion of an Idumean family that had converted to Judaism under Alexander Jannai, and a member by marriage of the Hasmonean family. To the Romans, he presented himself as a Roman. Nonetheless, he repeatedly offended Jewish sensibilities. He had a golden eagle – a pagan Roman emblem – placed atop the gateway of the Temple. He appointed and deposed high priests at will, thus completing the protracted process of undermining this office.

To be sure, many of the Pharisees had welcomed his reign as an alternative to war, choosing religious tolerance over political independence. In turn, Herod accommodated the Pharisees by not requiring them to swear an oath of allegiance, which in any case would have been largely superfluous, given the severity of his rule. At the same time, the relationship between the sects grew more complex during the reign of Herod, as multiple factions emerged within the ranks of the Pharisees, and new sects appeared.

The sources regarding the sects are decidedly biased, particularly with respect to the Pharisees. The early Christians regarded the Pharisees as a "brood of vipers." The authors of rabbinic writings regarded the Pharisees as their own forebears. The other source, the writings of Josephus Flavius, is replete with a variety of biases. Nonetheless, it is still possible, using these biased sources together, to form a reasonable composite picture of the sects as they matured during the reign of Herod.

Sectarian divisions were not rigid. There were undoubtedly Jews who picked and chose between sects. Moreover, despite differences, all Jewish sects shared certain beliefs in common: God, the Land of Israel, a common heritage and mythical tradition. In addition, the sects had more connection with each other than they had with Gentiles, even alongside growing intersectarian antipathy.

The Sadducees, though originally a Jerusalem-centered, priestly upper class, relocated along with the Jerusalem patricians to Galilee under the Hasmoneans, becoming a more rural landed aristocracy. When their descendants eventually returned to Jerusalem, they brought with them a more rural outlook that was parochial, politically conservative, and often hostile to education. They regarded the Temple service as the only legitimate form of prayer.

By contrast, the Pharisees tended to be more refined, educated, subtle, open to innovation, moderate, and fluid. Virtually any Jew could join their ranks by accepting their doctrines, regardless of background. At the same time, the Pharisees maintained sharp divisions between members and non-members; the latter they referred to as *Am Ha'aretz* (literally, people of the land). The Pharisees, who had earlier introduced prayer as an alternative to sacrifice, came to regard personal prayer as a superior form of worship, thus recalling earlier prophetic critiques of the sacrificial cult. Pharisaic doctrine also had a key social implication. The Pharisees were, by nature, a proselytizing sect. It was not enough for them to be pure. Rather, they needed everyone they came into contact with – through business or otherwise – to be pure.

Furthermore, the Pharisees were often critical of the openly Hellenistic demeanor of the Sadducees. To be sure, the Pharisees were also influenced by Hellenistic culture, but only indirectly. The Pharisees periodically incorporated Hellenistic concepts and rituals into Pharisaic Judaism by replacing the essential element with a Jewish equivalent. The symposium, for example, was a Hellenistic ritual in which participants discussed Greek philosophy while lounging around a table and eating a large feast. The Pharisees replaced the philosophical discussion with an annual recounting of the Exodus from Egypt – a ritual that came to be known as the Passover Seder. More broadly, there was originally no Jewish concept of man-made law; rather, all law had to come from Scripture. The Greeks, by contrast, had a long-standing tradition of human law that dated back to Aeschylus's *Eumenides*, which climaxes in the divine system of justice – the Furies – being transformed into the Athenian system of justice. The Pharisees emulated this concept of human law, but rooted it in the existing framework of biblical scripture, thus expanding Ezra's exegesis of Midrash.

By the end of the reign of Herod, an additional sect appeared alongside the Pharisees and Sadducees: the Essenes. Much of what is known about this sect comes from the Dead Sea Scrolls, a collections of parchments discovered in the Dead Sea region in 1947. The Essenes were an offshoot of the Sadducees, but shared some characteristics with the Pharisees. They regarded themselves as the true heirs of the priesthood, and were disillusioned with the deteriorating integrity of the Jerusalem priesthood. In response, they withdrew from mainstream Judean and Galilean society to a monastic lifestyle in the caves near Qumran.

Like the Pharisees, the Essenes regarded all other sects as ritually impure, especially the Sadducees and the Jerusalem priesthood. Also like the Pharisees, they stressed ritual purity, but went to far greater lengths to achieve it. They immersed themselves multiple times each day in a *mikveh* (ritual bath; *baptisma* in Greek). They regarded personal prayer as having superseded sacrifice as the true form of worship, yet prayed for a new age in which they would be the new, purified priesthood. The Essenes, moreover, believed in a cosmic struggle between the armies of light and darkness that would be set in motion by a new set of divine instructions. Accordingly, they practiced celibacy in preparation for what they regarded as an imminent moment of revelation. Since, they reasoned, the Israelites had been instructed by Moses to be celibate for three days prior to revelation at Sinai, not knowing when revelation would take place required them to remain celibate at all times. By the time Herod died in 4 C.E., then, there were at least three distinct forms of Judaism in Judea. During the first century C.E., a fourth sect would emerge that would ultimately upend the delicate relationship between Rome and Jerusalem: the Zealots.

The Zealot tradition and the age of revolt

For all his achievements, Herod left behind chronic tensions between Jews and pagans, between Jews and local Roman officialdom, between the sects, and between Jerusalem and the countryside. In retrospect, it is remarkable that it took more than sixty years after Herod's death for these tensions to erupt in the form of armed Jewish revolt. Two factors held these tensions in check for more than half a century: First, Roman rule continued to improve the material quality of life in Judea. Second, each of the Jewish sects had an ideological justification for not revolting. For the Sadducees, the Temple and its cultic service were largely undisturbed. For the Pharisees, the Romans did not impede their religious practice. For the Essenes, revolt was irrelevant while awaiting the "day of the Lord."

In this regard, a key element in the eventual outbreak of revolt was the emergence of the Zealots. The Zealots were the most uncompromising of the sects, even more rigid in their beliefs than the most parochial of the Sadducees. They rejected foreign rule, as the Maccabees had done a century earlier, but with far greater intensity, their singular goal being to eliminate all traces of Roman rule from the Land of Israel. They were most active in Galilee, where Jews were by and large the least educated and the most crude, and where the presence of foreigners and foreign culture was the most widespread. Like other freedom-fighters, the Zealots distrusted everyone, even members of other Zealot cells. They carried out sporadic attacks on Romans and Hellenized Jews, adding to the growing tensions in first-century Judea following the death of Herod.

Since Herod had virtually eliminated all indigenous Jewish forms of leadership, following his death the administration of Judea transferred into the hands of Roman procurators. In 7 C.E., Judea reverted to the status of a Roman province, and was subject to all the associated requirements. The procurators raised taxes and imposed new ones, and were generally insensitive to Jewish concerns. Rising taxes, along with periodic droughts, forced many small farmers to sell their farms and sharecrop or find work as day laborers in Jerusalem. The situation reached a low point in 37 when the emperor Caligula, obsessed with being worshiped as a deity all over the empire, ordered that a statue of himself be erected in the Temple.

This crisis, though, passed when Caligula died in 41. He was succeeded by Agrippa, tetrarch of Transjordan, who was crowned king of Judea. Agrippa, the grandson of Herod and Mariamne, was the last surviving member of the Hasmoneans, and thus popular in Judea. He enhanced his favorable standing by presenting himself as a pious Jew, although it is clear that he did this only in Jerusalem; elsewhere he was indifferent to Judaism, and a patron of Hellenistic culture. For a few years, it appeared that the golden age of the Hasmoneans might return. Such expectations, however, were short-lived. Agrippa died in 44, and the procurators returned as rulers of Judea. His son, Agrippa II, who ruled in Lebanon, was placed in charge of the Temple in 49, but this was a far cry from the rule of his father.

Circumstances during the 50s indicated that conditions were worsening. In 52, when a Galilean Jew was murdered by Samaritans, fighting broke out and spread to Jerusalem. Two Zealot leaders led an expedition to Samaria to wreak vengeance. At the request of Agrippa II, Emperor Claudius intervened, punishing the original Samaritan criminals and dismissing the procurator.

The emperor also gave Agrippa additional territory, including part of Galilee in 53. Like his father, the younger Agrippa made an effort in good faith to understand Judaism and to diffuse the growing tensions in Judean society. This became more difficult in 64, when the renovations of the Temple that had begun under Herod were finally completed, leading to massive unemployment of day laborers in Jerusalem. In retrospect, Judea teetered on the verge of revolt by the mid 60s, awaiting a spark to ignite the entire situation.

The spark came in 65, when Greek inhabitants in Caesarea built a pagan altar and temple on the grounds adjacent to a local synagogue, blocking the entrance. Soon after, fighting broke out between local Jews and pagans. When Emperor Nero sided with the Greeks in 66, the Zealots joined in and the fighting spread from Caesarea throughout Galilee and Judea. By 67, the majority of the Jewish population of Judea, Galilee, Idumea, and Samaria was in open revolt against Rome.

Most Jewish leaders – including Agrippa II and leading Pharisees and Sadducees – tried to end the conflict, with little success. The Zealots continued fighting, capturing several Herodian fortresses, including Masada, and occupying the Temple. At this point, daily sacrifices in the Temple came to an end. The Zealots aimed at driving the Romans out of Judea and Galilee, and redistributing the land out of the hands of the Sadducees, especially in Galilee.

The leadership of the revolt wavered between the Zealots and the Sanhedrin. The latter appointed Josephus Flavius as general of rebel troops, and he scored some initial victories in 66. In 67, however, Nero sent Vespasian to take charge of the Roman campaign against the revolt. By the end of 67, Vespasian had conquered the whole of Galilee, and pinned Josephus's forces down to a last holdout at Jotapata, at which point Josephus surrendered.

Fighting in Jerusalem continued for nearly three more years. Signs of disunity began to appear within the Jewish camp as the Zealots blamed the Pharisees and Sadducees for being too accommodating to the Romans. By the end of 68, Jerusalem was in the hands of the Zealots; surrender and negotiation were no longer viable options. By 69, three groups of Zealots were fighting in Jerusalem, one group in the lower city, one group in the upper city, and one group in the Temple. The Temple cell eventually wiped out the other two Zealot groups. In 69, when Vespasian became emperor of Rome, he sent his son Titus to crush the rebels in Jerusalem. This Titus did in the summer of 70, conquering Jerusalem and destroying the Temple.

The defeat of the revolt had profound consequences. First and foremost, the destruction of the Temple brought an end to the sacrificial cult. The Temple was also the political and economic center of the Jews in Judea and elsewhere in the Land of Israel. Thousands of Jews, moreover, were carried off into captivity to various parts of the Roman Empire.

It is useful to ask why the revolt against Rome failed while the Maccabean revolt succeeded. During the Great Revolt, there was no Jewish military leadership comparable to the Maccabees. In addition, whereas the Jews of Judea had united around the Hasmoneans, disunity between the sects and among the Zealots had weakened the revolt against Rome. Ultimately, the disparate outcomes of the two revolt reflected the strength of the opponent. The Seleucid Empire was on the wane during the Maccabean Revolt. By contrast, Rome was unbeatable in 70 C.E. It is remarkable that the Jews lasted as long as they did.

Yet Judaism survived the destruction of the Temple and the conquest of Jerusalem by the Romans, owing to a combination of preexisting developments in Judaism and Roman policy, and subsequent tactics by Jewish leaders. Jews had already experienced the destruction of the Temple, and thus already had a theological framework with which to explain it. Unlike in 586 B.C.E., they did not have to reinvent Judaism in order to come to terms with this calamity. In addition, by 70 C.E., Jews had centuries of experience living under foreign rule, both in the Land of Israel and in the diaspora. Also, the development of a personal religion by the Pharisees would prove crucial in allowing Jews to function without the Temple or the sacrificial cult.

Roman policies complemented these developments. The Roman campaign in Judea was a political campaign with few or no religious overtones; thus, the Romans left the Jews physically intact, with no reprisals or mass killings. Moreover, the Romans left the status of Judaism intact. Judaism remained a legal religion after the revolt, and Jews elsewhere in the empire were largely unaffected. The Sanhedrin was allowed to reassemble in the southern Judean town of Javneh.

For the Zealots, the end of the revolt did not signal the end of the campaign against Roman rule. Many of the surviving Zealots and their families fled to Masada, where for the next three years they conducted a campaign of guerrilla warfare against Roman soldiers, pagans, and Jews who were suspected of being overly Hellenized or too accommodating of Roman rule.

In 73, the emperor sent in Silva and the Roman Tenth Legion to deal with the Zealots at Masada. Fresh from its previous mission – the conquest of most of Africa – the Tenth Legion laid siege to Masada. After several months, the Romans mounted an assault on the seemingly impregnable mountain fortress. According to Josephus Flavius's problematic account, the Zealots, facing certain defeat and enslavement, chose mass suicide over surrender. The account is problematic because this story was never mentioned in any Roman source (by contrast, the Romans minted coins to commemorate the conquest of Jerusalem and the destruction of the Temple). Archeological remains unearthed at Masada indicate that the Zealots were prepared for battle. Yet the only piece of evidence that attests to the suicide, a shard etched with the name of the Zealots' leader, Eleazar ben Yair – who, according to Josephus, had used such shards to draw lots to determine who would be the last to die – lends a measure of credibility to this account. On the other hand, the fact that Josephus had been in a similar situation two years earlier in Jotapata and had opted for surrender over a heroic death suggests that he might have fabricated all or part of the story to compensate for his own lack of heroism.

Following the defeat of the Zealots at Masada, conditions stabilized in the Land of Israel. For nearly sixty years, the Romans ruled without armed conflict while the Sanhedrin continued to legislate and rule on religious matters. Small cells of Zealots occasionally caused trouble, but nothing concerted enough to bother the Romans rulers.

This situation changed during the 130s during the reign of Emperor Hadrian. A builder like Herod, in 132 Hadrian began a new construction project in Jerusalem. This raised expectations among Jews in Judea for some form of divine redemption. After all, 132 was nearly seventy years after the destruction of the Temple; Jeremiah's promise of redemption after seventy years began to resonate. In addition, in 132 the Roman Empire appeared to be facing serious threats, which appeared to some to be the pre-messianic fall of the Fourth Empire as prophesied by Daniel. Thus, some Jews believed that Hadrian might be rebuilding the Temple.

When it became known that, far from rebuilding the Temple, Hadrian was building a pagan temple in Jerusalem, disillusionment led to another Zealot-led revolt under the leadership of Simon bar Cosiba, later renamed bar Kochba by his followers. This revolt lasted three years. When Hadrian sent in troops from Gaul in 135, the rebels were quickly beaten back to Betar, where they made a final stand. When bar Kochba was killed (according to Jewish legend, by a snake and not by a Roman), the revolt collapsed.

Sensing perhaps that Vespasian had been too lenient after defeating the Jews in 70, Hadrian undertook a series of harsh measures against the Jews of Judea. He razed Judea to the ground and salted the earth. He outlawed the practice of Judaism and the teaching of the Torah; when ten leading Jewish scholars defied this decree, they were arrested, tortured, and executed. Hadrian also banned Jews from Jerusalem, except on the ninth of Av, when they were allowed to lament the destruction of the Temple. He renamed Jerusalem Aelia Capitolina and renamed Judea Palestina.

The impact of the defeat of the revolt and the ensuing decrees was far-reaching. Defeat brought an end to the Zealots and their tradition of armed revolt; accommodating foreign rule rather than revolting against it would be the predominant political tactic for Jews for more than 1,700 years. The promise of divine redemption was deferred from the immediate or near future to the end of time. The destruction of Judea would lead the Sanhedrin to move from Judea to Galilee.

The Hellenistic diaspora: Alexandria and Rome

The most important Jewish communities in the Roman Empire outside the Land of Israel, those of Alexandria and Rome, were minimally affected by events in Judea. Jewish settlement in Alexandria began as early as the third century C.E. While initially confined to the eastern sector of the city, by the Roman era Jews resided and had erected synagogues throughout the city, and two of the five city districts had large numbers of Jews. Most Jews in Alexandria were artisans, and a few were wealthy merchants. The Jews had been granted the status of a *politeuma* (autonomous community) under the Ptolemies. During this period, many Jews acquired citizenship. During the reign of Ptolemaeus III Philadelphus, an open exchange between Jewish and Greek culture unfolded, culminating with the publication of the Septuagint, a Greek translation of the Torah. This exchange peaked during the first century, as exemplified by the synthesis between Judaism and Greek philosophy.

Conditions deteriorated somewhat under Roman rule. The Romans granted citizenship to the Greek residents of the city but defined the Egyptians as a subject people, which meant their paying a poll tax. Alexandrian Jews tried to obtain citizenship as Greeks, prompting anti-Jewish propaganda. In 38 C.E., riots broke out against the Jews of Alexandria, resulting in Jewish fatalities, the scourging of Jewish notables, and the defiling of synagogues. In response, the Jews armed themselves and attacked their assailants. Claudius, recently crowned emperor, restored order. He also restored to Jews the national and religious privileges they had lost during the period of the riots, but forbade them to claim citizenship.

Culturally, the Jews of Alexandria were among the most Hellenized Jews in the world, but maintained strong ties to Jewish tradition. Emblematic of the balance between Judaism and Hellenism were the works of Philo, the first Jewish philosopher. Little is known about him. He came from a prominent family and participated in the Jewish delegation to Caligula in 40 C.E. His many works have been preserved, albeit by happenstance (they were preserved by the early church fathers; Jews discovered him only much later). Philo was not the first Jew to ask philosophical questions, or the first to study Greek philosophy, but he was the first to systematically synthesize Jewish law and lore with Greek wisdom. This synthesis would be the dominant mode of Jewish philosophy until the seventeenth century, when Baruch Spinoza would divorce Jewish thought from Greek philosophy.

Philo exemplified the exceptional impact of Hellenism on Jews. Other peoples embraced Greek wisdom at the expense of their own traditions and beliefs. For example, Hellenized Egyptians replaced their Egyptian gods such as Ammon with Greek gods such as Zeus. Jews incorporated Greek wisdom without giving up their own. In this respect, Philo's sense of Jewishness recalled the original encounter between Jews and Hellenistic culture.

Philo's work embodied more than the coexistence between Jewish and Hellenistic culture, and the blurred boundary between sectarian Jewish identities. In his thought, it is possible to detect both Sadducean and Pharisaic tendencies. Like the Sadducees, he interpreted the Torah allegorically; like the Pharisees, he believed in the immortality of the soul. Moreover, he was well versed in the oral tradition of the Pharisees, and used it to interpret the Torah.

Philo played an important role in defending Judaism against its critics. In the face of pagan criticisms of Judaism as a godless, antisocial religion, Philo offered a threefold defense. He argued that Jews rejected heathen deities, but were not atheists; that Jewish law was particular, but not inhospitable; and that Jewish religious practices were different than pagan practices, but were not superstitious. To Jews whose allegorical reading of the Torah led them to conclude that Judaism was no longer necessary in light of Greek philosophy, Philo elevated the laws of the Torah over philosophy, arguing that philosophy is a tool with which to understand more fully the divine revelation of the Torah's laws. Philo was not alone in this respect. Josephus Flavius also defended Judaism against its critics, notably from the criticisms of an Egyptian priest named Apion.

Philo also provided one of the few extant descriptions of Jewish spiritual life in the late Hellenistic diaspora. In *On the Contemplative Life*, he described a monastic Jewish community outside of Alexandria along Lake Mareotis, known as the Therapeutic Society. The members of this enclave included men and women who devoted their entire lives to philosophic contemplation – a Hellenized parallel to the Essenes. They prayed at dusk and dawn and studied the Bible allegorically the rest of the day. Like the Essenes, they lived simple and chaste lives.

For Therapeutic women in particular, participating in this society meant abandoning what was conventionally the primary function and responsibility of Jewish women in the ancient world: bearing and rearing children. Instead, these women, many of whom had means and a Hellenistic education, opted for a life of learning and contemplation even at the cost of being childless. In this regard, Therapeutic women, though atypical of Jewish women generally, underscore the availability of alternatives for Jewish women to the highly subservient role defined by biblical and, later, rabbinic law (as will be discussed in the next chapter).

If Philo and the Jews of Alexandria defined the cultural possibilities for diaspora Jews, the situation of the Jews of Rome defined the political parameters of diaspora Jewish life. Soon after the emergence of a small Jewish community in Rome, Jews were faced with a key decision around 60 B.C.E. during a contest for the imperial crown between two powerful generals: Pompey, who had recently conquered Judea, and the soon to be Julius Caesar. The Jews sided with Julius Caesar, who in return granted them a series of rights. He exempted Jews from military service, and excused them from having to attend court on the Sabbath. He also allowed Jews to send annual contributions to the Temple in Jerusalem. These privileges would define the parameters of Jewish communal autonomy for the next 1,700 years, surviving the abrupt shift in Roman policy toward Jews during the fourth century, as Rome was transformed from a pagan to a Christian empire. The Roman Empire would be the first major arena where Judaism and Christianity would confront one another, and where Jews would first be subjugated to Christian rule.

Judaism and Christianity in conflict

The emergence of Christianity as a major western religion, and as the dominant religion of the Roman Empire by the fourth century, profoundly altered the situation of Jews in the Roman Empire. While beginning as a sect of Judaism during the first century C.E., Christianity eventually posed the most serious and sustained challenge to the claim by Rabbinic Judaism of being the sole heir to the religion of ancient Israel. For this reason, it is important to understand the early relationship between Christianity and Judaism as rival religious traditions claiming to be the authentic expression and realization of the biblical covenant and prophetic tradition. The challenge in fleshing out this relationship is complicated by the absence of contemporary accounts of the life of Jesus and early Christianity. The earliest books of the Christian New Testament were written a generation or more after his death. There is little or no mention of Jesus in Jewish sources until the second century, and no mention of Jesus in Roman records until 130 C.E.

Despite these methodological difficulties, the ingenuity of Bible scholars and historians of Christianity and first-century Judea has made clear that most core Christian doctrines – notably the Virgin Birth and the Resurrection – seem to have been added later. The initial impressions of Jesus vary between the historically reliable passages of the Gospels that regard Jesus as an apocalyptic prophet, and Josephus Flavius, who refers to Jesus as the "Messiah of the Jews." What is clear is that, as one historian noted, Christianity evolved during the first century from the religion of Jesus to the religion about Jesus.

Jesus was most likely born in Nazareth or somewhere in Galilee. His putative birth in Bethlehem was apparently added to give him a Davidic pedigree – an important prerequisite for a messianic claimant. His familiarity with Pharisaic law suggests he was a Pharisee, but he clearly had adopted some Essene views as well. His dynamic oratory and charisma won him a growing following. His message was primarily religious and moral in nature, and not overtly political. Like the Essenes, he preached a non-violent, passive resistance to Roman and Sadducean corruption.

Eventually he was arrested, tried, and convicted by the Sanhedrin for treason and heresy. The notion that the Jews crucified him is belied by the fact that the Sanhedrin had lacked authority to execute anyone since the reign of Herod. Rather, the Sanhedrin gave him to the Romans, who sentenced him to crucifixion – a common and brutally Roman-style form of capital and corporal punishment.

In general, Jesus attracted the same types of individuals that were attracted to Pharisaic Judaism and, later, to the rabbinic movement. He appealed to the lower classes without being ascetic, and to propertied people with being elitist. His widest appeal was in Galilee, where his followers included Zealots such as Simon the Zealot and Judas Iscariot. He attracted many followers in the synagogue, especially in the diaspora.

Like other Jewish sects, early Christians referred to the Hebrew Bible for legitimacy. They reinterpreted the notion of a "new covenant" referred to in Jeremiah 31; and the notion of a "cornerstone rejected by the builders" in Psalm 118 as the Jewish rejection of Jesus. They personified the suffering servant in Isaiah 53 – originally a reference to the people of Israel in exile – as the suffering of Jesus himself; and they based the claim of Jesus' divinity by reinterpreting Daniel 7:13. In retrospect, each of these Christological interpretations is problematic from an exegetical point of view, and the Christological interpretation of Isaiah 7:14 as presaging the Virgin Birth is an outright misreading. Yet for those who began with the premise that Jesus was the Messiah and the Son of God, each of these interpretations was tenable and plausible.

Five factors helped the spread of Christianity during the first three centuries. First, Christianity claimed to be the true heir of Judaism, which was highly respected in the Hellenistic world as a cult of piety and moral values. Second, Christianity's apocalyptic and sectarian organization facilitated intense commitment from its membership. Third, the general mobility of peoples in the Hellenistic world aided Christian missionaries in their efforts to spread the teachings of Jesus and win adherents.

Fourth, Jesus' message appealed to the large population of economically viable but low-status people. Skilled artisans, for example, at times had above average economic security, but low status. The workshop was a good place to proselytize. Conversations between customers and tradesmen or between masters and apprentices could attract new followers.

Similarly, tax collectors and prostitutes, who were considered disreputable by Pharisees and Sadducees, found Christians to be more welcoming. "God-fearing" Gentiles who were interested in Judaism and attended synagogue but were unwilling to become fully Jewish – generally because of circumcision – chose Christianity as an alternative. Also, accomplished women could overcome their secondary status in Pharisaic or Sadducean society by becoming Christian.

Finally, Christian missionaries, beginning with Paul, were able to attract not only Jews but also pagans. Paul, in particular, was a major catalyst in the spread of Christianity. In 60 C.E., Christianity was still largely centered on the Land of Israel, and most converts had either once belonged or still belonged to one or another Jewish sect. It is useful in this regard to compare Paul's path to Christian belief with that of James. James came to Christianity as an extension of his Jewish beliefs. Paul, born Saul of Tarsus, was a Hellenized diaspora Jew who converted to Pharisaic Judaism, then later to Christianity. He never knew Jesus personally. According to the Gospel of Luke, Paul had a vision of Jesus while on the road to Damascus to preach Pharisaic Judaism, which precipitated an ecstatic experience and his conversion to Christianity.

As a Christian, he struggled to reconcile his new belief in Jesus with his Pharisaic belief in the primacy of the oral tradition of Jewish law. If he believed that the observance of the law and acceptance of the oral tradition was the medium of salvation, he could not have accepted Jesus as the Messiah since Jewish tradition said nothing about believing in or expecting a crucified Messiah. Paul's resolution was simple: once Christ was crucified, belief in and observance of law ceased to be the medium of salvation. As is frequently the case with converts, he believed first, and then he revalued Pharisaic Judaism to suit his postconversion theology.

Once converted, Paul became the most outspoken missionary for Christianity. Each of his epistles addressed a problem in one of the churches he had founded. To the Corinthians, he stressed the necessity to be ethical in addition to having faith. In his epistle to the Galatians, he rejected the claims of other missionaries who insisted that Christians were obligated to observe Jewish law. He disagreed with other Christians regarding the status of Jewish law. James, for example, had defended the Pharisaic notion of the dietary restrictions, teaching that Jews and Gentiles should not eat together. Paul claimed that all Christians, whether Jewish or Gentile, should eat together for the sake of Christian unity; as he said in Romans 14:20: "Do not for the sake of food destroy God's work."

Circumcision turned out to be the crucial issue for Paul. This ritual was the central element in male conversion to Judaism, and a major impediment to the converting of pagans to Christianity. Paul argued that circumcision was no longer necessary to convert to Christianity. He replaced "circumcision of the flesh" with "circumcision of the heart." This ultimately was the first step in the parting of the ways between Judaism and Christianity, although the split took several decades. By 96 C.E., it was clear that these were separate faiths, attested to by the fact that the Romans exempted Christians from the *fiscus judaicus*, thus imposing separate tax regulations on Jews and Christians.

For the next two centuries, Judaism would have preferable status under Roman rule. Judaism had been defined by Roman law since the time of Julius Caesar as a *religio licita* (legal religion). By contrast, Christianity was regarded as an upstart religion, and seen as a threat to the stability and hierarchy of the empire. Until 250 C.E., Christians were periodically persecuted, mainly for disturbing the peace and challenging the notion of family. Thereafter, a series of anti-Christian Roman laws appeared. For Christians, their secondary status alongside the preferred status of Jews bred resentment of Jews; the superior status of Judaism contradicted the foundational Christian notion that the Jews had been rejected by God for rejecting Christ. Already in the Gospel of John such resentment began to be expressed. Prior to the fourth century, although the number of Christians and the influence of Christianity continued to grow rapidly, as long as the Roman upper class and reigning dynasty were pagan, Christian power was limited.

By the fourth century, though, the influence of Christian bishops and confessors extended into the upper classes of Roman society, notably the emperor

Constantine. In 313, Constantine issued the Edict of Milan, which redefined Christianity as the official religion of the empire. Two years later, Constantine converted on his deathbed. Whether or not this was a sincere conversion is still a matter of debate; some claim he was hedging his bets to avoid the possibility of eternal damnation in the afterlife. In any case, when he converted, the entire Roman aristocracy converted with him. Suddenly the status of Jews and Christians became inverted, leaving Jews in a precarious position for more than a millennium.

There was a moment of reprieve for Jews under Julian (361–6), the grandson of Constantine. Julian, ostensibly a Christian priest and bishop, was a closet pagan. Once emperor, he revealed his true pagan nature and a bitter contempt for Christians and Christianity. In order to undermine the spread and popularity of Christianity, he attempted to revive pre-Christian religion. To this end, he invited Jews to rebuild the Temple. This offer was short-lived, however. In 366, Julian was assassinated by his Christian weapon-bearer during a campaign against the Sassanian Persians.

The surging confidence and power of Christians bred a growing hostility toward Jews, particularly in cities such as Antioch, where Christians and Jews lived in close quarters. Antioch, a wild, cosmopolitan city, was full of Jews, Christians, and pagans. There, a leading preacher named John Chrysostum was disturbed by the influence that Judaism continued to exert on local Christians, and particularly by Christians celebrating Jewish holidays. In response, he preached hostility toward, and violence against, Jews. In retrospect, this was a dangerous moment for Jews. Had Roman policy followed the teachings of John Chrysostum, the Roman Empire could have eradicated a majority of world Jewry.

That Roman policy continued to tolerate Jews stemmed from the teachings of Augustine of Hippo. Augustine lived in isolation, and not in a big city, and thus had a more idealistic outlook than John Chrysostum. Augustine preached toleration of Jews, citing four theological reasons. First, he pointed out that Christ had begged mercy for the Jews. Second, Augustine claimed that Jews were indispensable as preservers of Hebrew Scripture, and as conduits through which to understand its true meaning. Third, he argued that the ongoing suffering of Jews attested to the truth of Christianity. Finally, he noted that the eventual conversion of Jews to Christianity was a precondition for the Second Coming of Christ; thus Jews must be around at the end of days. From these arguments, Augustine concluded that Christians must neither kill Jews nor forcibly convert them to Christianity. The beauty and magnificence of Christianity, he argued, would in time bring Jews to the baptismal font voluntarily. At the same time, he argued that Jews must suffer.

The fact that Christians periodically killed or forcibly converted Jews thereafter suggests that, while Augustine's notion of Christian toleration of Jews was the predominant mainstream Christian doctrine, the more antagonistic view of John Chrysostum survived as a countercurrent to the notion of toleration. Nonetheless, by the beginning of the fifth century these teachings and conclusions had been woven into the fabric of papal and patriarchal dogma, and into Roman law, both in the Western Roman Empire and in Byzantium. In 591, Pope Gregory I scolded the bishop of Marseilles for allowing Jews to be forcibly baptized. The law codes of Emperors Theodosius and Justinian, moreover, have a distinctly Augustinian tone. Justinian's Novella 146 recognized Judaism as a tolerated religion, and outlawed the destroying or defacing of existing synagogues. Clearly, though, there were limits to Christian toleration. Justinian, while protecting existing synagogues, banned the construction of new ones. More important, in 425 he closed down the Sanhedrin for good, thus prompting a shift in the center of Jewish life from the Land of Israel to Babylonia, which was beyond the influence of Roman and Byzantine emperors and Christian dogma.

The harshness of Christian rule would be reflected in ways that Judaism, particularly Rabbinic Judaism, would develop. In the Land of Israel and its environs, Jews would exhibit a greater sense of insularity as a response to the harshness of Byzantium. In Babylonia, Judaism would be more open to worldly ideas, in response to the kinder environment.

Chapter 3

The rise of Rabbinic Judaism

During the first millennium C.E., Rabbinic Judaism expanded and developed from the religion of a small Jewish scholarly elite into the dominant form of Judaism worldwide. To be sure, the emergence of Rabbinic Judaism as normative Judaism worldwide was neither inevitable nor immediate. It took rabbinic leaders more than eight centuries to establish their teachings as the sole standards of Jewish belief and practices. Moreover, for all their scholarly and pedagogic efforts, the rabbis would most likely not have succeeded had broader political developments not intervened on their behalf, particularly the Islamic conquest of the Jewish world that began in the seventh century. Even aided by such developments, it still took the rabbis an additional two or three centuries to impose their brand of Judaism across the diaspora.

Until the fifth or even sixth century C.E., Rabbinic Judaism defined the lives of the Jewish intellectual elite; the beliefs and practices of the mass of Jews remained comfortably outside the realm of the rabbis. Even the redaction and dissemination of the Mishnah (a summary of oral traditions) at the end of the second century C.E. and the Babylonian Talmud at the beginning of the sixth century, important steps in the crystallization of Rabbinic Judaism, reflected in their time at best a partial victory. Rather, it is more accurate to see the rise of Rabbinic Judaism as a tortuous path to Judaism itself, aided by circumstances whose endpoint was, for several centuries, far from certain.

The early rabbis saw themselves as the intellectual and spiritual heirs of the Pharisees, and with good reason. The rabbis embraced the conceptual framework, content, and exegetical method of the Pharisees' oral tradition of law, and expanded this tradition steadily from the first century C.E. onward. They embraced the Pharisaic emphasis on personal prayer, the centrality of the synagogue, and many of the Pharisees' core beliefs: an afterlife, the balance between free will and predetermination, divine reward and punishment, resurrection of the dead, and messianic redemption at the end of time. The rabbis, moreover, internalized the accommodating political outlook of the Pharisees, adapting it to life in the diaspora.

There were, of course, subtle differences between the Pharisees and the rabbis. The Pharisaic oral tradition was a loose assemblage of teachings and sayings. The rabbis refined this tradition by defining the parameters of religious belief and practice more sharply. Furthermore, the Pharisees transmitted this tradition from one generation to the next in an ad hoc manner. The rabbis regularized this process of transmission by creating academies of learning that fostered a more disciplined and regularized relationship between master and disciple. Indeed, the word "rabbi," often colloquially translated as teacher, derived from the Hebrew word for master. The relationship between the rabbi and his student was like that of a master craftsman and his apprentice; and the world of the rabbis much like the exclusive world of a guild.

The early development of Rabbinic Judaism can be divided into two periods: the Tannaitic period, from 50 B.C.E. to 200 C.E., and the Amoraic period, from 200 to 500 C.E. The Tannaitic period, derived from "Tanna," the term that rabbinic tradition uses to refer to the scholars of the Mishneh and contemporary works, revolved principally around two collections of teachings: Midrash and Mishneh. Midrash, a Hebrew term for "that which is pursued," refers at once to a method of interpretation and to the amalgamation of teachings derived using this method. As a literary collection, Midrash is divided into two genres, Midrash Halacha and Midrash Aggadah. Midrash Halacha refers to laws and beliefs derived from the text of the Hebrew Bible. In some cases, this meant setting aside a literal reading of biblical law. For example, the biblical injunction "an eye for an eye" was reinterpreted in the Midrash to mean monetary compensation for bodily harm. Elsewhere, the Midrash derived concrete meaning from more abstract biblical terms. For example, on the basis of the verses "Honor your father and mother" and "A person should fear his mother and father," the Midrash derived more concrete understandings of the meaning of fear and respect.

Elsewhere, Midrash Halacha defined concretely vague biblical concepts, such as the definition of work that is prohibited on the Sabbath and festival days. The Midrash, noting that the Bible uses the terms *Melacha* (literally, labor) and *'Avoda* (literally, service) to refer to different forms of work, derived distinct prohibitions of work on the Sabbath and festivals. The scriptural basis of work prohibited on the Sabbath, *Kol Melacha lo ta'asu* ("You shall refrain from all forms of labor"), was less specific and hence more inclusive than the prohibition of work on festivals, *Kol melechet 'avoda lo ta'asu* ("You shall refrain from all forms of laborious service") – hence the conclusion that certain forms of work that are prohibited on the Sabbath are permitted on festivals.

In contrast to the legal aims of Midrash Halacha, Midrash Aggadah refers to folk tales about biblical figures and events. At times these tales romanticized the gaps in the narratives of the Hebrew Bible. For example, the Midrash explains how the patriarch Abraham came to discover monotheism.

Abraham, while contemplating the sun, moon, and other natural phenomena as all-powerful, only to see each one "fall" from omnipotence, recognized God as an incorporeal omnipotent deity who ruled over nature and the world. Elsewhere, an Aggadah (oral tradition) explains Isaac's poor vision as the result of angels' tears dropping into his eyes during his binding; or Leah's unattractive appearance as the result of her crying out of fear lest she be betrothed to her cousin Esau.

In other cases, the tales are themselves a vehicle for illustrating a law or legal principle. When explaining how the serpent enticed Eve to eat the forbidden fruit in the Garden of Eden, the Aggadic tradition notes a discrepancy between God's instruction to Adam ("Do not eat from the Tree of Knowledge") and Adam's instruction to Eve ("Neither eat from nor touch the Tree of Knowledge"). By adding to God's instruction, Adam inadvertently allowed the serpent to confound Eve's sense of obedience when she touched the tree without consequence. From this, the Midrash derives the legal-ethical principle *"ba'al tosif,"* or improperly augmenting how a commandment is to be observed (such as praying four times a day rather than three). Elsewhere, in the Book of Numbers, the Midrash imagines Moses scolding Zimri ben Salu for cohabitating with a Midianite women. Zimri retorts by noting that the prohibition of cohabiting with a Midiante women would be issued only in the Book of Deuteronomy, rendering this act technically permissible, since Numbers precedes Deuteronomy. The Midrash disparagingly terms this and similar forms of loopholing *vikuach Zimri*, the reasoning of Zimri.

The legal and folkloristic dimensions of Midrash were complemented by a parallel oral tradition of apodictic teachings that were eventually redacted at the end of the second century C.E. as the Mishneh. The bulk of these legal dicta expanded and applied the laws of the Torah. For example, this collection included a more specific definition of the Torah's rather vague definition of work by enumerating thirty-nine categories of work based on the forms of work performed in the construction and operation of the Temple.

Some dicta addressed civil matters. One tractate, eventually redacted as *Baba Kama*, defining four types of civil damage by systematizing and expounding the laws enumerated in Exodus 21:28–35. Other dicta defined the rules governing marital and divorce proceedings, and fixed the Jewish calendar by establishing a protocol for determining the beginning of a new month and fiscal, ritual, agricultural, and historical new years.

These legal dicta at times had a philosophical undertone. For example, the Mishneh defined the procedure for adjudicating capital cases so as to make it difficult if not impossible to convict a person of a capital crime. This reflected a deep wariness of executing an innocent person, and an implicit preference to risk letting a guilty man go free. The presumption was that God would ultimately bring this individual to justice.

That Tannaitic teachings remained dynamic and never stagnated owed in no small part to the emergence in the first century B.C.E. of *zuggot*, pairs of scholars who, while embracing the same corpus of beliefs and exegetical method, often articulated conflicting interpretations of specific practices. This dynamism born of disagreement was not new to the rise of rabbinic Judaism; tensions between kings and prophets, priests and scribes, and Pharisees and Sadducees had animated the development of Israelite and early Jewish culture. During the first century B.C.E., a highly productive and constructive incarnation of this animating tension appeared in the debates and disputes between the first of these *zuggot,* transitional figures between the Pharisees and the rabbis: Hillel and Shammai.

As Louis Finkelstein suggested decades ago, Hillel and Shammai represented two types of Pharisees that then presaged the two mentalities within the realm of rabbinic Judaism. Hillel, Finkelstein noted, was a plebeian Pharisee; Shammai was a patrician Pharisee with Saducean tendencies. Shammai tended to interpret Scripture more conservatively and literally. Hillel, more attuned to what later generations of rabbis would call *inyana de-yoma* (affairs of the day), would adapt biblical tradition more liberally.

In addition, Shammai, like other landed patricians and Sadducees, was more interested than Hillel in agricultural matters. Hillel was more sensitive to the economic implications of agricultural commandments like the Shmita (sabbatical year). According to the Bible, every seven years the land was to lie fallow and debts were to be cancelled. Hillel, noting the reluctance of creditors to lend money as the sabbatical year approached, and the potential economic devastation that could ensue, modified the cancelling of debts with the *prozbol*, a caviat that allowed creditors to place certain type of debt in escrow during the sabbatical year, and then collect them the following year.

The disparate outlooks between Hillel and Shammai carried over to and were developed by their disciples, Bet Hillel and Bet Shammai (literally, the School of Hillel and the School of Shammai). A disagreement over the proper way to kindle the Hanukkah lights, for example, reflected a broader philosophical understanding of the nature of holiness. Bet Shammai advocated lighting the lights in a diminishing order, eight on the first day down to one on the last, arguing that one can descend in holiness but not ascend. Bet Hillel advocated lighting the lights in ascending order, arguing that one only ascends in holiness. In other words, Bet Shammai regarded holiness as ultimately finite and diminishing, while Bet Hillel regarded holiness as infinite and ever-expanding.

An equally revealing dispute was over the proper way to greet a bride on her wedding day. The disciples of Shammai advocated *kalah k'mot she-hi* (speaking to the bride truthfully no matter what). The disciples of Hillel, by contrast, advocated *kalah na'a va-hasida* (telling the bride she is beautiful and pleasant). This underscored the overriding Shammaite concern with the letter of the law, as opposed to the Hillelite concern with both the letter and the spirit of the law and its social and emotional affect. Gradually, the disciples of Hillel emerged as the leaders of the rabbinic movement as the latter emerged dominant after 70 C.E.

The rise to prominence of the rabbis stemmed in large part from the latter's Pharisaic heritage. The rabbis had appropriated those elements of Pharisaic Judaism most viable without a temple and a priesthood: personal prayer and faith, and oral tradition. Moreover, the rabbis inherited the Pharisees' ability to accommodate and thrive under foreign rule. The leading rabbinic figure after 70 C.E. was Yohanan ben Zakkai, a disciple of Hillel. According to legend, during the Great Revolt, ben Zakkai had negotiated a deal with the Romans, allowing him to reconvene the Sanhedrin in Yavneh. Whether this story was true or apocryphal, by the mid-second century the Romans recognized the religious authority of the patriarch, the presiding officer of the Sanhedrin confirmed by the Romans, who after 70 C.E. replaced the high priest as the central Jewish leader. In exchange, ben Zakkai and his successors agreed to abide by a Roman-imposed truncation of the Sanhedrin's authority to religious affairs. From 85 C.E. on, the patriarch was a descendant of Hillel, thus affirming the triumph of the Hillelite dynasty.

The constructive tensions within the ranks of the rabbis persisted under the leadership of the Hillelites. The disparate interpretive approaches of Ishmael and Akiva, two disciples of Ben Zakkai, illustrate the continuation of the dualist scholarly tradition. Ishmael, an exegetical minimalist, approached scripture with the mantra "dibra Torah bilshon bnai adam" (the Torah speaks in plain human language). This axiom, he believed, precluded the need for extensive or overly expansive interpretation. To this end, he laid down thirteen rules of exegesis and insisted that these were the only legitimate tools for interpreting the Torah. Most notable among these are kal va-homer and gezera shava.

Kal va-homer (literally, lenient and stringent) meant that a prohibition imposed in a lenient case could be implicitly presumed in a more stringent case, and that which was allowed in a more stringent case could be implicitly presumed to be permitted in a more lenient case. For example, the laws prohibiting work were more stringent regarding the Sabbath than festivals. Thus, work permitted on the Sabbath was presumed to be permitted on festival days, and work prohibited on festival days was presumed to be prohibited on the Sabbath.

Gezera shava (literally, equal or parallel pronouncement) meant that an explicit understanding of a word or phrase in one part of the Bible could be applied to the word or term anywhere it appeared in the Bible. This principle was employed, for example, in attributing each of the three daily prayer services to one of the biblical patriarchs. Abraham was credited with instituting the morning service on the basis of a verse in Genesis, "Abraham arose early in the morning." Elsewhere, the terms "arose early" referred explicitly to prayer; thus, the Midrash concluded that Abraham arose early to pray. Similar reasoning credited Isaac with instituting the afternoon, since he was "meditating in the field at twilight;" and Jacob with the evening service, since he "halted at that place" before retiring for the night.

Akiva's understanding of scripture was extremely expansive. He believed in an almost infinite possibility of interpretation, epitomized by his mantra *Kozo Shel Yud* (Tip of the Yud), which meant that, in addition to inferring meaning from verses and individual words, one could read meaning into the juxtaposition of words and letters, and that even the tip of the yud, the smallest Hebrew letter, could yield meaning. Akiva was thus the father of the mystical tradition. In a key rabbinic legend, Akiva is the only one of four rabbis to emerge unscathed from Pardes, the heavenly orchard and the mystical gateway to the heavenly chariot and throne described in Ezekiel 1. Akiva's disciple Simon Bar Yochai is credited (ahistorically) by rabbinic tradition as the author of the Zohar, the central text of the Kabala. The term "Pardes" was given a second meaning as an acronym for Akiva's broader interpretive method. PaRDeS stood for *peshat* (literal meaning), *remez* (the implied meaning), *drash* (the derived meaning, akin to Midrash), and *sod* (the hidden meaning).

After the defeat of the Bar Kochba revolt and the ensuing decrees of Hadrian, the impulse to codify the hitherto oral tradition of laws and teachings intensified. The execution of ten leading scholars, coupled with the proliferation of interpretation and the dislocating shift of the center of Jewish life from Judea to Galilee, prompted Rabbi Judah the Patriarch to redact many of the extant legal dicta into a single collection: the Mishneh. He divided this legal corpus into six orders, each of which was made up of multiple tractates that were themselves divided into chapters and individual statements. Other contemporary legal dicta known as Baraita and Tosefta, though not incorporated into the Mishneh, nonetheless retained the same degree of authority.

The codification of Mishneh reflected the triumph of the patriarchate over Jewish society. In addition, the emergence of the Mishneh reflected the impulse among rabbinic leaders to present Judaism to non-Jewish society as uniform and united. To this end, the rabbis equated the act of informing on fellow Jews to the Romans with outright apostasy. What is more, there was no serious attempt to dislodge the Hillelite patriarchy. Direct challenges to the authority of the patriarch were deemed intolerable. Rabbi Eliezer ben Hyrcanus – the patriarch's brother-in-law – was expelled from the Sanhedrin for not accepting the rule of the majority. More dramatically, when Rabbi Joshua disagreed with the Patriarch

Gamaliel's determination of the calendar, he was required to followed the latter's calendar, and to eat and show up for work on the day he believed was the Day of Atonement.

At the same time, early rabbinic tradition was not entirely uniform. Built into this legal corpus was the right of rabbis to disagree with one another. Moreover, unity and uniformity did not lead to a complete centralization of authority in the Sanhedrin or the patriarchate. Local tribunals and academies existed alongside those of the patriarch. Any three Jews could form a tribunal. At the same time, although all Jews presumably had equal access to Scripture once it was canonized, the rabbis arrogated the right to interpret and apply law and prophetic instruction to contemporary life.

The codification of the Mishneh prompted almost immediately a new oral tradition of discussion, interpretation, and dispute that would last for nearly three centuries. During the fifth century, this tradition would itself be redacted into two large collections, one in Babylonia and the other in the Land of Israel, that would eventually be known as the Babylonian and Jerusalem Talmuds. The codification of this post-Mishnaic oral tradition coincided with the decline of Jewish life in the Land of Israel under Byzantine rule, and the rise of Babylonia as a center of Jewish life and scholarship by the fifth century. In retrospect, the shift to Babylonia is evident by around the year 350, when the Byzantine emperor curtailed the Sanhedrin's right to fix the calendar. In response, a Babylonian rabbi named Hillel, a descendant of the original Hillel, fashioned a new method for determining the calendar by designing a preset calendar that functioned independently of the Sanhedrin and the Patriarch. When the Sanhedrin was closed down for good by the Byzantine emperor Theodosius II in 425 C.E., the Jews of Babylonia had already laid the groundwork to step forward as leaders of the Jewish world.

Although it dated back to the sixth century B.C.E., relatively little is known about the Jewish community of Babylonia prior to the third century C.E. Until 226 C.E., Jews fared well under the Parthians, who granted them autonomy and left them alone if they paid an annual poll tax. The situation of Jews, or at least the Jewish elite, was enhanced by the emergence of the Resh Galuta (exilarch) as a state-recognized leader of the Jews. By contrast, rabbinic tradition described the rank-and-file Jews of Babylonia as the most impoverished in the world ("God bequeathed nine out of ten measures of poverty on the Jews of Babylonia").

The exilarch was believed to be a descendant of David, and heir-in-exile to the Davidic throne. While some scholars have suggested that this office dates back to the exiled Judean king Jehojachim, historically the existence of the exilarch can be attested to only from 140 C.E. The exilarch was regarded as royalty and was part of the reigning monarch's personal court.

Moreover, Judah the Patriarch recognized the authority of the exilarch as higher even than his own, because of the exilarch's Davidic lineage. By the third century, rabbinic leadership emerged in Babylonia alongside that of the exilarch, punctuated by the arrival in Babylonia of two of Judah the Patriarch's leading disciples, Rav and Samuel. Rav was born in Babylonia, studied under Judah in the Land of Israel, and then returned home in 219, where he founded a rabbinic academy in Sura. According to one of Rav's students, Rav put Babylonian Jewry on a par with Jews in the Land of Israel by claiming that "studying Torah is more important than sacrifices or even rebuilding the Temple." Samuel's concurrent arrival in Babylonia further enhanced the prestige of the Babylonian rabbinate. Contemporary observers assigned to each an area of legal expertise: *Halacha ke-rav be dinai u-che-shmuel be-isurai* "The law is according to Rav in civil matters, and according to Samuel in ritual matters." As rival rabbinic figures, Rav and Samuel assured that the dynamism of Rabbinic Judaism that had existed since the time of Hillel and Shammai would continue.

Until the mid-third century, the rabbis in Babylonia were subordinate to the exilarch. The two forms of leadership complemented one another. The support of the exilarch empowered the rabbis to enforce Jewish law. In turn, the rabbis gave the exilarch legitimacy by affirming his Davidic lineage. Eventually, though, the rabbinate and the exilarchate began to clash. At the heart of this clash were competing views of biblical tradition. The rabbis emphasized law, the exilarchate emphasized kingship. In 241, King Shapir I placed the rabbis on equal footing with the exilarch. In response, the exilarch regained influence by taking over the rabbinic academy at Pumbedita. By 500 C.E., the rabbinate and the exilarchate had forged a working relationship. At this point, three centuries of discussions of the Mishneh were compiled and written down as the Gemara, which comprises the bulk of the Talmud.

At its heart, the Talmud is a legal code surrounded by a philosophical and ethical code, which expands the ideas of the Mishneh and the Midrash. The Amoraim, or scholars of the Talmud, laid down a series of systemic legal and interpretive principles. First and foremost, they codified the distinctions between the two categories of law, biblical and rabbinic. For example, one systemic legal principle holds that an uncertainty regarding a biblical law mandates a stringent interpretation, while an uncertainty regarding a rabbinic law allows for a lenient interpretation. Other principles defined the authority of the rabbis vis-à-vis their own legal forebears. The principle *hitkatnut ha-dorot* (literally diminishing of the generations) held that an Amoraic scholar may not contradict a Tannaitic teaching, a rabbinic analog to the American legal principle *stare decisis et non quieta movere* ("maintain what has been decided"; do not altar precedent). Most of the discourse found in the Gemara consists of Amoraic scholars attempting to harmonize ostensibly contradictory Tannaitic statements, since Amoraic scholars had to agree with both sides of the apparent contradiction. At the same time, the principle *hilchata ke-vatra-ei* (literally, the law follows the later one) holds that once a later scholar properly reinterprets an earlier ruling, the later ruling becomes the definitive one.

The right to disagree, moreover, and the importance of minority opinion were central elements of talmudic discourse, to the point where not every dispute between Amoraic scholars had to be resolved. *Teku* (a shortened form of *tekum*, meaning "let it stand") is a periodic conclusion to talmudic discussions. Recognizing the importance of allowing disputes to remain unresolved, the rabbis assigned a larger meaning to this ordinary legal term by fashioning the acronym *Tishby yetaretz kushiyot ve-aba'ayot* ("the prophet Elijah the Tishbite will, at the onset of the Messianic Age, resolve all lingering questions and disputes").

In addition, talmudic discourse tried to validate and clarify unsubstantiated or puzzling Tannaitic statements. For example, the Mishnaic tractate on marriage stipulated that "a virgin marries on Wednesday," but offered only a partial explanation. The Mishneh explained that in the case of a presumed virgin bride who turns out on the wedding night not to be a virgin – thus introducing the possibility of an adulterous or other illicit sexual relation that would preclude the married couple from consummating the marriage – the smitten groom might choose to remain in the adulterous marriage if he had to wait a day or two before bringing the matter to court. Thus, the Mishneh insisted that the couple marry on the day before court was in session, so that "the groom could arise and come to court the very next morning." The rabbis of the Talmud, however, noted that although court was in session on Monday and Thursday, the Mishneh stipulated only Wednesday but not Monday – each being the day before court was in session. The Gemara's rabbis answered, "The rabbis of the Mishneh were concerned with the welfare of the daughters of Israel," and believed every bride was entitled to a wedding that took three days to prepare. Since preparation on the Sabbath for a post-Sabbath event was not permitted, a Monday wedding would allow only one day of preparation – hence the statement "A virgin marries on Wednesday."

Beyond resolving disputes, a central goal of the Talmud is to regulate all aspects of Jewish life, mundane and sacred, while discovering the potentially sacred in all things. This aim is exemplified by the broad range of rabbinically composed benedictions regarding even the most mundane of activities: going to the bathroom. The rabbis defined the bathroom as a decidedly unsacred space, where, for example, one was forbidden to pray. At the same time, the rabbis of the Talmud recognized the miraculous nature of going to the bathroom, and composed a benediction accordingly: "Blessed are you, Lord our God, king of the universe, who has created man wisely, fashioning orifices and openings, clear and known to the throne of his glory, such that if one of these orifices should burst or become obstructed, it would not be possible to exist and stand reverently before God."

While dealing predominantly with legal questions pertaining to religious and civil matters, talmudic discourse periodically addressed philosophical questions, sometimes explicitly and sometimes implicitly. At times, a mundane legal discussion took a philosophical and speculative turn. For example, in defining the obligation to return a lost article to its owner, the Mishneh had explicated the biblical injunction by defining two types of lost articles that had to be returned: a clearly marked article, and an article of great value. The Gemara inferred that the overarching principle that determines when one has to return a lost article is *yeush* (despair). That is, if the finder can reasonably assume that the person who lost the article has despaired of ever recovering it, the finder can keep the lost article. If the lost article is something the owner will try to retrieve, the article must be returned.

At this point, two Amoraic scholars, Rava and Abaye, push the discussion a step further by positing the case of the lost article whose owner is not yet aware that the article has been lost. If the article is clearly the type that the owner will despair of finding, but no such despair has taken hold in the owner's mind because the owner is unaware of its loss can the finder then keep the article? The larger, philosophical question, in a way anticipating (Bishop) George Berkeley by more than a thousand years, asks whether "lostness" is an innate quality that is defined only by human perception.

Other philosophical musings are more explicit, such as the extent of rabbinic authority with respect to divine authority. In a celebrated case, a group of scholars disagree as to whether the oven of a certain Achnai can be made kosher. During the ensuing debate, Rabbi Jeremiah takes a position contrary to everyone else. After having numerous exegetical proofs rebuffed, Rabbi Jeremiah invokes a series of supernatural proofs: "If the law is as I say, let that carob tree walk four hundred cubits ... let the current in that stream change direction ... let the walls of this house of study collapse upon us." In each case, this supernatural proof is rejected. "We do not accept proof from walking trees ... water changing direction ... walls of a house of study." At this point, Rabbi Jeremiah says dramatically, "If the law is as I say, let the proof come from heaven." Yet when a heavenly voice affirms the position of Rabbi Jeremiah, the other scholars reject this proof, too, saying that God has given the rabbis the ability and the right to interpret laws and make legal decisions – a remarkable delineation between the ontological realms of heaven and earth in legal matters.

In addition, talmudic discourse betrays a discernible social and political agenda. The former is perhaps most evident with respect to the status of women. Taking a hierarchical view of Jewish society, the rabbis often relegated women to a second-class status. This has prompted recent scholars to debate the status and image of women in talmudic discourse. Some scholars, notably Judith Baskin, have noted that the rabbis fashioned a Jewish world that regarded men as the ideal and women as an inferior other. Thus, Baskin argued, the rabbis dealt with women only insofar as they came in contact with or affected the lives of their fathers, husbands, brothers, or sons. The Mishneh, she noted, presented women largely as possessions to be acquired by their husband from the bride's father – thus precluding a wife from initiating a divorce. Women, in other words, had little or no autonomous identity. Other scholars, noted Judith Hauptman, revised some of the recriminations against rabbinic tradition by noting a measure of improvement in the status of women in the Gemara in comparison with the status of women in the Mishneh. The Tannaitic denial to women of any participation or say in marriage and divorce arrangements, was modified in the Talmud to preclude a women being married against her will and allowing a woman who wanted a divorce from an unwilling husband to obtain a divorce with the intervention of the Jewish community.

More problematic perhaps was the Mishneh's unsubstantiated exemption of women from all positive time-bound commandments. When coupled with injunctions that restrict the performance of a public or communal ritual to those who are themselves obligated, this exemption eventually resulted in the exclusion of women from communal roles in the synagogue and as witnesses in Jewish tribunals. This became the basis of women's second-class status in Jewish communal life until the twentieth century.

The Babylonian Talmud also contains a political theory of the diaspora, most notably a justification of accommodating foreign rule in the diaspora by completing the sublimation of national impulses. Drawing on Jeremiah's instruction to the exiled, Samuel reaffirmed the legitimacy of serving a Gentile sovereign by deriving the principle *dina di-malchuta dina* ("the law of the land is the law"). A similar sentiment is expressed in a Midrashic commentary on the Song of Songs, in which God extracts a promise from Jews in exile not to rebel, not to attempt to hasten the arrival of the Messianic Age, and not to return prematurely to Zion. In exchange, God extracts a promise from the nations of the world not to persecute or place undue burdens on the Jews. This willingness to submit to foreign rule is manifest in the revaluing of the story of Hanukah. Once this was a celebration of a miraculous Maccabean military victory, but the rabbis of the Talmud reinterpreted the miracle in ritualistic rather than military terms: divine intervention allowed one day's worth of purified olive oil to burn for eight days.

Yet despite the redaction of the Babylonian Talmud at the end of the fifth century, and the emergence of Babylonia as a center of Jewish scholarship, the constituency of Rabbinic Judaism was still decidedly limited, in two respects. First, the rabbis were an elite intellectual caste, atypical of the mass of rank-and-file Jews. The latter practiced more diverse forms of Judaism that combined the teachings and dictates of the rabbis with non-rabbinic customs and practices, some of which predated the development of Rabbinic Judaism. In addition, in parts of the Jewish world the authority of the Babylonian Talmud lacked the intensity that it had in Babylonia and its immediate environs. It would take several centuries until the Babylonian rabbinate was able to extend its authority to the far reaches of the Jewish world. The first step in this protracted and tortuous process would be the rise and spread of Islam.

Chapter 4

The Jews of Islam

The emergence of Islam as a major western religion during the seventh century C.E. fundamentally altered the political and cultural landscape of the Jewish world. For much of world Jewry, the Islamic conquest brought a reprieve from the harshness of Byzantine rule. In addition, the uniting of the heretofore separate Jewish populations of Byzantium and Sassanid Persia under a single Islamic ruler would prove critical in the emergence of Rabbinic Judaism for the first time as the normative Judaism for most of the Jewish world.

Furthermore, by the end of the eight century the influence of Islamic culture on Jewish culture, reminiscent of the impact of Hellenism a millennium earlier, would expand the cultural and intellectual boundaries of Judaism to include the philosophical tradition of the ancient Greeks, refashioning the archetypical Jewish scholar as a master of rabbinic text and Greek wisdom. As with earlier encounters between Judaism and non-Jewish cultures, the encounter with Islamic culture would engender the emergence of two rival traditions claiming to be the one authentic and legitimate Judaism: Rabbinic Judaism and Karaism. Karaism would pose the greatest challenge to Rabbinic Judaism, and be the focal point of rabbinic efforts to establish Rabbinic Judaism as normative Judaism.

Historians have disagreed in assessing the favorable and deleterious aspects of Jewish life under Islam. In response to a long-time prevailing assumption that the Jews of Islam fared better, on the whole, than Jews under Christendom, several historians asserted that the Jewish experience under Islam amounted to little else than 1,300 years of uninterrupted adversity and persecution. This point of view, labeled by its detractors as a "neo-lachrymose" view of Islamic Jewish history, in reference to an older "lachrymose view" of endless Jewish suffering in the Christian world (to be discussed in the next chapter), presumes above all that Qur'anic doctrine exerted a decisive and overarching influence on Islamic policy and popular attitudes toward Jews, and that the disparaging view of Jews expressed in the Qur'an translated directly into the political and social status of Jews. This claim has recently been called into question, particularly in light of three episodes in the history of Jews in the Islamic world that contradict this view: eighth- and ninth-century Baghdad, tenth- and eleventh-century Spain, and the early-sixteenth- through late-seventeenth-century Ottoman Empire. Each of these three episodes reflects a significant gap between the theological and the sociopolitical attitudes toward Jews.

The status of Jews under Islam, and the ways that it differed from the status of Jews under Christendom, reflected a combination of theological and political factors that stemmed partly from the initial Islamic and Christian encounters with Jews and Judaism. Early Christianity was one of several Jewish sects competing for hegemony in a land where Judaism was the dominant and majority religion. By contrast, Muhammad encountered Jews as a minority, and thus did not see Judaism as a rival religion. Moreover, by Muhammad's time, Judaism itself had developed beyond the laws of the Bible and the moral teachings of the prophets; Muhammad drew on a much larger corpus of rabbinic teachings in conceptualizing Judaism as a precursor to Islam. For example, the Midrashic story of Abraham's path to monotheism was retold in the Qur'an as Abraham's path to Allah. While the theological image and view of Jews in Muslim theology were ambiguous, at best, at no point did the Qur'an or Hadith villainize Jews the way Christian doctrine had. Simply put, there was no Islamic belief that Jews had murdered Allah or his son, or that Allah had singled out the Jews to be persecuted for all eternity. The notion that Islam had supplanted Judaism (and Christianity) was far less antagonistic toward Jews than the Christian notion of divine rejection and condemnation.

There was also a crucial difference between the Muslim *ulam* and caliph on the one hand and the Catholic priest and king on the other – a difference that stems from the disparate roles that Jesus and Muhammad played as founders of their respective religions. Jesus' leadership was exclusively religious. He never ruled an empire in the temporal sense, envisioning Christendom exclusively as a theological realm. As a result, Christian sovereigns, while periodically acting independently of, or contrary to, Christian theology, on the whole regarded their domain as a *Regnum Marianum*, limiting the theological and political space for Jews in the world of Christendom.

By contrast, Muhammad was a political leader in addition to founding a religious faith. Hard-wired into the fabric of Islamic civilization, therefore, was a dimension of politics and statecraft that was independent of theology. Hanafi, one of the schools of jurisprudence in Sunni Islam, allowed political leaders to make decisions based on reason and the demands of circumstance. All in all, Islamic leaders had greater freedom to act pragmatically, independent of religious doctrine; their decisions that determined the privileges, obligations, and restrictions imposed on their subjects were based in no small part on non-religious considerations such as economic utility and political allegiance.

The specific relationship between Muslims and non-believers was defined by circumstances. The status of Jews in Islam was defined first during Muhammad's initial encounters with Jews on the Arabian Peninsula, and then in the vast territory conquered during a century or more of Islamic expansion. Muhammad's first encounters with Jews quickly turned violent, with Muhammad eradicating one of the three Jewish tribes living in Medina and forcing the others to flee to an oasis at Khaybar. Later, after laying siege to Khaybar, he forced the Jews to surrender and pay an annual tribute. Soon afterward, he expelled the Jews from the Hijaz, the Arabian Peninsula and heart of Muhammad's empire.

During the ensuing period of expansion and conquest, Muhammad and his Muslim followers became increasingly a small minority ruling a large non-Muslim population. The conquest of the Sassanid Persian and Byzantine Empires brought a large Christian and Jewish population under Islamic rule. Eventually, Muslims, Jews, and Christians found a common adversary in the polytheistic pagan population. This was to prove decisive in defining the theological and legal status of Jews and Christians.

Theologically, Islam divides the world into two great realms, *Dar al-Islam* (House of Islam) and *Dar al-Harb* (House of the Sword), and believes that a perpetual state of war existed between the two. Most non-Muslims, once conquered, were given the choice of entering *Dar al-Islam* through conversion, or being put to death. Because Islam defined Jews, Christians, and Zoroastrians as *ahl-al-kitab* (peoples of the book) who had recognized part of the truth of Islam, they were exempted from this choice. They were given a special pact of protection, and known as *dhimmi*: people of the pact, or protected peoples. *Dhimmi* status meant having the right to live, and to practice one's scriptural religion unmolested by the populace, as long as one recognized one's inferior status. This the *dhimmi* were expected to do principally through the payment of special taxes such as the *jizya* and *kharaj* and by acting at all times with humble deference to Muslims.

The legal status of the *dhimmi* was codified in the Pact of Umar, a late-seventh-century agreement concluded initially between Muhammad's successor and the Christians of Damascus. The heart of this agreement was the obligation of the *dhimmi* to show deference to Muslims, and to remain culturally distinct from the Muslim population. To be sure, neither *dhimmi* status nor the Pact of Umar was applied uniformly. To orthodox Muslim leaders, it meant protection with humility. In other instances, *dhimmi* status was applied with excessive harshness or lenience.

In a sense, Jews had certain advantages over Christians in adapting to Muslim rule. The ongoing and seemingly endless wars between Islam and Christendom fostered an adversarial attitude on the part of Muslims toward

Christians. In addition, while Byzantine Christians had to adapt to a second-class status after having been the dominant religious group since the fourth century, Jews were already prepared for a subordinate role. For Jews, the Islamic conquest entailed largely a change in overlords. In the case of the Byzantine Jews, this meant a significant improvement.

The Muslim conquest of Persia and Byzantium united most of world Jewry under a single rule for the first time in over a millennium. The center of this united Jewish world was naturally the capital of the Islamic world. Under the Umayyad dynasty, this meant Damascus. Following the Abbasid conquest of the Umayyads in 750, the capital moved to Baghdad. The proximity of the new capital to Sura and Pumbedita, the intellectual centers of Babylonian Jewry, significantly enhanced the prestige and authority of the Jews of Babylonia. Coupled with the decline of the rabbinate in the Land of Israel, the proximity of the new capital to Sura and Pombedita, the intellectual centers of Babylonian Jewry, significantly enhanced the prestige and authority of the Jews of Babylonian Jewry. The Jews of Baghdad, in particular, would soon become the undisputed leadership of world Jewry.

The leadership of Babylonian Jewry lay in the hands of three groups: the exilarch, a coterie of leading Jewish families, and the Gaonate. The exilarch was the liaison between the Jews and the Muslim caliph. As a scion of the Davidic dynasty, he was treated as royalty. While nominally tagged with *dhimmi* status, he was allowed a royal entourage and had unimpeded access to the court of the caliph. His stature was buttressed by the support of leading Jewish families in Baghdad. The installation of the exilarch took place in the magnificent home of one of these families.

Gaon (the plural is "geonim"), the title given to the heads of the rabbinic academies in Sura and Pumbedita, was a shortened version of *Rosh Yeshiva Ga'on Bet Ya'akov* (Head of the Academy and Sage of the House of Jacob). Each gaon regarded himself as an heir of the Amoraic scholars who had participated in the deliberation of the Gemara via the Savoraim, a transitional group of scholars who lived and adjudicated immediately after *Sof Hora'a* (literally, the end of instruction), the rabbinic epithet that placed the interpretive authority of the Amoraim on a superior footing even to that of their immediate successors following the redaction of the Babylonian Talmud – that is, from the mid-sixth through the mid-eighth century. The geonim, while acknowledging their inferior authority vis-à-vis the Amoraim, regarded themselves as the authoritative voices of their age. In particular, this meant elevating the Babylonian Gaonate over the rabbis of the leading academy in the Land of Israel, located mainly in Tiberius, despite the latter's similar pedigree. By the end of the ninth century, the geonim had managed the arduous task of extending Rabbinic Judaism and imposing rabbinic authority through much of the Jewish world. As H. L. Ginsburg noted, "The Amoraim of Babylonia wrote a Talmud; the Geonim made it the Talmud."

This remarkable achievement was facilitated by the general mobility in the Abassid Empire, which allowed the gaonic leaders to send emissaries throughout the Jewish world. The task of these emissaries was further aided by the Radhanite merchants, a coterie of international Jewish merchants who traveled and traded from the Far East to Spain. By the end of the ninth century, the families of the Radhanites and the geonim merged through intermarriage. Under these favorable conditions, the emissaries collected donations for the rabbinic academies, and brought religious queries to the Geonim from Jews throughout the Jewish world. The replies of the geonim to these queries, eventually published as responsa, expanded the religious authority of the geonim. Emblematic of the impact of this achievement was the *Seder 'Amram* (Order of Amram), written by Amram Gaon toward the end of the ninth century in response to a query from the Jews of Spain, which regularized the order of Jewish prayer into what is, in large part, still the liturgy used in most traditional communities to this day.

In addition to uniting the Jewish world and facilitating the extension of Rabbinic Judaism, the Islamic conquest also began a period of Arabization of Jewish culture. Arabic replaced Greek and Aramaic as the language of Jewish high culture at the moment when the Arabic world discovered the wisdom of the Greeks, and when Arabic became the language of science. This led to the emergence of a new image of the ideal rabbinic scholar. Previously, the ideal scholar had been a master of biblical, Tannaitic, Amoraic, and gaonic literature. By the ninth century, knowledge of the Kalam – the Arabic translation and interpretation of Greek philosophy – and the ability to interpret biblical and rabbinic teachings philosophically as well as exetegically was an essential element of the ideal Jewish scholar.

A towering example of this new scholarly ideal, and the leading figure of ninth- and tenth-century Baghdad Jewry, was Sa'adia Gaon (882–942). His life and career embodies not only the intellectual achievements of the age, but also the conflicts. Sa'adia was born in humble circumstances in Egypt, but his intellectual prowess propelled him by early adulthood to the upper echelon of the Jewish intellectual elite. In 910, he was brought to Baghdad to help mediate a conflict between the exilarchate and the Gaonate, and was rewarded by being appointed the gaon of Sura. Sura, which had recently been overshadowed by Pumbedita, regained its scholarly primacy under Sa'adia Gaon's leadership. During his years as gaon of Sura, he authored his major works: the *Tafzir*, a commentary on the Hebrew Bible written in Judeo-Arabic; and *The Book of Opinion and Beliefs*, a philosophical treatise in Arabic. The latter was the first to present the laws, beliefs, and principles of Judaism systematically. In addition, he authored numerous *piyyutim* (religious hymns) that were hailed by later Jewish poets for their poetic virtuosity.

The overarching goal of Sa'adia's philosophical and rabbinic works was to defend Judaism's validity by demonstrating its philosophical and rational underpinnings. For example, he explained why the Jewish belief in revelation did not belie the primacy of reason. Revelation, he argued, augmented the human power of reason. Theoretically, he suggested, it was possible to grasp the divine will through reason alone. Revelation provided a means to accomplish this task for those who lacked the intellectual ability to reason philosophically or rationally. Revelation also provided a shortcut to rational truth – that is, something to believe in while trying to understand the divine will philosophically.

The cultural and intellectual achievements of Sa'adia Gaon and other Babylonian Jewish scholars, however, did not ensure the predominance of Babylonian Jewry. Beginning in the 920s, Sa'adia played a major role in the two arduous struggles waged by the Babylonian Gaonate, the first against the Gaonate of the Land of Israel over the right to determine the calendar, the other against the Karaites (see below) over the exclusive authority of the Babylonian Talmud. In 920, Rabbi Aaron ben Meir and the rabbinate of the Land of Israel attempted to revive and reclaim the rabbinate in the Land of Israel's practice of determining the Jewish calendar on a monthly and yearly basis, a practice that had been discontinued nearly six hundred years earlier.

This was no small challenge. The uniformity of the Jewish calendar allowed Jews to travel anywhere in the Jewish world safe in the knowledge that festivals and fast days would be observed on a given day. The ability to determine the calendar was a foundation stone of world Jewish leadership. In a larger sense, the dispute reflected the discontent of the Gaonate in the Land of Israel at the Babylonian effort to usurp world leadership. More specifically, in 835, the gaon of Sura had solicited instruction from the rabbis in the Land of Israel regarding the calendar, only to then claim superior knowledge of and authority over it, in the face of Amoraic statements that reserved the right to determine a Jewish leap year to the rabbis in the Land of Israel.

Buttressed by the support of an Egyptian sovereign trying to assert his independence from Abbasid rule, ben Meir reinstated the older calendar practice over the objections and condemnations of the Gaonate. Unprecedented in the history of the diaspora before or since, in 921 the Jews in the Land of Israel followed a different calendar and observed holidays on different days than the rest of the Jewish world. In response, Sa'adia Gaon published *Sefer ha-Mo'adim*, a compendium of laws concerning the Jewish calendar and festival. In addition, he spearheaded a campaign to win the support of the Jewish world for the Babylonian rabbinate. By 923, Sa'adia Gaon had persuaded ben Meir and the other rabbis to acquiesce.

Nonetheless, this episode demonstrated the limits of Babylonian hegemony as late as the early tenth century. The calendar controversy might not have been so contentious had it not taken place against the background of a second, larger challenge to the authority of the Babylonian Gaonate: Karaism. The Karaites were a sectarian movement that originated in the maverick biblical interpretations of Anan ben David, an eighth-century member of the exilarch's family. Anan articulated an alternative interpretation of the Torah that contradicted conventional rabbinic tradition. Some of his stricter interpretations of the Torah suggest a more literal reading. For example, whereas as the rabbis interpreted Exodus 35:3 ("You shall not kindle a flame in all your domain on the Sabbath") as not precluding the use of a flame that had been kindled prior to the Sabbath, Ananite tradition banned the use of any flame. In fact, this stricter interpretation derived from Anan's use of some of the same exegetical tools that the rabbis used; he simply drew different conclusions. Among other things, Anan and subsequently his Karaite followers observed the older, Land of Israel-dominated system of determining the Jewish calendar.

By the beginning of the tenth century, the followers of Anan had expanded and crystallized his system of interpretation to form a distinct brand of Judaism: Karaism. As Karaism came into conflict with conventional Rabbinic Judaism, Karaite scholars looked for ways to defend themselves. For example, Jacob al-Kirkisani's history of Jewish sects argued that sectarian movements, from the Sadducees to the Karaites, were an inherent part of Judaism's natural development and survival. Sa'adia Gaon spearheaded the campaign against Karaism. Bringing to bear an arsenal of rabbinic and philosophical modes of argument, he denied Karaism entry to the Jewish mainstream. While recognized as a Jewish sect by the Abbasid caliphate, by the end of the tenth century Karaism was regarded by mainstream Jewish society as an illegitimate form of Judaism. In retrospect, Karaism was not the first challenge to the hegemony of Rabbinic Judaism. Rather, it was the last gasp of non-rabbinic forms of Judaism that had coexisted with Rabbinic Judaism for centuries. In the end, though, the preeminent position of Babylonia and Baghdad was relatively short-lived. By the beginning of the tenth century, rival Jewish centers began to appear in the Islamic world in Egypt, Kairowan, and, most notably, Spain.

"Convivencia": the Jews of Muslim Spain

By the end of the tenth century, the breakup of the united Abbasid caliphate led to the emergence of new Islamic kingdoms in Egypt, North Africa, and Spain. Concurrently, new centers of Jewish life emerged in each of these new caliphates, most notably in Spain. Until recently, historians generally regarded Muslim Spain as a highly favorable situation for Jews, a view that was often telescoped into a single Spanish term: convivencia. This term referred to an extended, relatively peaceful coexistence of Muslims, Christians, and Jews in Spain from the eighth through the end of the tenth century, often characterized as a golden age in the history of the diaspora. To be sure, Spain was the only country in Europe where three major religions coexisted for an extended period of time, and where Jews were not the only religious minority. Yet the notion of a golden age for Jews in Muslim Spain, while perhaps tenable from the vantage point of Jewish culture, is harder to defend in light of the tumultuous political climate of the Iberian Peninsula. From the eighth through the end of the fifteenth century, Christendom and Islam met and fought in Spain. In addition, during the eleventh and early twelfth centuries, war between Muslim states continued unabated. Still, Muslim Spain was at least no less hospitable to Jews than other parts of the Muslim world, and considerably better for Jews than any part of Christendom prior to fifteenth-century Poland.

The origins of Jews in Spain are a melange of mythical, semi-historical, and historical accounts. The mythical origins trace Jewish life in Spain back to the time of Solomon, who, according to legend, sent a tax collector to Spain, who died and was buried there. The prophet Obadiah made reference to "captivity in Sepharad," which later became an epithet for Spain. There were also tales of Jewish refugees from Babylonian and Roman captivity settling in Spain. Semihistorical accounts, based on historical suppositions or circumstantial evidence, include an assertion that since the apostle Paul had traveled to Spain, there must have been Jews there, else why would he have gone there in search of converts? Similarly, there was the presumption that the Jewish presence extended to the farthest reaches of the Roman Empire, which included Spain. The earliest historical evidence of Jewish life in Spain, a tombstone of Anna Salo (Hanna bat Solomon), dates to the third century C.E.

Crucial in understanding the situation of Jews in Spain is the fact that Spain was a frontier region with respect to the early Christian and early Islamic worlds. Thus, conditions in Spain until the high Middle Ages often deviated from conditions closer to the center, sometimes to the advantage and sometimes to the detriment of Jews. In fourth-century Spain, one of the few extant sources from this period, the proceedings of a church council in Elvira, suggests a close relationship between Jews and Christians, in contrast to the deteriorating relations between Christians in Jews in points to the east. This council found it necessary to issue a ban on Christians eating with and marrying Jews, and Christians asking Jews to bless their crops.

This situation inverted following the Visigothic conquest of Spain during the sixth century. The Visigoths, extremist Christians, went to great lengths to limit the comforts of Jews in Spain. They heaped all sorts of restrictions on them, culminating in efforts to force them to convert, in violation of Augustine's injunction to the contrary. By the beginning of the eight century, Jewish life in Spain was on the verge of ending.

The conquest of the Iberian Peninsula by the Muslim forces of Al-Tariq in 711 brought a major reprieve for Jews. As his army gained ground, he recruited Jews in conquered towns to be standing garrisons, while Muslim armies advanced. Later, Spanish Christians would accuse Jews of betrayal, even though most Christians had fled before the Muslims arrived. The Muslims extended to Jews, along with Christians, *dhimmi* status, a quarter of their own in each town, and, in violation of the Pact of Umar, the right to bear arms.

Until 756, Muslim Spain was ruled by military governors from Muslim North Africa, leading to a period of instability, anarchy, assassinations, and tensions between Arabs, and Berbers, and Slavs. The situation improved after 750 following the Abbasid conquest of the Umayyad Dynasty. The lone Umayyad survivor of the Abbasid slaughter was Abd-ar-Rachman, who fled to Spain. After subduing the local rivals, he was proclaimed emir of al-Andalus in 756. During his thirty-year reign, he ended the internal strife that had plagued Iberia.

Distrustful of other Muslims, Abd-ar-Rachman implemented a broad policy of toleration of Jews and Christians, a policy that was pursued by his successors as well. By the reign of Abd-ar-Rachman II (822–52), Spain had become an international power with fleets and foreign embassies. Abd-ar-Rachman II forged an alliance with Byzantium in order to fight their common enemy: the Abbasid caliphate.

The rise of Muslim Spain as an important center of Jewish life coincided with emergence of Spain as an independent caliphate. Full independence was achieved during the reign of Abd-ar-Rachman III. In addition, this caliph wanted to create a royal court that would rival the imperial court in Baghdad. To this end, he invited leading Muslim, Christian, and Jewish intellectuals to join his court. This coincided with the decline of the exilarchy and the Gaonate in Baghdad.

The independence of Jews in Spain from the Jews of Baghdad was completed under the leadership of Hasdai ibn Shaprut, a Jewish parallel to Abd-ar-Rachman III. Hasdai ibn Shaprut was a wealthy, well-connected courtier, and thus a natural leader of Jews in Spain. He was also an accomplished scholar, characteristic of Jewish courtiers. In this sense, he combined the religious leadership of a gaon with the political leadership of the exilarch.

His patronage, moreover, was instrumental in the flourishing of Jewish culture in Spain. He imported volumes of the (Babylonian and Jerusalem) Talmuds and spent lavishly to obtain correct talmudic manuscripts. Until Hasdai expanded the parameters of Jewish culture according to the Islamic Jewish model, there was no evidence of non-traditional Jewish culture in Spain. The court of Abd-ar-Rachman III in Córdoba was worthy of emulation, and, in addition, the royal policy of toleration encouraged interpenetration of Islamic, Christian, and Jewish culture, based partly on religious competition. Finally, the personal example of Hasdai himself spurred other Jews to expand their cultural horizons.

As a patron of the arts, Hasdai sponsored many promising young scholars. Principal among them were Menachem ibn Saruk and Dunash ibn Labrat.

Ibn Saruk, Hasdai's secretary, compiled the first Hebrew dictionary. Eventually he met a tragic end, when he was suspected of being a Karaite and chased out of Córdoba. Ibn Labrat was born in Fez, Morocco, and educated in Babylonia. Under Hasdai's tutelage, he became the first Hebrew poet in the Muslim world, and the first secular Hebrew poet since ancient times. He introduced Arabic meter into Hebrew poetry. Though not a great poet, he prepared the ground for the great poets who would follow.

Hasdai was also involved in the discovery of the Khazars by the Jews in Europe and the Middle East. The Khazars were a pagan people in Central Asia whose king had converted himself and then his people to Judaism in the eight century C.E., for reasons unknown. In Hasdai's correspondence with the king of the Khazars, he attempted to present himself as near-royalty, comparable to the Jewish king of Khazaria.

The cultural development of Jews in Muslim Spain reached a high point at the end of the tenth century during the life of Samuel ibn Nagrela (997–1056), the most accomplished and successful Jew in Spain, if not in the entire history of the diaspora. He was a product of the cultural developments that preceded him. He received a dual education, Jewish and Arabic. He was an accomplished talmudic scholar, but also a great poet, Arabic scholar, statesman, and military leader. He would eventually hold the highest position obtained by any Jew in the diaspora.

Ibn Nagrela was born at a time of growing political instability during the breakup of the caliphate of Abd-ar-Rachman III at the end of the tenth century. In 1013, a series of civil wars climaxed with the Berbers capturing Córdoba, and the ensuing emergence of many petty states. The Berbers were far less tolerant of non-Muslims than the Arabs had been, prompting the center of Jewish life to shift from Córdoba to Grenada.

Against this background, Ibn Nagrela rose from humble beginnings to greatness. As a young man, his knowledge of Hebrew and Arabic earned him a job as a scribe, first for a local official and then for a courtier of King Habus of Grenada, and finally for the king himself. In 1020, Habus appointed Ibn Nagrela royal vizier owing to his skill as a scribe, and because the Berber king ruled an Arab majority and deemed Jews to be the most trustworthy of his subjects. As vizier, Ibn Nagrela had authority over all Muslims except the king, and even led the Muslim troops into battle.

In 1027, he assumed the title of *nagid* of Granada, the *de facto* leader of the city's Jews. In this capacity, he supported academies not only in Granada and elsewhere in Spain, but also in Babylonia and Jerusalem. He purchased manuscripts for poor Spanish Jews, and was a patron of leading Jewish scholars such as the biblical commentator Abraham ibn Ezra, and leading Jewish poets such as Moses ibn Ezra and Solomon ibn Gabirol.

The biblical commentary of Abraham ibn Ezra, in particular, underscores the complexity of Jewish culture in Muslim Spain. Building on the work of Sa'adia Gaon, Ibn Ezra composed one of the most elegant commentaries on the Hebrew Bible. It combined mastery of rabbinic literature, Aristotelian philosophy, and the literary and linguistic sensitivities of the age. Commenting on Deuteronomy 6:5, "You shall love the Lord your God with all your heart and all your soul," Ibn Ezra notes, "The heart is knowledge and is the pseudonym for the enlightening spirit and the prime mover. ... The soul is spirit of the body of the body that desires."

Ibn Ezra, moreover, periodically used his commentary on the Torah as a vehicle to defend Judaism from its Muslim, Christian, and philosophical assailants. For example, by the tenth century there was a prevailing notion among Christian and Muslim astrologers that Jews were closely aligned with the planet Saturn, regarded by astrologers as the most malevolent of the planets. This notion had originated much earlier among Roman astrologers such as Tacitus before finding its way into the writings of Saint Augustine and Muslim philosophers such as Abu Ma'shar, and would remain a core element of Christian and Muslim critiques of Judaism until the sixteenth century.

In response, Ibn Ezra recast the influence of Saturn in a more positive light from malevolence to fear of heaven, initially in his work on astrology, *Reshit Hokhma*, and later in his biblical commentary. In his commentary on the Ten Commandments, Ibn Ezra linked the nine known planets to the last nine of the ten commandments. Saturn, he claimed, coincided with the commandment to keep the Sabbath, noting, "It is therefore unfit for one to occupy himself on that day with everyday matters. On the contrary, one should devote himself on the Sabbath day solely to the fear of God."

Ibn Nagrela was also an accomplished scholar in his own right. He was the greatest theologian of Islam anywhere in Spain, and wrote a critique of the Qur'an. He composed poetry using the finest metric virtuosity of any premodern Hebrew poetry. He developed the wine-song to its apex, and wrote war poems in Hebrew in which he attributed his military victories to divine providence. Typical among these, and indicative of his profound sense of greatness, was the poem *"Ani David Le-Dori"* (I am the David of my generation).

His stature as *nagid* and vizier challenged the notion that Jews' lack of sovereignty was a result of a divine punishment. For this reason, some Muslims regarded his high position as scandalous and a violation of Muslim law. Such discontent was galvanized by Ibn Nagrela's arrogance. During his lifetime, though, criticism against him remained muted and dormant.

After his death in 1056, these tensions surfaced and were directed at his son, Joseph ibn Samuel. Ibn Samuel inherited his father's status as *nagid* and was a courtier, but was not the royal vizier. Soon after his father's death, there appeared a scathing polemical attack against him. In 1066, Muslim rioters destroyed the Jewish community of Granada, in retrospect the beginning of the end of Jewish life in Muslim Spain. During the ensuing decades, a Berber invasion brought to power a series of fundamentalist Muslim rulers who were intolerant of Jews.

The collapse of Jewish life in Muslim Spain elicited three responses from the Jews, each of which reflected a distinct view of the future of Jewish life in the diaspora: migration to elsewhere in the Muslim world, migration to the Land of Israel, and migration to Christian northern Spain. The contours of each of these responses can be described with reference to the lives of Moses Maimonides, Yehuda Halevi, and the Ibn Ezra family respectively.

The family of Moses Maimonides was among those who opted to migrate elsewhere in the Muslim world. Maimonides was born in Córdoba in 1135. When he was 13, Córdoba was conquered by the Almohads, Muslim fundamentalists from North Africa. The ensuing religious persecution prompted the Maimon family to leave Córdoba and, after wandering for twelve years, to settle in Fez, Morocco, by 1160. There Moses Maimonides studied with Judah ha-Cohen ibn Susan. In 1165, Ibn Susan chose martyrdom over forced conversion – a subtext of Maimonides' treatise on the subject of forced conversion. The Maimon family then moved to Cairo, so that Moses could fight against the Karaites. Until 1168, Moses was supported by his brother David, a physician. When David died in 1168, Moses studied medicine so as not to have to earn a livelihood from the study of the Torah.

By 1177, Moses Maimonides was appointed the head of Jewish community of Fustat, a suburb of Cairo, and would often be referred to as the Sage of Fustat. In 1185, he was appointed the physician of Al-Fadil, royal vizier of Egypt. From this point, he worked nearly around the clock as royal physician and physician to the Jewish community. On the Sabbath, he addressed legal and theological questions all day. Given this full schedule, it is hard to imagine when Maimonides slept, let alone found the time to write books. Nonetheless, he was a prolific scholar, producing some of the most influential legal and philosophical works of his time. Chief among these was his legal code, *Mishneh Torah*, written in clear, concise Hebrew for a broad Jewish audience. His philosophical treatise *Guide to the Perplexed*, which he wrote in Arabic for the older children of the Jewish elite, was intended to resolve tensions between Judaism and Greek philosophy; and his numerous epistles dealt with a diverse array of subjects such as the Messiah and the status of converts in Jewish communal life. A common thread in his varied works was a sense of dislocation. In his introduction to the Mishneh Torah, as well as his introduction to his commentary on the Mishneh, he noted a concern lest the transmission of scholarship be interrupted by the travails of the time.

Yet neither the Maimon family's response to the decline of Jewish Muslim Spain nor the writings of Moses Maimonides revealed a sense of disillusionment with the future of Jewish life in the diaspora, but only with Muslim Spain. This was in contrast to the response of Yehuda Halevi, who despaired of any future for Jewish life anywhere in the diaspora. Halevi, the greatest Jewish poet in the history of the diaspora, was born *c.* 1075 in Toledo amid the tempestuous transition in Spain from Muslim to Christian rule. His friendly demeanor gained him access to elite circles. He won an Ibn Ezra poem improvisation competition, and the admiration and support of the Ibn Ezra family, who invited Halevi to Granada. There he remained until 1090, when the Muslim fundamentalist Ibn Tashfin captured the city.

At this point, Halevi began to travel, and spent time in Lucenna and Seville. Eventually he settled in Córdoba, which was still home to Jewish scholars and writers. He earned a living as a physician, and became rich. His literary output marked the pinnacle of Hebrew poetry in Spain. More of his poems were incorporated into the Jewish liturgy than those of any other poet.

Most striking among his poems were those in which he expressed his yearning for Zion, such as *"Libi ba-Mizrach"* (My heart is in the east). Unlike his contemporaries, Halevi believed that the Muslim–Christian conflict in Spain was a microcosm of global conflict. He saw Spanish Jews as caught between hammer and anvil, tottering on a precipice, and felt that Spain was at best only a temporary refuge. He argued that Jews should return to Zion. Centuries later, proponents of Zionism would (anachronistically) claim him as a precursor. In fact, his yearning for Zion reflected a traditional messianic belief, with one modification: that Jews should wait for the Messiah in Israel in order to hasten the arrival of the Messianic Age.

Parallel to his disillusionment with the prospects for Jewish life in Spain was his critique of the influence of philosophy in Jewish intellectual life. In the greatest of his works, *Kuzari: A Defense of a Despised Religion*, Halevi produced what has been described as a philosophical critique of philosophy. In this work, he imagined the decision-making process that led the king of the Khazars to convert to Judaism. In a series of dialogues, the king listens and dismisses the arguments of a Muslim, a Christian, and a philosopher. He then listens and accepts the arguments of a rabbi, deciding that Judaism is the bearer of divine truth.

In the end, though, while Maimonides and Yehuda Halevi were undoubtedly not the only Spanish Jews to leave Spain, many others remained in Spain by migrating northward to Christian Spain. Notable among these Jews were Abraham ibn Daud and the Ibn Ezra family, who were able to reestablish themselves in the comparatively less contentious climate of the Christian North. There they would encounter a whole new set of challenges and opportunities in the world of European Christendom.

Chapter 5

The Jews of medieval Christendom

The historical experience of Jews in medieval Christian Europe has conventionally been presented as the epitome of what Salo Baron termed "the lachrymose view of Jewish history." This 700-year experience was undeniably marked by numerous episodes of adversity, beginning with the First Crusade and ending with the expulsion of the Jews from Spain. Nonetheless, rather than define this extended period simplistically as an unyielding age of persecution and Jewish suffering, it is more accurate to explore the ebb and flow of Jewish life in medieval Christian Europe in terms of a combination of three broader factors. First, law in medieval Christian Europe combined elements of Christian doctrine and Roman law; the legal status of Jews was often an amalgam of Christian and Roman policy and tactics. Second, the situation of Jews often reflected the give and take between temporal (royal and noble) and ecclesiastic authorities ("throne, sword, and altar"). Third, as in the world of Islam, there was consistently a discrepancy between law and its actual implementation and enforcement.

This discrepancy is both elusive and crucial – elusive because legal statutes are one of the main sources of information about medieval Christendom, particularly with respect to Jews; crucial because of the widely varying application of legal dicta, particularly between political centers, where social reality coincided more closely with legal pronouncements, and frontier and border regions, where, for better or worse, social reality fluctuated widely from the letter of the law. For Jews in centers of Christendom such as Rome, that status remained consistent and stable, as evidenced by the fact that the pope, who ruled Rome throughout the Middle Ages, was one of the few political leaders who never expelled the Jews. In frontier regions, such as ninth-century France and pre-1250 Christian Spain, the situation of Jews oscillated from exceptionally favorable to exceptionally deleterious. Such shifts were in some cases set in motion by a realignment in the political hierarchy, in which royal and papal authority worked increasingly in a more complementary fashion, often at the expense of the nobles.

By the reign of Charlemagne, the legal status of Jews had been defined, principally by Pope Gregory VII. In the more outlying parts of Christian

Europe, though, real authority rested in the hands of local nobles. Jews in these regions obtained privileges and were given restrictions locally; thus, these privileges and restrictions were generally defined in terms of the immediate economic needs of the nobles rather than larger theological concerns. In a frontier-like area that was generally underpopulated, it is not surprising that Jews played an important role in the local economy. By the tenth century, Jews were also an important element of the small but growing urban population.

This was more the case in France than in the Rhineland. Jews who lived in French towns were not segregated in a Jewish quarter but settled in various parts of the town. Contacts between Jews and non-Jews were more extensive in France than in Germany, where economic contacts laid the basis for cultural and social contacts. By the end of the tenth century, Jewish scholars such as Rashi were using French words to aid in explicating biblical texts. Jewish women in France frequently used French names. An injunction against Christians eating meals with their Jewish neighbors issued by the leaders of the church in France in 888 suggests that social contacts between Jews and Christians were not particularly uncommon.

An interesting episode that reflected the stabilizing of the situation of the Jews took place during the reign of Charlemagne. Like those of nobles, Charlemagne's Jewish policies were dictated by non-religious in addition to theological concerns. By assuming the title of Holy Roman Emperor during the eighth century, he made an enemy of the Byzantine Empire, which had the same imperial claim. The endless wars between Charlemagne and his Byzantine rival led to an initiative to make an alliance with Persia, which was situated on the other side of Byzantium. To this end, around 800 C.E. Charlemagne dispatched a three-man delegation: two Christians and a Jew named Isaac. When Isaac returned with a treaty in hand, Charlemagne rewarded him with a series of privileges. Noting that Isaac's commercial and familial connections in the Muslim world had helped secure the treaty, the emperor eventually extended these privileges to other loyal Jewish subjects, in order to encourage other loyal and useful Jews to settle in his domain.

These privileges included, first and foremost, the coveted right to life and property, the right to own allodial (absolutely owned) land, the right to own and import slaves, and the right to employ free Christians as servants. Charlemagne also imposed a fine of ten gold pounds on anyone who harmed Jews or incited violence against them, payable to the royal treasury. He required a Christian bringing suit against a Jew to bring three Jewish witnesses in addition to three Christian witnesses. Under Charlemagne's and his sons' protection, the first Jewish communities took shape in the eastern part of the Holy Roman Empire in Metz in 868 and in Mayence (Mainz) in 906. By the end of the tenth century, there were two clusters of Jewish communities: Narbonne, Trois (Troyes), and Lyon in addition to Metz in France; and Worms and Speyer in addition to Mayence along the Rhine.

After the death of Charlemagne, the ensuing fragmentation of his empire underscored the importance of the protection that Jews received from a noble benefactor, despite the growing influence of archbishops. Often archbishops and other ranking clergy were concurrently counts and barons for whom economic and other temporal concerns superseded theological ones. The latter coincided with a backlash against Charlemagne's policy of Jewish toleration, spurred, among other things, by the conversion of Bodo the priest to Judaism. During the 820s, Archbishop Agobard of Lyon, advocating that "true Christians separate themselves from the company of infidels," embarked on a campaign to curtail the right of Jews to reside in France. This effort culminated when he tried to convert Jewish children en masse to Christianity. Though this effort failed when Louis the Pious, the heir of Charlemagne, intervened, it reflected the discontent with the expansion of privileges of the Jews by royal and noble benefactors. Agobard's successor and protégé, Amulo, continued the efforts of his mentor, albeit in muted form. While reiterating Louis the Pious's prohibition on violence against Jews, Amulo encouraged bishops to missionize intensely and to deliver sermons in synagogues.

Conditions for Jews remained relatively stable throughout the eleventh century, despite occasional setbacks. In 1007, rumors of anti-Christian acts in the Muslim world prompted anti-Jewish riots and forced conversion in the empire. At the request of Jacob ben Yekutiel, a leading Jew, the pope intervened. In 1012, Emperor Henry II expelled the Jews from Mayence after a local priest converted to Judaism. Within a year, though, he invited them back for trade reasons. The upshot is that temporal interests generally trumped theological aims during the first several centuries of Jewish life in Christian Europe.

Emblematic of this stability was the charter that Bishop Rudiger of Speyer gave to the Jews of Speyer in 1084. This charter, one of the oldest extant, resulted from an attempt by the bishop to attract Jews to Speyer after a fire had displaced them from Mayence. The charter contained the basic contractual elements embedded in subsequent Christians charters: the sovereign's protection in exchange for Jews paying an annual tax.

The language of this remarkable document underlines the bishop's practical and economic rather than theological aims: "When I wished to make a city out of the village of Speyer, I ... decided that the glory of our town would be augmented a thousandfold if I were to bring Jews." The bishop then delineated what would become a template for Jewish privileges and obligations in Christian Europe for the next seven or eight centuries. In exchange for an annual payment of three and a half pounds in Speyer currency, Jews were granted the right to live in a Jewish quarter protected by a wall, the obligation to police the Jewish quarter, land for burial (given in perpetuity), the right to quarter Jews from other communities, the right to employ Christians as wet nurses and servants, and the right to slaughter kosher meat and even sell meat to Christians. Most important, the leaders of the Jewish community were given the right to "adjudicate any quarrel that might arise among or against" the Jews. Six years later, the Holy Roman Emperor gave his Jewish subjects an expanded version of this charter.

It is useful to note a contrast between the charter of Rudiger of Speyer and the Pact of Umar, the legal template for Jews in Islamic lands. The latter imposed a series of restrictions on a broad array of implied occupational and residential privileges; Jews in the Islamic world were generally more integrated into the mainstream economy and allowed to reside with minimal impediment outside the Arabian Peninsula. By contrast, Christian charters granted a series of privileges atop a broad array of implied restrictions.

Though the relationship between Jews and their Christian rulers was lopsided in favor of the latter, it was still contractual: sovereigns needed the revenue from Jews as much as Jews needed protection. In an age when war was endless, sovereigns had a chronic need for liquid capital to pay and provision their armies. Jews were rare among taxable subjects in that they had liquid capital. Peasants often fulfilled their tax obligation in kind or through some form of labor. Nobles and church leaders, though they had capital, were tax-exempt. As a result, kings, bishops, noblemen, and town councils at times vied with one another to be the one who gave Jews their charter and collected tax revenue from them, partly for economic reasons but also as a measure of hegemony.

In general, Jews preferred to obtain charters from the highest possible authority. Hannah Arendt, commenting on this situation in the twentieth century, referred to this political strategy as the "royal alliance." Jews described this strategy in more poetic terms. The fourteenth-century Spanish Jew Bahya Ibn Asher, commenting on Deuteronomy 28:10, noted, "He who is a servant to a vassal of the king is not in as favorable position as he who is himself a servant of the king." A century later, Isaac ben Moses Arama echoed this sentiment: "We are the servants of kings, and not the servants of servants." This political outlook was not unique to Jews: a common aim of most subjects in the Middle Ages was to have as direct a relationship as possible with the highest possible authority.

Alongside this standardized political status emerged an overarching occupational profile: the concentration of Jews in commerce and money-lending. This economic trend resulted not, as some would later argue, from any Jewish affinity for these occupations; rather, it came about because of larger economic developments in the Christian world. A religious-based stigma discouraged Christians from doing business or lending money at interest. In addition, agriculture and artisanship were becoming more Christianized, involving a Christian oath with increasing frequency. Finally, dealing in liquid capital, like all specialized occupations, carried a certain power with it. Sovereigns did not want something as potentially powerful as the amassing of liquid capital to fall into the hands of someone who might aspire to the throne. Consequently, occupations such as moneylending, forging metal, alchemy, and sorcery fell into the hands of outsiders, foreigners – in other words, the politically emasculated. All in all, the concentration of Jews in commerce and moneylending fortified their relationship with the sovereign, and ensured for the most part royal or imperial protection. In this way, the benefits of protecting Jews for economic reasons dovetailed with the Augustinian injunction not to kill or forcibly convert Jews.

Political and economic stability by the eleventh century facilitated the development of Ashkenazic Jewish communal and intercommunal life. The demographic origins of Ashkenazic Jewry posed a problem to Ashkenazic Jews that their Sephardic counterparts did not have to face. The Jews of Spain originated in Babylonia and other parts of the Islamic world. Spain and Babylonia were part of a single Islamic world, with easy access from one to the other. Thus communal leaders of the Jews of Spain had a direct, unimpeded link to the Babylonian Gaonate – and a uncomplicated legitimizing of their authority. Ashekanzic Jewry traced its origins back to the Land of Israel via Italy; in 917, for example, the Kalonymus family – a leading Italian Jewish family – migrated to Mayence. By the tenth century, the Rhineland and the Land of Israel were on opposite sides of the grand border between Christendom and Islam; thus, Ashkenazic Jews were largely cut off from their rabbinic forbears in the Holy Land. While rabbinic and lay leaders in Spain claimed to be the heirs of the Jews of Baghdad, through such means as the gaonic responsum, Ashkenazic Jewish leaders had no such luxury. Rather, they had to justify their leadership without the inherited authority of a Palestinian patriarch or Babylonian gaon or exilarch.

Instead, they derived their authority through mutual consent from their constituents. That is, the members of the Ashkenazic communities bound themselves to a common set of laws, investing their leaders with the authority to enforce them. The self-derived communal authority of Ashkenazic communities provided a system of courts for Jews in an age when other existing courts were inadequate. Royal, ecclesiastical, and feudal courts assumed that Jews would handle their own legal and juridical problems. Manorial courts lacked the sophistication to deal with commercial matters.

At the heart of these laws was the *herem Bet Din*, the right to adjudicate cases and, more important, to excommunicate a member of the community who refused to comply with communal statutes. In an age that did not allow an individual to be *religionslos* (without a religion), excommunication from the Jewish community left no alternative but conversion. Short of converting, the only alternatives when facing a threat of excommunication were joining a different community, which was enormously difficult since new members were expected to bring a letter of reference from the previous community; or recanting. Most Jews who were threatened with excommunication chose the latter.

At the heart of this system was an Aristotle-esque assumption that proper-tied individuals were the best suited to act in the best interests of the community. As one of Rabbenu Gershom's statutes eloquently concluded, "All decisions according to the view of communal elders, the customs of old, and the needs of the day." Beyond the general rights of adjudication and ostracism, these statutes empowered communal leaders to protect individual and communal property (*Herem ha-Ikkul*) and to decide whether or not a new-comer could join the community (*Herem ha-Yishuv*). In addition, communal leaders had the right to impose communal taxes to support communal insti-tutions and send a communal donation to the Jews in the Land of Israel.

Communal leaders also derived a a notion of majority rule – not the mod-ern democratic notion, to be sure, rather the right of the majority to coerce the minority to concur. To counterbalance the power of the majority, the authority of the leadership, and the natural influence of the affluent, individ-ual members were given ways to voice a grievance by interrupting the prayer service in the synagogue. In such a case, the service could not resume until the grievance was redressed to the satisfaction of the plaintiff.

At the center of this new communal administration was the first great Ashkenazic rabbi, Gershom ben Meir, commonly known as Rabbenu Gershom (mentioned earlier). He had come to Mayence from Italy. Beyond helping to establish a system of communal administration, he established rabbinic learn-ing in France on a sound basis, reintroduced the lawmaking function of the rabbi, and united the scattered communities of the Ashkenazic world into a federation by establishing a measure of uniformity in the face of local cus-toms. His decrees (*takkanot*), approved by rabbinic synods, dealt mainly with marriage, social relations, and intercommunal relations.

Most famous is his ban on polygamy. This ban reflected an economic con-cern that Jewish men in an upstart communal and commercial world would have difficulty supporting more than one wife; and a concern lest the Jews be the only ones practicing polygamy in a monogamous Christian society. He also prohibited a husband from divorcing his wife against her will without the consent of the court, a marked deviation from classical rabbinic law.

With respect to social relations, he prohibited the insulting of former apostates who converted back to Judaism, the renting of domiciles from gen-tile tenants who had evicted Jews, and the reading of private mail. With respect to intercommunal relations, he extended the jurisdiction of a Jewish court to any Jew who happened to be in the community concerned, even non-residents. He allowed an individual to interrupt the prayers only after the individual had made three bona fide attempts to redress his grievance at the end of service. He disallowed the owners of synagogues from excluding any-one from attending. He required anyone with information regarding a lost article to come forward once the owner had made a public declaration. Rabbenu Gershom's accomplishments with respect to communal administra-tion marked the first step in the development of the Ashkenazic world.

As Ashkenazic Judaism developed, rabbinic scholars and affluent laity formed a natural communal leadership, largely because of the corporate status of the Jewish community. Scholarly and wealthy families often intermarried, forming communal dynasties. Jewish self-government reflected the overall corporate organization of medieval society: an amalgamation of corporate groups, each with its own set of privileges and obligations.

As a corporate entity, each Jewish community paid a single corporate tax to the governing sovereign. The leadership of the Jewish community was empowered by the sovereign to assess and collect taxes on its constituent members, the *kehilla*. The ability of a Jewish community to meet this annual obligation was the linchpin of its existence. For this reason, the ability of the few affluent families to cover much or all of the communal tax obligation and, when necessary, to secure protection through their connections with powerful people made them the guarantor of the community's very existence. In addition, wealthy Jews periodically contracted with the sovereign to collect taxes from individual Jewish households in exchange for a portion of the tax revenue – an occupation known as tax farming.

The other pillar of corporate Jewish autonomy, the Jews' right to govern themselves according to their own laws, elevated the scholarly elite into a position of communal leadership. In this situation, who better to interpret and adjudicate disputes and other matters in a situation where Jewish law had actual authority? Among other things, this meant that the communal leadership had the ability to enforce Jewish law. Observance of Jewish law, like affiliation with the Jewish community, was mandatory – a situation that would remain universal until the end of the eighteenth century.

The Jewish community also imposed its own taxes on its members, largely to help maintain a network of Jewish communal institutions, typically synagogue, school, and cemetery. In addition, individual members formed voluntary societies for predominantly religious purposes. These voluntary societies provided the means for social life and ordinary social intercourse among Jews. That these voluntary societies were almost exclusively formed for religious purposes – the study of rabbinic texts, collecting charity, caring for orphans, visiting the sick – reflects the all-encompassing nature of Jewish life in this world.

Jewish communal authority was based on a combination of state sponsorship – to go against communal leaders was to go against the king – and the threat of excommunication, a real threat because religion was mandatory. In addition, the rabbis derived their legal authority from a divine source, a belief in a chain of tradition that dated back to Moses and the revelation at Mount Sinai. The rabbis themselves were ordinary men; but their teachings were seen as divine. This was a common theme in the Middle Ages: power of the past over the present. Precedent and tradition were all-powerful. The authority of the rabbis and wealthy was symptomatic of the hierarchical nature of medieval Jewish society. Wealth and scholarship set rabbis and lay leaders apart from rank-and-file Jews.

Still, it is important to remember that, the growing complexity of communal life notwithstanding, Jewish communities in the Middle Ages were small, and without deep roots. Indicative of this characteristic was the status of Jewish women. Jewish society was generally highly patriarchal in nature, with communal leadership and public life dominated by men. Women, consigned (at least ideally) to the home, had domain over family life and the private sphere.

In more recently established Jewish communities, however, women and other groups who were relegated to subordinate status in more developed communities were given greater latitude. Thus, women in these communities were given a larger voice in communal matters, particularly more affluent women. They were also given greater leeway in marriage and divorce. Most noteworthy in this regard was Gershom's ban on polygamy, the need for which is a telling indicator of the subordinate status of women. In general, Ashekanazic women were less encumbered by local custom than their counterparts in the Islamic world.

The next major step in this direction was taken a generation later by one of his intellectual progeny, Rabbi Solomon ben Isaac (1040–1105), commonly known by his rabbinic epithet, Rashi. Born in Trois, Rashi studied in Mayence with one of Gershom's students. Later, he returned to Trois and founded an academy there in 1070.

Though no less involved in communal decision making and economic life, Rashi's main contribution was in the area of Jewish learning. His glosses on the Bible and the Talmud were lucid and easy to understand, and would eventually become a staple of biblical commentary and Talmudic study. He clarified difficult words or concepts, sometimes using a medieval French word to explain. He often appended a Midrashic tale to a legalistic interpretation, to appeal to children.

In addition, Rashi, like other commentators such as Ibn Ezra, engaged critics of Judaism through his biblical commentary. Commenting on Genesis 1:1, Rashi asked why the Torah began with the story of creation rather than the first commandment given to Jews. His answer: "The whole world belongs to the Holy One, blessed is he; he created it and gave it to whomever he deemed fit. Through divine will it was given to them [i.e. Muslims or Christians] and through divine will it can be taken from them and given to us" – a striking comment for a Jewish exegete to make at the moment when Christians were claiming control over of the Land of Israel. Rashi was not the only Jewish scholar to polemicize against Christian ideas. Two anonymous texts appeared at around this time as well. The first, *Toldot Yeshu* (History of Jesus), retold the life of Jesus as the story of a charlatan who deceived his followers by the improper use of magic through which he unlocked the magical powers of the tetragrammaton. The other, *Nizahon Vitus*, assembled Christological interpretations of the Hebrew Bible and then refuted them one by one – and then challenged the plausibility of the Christian Gospels.

Rashi's commentary on the Talmud, in particular, made this rich, complex corpus of laws and other material accessible to generations of Ashkenazic Jews. By the eve of the First Crusade, Ashkenazic Jews had established a stable relationship with the governing powers that be, an effective communal administration that balanced uniformity and diversity. They had also created a center of Jewish learning that, while not yet as sophisticated as the older centers in Spain and Baghdad, was narrowing the gap.

The crusades

The first major setback suffered by Ashkenazic Jews began in 1096 with the outbreak of violence during the First Crusade. While anti-Jewish violence accompanied virtually every crusade, the intensity of violence during the First Crusade caught both temporal and ecclesiastical leaders by surprise, preventing them from adequately protecting their Jewish subjects. During subsequent crusades, increased preparedness would limit the extent and effects of anti-Jewish violence.

The long-term origins of the First Crusade include several eleventh-century developments: the sense of Christian vigor that accompanied victories over Muslims in northern Spain and over Byzantium in Italy, a reassertion of papal authority, the general anarchic temperament of the period, and the search by younger sons of nobility for a valorous cause in an age of primogeniture. More immediately, the crusade had been summoned in late 1095 by Pope Urban II to liberate Jerusalem and the Holy Land from the infidel Moors.

Amid this heightened animosity against infidels, Christians in Europe turned against the Jews, the only infidels who were in plain sight. The pope's responsibility in this regard is a matter of historical debate. On the one hand, he had initiated a preaching campaign to stir up popular support for this massive and costly campaign. Whether intentionally or not, this helped transform a relatively restricted army of nobles on horseback into an undisciplined mass movement. At the same time, like all political figures, the pope was adamantly wary of inciting a breakdown in law and order of any kind. A riot against Jews, after, all could easily escalate into general mayhem.

Anti-Jewish violence appeared in multiple forms. More destructive than the violence perpetrated by baronial armies were the violent acts committed by Christian mobs. When incited by preachers such as Peter the Hermit, mob violence might result in random killings of Jews or in premeditated assaults on entire Jewish communities, notably those of Speyer, Cologne, and Worms.

Jewish responses to the violence varied accordingly. They attempted to negotiate with the crusaders by offering money, with limited success. The followers of Peter the Hermit and Duke Godfrey were assuaged. The followers of Enicho of Leiningem were not. At other times, Jews turned to their Christian burgher neighbors for assistance, and to the political authorities for protection. In general, where violence was poorly organized and sporadic, authorities could arrive in time and help. If it was organized and sustained, they could not. Some Jews chose the less conventional option of apostasy when facing the threat of immediate death. While rabbinic tradition makes little or no mention of voluntary abandonment of Judaism as a way of escaping death, in retrospect it was a reasonable choice in the face of brutal physical coercion.

More difficult to explain are those Jews who chose martyrdom and, in particular, who martyred their own children in the face of death or forced conversion. One would expect, given the traditional Jewish taboo against martyrdom, that Jews would have chosen this option as a last resort, perhaps reluctantly. According to the chronicles written by Jews immediately after the First Crusade, however, some Jews enthusiastically embraced martyrdom.

Historians have adduced several explanations. Some have explained this choice simply as a spontaneous reaction to frightening circumstances. Others have suggested the influence of preexisting rabbinic precedents that could potentially feed the urge to martyrdom: the commandment to proclaim the unity of God (*Shema Yisrael*), to worship no other deity, to love the Lord your God with all your faculties (*bechol me'odecha*), and to sanctify the name of God (*Kiddush Hashem*), and the Halachic injunction to choose death over apostasy. Still other historians pointed to historical precedents such as the Hasideans, the ten martyrs at the time of Hadrian, and Hannah who martyred her seven children rather than allowing them to be forcibly converted into Pagans during the Maccabean Revolt.

Most engaging, though, is what Robert Chazan described as a "counter-crusade." Chazan noted five parallels between the mentality of the Jews who chose martyrdom and that of the crusaders themselves: a sense of cosmic confrontation, a conviction of the absolute validity of their religious beliefs, an emphasis on profound self-sacrifice, a certainty of eternal reward for martyrdom, and belief in ultimate victory.

In the aftermath of the violence, sovereigns and rabbis tried to undo some of the damage, particularly with respect to Jews who were forcibly converted. In 1103, Holy Roman Emperor Henry IV issued the *Landfried*, which allowed forcibly converted Jews to return to Judaism, albeit for a price; from this point on, Jews would pay more for imperial protection. The rabbinic response was expressed most succinctly by Rashi, who welcomed the forced converts back to Judaism using the rabbinic aphorism *Af al pi she-hata Yisrael hu"* ("Although he transgressed, he is still a part of Israel").

The scale and extent of the violence during the First Crusade were not repeated during subsequent crusades, owing in large part to the efforts of imperial and ecclesiastical authorities to curb such violence. Bernard, the abbot of Clairvaux, when addressing the assembled knights prior to their expedition to the Holy Land, reminded them of Augustine's injunction against killing or forcibly converting Jews, reiterating Augustine's reasons for tolerating Jews:

> The Jews are not to be persecuted, killed, or even put to flight. ... The Jews are for us the living words of Scripture, for they remind us always of what our Lord suffered. They are dispersed all over the world so that by expiating their crime they may everywhere be the living witnesses of our redemption. ... If the Jews are utterly wiped out, what will become of our hope for their promised salvation, their promised conversion?

To be sure, the abbot reiterated some of the iniquities of the Jews, such as moneylending, which undoubtedly spurred some violence. Still, he redirected at least some of the crusaders' zealous animosity toward the infidel away from the Jews.

From this point on, Jews sought more reliable protection from the authorities, and were willing to pay more for it, crystallizing in a newly emerging status of the Jews: *servi camari nostrum* (literally, servants of our chamber, i.e. the royal or imperial treasury). This new status entailed a stricter array of restrictions, mainly in terms of residence and occupation.

Moreover, Jews were gradually excluded from most major European cities. A "city" in the twelfth century was not defined by size or population; rather, it was a legal category. Cities had royal, imperial, or ecclesiastical charters that gave them a measure of autonomy and certain rights. Typical among the latter was *De non tolerandis Judais*, the right to exclude Jews. The motivation behind this exclusion was largely economic – that is, Christian burghers and artisans not wanting to compete with Jewish merchants and artisans. The lone exceptions to this residential exclusion were cities that housed the seat of an imperial or royal throne. In such places, the sovereign was able to override the right of exclusion for his own benefit. This was the case in Prague and later in Kraków.

Jews were also gradually excluded from most occupations. They could not own or farm land, thus they could not be farmers or landowners. They could not attend university, thus they were excluded from the free professions. They could not join Christian guilds, thus they could not be artisans. What remained were commerce and moneylending, which ranged from peddling to international trade, and from pawnbroking to large-scale lending.

In addition, the experience of the crusades left an imprint on the Ashkenazic worldview. In this regard, it is useful to contrast Rashi's commentary with that of his Spanish counterpart, Abraham ibn Ezra. As compared with Ibn Ezra's philosophical commentary on Deuteronomy 6:5, "Thou shalt love the Lord your God with all your heart and with all your soul," Rashi's comment is more pietistic and indicates his awareness of the traumatic experience of the martyrs: "Even if he should take your life."

Ashkenazic culture and community: Pietists and Tosafists

The devastating effects of the First Crusade did not bring an end to Jewish life in the Rhineland. The main Jewish communities in the Rhineland – Speyer, Worms, and Mayence – were destroyed in 1096, but they were rebuilt and restored within a generation. This was due in part to the fact that the Jews in the smaller villages surrounding these towns were left alone. After order was restored, they eventually relocated to the towns and rebuilt the Jewish communities. At the same time, the crusades accelerated the westward movement of Jews from the Rhineland to northern France. In both cases, owing to the resilience of Ashkenazic Jews, less than a century after the First Crusade, a period of cultural explosion ensued.

Two differences are detectable between the Ashkenazic culture and the culture of Sephardic Jews and other Jews in the Islamic world. While both Ashkenazic and non-Ashkenazic Jews established an extensive network of yeshivot (rabbinical schools), a typical Ashkenazic yeshiva tended to be smaller and more elitist than its non-Ashkenazic counterpart. Moreover, in contrast to non-Ashkenazic culture, which combined religious and secular components, Ashkenazic culture was largely religious in nature, focusing primarily on the study of rabbinic texts.

Still, it is important not to overstate the difference between Ashkenazic and non-Ashkenazic culture. In the non-Ashkenazic world, despite the extra-talmudic focus, talmudic study was still the centerpiece of learning. The Ashkenazic focus on rabbinic texts did not preclude the study of Jewish philosophers such as Sa'adia Gaon, Maimonides, and Yehuda Halevi, and the writing of non-legal genres such as religious poetry.

The main currents of Ashkenazic culture took shape beginning in the twelfth century, each with distinct theological underpinnings and social philosophy, beginning with the *Hasidei Ashkenaz*, the Pietists of Ashkenaz. Despite the name, this group was connected neither to the pietists at the time of the Maccabees nor to present-day Hasidic Jews. The origins of this movement are unclear. The historian Yitzhak Baer pointed to a parallel between these pietists and coterminous Christian counterparts such as the Albigenses. Other historians have argued that their pietistic, ascetic, and mystical outlook was a response to the trauma and martyrdom of the First Crusade, an intense moment engendering an intense response. Critics of both contentions point to the pre-crusade roots of Ashkenazic pietism, notably within the Kalonymus family, prominent in the development of Jewish learning in Germany. Most compelling, though, is the assertion that this movement arose as a response to Rashi's disciples relocating themselves and the center of rabbinic scholarship from the Rhineland to northern France after the First Crusade, leaving behind a corps of intensely spiritual and ascetic pietists.

As noted by Eleazar of Worms, Yehuda ha-Hasid's *Sefer Ha-Hasidim* (The Book of the Pietists), the central text and one of the few extant texts of this movement, shows that the pietists were critical of conventional Judaism in two respects. First, they regarded it as minimalist – that is, as a body of beliefs and practices that demanded little beyond the fulfillment of the minimum requirements. For example, mainstream Judaism required Jews to pray three times a day. Pietists, while observing this requirement meticulously, composed and recited additional prayers for other occasions, such as midnight meditations and all-night recitations of psalms.

In addition, the pietists regarded mainstream Judaism as too theologically passive, with little or no active attempt to understand and carry out the will of the Creator (*Rezon ha-Bore*). Ordinary Jews, for example, rarely or never engaged directly the evil inclination that resides in the heart of every individual. The pietists would stare temptation in the face by placing themselves in the midst of overwhelming temptation and then resisting the urge to transgress. Notoriously, according to *Sefer Ha-Hasidim*, some pietists would spend the night in a brothel in order to resist partaking of the available pleasures. The number of pietists who participated in this movement was never very large. Some historians have speculated that the mentality of this movement was eventually carried eastward to Poland and left an imprint on the religious outlook of Polish Jewry during the fifteenth and sixteenth centuries.

More significant in terms of impact were the Tosafists (Hebrew: *Tosfot*), a highly skilled group of biblical and talmudic exegetes. Derived from the Hebrew term *tosefet* (gloss), the Tosafists were the intellectual progeny of Rashi and his school (and in some cases his actual progeny) who expanded or critiqued (or both) Rashi's interpretation of the Talmud. Most of the Tosafists are known only from their commentary. Some, such as Rashi's grandson, Tam ben Meir (also known as Rabbenu Tam), were also communal leaders.

As exegetes, the Tosafists faced the problem of adapting existing rabbinic laws and customs, which had been fashioned centuries earlier in the Land of Israel and Babylonia and then adapted by the geonim to life under Islam, to the particular circumstances of twelfth- and thirteenth-century central Europe. To this end, the Tosafists brought to bear an impressive intellectual arsenal that included all extant facets of rabbinic literature: the Babylonian and Jerusalem Talmuds, commentaries and responsa of the geonim, commentaries from Muslim Spain, works of Italian rabbis such as Gerson ben Meir, and of course the writings of Rashi. With this vast corpus in hand, they employed a dialectical process called *pilpul* (casuistry), an intense and rigorous analysis of existing rabbinic texts. Moreover, they were confident enough to second-guess earlier authorities such as Rashi, the geonim, and even the Talmud. In this way, they were able to apply talmudic and other dicta to their own circumstances. At times this meant invoking the talmudic principle such as *Ha Lan ha lehu* (Is this really so?) to legitimize distinct Ashkenazic customs in the face of older existing customs elsewhere. This was instrumental in the appearance of the first Ashkenazic prayer book, the *Vitri Mahzor*.

More than anything else, this exegetical method allowed the Tosafists to address immediate problems. For example, biblical and talmudic law prohibited Jews from lending money to other Jews at interest. The economic reality of the twelfth century required it, however; Jews needed money from lending at interest to pay taxes. The Tosafists fashioned a loophole, allowing Jews to use Christians as middlemen in credit transactions. Another major source of income for Jews in the Champagne region was from the sale of wine. The Talmud forbade Jews to handle or derive benefit from wine produced by non-Jews on the chance that it might have been consecrated to a foreign god or used for ritual purposes. The Tosafists distinguished between wine made by Christians and wine made by pagans, arguing that the earlier taboos referred only to the latter, thus allowing Jews to sell Christian-produced wine.

The upshot is that after Rashi made rabbinic literature accessible, the Tosafists made it applicable to their own day. Often, as Haim Soloveitschik noted about two decades ago, "the prevalent would not only expand the normative; it would become the normative." Under the religious and intellectual leadership of the Tosafists, Ashkenazic Judaism became an all-encompassing way of life, regulating all aspects of Jewish existence. Emblematic in this regard were the responsa of Meir of Rothenberg, which cover virtually every facet of life, from the sublime to the mundane; and the publication of the Tur, an easily accessible code of Jewish law, which was as user-friendly as Maimonides' Mishneh Torah.

To be sure, the Ashkenazic Jewish community was not hermetically sealed from the neighboring non-Jewish world. While most Jews resided in the Jewish quarter of the city or town, the market square was typically an arena for interaction between Jews and non-Jews. Moreover, there were often contacts between Jewish and Christian women. In England, for example, less affluent Christian women tended to borrow money from small-scale female Jewish moneylenders. What is more, historian Elisheva Baumgarten discovered in the medieval Ashkenazic world a camaraderie and extensive interaction between Jewish and Christian wet nurses and midwives. This suggests that the image of the Ashkenazic Jewish community as insular and isolated may be largely exaggerated. Given the small size of the Jewish community, and despite the social barriers between Jews and non-Jews erected by Jewish law and Christine doctrine, it was virtually impossible for Jews to function on a daily basis without extensive interaction – economic and social – with non-Jewish people.

Jewish–Christian relations during the thirteenth century

The thirteenth century witnessed a steady deterioration in the condition of Jews at a time of cultural flourishing and communal development. This was due largely to a general rise in Christian piety, from above and from below, and growing influence of the pope and the Christian clergy on Christian sovereigns. From above, the papacy reasserted its influence over the lives of European Christians in 1215 at the Fourth Lateran Council. While its edicts dealt primarily with the regulation of Christian life, Canons 67–70 had a direct bearing on Jews. Canon 67 placed a limit on the rate of interest Jewish creditors could charge Christian debtors and cancelled the debts owed to Jewish creditors by crusaders. Canon 68 required Jews to wear a distinguishing badge or form of dress, and forbade Jews (and Muslims) from appearing in public on Christian holidays. Canon 69 forbade Jews from holding public office, apparently a common practice hitherto. Canon 70 encouraged Christian clergy to prevent Jewish converts to Christianity from converting back to Judaism. The impact of these decrees depended on the willingness of Christian sovereigns to enforce them, which varied from state to state. On the whole, they led to the increasing impoverishment of Jews and to a growing separation of Jews from the Christian population, particularly in France. To aid in the papal efforts to heighten Christian piety, the pope created the Papal Inquisition in 1233 (not to be confused with its Spanish counterpart, which was formed more than two centuries later).

Papal attempts to revivify Christendom were complemented by grassroots initiatives within the church, notably the emergence of two mendicant orders, the Franciscans and the Dominicans. More than anyone else, the mendicant orders spearheaded the assault on Christian heresy and religious laxity. They attributed the decline of Christian piety in part to excess contact between Christians and Jews and to the material success of Jews despite the Augustinian instruction that Jews be made to suffer.

In assessing the presence of Jews in Christian Europe, Dominican scholars such as Raymond Martini reinterpreted two of Augustine's four reasons for Christian toleration of Jews. A pervading notion in the thirteenth century that the Second Coming of Christ was imminent diminished the urgency of Augustine's notion that Jews must be allowed to remain Jews until the end of time. This led to an escalation of missionary efforts among Jews. More important, perhaps, during the thirteenth century Christian scholars discovered the existence of postbiblical Judaism; hitherto, they had apparently presumed Judaism to be the Judaism of the Bible and the time of Christ. Because Augustine had rooted toleration of Jews in the role of Jews as preservers of Scripture, there was no basis for tolerating postbiblical – that is, Rabbinic – Judaism. This led to two forms of attack on the Talmud: actual burning of volumes of the Talmud, and polemical attacks in the form of forced sermons and public disputations.

The impact of such attacks was enhanced because their initial appearance coincided with a major internal Jewish dispute over the writings of Maimonides during the 1220s, known as the Maimonidean Controversy. In 1205, Maimonides' esoteric philosophical treatise *Guide to the Perplexed*, originally written in Arabic for a select audience, was translated posthumously, against his instructions, into Hebrew, thus becoming available to a much wider Jewish audience. This elicited criticism, particularly from antirationalist thinkers such as Abraham ben David of Posquierres. In the late 1220s, Rabbi Shlomo of Montpelier (known also by the literary epithet RaShBaM) condemned Maimonides' allegorical understanding of the Bible and the Midrash, especially his allegorizing of anthropomorphic images of God. He then issued a ban on *Guide to the Perplexed*, and on "The Book of Knowledge" section of Maimonides' Mishneh Torah. Other rabbis, particularly in northern France, supported the ban.

In response, rabbis in Provence defended Maimonides, and appealed to the Jews of Spain to arbitrate the dispute. When the rabbis of Spain divided over this issue, too, Jewish laity in Spain were asked to arbitrate; they, too, divided. As the Jewish communities of France and Spain teetered on the brink of a major schism, Rabbi Moses ben Nachman of Gerona (also known as Nachmanides or Ramban) was asked to arbitrate. Initially an anti-Maimonist who agreed that the study of philosophy could have deleterious effects on less educated Jews, ultimately he elevated Jewish unity over the importance of ideas by advocating a compromise. He ordered both sides to cease issuing bans against the other. He concluded that, in moderation, philosophy could be acceptable and even beneficial. He argued for a graded curriculum, meaning that philosophy could be studied only by those who had already mastered the fundamentals of rabbinic literature.

Yet the conflict did not end there. The pro-Maimonists sent David Kimchi, a defender of *Guide to the Perplexed*, to gather renewed support among lay leaders. The anti-Maimonists, fearing that the spread of philosophy would lead to the allegorizing of biblical and rabbinic texts out of existence, turned in 1233 to the Papal Inquisition, handing over *Guide to the Perplexed* and the "Book of Knowledge." The Inquisition ordered that these volumes be burned.

The internal mayhem over the writings of Maimonides coincided with an external assault on Rabbinic Judaism. In 1239, the king of France ordered a public disputation between Jews and Christians in Paris. While ostensibly an open debate on the relative merits of Judaism and Christianity, this disputation devolved into an inquisition, with Rabbi Yechiel of Paris being interrogated by the Jewish apostate-turned-Christian disputant Nicholas Donin. At the conclusion of this disputation, the king declared Donin and the Christianity the winner, and a year later ordered the burning of all volumes of the Talmud.

The deleterious impact of papal legislation and mendicant preaching on Jews was aggravated by the deterioration of the image of Jews in the popular imagination of ordinary Christians. In general, medieval Jew-hatred was expressed primarily in religious terms, with an economic undercurrent. The Jew was regarded as a usurer and a devious commercial adversary of Christian merchants.

At the heart of the negative image of Jews was an increasingly entrenched notion of a connection between Jews and Satan. For medieval Christians, Satan was as immediate as God and Christ, and tried on a daily basis to destroy all that was good. It was commonly believed that the same stubbornness that prevented Jews from recognizing the truth of Christianity made them defenseless against Satan. In many medieval depictions and tales, there is a confrontation between a Jew and the devil, in which the Jew always succumbs: "Thus can the devil lead into error the minds of those whose hearts do not cleave to God's word." For this reason, Jewish rituals in the synagogue or ritual bath were often depicted in medieval art as Satanic, with Satan actually participating.

In Christian folklore, the Jew was often depicted as the Antichrist. In one legend, a Jewish prostitute offers herself to her lover, the devil, in order to sire a superhuman offspring through whom "Christendom will be destroyed and Judaism raised up again." The child is reared by Satan, and when trained appears first among Jews, who recognize him as their Messiah. Such notions resonated with the terrifying Mongol invasions of the thirteenth century. Jews, it was believed, greeted these invasions with renewed hope, as some form of redemption. The fearful Christians, saw the Mongols as minions of the Antichrist, thus reinforcing the notion that the Antichrist was a Jew.

The identification of Jews and Satan was affirmed by the image that Jews – like Satan – had horns, a billy-goat beard, and a tail. The image of Jews having horns originated in a mistranslation of Exodus 34:29–30, which describes Moses descending from Mount Sinai: "*Ve-hineh karan or panav.*" The Hebrew word *karan* is related to the Hebrew homonym *keren*, which can mean horn or ray. Older translations rendered this verse as "and behold rays of light emanated from his face." In early Christian translations such as the Vulgate and the Aquila, the verse was rendered "and behold horns emanated from his face." As a result, sometimes Jews were forced to wear horns as distinct dress. In Vienna in 1267, for example, Jews were forced to wear a *pileum cornutum* (horned hat). The notion of a supernatural being with horns, per se, was not original. Babylonian and Egyptian mythology was full of horned deities. In Hellenistic culture, horns were a symbol of might and power. The Qur'an depicts Alexander the Great as having two horns.

The image of the Jews as having a beard and tail stemmed from an association of Jews and goats, the goat being Satan's helper. A common popular belief held that good spirits gave off a pleasant odor, while evil spirits were identifiable by their foul stench. Thus, the notion of a goat-like *foetor judaicus*

(Jewish smell) reflected the association of Jews with the supernatural realm of evil. The thirteenth-century Austrian poet Seifried Helbling claimed, "There was never a state so large that a mere thirty Jews would not saturate it with stench and unbelief." Some Christians believed that even if a Jew accepted baptism, he could not shed the stench. Some historians have argued, somewhat anachronistically, that the belief in a Jewish stench marked the beginnings of biological or proto-racial Jew-hatred.

Once Jews were seen as allies of the devil or as the Antichrist, it was possible to accuse them of iniquitous crimes such as Host desecration, ritual murder, and well poisoning. Host desecration referred to Jews being accused of stabbing Communion wafers and defiling sacramental wine, thereby reenacting the Crucifixion again and again. In retrospect, this accusation was absurd: Jews did not believe in the doctrine of transsubstantiation. Yet in the odd logic of the medieval Christendom, once the church propounded some dogma, it was regarded as necessarily true, and all Christians were required to believe it.

More devastating was the accusation of ritual murder, also known as the blood libel. Jews were accused of killing a Christian child in order to use the blood of the victim for sacramental purposes, such as making Passover matzoth. This accusation derived from a medieval notion that blood had certain power; it was also used in sorcery, witchcraft, and healing rituals. Recently, some historians have suggested that the Christian belief in the blood libel originated during the First Crusade, when rumors abounded about Jewish parents killing their own children in a fit of piety. Once the possibility of Jews killing their own children was introduced, the argument goes, it was not especially far-fetched to presume that Jews would kill a Christian child for sacramental purposes. Originally, these accusations were not associated with Passover, but they often coincided with Passion Week. The belief was that Jews killed a Christian child in order to mock the Christian commemoration of the Crucifixion.

The earliest recorded blood libel took place in Norwich, England, in 1144. Subsequent blood libels took place in Gloucester in 1168, in Blois in 1171, and in Saragossa in 1182. During the thirteenth century, one of the more notorious incidents took place in Lincoln in 1255. The day after a local wedding, the body of a boy named Hugh of Lincoln, who had been missing for over three weeks, was found in a cesspool. According to an alleged eyewitness, Matthew Paris, the child had first been fattened for ten days with white bread and milk, and then Jews from all over England were invited to attend a mock crucifixion. Subsequently, a Jew named Copin was forced to confess that the boy had been mock-crucified to injure Christ before being killed. One hundred Jews were arrested, including Copin, and nineteen were hanged without trial. The rest were saved when Richard of Cornwall, to whom most Jews in England at the time paid taxes, interceded to protect his property.

Ultimately the most devastating accusation was the claim that Jews poisoned wells. A proliferation of Jewish physicians during the high Middle Ages lent false credibility to the notion that Jews controlled life and death, and had the scientific know-how to kill undetected. This accusation ran wild in 1348 during the outbreak and spread of the Black Death. In May 1348, rumors of Jews poisoning wells circulated in Provence, leading rioters to burn entire Jewish communities. Waves of riots against Jews ensued through much of continental Europe. Often, rumors of Jews causing the plague spread faster than the plague itself. In May 1349, the city fathers of Brandenburg passed a law a priori condemning Jews of well poisoning:

> Should it become evident and proved by reliable men that the Jews have caused or will cause in the future the death of Christians, they shall suffer the penalties prescribed by law, as it is said that the Jews have elsewhere dispatched many person through poisoning.

On July 6, 1349, Pope Clement tried to curb anti-Jewish violence by issuing a papal bull. Its effectiveness was limited by the Holy Roman Emperor Charles IV, who made arrangements for the disposal of Jewish property in the event of a riot, implicitly giving immunity to rioters in advance.

The combination of papal initiatives, aggressive missionizing, and popular violence furthered the political and material decline of Jews in England, France, and the Holy Roman Empire, culminating in a series of expulsions at the beginning of the fourteenth century. In general, five factors led to expulsion: the growing influence of the popes on kings, and the ensuing stricter enforcement of the Fourth Lateran Council's canons on Jews; the growing influence of mendicant friars on the pope, on kings, and in the dissemination of negative popular images of Jews; the Jews' economic decline through impoverishment and the rise of a Christian merchant and moneylending class; the rise of nation-states, with an accompanying notion of an ideal homogeneous Christian population; and a general rise of intolerance toward those perceived as inherently alien to Christian society, such as Jews and homosexuals.

The specific path to expulsion, while reflecting some combination of these broader factors, followed a distinct path in each state. For Jews in England, the key moment was their impoverishment after 1190. Until 1189, royal protection had preserved stable conditions for Jews as a way of guranteeing the revenue that they provided to the royal treasury. In 1189, King Henry II died, and was replaced by Richard the Lion-hearted. The latter was more pious, excluding Jews and women from his coronation. Those Jews who sneaked in were trampled to death. When Richard then left for the Third Crusade in 1190, the ensuing breakdown of royal authority, coupled with the level of piety, climaxed in the York Massacre.

Although the riots were sparked by religious fanatics, the rioters had an economic aim as well, looting the property of the Jews of York. When Richard was captured several years later, the Jews were forced to contribute a large sum of money toward his ransom. Upon his return, Richard investigated and seized all loot taken from Jews during the riot. In order to preserve Jewish economic records, contracts, and deeds in case of future violence, he created a royal exchequer of Jews as a branch of royal administration. By the end of his reign, the Jews were able to contribute significantly less in tax revenue, but at least their situation had restabilized.

Conditions for Jews worsened during the reign of King John. Facing a near-bankrupt treasury, the loss of Normandy, and severed ties with France, and with a limited understanding of economics, in 1210 he tried to extort a large sum from Jews in a single act. He had all Jews arrested and fined, seized some Jewish assets, and taxed the remaining assets rather than the income they produced. This led to widespread Jewish impoverishment by the 1220s. John also required the children of deceased Jews to settle debts with the treasury, precluding any economic recovery. Jewish capital and revenue from Jews declined rapidly.

At the same time, English bishops became increasingly anti-Jewish, telling Christians not to sell food to Jews. By 1253, the only Jews who remained in England were those who provided a direct benefit to the king. Edward I formalized this situation 1272 by banishing poor Jews. Then, in 1275, he tried to move Jews experimentally into more productive occupations. He forbade Jews from lending at interest by withdrawing state enforcement, and then allowed them to become merchants and artisans, and to lease land. The experiment failed.

By 1290, the Jewish community of England was only a shadow of what it had been a century earlier. Thus, the expulsion edict of 1290 was more a culmination of a century of economic decline than a sudden change of royal policy. Interestingly, contemporary chronicles attributed the expulsion – in addition to the influence of Dominicans on the queen mother, economic excesses such as coin clipping, and impoverishment – to Edward's expulsion of the Jews from Gascony, an English holding on the Continent, a year earlier. They regarded the expulsion from England as part of a larger effort toward political and territorial consolidation, a way to bring all English territory under a uniform royal law, and to rid all English crown lands of Jews. The expulsion left the economic difficulties unresolved. As late as 1327, the crown was still trying to collect money owed to Jews.

The expulsion of Jews from France was more complex and protracted, punctuated by impetuous royal economic policies and complicated by the inability of the king of France to subordinate the landed nobles. The situation of French Jews began to deteriorate by the late twelfth century during the reign of the pious and anti-Jewish Philip II Augustus (1179–1223), whose anti-Jewish policies won support from bishops. In need of liquid capital to subdue the feudal barons, in 1181 he arrested Jews in Paris in the synagogue, and demanded a substantial ransom. A year later, he expelled the Jews, and cancelled all debts owed to Jews if the debtor paid 20 percent to the royal treasury. The Jews, though they lost much of their property, found refuge on the estates of the neighboring feudal barons. In 1198, once again short of cash, Philip allowed the Jews to return, and forced the barons to release them. He gave the Jews a new charter that regulated Jewish life to the benefit of the crown.

A century later, Louis IX, needing money and hoping to gather a large sum in one fell swoop, banished the Jews in 1306 but forced them to leave their property behind. He struggled to appropriate their property, and was unable to collect the debts owed to Jews by Christians. In 1315, facing a dearth of credit, Louis X recalled the Jews immediately upon his ascension to the throne. He allowed them to regain all previous residential privileges, and to lend money at high rates of interest. The readmission, however, was only for a period of twelve years, at which point the arrangement would be renegotiated.

In the interim, a popular uprising known as the Shepherd's Crusade led to a series of massacres of Jews in 1320–1. A year later, Jews were blamed for an outbreak of leprosy, leading to more massacres. These massacres left the Jews of France seriously depleted. By 1359, a small number of Jews remained in France. These Jews were given a new charter for twenty years. It was renewed once, in 1379. By 1394, amid increasing anti-Jewish pressures, Charles VI expelled the Jews in perpetuity.

In the Holy Roman Empire, the situation of Jews improved slowly after the ravages of the Black Death subsided. During the 1350s, Jews were invited back to communities from which they had been driven out by rioters, although on less favorable terms. They were confined largely to small-scale money lending, forced to pay a special imperial tax called the "golden penny," subjected to harsher residential restrictions, and forced to wear a badge.

However, because the empire was a confederation of autonomous states, no full-scale imperial expulsion edict was ever issued, simply because neither the emperor nor any other temporal or ecclesiastical authority had the power to expel Jews from any domains other than his own personal holdings. Instead, a series of local expulsions began during the late fourteenth and early fifteenth centuries. Typically, when evicted from one state, the Jews would migrate to the nearest state that would admit them. This series of local expulsions gave credence to the image of the wandering Jew.

The Jews of Christian Spain

By the end of the fourteenth century, the only part of Western Europe with a permanent Jewish community was Spain. This was not surprising. Spain was on a different timetable than the rest of European Christendom, as were the

Jews of Spain. Spain was, after all, the meeting point of Islam and Christendom – two very different situations.

It should be noted that until 1470 there was no country called Spain. Rather, the Iberian Peninsula was a collage of separate states, each with its own laws and ruling house. The first steps toward a united Spain were taken in 1230, when Leon and Castille united under Ferdinand III, and Aragon annexed Catalonia and Valencia. From this point until 1470, Castille and Aragon comprised most of what would be become Spain. Thus, it would be more accurate to speak of Spanish Jewries until 1470.

Castille and Aragon were different places in certain respects. Castille was more independent of foreign influence. Aragon was more influenced by the pope, the king of France, and European trends, including European attitudes toward Jews.

A telling difference between Christian Spain and the rest of Europe stemmed from a very different experience with regard to the Crusades. In Spain, the great battle between Christendom and Islam was not fought thousands of miles away in the Holy Land, but on the Iberian Peninsula. Thus, there was no cause for zealous Christians to assault Jews as surrogate infidels; the actual Muslim infidels were right there. In Christian Spain, therefore, the great Christian campaign against Islam – known as the *Reconquista* – worked to the benefit of Jews. The status of Jews in Christian Spain would rise and fall with the course of the *Reconquista* itself.

Until the mid-thirteenth century, when the southern half of Spain was still in Muslim hands, Jews flourished in Christian Spain. Jews were well treated by the Christian conquerors, as they had been by the Muslim conquerors in the eighth century. For example, when Alphonso VI conquered Toledo, he appointed a Jewish adviser. The Jews of Toledo were guaranteed horses and property, and fortified quarters. At a time when Jews in the rest of Christian Europe began to languish under increasingly harsh conditions during the thirteenth century, those in Spain reached a high point. After 1250, when all but the southern tip of Spain, Granada, had been reconquered, the situation of Spanish Jews plateaued and then, at the end of the fourteenth century, entered a period of decline.

There were several key differences for Jews in Muslim as compared with Christian Spain. In Muslim Spain, Jews had a blank slate with Muslim rulers. In Christian Spain, the church had a legacy of 1,000 years during which it had formed attitudes, laws, and a theological attitude toward Jews. Moreover, Muslim Spain reached its heyday at the tail-end of the golden age of Islam, when Islamic culture was ripe, and somewhat decadent. Christian Spain reached its heyday when Christianity was beginning a period of resurgence.

However, it is important not to overstate the difference. Massacres and wholesale expulsion were part of the waning days of Jewish life in late-eleventh-century Muslim Spain, not unlike in late-fifteenth-century Christian Spain. In both cases, Jews became outcasts at the moment when their Muslim or Christian benefactors no longer needed them as supporters in the struggle against their Christian or Muslim adversaries.

The Jews of Christian Spain inherited both the communal organization and much of the cultural heritage of their forebears in Muslim Spain. Typical of Jewish communities throughout the diaspora, each Jewish community governed by an *aljama* (the Arabic equivalent of kehilla), a communal board empowered by the state to govern the entire community. The range of authority enjoyed by the *aljama*, though, was virtually unprecedented. The Aljama issued ordinances (*takanot*); established and maintained a system of courts; assessed and collected communal taxes and fines; administered communal charity, schools, and synagogues; managed communal property and emergencies; repaired walls and gates; regulated markets and prices; and, if necessary, excommunicated recalcitrant members. Unlike any other Jewish communal board, however, the *aljama* supervised the moral behavior of the community through a special committee called *Birurei Averot*, and flogged and even imprisoned troublesome members.

The *aljama*'s power was concentrated in very few hands – thirty lay leaders in Barcelona, for example. Yet the extensive authority of these individuals was limited by a system of checks and balances. The rabbinate at times disputed the rulings of the lay *aljama* board by referring to legal precedents within rabbinic tradition. At the same time, learned lay leaders could dispute the claims of the rabbis. All ordinances proposed by the *aljama* had to be ratified by a majority of the general communal membership at a public assembly, checking the combined influence of the lay and rabbinic elite. In the long run, the authority of the *aljama* was made possible by an underlying consent of the governed, a deeply rooted loyalty to Jewish law, and a sense of peoplehood.

The cultural world of the Jews in Christian Spain also had origins in Muslim Spain. The Jewish courtiers in Christian Spain generally received a dual education, as had their earlier counterparts: the Bible, the Talmud, Hebrew, coupled with philosophy, poetry, and often medicine. Jews in Christian Spain, moreover, maintained Arabic high culture into the thirteenth century. At the same time, there were curricular differences. Jews in Christian Spain increasingly gravitated toward a different philosophical tradition than their forebears, opting for Neoplatonic rather than Aristotelian philosophy. Hasdai ibn Crescas, one of the leading Jewish philosophers in Christian Spain, was a sharp critic of Aristotle. Among other things, the impact of Neoplatonism introduced an element of non-rational thinking, complemented by the inclusion of Kabbala on the Jewish side of the curriculum.

The emergence of a systematic Jewish mystical tradition known as Kabbala reached a high point with the appearence of the first full-length systematic treatment of this tradition, *Sefer ha-Zohar* (The Book of Radiance). Compiled and published in the thirteenth century in southern France by Moses de Leon, it was attributed pseudonymously to Simon bar Yochai, a disciple of Rabbi Akiva. This text, a commentary on the Torah and a recapitulation of Bar Yochai's mystical journeys, is largely a theosophic attempt to understand the true nature of God, and to unite with those parts of God that are understandable to human being. The Kabbalists themselves admitted that not everything about God is comprehensible, even to Kabbalists. This kabbalistic tradition would reach full expression in Christian Spain during the thirteenth century, particularly under the tutelage of Moses ben Nachman of Gerona.

Moses ben Nachman, also known as Ramban or Nachmanides, embodied this cultural tradition: a master commentator on the Bible and Talmud and an accomplished philosopher, he was also the leading kabbalistic scholar of the thirteenth century. His integration of conventional biblical interpretation with kabbalistic writing is evident in his commentary on Genesis 1:1. Noting Rashi's comment that the verse attested to God's bequeathing the Land of Israel to the Jews, Nachmanides questions Rashi's motive for wondering why Genesis began with creation:

> because in fact it is necessary to begin the Torah with "In the beginning" because the root of our faith and anyone who does not believe this and instead believes that the world is eternal is a blasphemer. Rather, the answer [i.e. why the Torah begins with "In the beginning"] is that the story of Creation [ma'aseh bereshit] is a deeply hidden secret that is not comprehensible from the text of the Torah and can known only from the words of the Kabbala.

In other words, Nachmanides implied a kabbalistic meaning embedded in a biblical verse without revealing this meaning to the readership of his commentary. Kabbala was to remain an esoteric tradition reserved only for the few who have merited studying it.

There was also a key cultural difference between Muslim and Christian Spain. In Muslim Spain, Arabic was the language of culture and religion, but also the spoken vernacular. In Christian Spain, Latin was the language of culture and religion, but Castilian was the language of the street. Thus, Arabic culture had a secular component; Latin culture was closely tied to religion and theology, thus limiting Jewish access to high culture. Hebrew poetry in Christian Spain drew virtually nothing from Latin poetry.

As a result, there was also a sharper divide between Jewish and Christian courtiers. Jewish courtiers in Christian Spain were more susceptible to court intrigue, leading to the emergence by the end of the thirteenth century of two types of Jewish courtiers. Some, like those in Muslim Spain, used their power and influence to help Jews. Others were guided more by self-interest, and were more prone to ape the Christian nobility, and distance themselves from the rest of the Jewish community.

Already during the second half of the thirteenth century, signs of precariousness began to appear. In 1273, for example, when King Alfonso X's chief tax-farmer, Don Culema ibn Zadok, died, the king confiscated his property and gave it to a cathedral in Seville. When Don Culema's son Don Isaac ibn Zadok inherited his father's position, he supported a revolt against Alfonso in 1276 by the king's son, Sancho. When Alfonso defeated the rebellion in 1279 and discovered Don Isaac's complicity, he imprisoned Don Isaac and other Jewish financiers, and then hanged Don Isaac as a traitor. Several years later, in 1281, Jews in Castille were arrested and released only on the promise of ransom of 4 million maravedis. The situation stabilized in 1284 when Sancho came to the throne and reinstated the status of Jewish courtiers.

For Jews in Christian Spain, the mid-thirteenth century was both a high point and a turning point. The dominant role played by Spanish Jews in the Maimonidean Controversy of the 1220s attested to the preeminent position of Spanish Jews. Moreover, the order by the pope in 1240 to burn the Talmud was totally ignored in Spain – a reflection of the Jews' power and influence.

A high point for Jews in Christian Spain was the Disputation of Barcelona in 1263. Jews come closer to winning this disputation than any other. King Jaime I of Aragon, who convened the disputation, apparently wanted it to be fair. Unlike the Disputation of Paris, this event did not devolve into an inquisition. Furthermore, the Jews had Nachmanides arguing their side. His towering stature overshadowed his opponent, Pablo Christiani. Although raised a Jew with a strong knowledge of rabbinic texts, Christiani was no match for Nachmanides. The disputation was called off after several weeks. Jewish and Christian accounts describe the outcome differently. The Christian account claimed victory for the Christian side. Nachmanides' account called it a draw. In the aftermath of the disputation, though, Nachmanides fled from Spain to the Land of Israel, a portent of the future unstable position of Jews in Christian Spain.

The Christian pressure that led to the disputation, moreover, was also felt by Spanish kings. In 1265, Alfonso X, king of Castille, responded to this pressure by regulating more closely the status of the Jews of Castille in *Las Siete Partidas,* a seven-part code of behavior. This code defined ten aspects of Jewish life. A Jew was defined as a believer in the laws of Moses, an implicit critique of Rabbinic Judaism and a license for Christian clergy to attack it. Jews were enjoined to live quietly among Christians and to refrain from blasphemy and proselytizing, and were barred from holding public office and from employing Christians or keeping Christian mistresses or concubines. Any Christian who converted to Judaism would be executed as a heretic. Christian men and women were prohibited from living in a Jew's house. Jews were prohibited from acquiring Christian slaves, and from convering Muslim or pagan slaves to Judaism. Finally, they were required to wear a distinguishing mark in accordance with the Fourth Lateran Council.

On the other hand, the synagogue was defined as a legal house of worship. Christians were prohibited from desecrating synagogues. No new synagogues could be constructed without royal permission, but existing ones could be renovated. Jews could not be subjected to compulsory labor on Saturday, except for those who had been convicted of a crime. Finally, forced conversion of Jews to Christianity was prohibited, though Jews who had converted were allowed to inherit from their Jewish parents.

The upshot is that this code was a mixed bag for Jews. Judaism was defined as legal, but rabbinic tradition implicitly opened to attack. Jews could not be compelled to work on the Sabbath, but Jewish economic life was restricted by the injunctions against employing Christians. More importantly, the very appearance of the code marked a step back for Jews in Christian Spain. For their counterparts elsewhere in Christian Europe, the privileges of a charter like this would have meant an improved situation. For Jews in Christian Spain, who had hitherto lived with few restrictions, much like Jews in the Islamic world, a Christian-style charter was an indication of decline.

Fortunately for Jews in the thirteenth century, there was a time lag of a century between the time this code was legislated and the time it was actually implemented and enforced. When the kings of Castille began enforcing it in the mid-fourteenth century, a period of decline ensued. Yet the implementation of *Las Siete Partidas* during the 1360s significantly did not drastically undermine the condition of Jewish life in Christian Spain. As late as 1390, Jewish life in Christian Spain bore much of the character it had done a century and half earlier.

The position would change dramatically with the outbreak of anti-Jewish riots in Spain in 1391. These riots destroyed dozens of Jewish communities in Aragon, and eventually spread elsewhere as well. Most of these Jewish communities recovered only partially, and many never recovered. In retrospect, these riots can be seen as the beginning of the end of Jewish life in Christian Spain.

In the aftermath of the riots, a wave of Jewish conversion to Christianity followed. The scale of this wave of conversions was largely unprecedented, leading historians to speculate as to the cause. Some, notably Yitzhak Baer, presumed that most of those who converted were from the ranks of Jewish courtiers. Thus, they attributed these conversion to the denuded Jewish identity and commitment of the Spanish Jewish elite, and contrasted the conversion of "assimilated" Spanish Jews with the martyrdom chosen by simple, pious Ashkenazic Jews during the First Crusade.

More recently, this conceptualization has been shown to be highly problematic and simplistic, leading other historians to adduce alternate explanations for the wave of conversions. A particularly compelling explanation situates these conversions in the context of the major victories by

Christendom over Islam. Previously, the specter of Islam as a more powerful force than Christendom deterred the mass of Jews from defecting to Christianity; after all, why join the weaker of two sides in a conflict? As the *Reconquista* approached ultimate victory at the end of the fourteenth century, with the heretofore seemingly invincible Moors pinned down in Granada, a surge of Christian confidence made conversion to Christianity a more attractive option for beleaguered and besieged Jews.

Among the Jewish converts was Joshua ha-Lorki. In 1412, in order to demonstrate his Christian conviction and to induce other Jews to convert, he persuaded Pope Benedict XIII to convene a disputation in Tortosa in 1412. Although the Jews had capable scholars arguing on their behalf, this disputation was, from the outset, designed more along the lines of its precursor in Paris rather than the one in Barcelona. It lasted more than two years, during which time the Jewish scholars were subjected to relentless interrogation. When the disputation finally ended in 1414, another wave of conversions followed. The conversions continued well into the fifteenth century. It is estimated that by 1450, 60,000 Jews had converted.

By the mid-fifteenth century, a growing concern among the Catholic clergy emerged regarding the sincerity of these conversions, resulting in a division within Spanish Christendom between Christians and *conversos*. A *converso* was any Christian whose religious pedigree did not predate 1391 – in other words, a Jew who had converted after the riots, presumably for pragmatic reasons rather than as a matter of true conviction. The growing suspicion that the *conversos* were not sincere Christians led in 1449 to a series of restrictions placed on them, *Limpieza de Sangre* (literally, purity of blood laws), which barred them from holding public office, engaging in certain occupations, and cohabiting too intimately with Christians – reminiscent of the restrictions placed on Jews by *Las Siete Partidas*.

Three decades later, shortly after the unification of Aragon and Castille into Spain, Queen Isabella and King Ferdinand authorized the creation of a Spanish branch of the Papal Inquisition under the direction of Tomás de Torquemada. Unlike the Papal Inquisition, which had been created to combat Christian heresy, the Spanish Inquisition was created to combat *converso* heresy. Hundreds of *conversos* suspected of heresy were brutally interrogated by the Inquisition on the pretense of saving their souls from eternal damnation. Many were executed as heretics immediately upon confessing.

Historians debate as to how to interpret the results of these interrogations, particularly about how many of these *conversos* were crypto-Jews, *conversos* who practiced Judaism in secret (also called *marranos*, a derogatory Castilian word for swine). Some historians, taking the claims of the inquisitors at face value, have argued that the confessions of heresy reflected widespread crypto-Judaism among the conversos. Others have suggested that the inquisitors exaggerated and that not many *conversos* were crypto-Jews.

In any case, the chronic presence of crypto-Jews eventually convinced Ferdinand and Isabella that the source of this infidelity was the presence of a large openly Jewish population; and that expelling the Jews would allow *conversos* to become true Christians. Yet the decision to expel the Jews was far from inevitable. As late as 1491, Don Isaac Abravanel, one of the last of the Jewish courtiers in Spain, signed a three-year commercial contract with the royal crown.

The final straw came in 1492 with the conquest of Granada and the completion of the *Reconquista*. Amid the surge of Christian jubilation over the uniting of all of Spain as a Christian kingdom under Christian rule, an edict of expulsion was issued in March 1492, which would go into effect in August 1492. A century of decline since 1492 had reduced the Jews of Spain numerically and economically, and eroded their political situation. Nonetheless, on an absolute scale, in 1492 Spanish Jewry was still one of the largest, most affluent, and most prestigious Jewish communities in the world. Thus, the expulsion set in motion a period of flux for world Jewry.

Chapter 6

World Jewry in flux, 1492–1750

The two and half centuries from 1492 to around 1750 were characterized by developments in the world of Christendom and Islam that distinguish this period from both the premodern and the modern periods, while marking a transition between the very different Jewish worlds of the late fifteenth and the late eighteenth centuries. First and foremost, extensive migration and the rise of print culture increased contact between heretofore mutually isolated parts of the Jewish world. Migration in this context meant not only a steady eastward migration, from Spain to the Ottoman Empire and from central Europe to Poland; but also a two-pronged demographic migration from out-lying small towns to larger cities and centers of urban commerce and culture, and from more established areas of settlement to frontier and border regions in Poland and the Ottoman Empire. These migration movements, moreover, brought together Jews from parts of the Jewish world that had heretofore been largely isolated from one another. The convergence of Ashkenazic and Sephardic Jews in the Italian states epitomized this trend, but it was true in the Ottoman Empire as well.

The rise of print culture following the invention of the printing press complemented this convergence of Jews by making it possible for literate Jews who did not meet face to face to read one another's written texts and exchange views on an unprecedented scale. A text like the *Shulchan Aruch* (Set Table), a code of Jewish law initially written by Joseph Karo in the Land of Israel, was eventually published in Poland with Karo's code and the Polish rabbi Moses Isserles' glosses (known as the *Mapah*, tablecloth) side by side – virtually unimaginable prior to the age of the printing press. Similarly, the publication of editions of the Hebrew Bible with commentaries by scholars from all over the Jewish world surrounding the biblical text was no less a product of print culture.

Migration and print culture had a homogenizing effect on the Jewish world, as customs and rabbinic precedents from one part of the Jewish world impacted on the understanding and practice of Judaism elsewhere. At the same time, as disparate customs were juxtaposed through face-to-face encounters and written exchanges, a tension emerged between the preexisting diversity and an emerging uniformity. Jewish communal leaders faced the challenge of maintaining a sense of unity amid this tension between uniformity and diversity.

A redefinition of the political and civic status of Jews, moreover, replaced a preexisting balance between religion and statecraft either with a polity that functioned independent of religion or with one that was completely overwhelmed by religion. The former took the form of absolutism in central Europe and liberalism in western Europe. The latter accompanied the Protestant Reformation and Catholic Counter-Reformation in the world of Christendom, and the triumph of less tolerant forms of Islam in Islamic states that were beyond the authoritative reach of the Ottoman Empire. To be sure, these new polities did not triumph everywhere. The most thriving centers of world Jewry during the early modern period – the Jews of Poland and the Ottoman Empire – were situated in states where the older balance between throne, sword, and altar remained largely intact well into the eighteenth century.

By the end of the seventeenth century, the expanding horizons and complexity of Jewish life, through the emergence of compartmentalized and non-rabbinic forms of Jewish identity, introduced a voluntary rather than mandatory observance of Jewish law and affiliation with the Jewish community, intensified communal cohesion through the subordination of the rabbinate to lay leadership, brought challenges to rabbinic authority from heretics and pietists, and created a religiously neutral society that blurred the boundary between Jews and non-Jews, in which Jews and non-Jews could interact freely.

The expulsion of Jews from Spain set this period of Jewish history in motion. It marked not only the end of open Jewish life in western Europe but also the end of one of the longest-lasting, most prosperous, and culturally most productive diasporas in Jewish history. The impact of this event was felt first by Jews on the Iberian Peninsula, but eventually reverberated elsewhere. Refugees from Spain, mainly Jewish but also *conversos*, fled first to Portugal and then to western Europe, the Italian states, and especially to the Ottoman Empire.

For many of these refugees, the expulsion had cosmic significance. Not surprisingly, some Spanish Jews and *conversos* understood this event in messianic terms. For some, such as the messianic pretender David Reuveni and his follower Solomon Molkho, it became the defining element in their identity. For others, such as the rabbinic scholar and Kabbalist Don Isaac Abravanel, the expulsion pointed to the imminent arrival of the messianic age.

In addition, some historians have argued that the expulsion from Spain led to a reorientation in the study of Kabbalah, particularly among Spanish Kabbalist refugees who settled in Safed in the Land of Israel during the sixteenth century and eventually founded a new center of Kabbala around the Kabbalist Isaac Luria. Lurianic Kabbala, as this new brand of

Jewish mysticism came to be known, exhibited a deep preoccupation with determining when the Messiah would arrive and hastening the arrival of the Messianic Age. Even if the expulsion was not the seminal event in the development of Jewish messianism that the twentieth-century historian Gershom Scholem and his disciples claimed, the heightened messianic expectations of the generation of the expulsion are indisputable.

For most Jewish refugees from Spain, the natural response to expulsion was to relocate to the closest refuge: Portugal. The influx of approximately 50,000 Jews presented the king of Portugal, for the first time, with the task of governing a large Jewish population. Within five years, he resolved this situation by forcibly converting all Jews in Portugal. While eliminating open Jewish life in Portugal, however, this drastic measure created in Portugal a more intense version of the *converso* problem that had plagued the throne and church in Spain during the fifteenth century. In contrast to the mass, and largely voluntary, conversion of Spanish Jews that had taken place over the course of a century, Portuguese Jews were converted against their will all at once. In addition, whereas Spanish *conversos* lived alongside a large normative Jewish community, after 1497 Portuguese *conversos* became the *de facto* Jews. As a result, as Yosef Yerushalmi demonstrated more than a quarter of century ago, Portuguese *conversos* maintained a more tenacious sense of Jewishness than their Spanish counterparts; and the problem of crypto-Judaism – or at least alleged crypto-Judaism – was more widespread in Portugal than it had been in Spain.

In response, King João III of Portugal established the Portuguese Inquisition in 1536 to deal with his *converso* problem. The ferocity and ruthlessness of the Portuguese Inquisition soon eclipsed that of its Spanish counterpart (the infamous burning of heretics at the stake is more commonly known by its Portuguese, not Spanish, epithet: *auto da fé*), prompting some Portuguese *conversos* to emigrate, in some cases even back to Spain. Those who returned to Spain found refuge only until 1580, when Spain and Portugal were united, along with their heretofore separate inquisitorial organizations. Portuguese *conversos* who fled the Iberian Peninsula often maintained connections with other *conversos*. During the seventeenth century, in fact, the term "men of the Portuguese nation" emerged as a coded reference to Portuguese *conversos*.

After 1492, and even more so after 1497, the majority of Jews who fled from Spain settled in the Ottoman Empire. Some Jewish refugees even saw the divine hand in the refuge that the Jews found in the Ottoman Empire. Samuel Usque, a Portuguese *converso* who returned to Judaism after settling in Ferrara, Italy, described "the great nation of Turkey" in 1553 as "a broad and expansive sea that the Lord has opened for you as Moses did for you during the exodus from Egypt." "There," he continued, "the gates of liberty are wide open to you so that you always fully practice your Judaism." Hyperbole aside, Usque's description of the Ottoman receptivity reflected the favorable conditions for Jews under Ottoman rule from the sixteenth through the eighteenth century.

The dominant form of Islam in the Ottoman Empire at this time, the Hanafi brand of Sunni Islam, emphasized and encouraged the use of reason and pragmatism in determining policy and adjudicating law. This allowed Ottoman sultans and officials to govern non-Muslims on the basis of demographic, political, and economic considerations rather than theological dicta. By the end of the fifteenth century, as the Ottoman Turks extended their empire from the Levant into the Middle East, North Africa, and the Balkans, the Turks had become an ethnic minority in their own empire. Ottoman expansion from the fifteenth through the seventeenth century brought under Ottoman rule vast areas where the Ottoman government needed to settle loyal subjects to counter disloyal or contentious elements within the local population. Thus, Ottoman policy placed a premium on the support and loyalty of ethnic and religious minorities, Jews in particular. As a result, Jews encountered in the Ottoman Empire a favorable interpretation and application of the legal category of the *dhimmi*, expanding their residential options to include major cities such as Istanbul, Salonika, Izmir (Smyrna), and Edirne (Adrianople).

Ottoman demographic strategies often worked to the advantage of Jewish settlers. Desperate to populate the recently conquered Istanbul (formerly Constantinople) at the end of the fifteenth century, the sultan invited Jews and others to settle there by allowing them to live virtually anywhere in the city; to practice Judaism and organize communal life with little or no intrusion, and to trade without any impediment; and to engage in a variety of occupations, including international commerce and such other lucrative endeavors as the feather trade, artisanal crafts, and medicine. This attracted Jews from all over the Jewish world.

Following the Turkish conquest of Istanbul by Sultan Mehmet II, much of the city's population was massacred, but the Jews were left alone. The sultan repopulated the capital quickly by transferring Muslims, Christians, and Jews from all over the empire, especially from Anatolia and the Balkans. Among these were Jews from Salonika, Bulgaria, and Macedonia. Jews in Istanbul were defined as a "millet," as were other religious communities, and divided by origin, including Romaniot, Ashkenazic, Italian, and Sephardic congregations. In a fashion reminiscent of Jewish success in earlier periods under Islamic rule, Jews in Istanbul rose in the ranks of Ottoman society to levels they had never reached under Christendom. Moses Hamon, the leading member of a prominent Sephardic family, served as royal physician to Sultan Suleiman I the Magnificent. This recalls the accomplishments of Samuel ibn Nagrela in Muslim Spain.

Equally diverse was the Jewish community of Salonika. Following the Turkish conquest of Salonika, an influx of Ashkenazic Jews from Bavaria began in 1470, followed by an influx of Sephardic Jews after 1492 from Spain, Portugal, North Africa, and southern Italy. Along with the indigenous Romaniot Jews, each of these Jewish communities created a separate network of communal institutions. The Jewish population of Salonika became one of the most diverse in the world. By 1553, there were 20,000 Jews in Salonika; by 1650, there were 30,000, comprising half of the total population. While Ottoman Jewry was an agglomeration of Jews from various parts of the Jewish world, Sephardic influence increasingly predominated in most major Jewish communities by the mid-seventeenth century. Indicative of the Sephardic influence was the widespread use of Ladino (Judeo-Spanish) in much of the empire, which eclipsed Jewish dialects of other vernaculars.

The favorable treatment of Jews in the Ottoman Empire extended as far as Ottoman rule itself. In Iraq, government rule alternated between Persia and the Ottoman Empire. When under Persian rule, from 1508 to 1534 and 1623 to 1638, Jews in Iraq languished under harsh restrictions. From 1534 to 1623 and from 1638 until the end of the eighteenth century, Jews in Iraq thrived under Ottoman rule. The Jews of Baghdad, in fact, commemorated the day that Ottomans recaptured Baghdad from the Persians as a *yom nes* (a day of miracles). The local governor appointed the leader of Baghdad Jewry as the *nasi*, who was not only the official leader and representative of the Jews of Iraq, but also in charge of the governor's treasury. By 1600, 2,500 out of the 25,000 houses in Baghdad belonged to Jews.

By contrast, in Persia proper the Shi'ite Safavid Dynasty, which ruled from 1502 to 1736, regarded non-Muslims as ritually unclean and tried to limit contact between Muslims and non-Muslims, with varied success. Exceptional in this regard was Abbas I at the beginning of the seventeenth century. Abbas was a social reformer who tried to weaken the influence of the Shi'ite clergy over Persian politics and society. He encouraged the immigration of foreign merchants and artisans from Turkey, Armenia, and Greece by granting them freedom of religion. This period of openness ended with Abbas's death in 1629. His successors, notably Abbas II (1642–66), were religious fundamentalists who restored the influence of Shi'ite Islam. After 1650, a campaign of forced conversion began. Reminiscent of what happened in fifteenth-century Iberia, many of the Jews who were forced to convert were then suspected of being insincere, and defined as "new Muslims," leading to the appearance of crypto-Judaism. In response, in 1661 Abbas II allowed Jews who had been forcibly converted to return to Judaism, and even relaxed some of the restrictions on Jews. In 1670, a European traveler noted that Jews in some Persian cities congregated in their synagogues on the Sabbath, holidays, and at the time of the new moon without disturbance.

The contrast between the Ottoman and non-Ottoman parts of Islam, in this respect, was paralleled by the contrast in the world of Christendom between the Jews of Italian states and central Europe, on the one hand, and those of Poland. Some of the Jews who fled from Spain in 1492 and Portugal, as well as some of the *conversos* who left the Iberian Peninsula during the sixteenth century, found refuge in Italy. Those who settled in the south soon had to relocate again when Spain conquered southern Italy and extended the expulsion edict and the Inquisition's jurisdiction there. In northern Italy, Jews found safe haven under the aegis of leading Italian magnate families, such as the Medicis in Florence and the Este family in Mantua, Padua, and Modena. These Jews arrived in northern Italy at the height of the Italian Renaissance.

In assessing how the Renaissance affected Jews, it is essential to note that, despite the emphasis on humanism, Renaissance culture was Christian culture. The participation of Jews in this cultural movement, therefore, varied from discipline to discipline between imitation and engagement. Jews largely abstained from the "plastic arts" – painting and sculpting – while fashioning a Jewish equivalent of other aspects of the new cultural movement. The renewed interest in Greek mythology, for example, led Italian rabbis such as Abraham Yagel to compose sermons using mythological in addition to biblical references, prompting one observer to note that "Christians baptized the pagan myths; Jews circumcised them." Akin to the growing interest in history among Renaissance Catholics, Azaria de Rossi of Mantua wrote *Meor Eynayim*, an early attempt at a history of the Jews that extended beyond the conventional *Shalshelet ha-Kaballah*, or chain of tradition genre, which had been the only form of Jewish historical writing since ancient times.

Jews also embraced Renaissance dancing and tennis, as indicated by the frequent complaints by Italian rabbis regarding young Jews who skipped Saturday morning services to play "the sport." More ambitious and engaging was the Jewish contribution to Renaissance rhetoric. David ben Judah Messer Leon of Padua, in his handbook on rhetoric, *Sefer Nofet Tzufim* (The Book of the Honeycomb's Flow), boldly claimed that the true font of rhetoric in the ancient world was not the Roman rhetorical tradition of Cicero and Tacitus, but rather that "every science, every rationally apprehended truth that any treatise may contain is present in our Holy Torah." The true font of rhetoric, he claimed, was the biblical orations of Moses and the prophets.

Most complex, though, was the Jewish engagement with Renaissance philosophy. That the rise of Renaissance culture coincided with the influx of Jews into Italy from Spain underscores the importance of distinguishing between those aspects of Renaissance culture that also represented a renaissance in Jewish culture, and those that did not. Renaissance philosophy belongs in the latter category. For Christians, the Renaissance expanded the study of Greek philosophy from a hitherto limited interest in Aristotelianism into a broader philosophical inquiry that incorporated the Neoplatonic school – that is, a revival of Plato. This was nothing new for Spanish and Provençal Jews such as Nachmanides, whose kabbalistic writings had reflected the influence of Neoplatonic philosophy as early as the thirteenth century.

This shift in Renaissance philosophy led to the appearance of Christian Kabbalists, Christian scholars who took a growing interest in Kabbala. Unlike the Christian Hebraists of the thirteenth century who learned Hebrew in order to attack rabbinic texts, Christian Kabbalists initially turned to the Kabbala in order to gain a more nuanced understanding of Christian teachings. Foremost among them was Giovanni Pico della Mirandola, who studied Hebrew and then Kabbala under his friend Yohannan Alemanno. Pico used kabbalistic teachings and exegesis to unravel the complexities and contradictions associated with Christian doctrines such as the Trinity and the Virgin Birth.

The participation of Jews in philosophical speculation during the Renaissance extended beyond Italy to other centers of Renaissance activity, notably Prague. David Gans studied philosophy and astronomy with Tycho Brahe and Johannes Kepler; his *Nehmad ve-Na'im* was a Hebrew-language text on astronomy (which in the sixteenth century included what we now call astrology). No less important in this regard was Rabbi Judah ben Bezalel Löw of Prague (MaHaRaL), commonly known in Jewish folklore as the creator of the golem. Löw was in fact a leading talmudic and kabbalistic scholar who made Prague a center of kabbalistic study for both Jews and Christians.

The kabbalistic atmosphere in Prague may offer an alternative explanation of one of the oddities of the city: an eight-foot cross with the biblical/liturgical verse *"Kadosh, kadosh, kadosh adonai Tzevaot Melo Hol ha-aretz kevodo"* (Holy, holy, holy is the Lord of Hosts; his glory fills the world) that adorns the Charles Bridge, made from golden letters attached to the top. The conventional explanation, which every local guide dutifully repeats, tells of a Catholic priest who saw a Jew spit on the cross and attached the Hebrew letters to prevent further such occurrences. Yet in a town saturated in kabbalistic study, it is no less plausible that a Christian kabbalist interpreted the verse Christologically to refer to the Trinity, and added it to the large cross accordingly.

Initially the scholarly endeavors of the Christian kabbalists led to a rapprochement between Jewish and Christian scholars. By the beginning of the sixteenth century, however, this growing interaction prompted a backlash. Erasmus, for example, disapproved of all forms of Christian Hebraism, arguing that the study of Hebrew texts deflected Christian scholars from Christ. Though a Renaissance scholar, Erasmus regarded Jewish learning as even more dangerous than medieval Christian obscurantism. This mentality led to the emergence of a more sophisticated expression of anti-Judaism, reminiscent of thirteenth-century Christian Hebraism, that was fortified by the revelation that Kabbala contained disparaging views of Christianity.

This anti-Judaism included a renewed desire to segregate Jews from Christians. In 1516, this mentality crystallized into actual state policy, when the leaders of the city of Venice confined all Jews in Venice and its environs to the newly created ghetto of Venice. The term *ghetto*, Italian for iron foundry, refers to an abandoned iron foundry situated in the part of Venice that became the Jewish ghetto. In retrospect, the decision to confine the Jews to the ghetto was an alternative to expulsion or forced conversion. The ghetto maintained a greater separation between Jews and Christians without forfeiting the tax revenue and commercial benefits provided by Jewish subjects and without creating a *converso* problem. As a physical and legal space for Jews, the ghetto had more in common with the classical Jewish quarter than, say, with the Nazi ghettos. Although Jews were confined to the ghetto at night, Jews and Christians were allowed to enter and exit the ghetto in Venice and other Italian ghettos freely during the day.

Moreover, although the original intention of the ghetto was to isolate and marginalize Jews by delineating a Jewish space, the ghetto assured a Jewish presence in Venice and other major Italian cities, a first step in the process of Jewish urbanization. Thus, the ghetto paradoxically provided a sense of stability amid harsh conditions, and fortified Jews with a greater sense of security and belonging. While intended to curtail interactions between Jews and Christians, which had increased during the Renaissance, Jews were instead situated in the heart of Venice and eventually every major Italian city, thus assuring that they would remain an integral part of urban life and culture in Italy. To be sure, the ghetto affected Jews differently. Poor Jews languished, while rich Jews were able to participate in the cultural world of the Baroque.

The new sense of security and confidence among Jews at the beginning of the sixteenth century was reflected in several Jewish defenses of usury. Abraham Fassisol, a Avignonese Jew living in Mantua, challenged the Aristotelian argument that because money was barren and therefore not subject to the law of supply and demand, it must be exchanged gratuitously – the heart of the Christian condemnation of Jewish usury. Don Isaac Abravanel, who settled in Italy after fleeing from Spain, incorporated a five-part defense of Jewish usury into his commentary on Deuteronomy. Other defenders of Judaism included Simone Luzzatto of Venice, whose treatise on the economic utility of Jews eventually became a blueprint for subsequent defenses of Judaism, and Leone Modena. At the beginning of the seventeenth century, Modena invited his composer friend Salomon de Rossi to compose a series of Baroque-style choral pieces for use in the synagogue. Though borrowing the style of the Baroque, this music was clearly Jewish because of its Hebrew text and function.

The emergence of the ghetto as a new standard for Jewish residence reflected an attempt to reinvigorate Catholicism and a concern regarding the religious commitment and intensity of Catholics. This concern would heighten precipitously during the sixteenth century following the challenge of Martin Luther and the Reformation. The Protestant Reformation linked two distinct waves of Jewish expulsions in the Holy Roman Empire and the Italian states, where the absence of a central authority had precluded any mass expulsion of Jews. From 1450 to 1520, momentum for expulsion had emanated largely from towns and the lower clergy. The papacy, prince-bishops, and other secular authorities generally remained aloof from such agitation. Typically, higher authorities eventually readmitted Jews, overriding the aims of locally issued edicts.

In Italy, the fate of Jews was often tied to the fate of a particular ruling house. In Tuscany, Jews were expelled along with the Medici family in 1501, but returned with it in 1513. By contrast, during the wave of expulsions from 1520 to 1570, the driving force included princes and bishops in addition to local elites and popular initiatives. This change was due largely to the impact of the Reformation.

Primarily a religious movement that was critical of Catholicism, the Reformation aimed at restoring the church to its pristine origins. In general, Luther and his followers advocated restoring a direct relationship between man and Christ, without the mediation of a priest or confessor. For example, Luther and others derided simony (the buying and selling of ecclesiastical positions) as a reflection of the corruption of the church. His Ninety-five Theses included the elimination of four of the seven Catholic sacraments, the elimination of tithes to Rome, and the reinterpretation of communion from transubstantiation to consubstantiation. At the same time, the Reformation also had an economic and political dimension, freeing temporal rulers from losing revenue that was paid to Rome as a tithe. Barons and dukes also regarded the Reformation as a way to throw off the yoke of the Holy Roman Emperor.

Initially, Luther regarded Jews amicably as potential supporters and followers. His mentor, Johannes Reuchlin, was a Christian Hebraist who had reached a favorable view of Judaism from his study of Kabbala. Luther believed that Jews and Protestants shared a common enemy in the Catholic Church. In 1523, Luther wrote "That Christ Was Born a Jew," in which he attributed the Jews' refusal to convert to the shortcomings and iniquities of the church and its "papal paganism":

> For our fools – popes, bishops, sophists, monks, the coarse blockheads! – have so treated the Jews that to be a good Christian one would have to become a Jew. And if I had been a Jew and had seen such idiots and blockheads ruling and teaching the Christian religion, I would rather have been a hog than a Christian.

By the end of the 1520s, as it became clear to Luther that Jews were not converting, his demeanor turned accordingly hostile, first toward Jewish usury and then to Jews in general. In 1543, he published a second essay about Jews, "On the Jews and Their Lies." In this essay, he advocated violent condemnation of Jews as rejectors of Christ:

> What then shall we Christians do with this damned, rejected race of Jews? Since they live among us and we know of their lying, blaspheming, and cursing, we cannot tolerate them if we do not wish to share in their lies, curses, and blasphemy. ... Their synagogues should be set on fire and whatever does not burn up should be covered or spread over with dirt so that no one may ever be able to see a single cinder or stone."

Luther's condemnation exceeded that of his contemporaries.

For their part, Jews were not passive onlookers during these tumultuous events. On the contrary, they used their conventional political strategy – *shtadlanut* (petitioning) – to safeguard themselves and even take advantage of these developments. In 1520, Josel of Rosheim, an Alsatian rabbi and the unofficial spokesman for Jews in the Holy Roman Empire, obtained a renewal of Jewish rights from Emperor Charles V. He and other Jews initially regarded Luther and his reform movement with guarded optimism. Some Jews felt that Luther's reexamination of scripture would ease Christian antagonism. A few even regarded the Reformation as a sign that messianic redemption was imminent, that Luther's challenge to the Roman Catholic Church, coupled with the Ottoman victories over the Holy Roman Empire, marked the fulfillment of the prophet Daniel's vision of the defeat of a fourth empire (later reinterpreted as Rome) as a prelude to redemption.

As Luther began to show hostility to Jews, the latter grew increasingly wary of him. Earlier hopes that he might benefit the Jews gave way to wariness and derision. Some Jews referred to him as *Lo Tahor*, a Hebrew play on words that meant impure. In 1543, Josel of Rosheim offered to debate Luther publicly.

Not all Protestant leaders were as openly hostile as Luther. John Calvin, for example, emphasizing law over theology, regarded the legal tradition of the Hebrew Bible more favorably than Luther, claiming that Jews had corrupted a once useful, and potentially still useful, tradition. Calvin challenged the widespread Christian rejection of moneylending, and argued that Jewish usury was an abuse of an otherwise acceptable occupation. For Calvin, who had little or no contact in Geneva with actual Jews, the real adversary was not Jews but rival Christian theologians such as the anti-Trinitarian Miguel Servetus, who Calvin claimed relied too much on the Hebrew Bible and Jewish commentaries. Calvin denounced Servetus as a Judaizer, and had him burned at the stake in 1553. Calvin's followers, though, tended to be more militant, expelling the Jews from Geneva in 1582.

As a series of wars between Catholics and Protestants consumed much of Europe during the second half of the sixteenth century, most Jews tried to remain neutral. Given the more overt hostility of Lutherans and Calvinists, Jews generally regarded Catholic sovereigns as less hostile and more predictable. The Peace of Augsburg, which ended the first wave of religious wars in 1555, introduced an element of uncertainty for Jews. This agreement between Catholics and Protestants to disagree was epitomized by the principle *cuius religio euis regio* (literally, whose realm, his religion). While reflecting a measure of mutual toleration between Catholics and Protestants – much to the outrage of the pope – this principle implied the theoretical possibility of outlawing, or at least curtailing, the practice of Judaism in a Catholic or Protestant state.

Events during the 1550s were indicative of this narrowing toleration of Jews. In 1552, a request by a Venetian Jewish publisher that the ecclesiastical censors investigate an edition of Maimonides' *Mishneh Torah* that a rival Jewish publisher had published with a controversial contemporary commentary led to a renewed accusation of blasphemy against Italian Jews. This renewed accusation dovetailed with the pietistic mood of the Counter-Reformation, culminating in the pope's order in 1553 to burn the Talmud. Two years later, the pope confined all Jews in and around Rome to a newly created ghetto.

Despite such setbacks, however, the Counter-Reformation prevented the complete collapse of Jewish life in the Holy Roman Empire and the Italian States. In 1544 and 1546, the emperor reaffirmed his protection over all Jews in the empire. As the Catholic princes and prince-bishops turned to the emperor for support against Lutherans, thereby extending imperial authority, renewed imperial protection took on greater importance. In addition, the emperor and Catholic princes regarded Jews as a counterweight against an often recalcitrant Protestant middle class. On the other hand, the emergence of the Jesuit order as a major player in politics led to new source of anti-Jewish hostility. The pope's about-face in 1553 reflected, among other things, the growing influence of the Jesuits on all ranks of the church.

On balance, the Reformation and Wars of Religion eventually worked to the advantage of Jews in central Europe, Luther's virulent anti-Judaism notwithstanding. The Protestant reinterpretation of Communion undermined the accusation of Host desecration. Moreover, the Thirty Years War – which began as the last great European war of religion in Europe – accelerated the reintegration of Jews into central European society that had begun slowly during the 1570s. As late as 1618, Jews had been excluded from much of the empire: from all larger states, except Bohemia and Hesse; from all major imperial free cities, except Prague, Frankfurt, and Hamburg; and from most lesser imperial cities.

The survival of Jewish life in the empire at the end of the sixteenth century was made possible by a combination of pro-Jewish attitudes on the part of most emperors, the support of ecclesiastical princes who helped Jews to offset influence of the Lutheran bourgeoisie and from the emergence of new political strategies such as mercantilism and early absolutism. To be sure, popular opposition to Jews continued. In 1614 and 1615, for example, anti-Jewish riots broke out in Frankfurt and Worms. The rioters were suppressed by imperial and ecclesiastical troops.

These factors allowed first *conversos* and then Jews to move beyond money-lending and a restricted array of commercial endeavors to more lucrative forms of commerce such as international trade. By 1618, Portuguese *conversos* were importing sugar and spices from Asian and African colonies. There was also a concurrent rise in the Jewish population of commercial centers such as Prague and Frankfurt. The Jewish population of Frankfurt increased from 400 in 1542 to 2,000 by 1600.

As sovereigns' need for money peaked during the Thirty Years War, toleration of Jews increased. Emperor Ferdinand II (1619–37), though militantly Catholic and overtly anti-Jewish, was bailed out of a financial crisis in 1620 by the Jews of Vienna, whose assistance allowed him to provision his troops. When Prague was sacked by the emperor in 1620 in his effort to reconquer the city from Protestant Czech rebels, the *Judenstadt* was left intact. During the 1620s, the *Judenstadt* was enlarged, and Protestant houses were confiscated and given to Jews. In 1627, the emperor granted all Jews open access to all Bohemian trade fairs. In Vienna, Jews were allowed to congregate in Leopoldstadt beginning in 1624. The Jewish population of Vienna increased from 50 families in 1625 to 2,000 by 1650.

The financial strain caused by the war also placed a premium on highly capable and resourceful Jewish merchants. Jacob Bassevi von Treuerberg (1580–1634), who dealt in silver, was ennobled by the emperor and granted the right

> to engage in any business whatever, in any part of the empire, whether cities, towns, or marketplaces, in Prague and Vienna, and other places where Jews are allowed to reside or are not; to acquire property and to reside anywhere he pleases. His property in any form is to be free from taxes, imposts, and duties; he is allowed to reside in the imperial quarters; and he is responsible to no tribunal, except that of the marshal of the court.

Such Jews were also able to provide protection to other Jews. When the Prague rabbi Yom Tov Lipmann Heller was arrested and fined 12,000 florins, Bassevi personally paid off nearly a quarter of the fine and helped secure his release.

Protestants, too, mollified their treatment of Jews for economic reasons. When the Swedes invaded and dominated central Europe during the 1630s, they imposed heavy taxes on Jews, but there was no retribution against Jews by the Swedish crown or the Lutheran populace under Swedish rule. When the Swedes "liberated" Prague from the Catholics in 1632, they sacked the city but spared its 7,000 Jews. Under Swedish rule, in 1639 the Jews of Mayence were allowed to build a synagogue for the first time in centuries.

The Treaty of Westphalia, which brought the Thirty Years War to a close in 1648, marked the end of the wars of religion; from this point on, European wars would be waged for economic, territorial, and political reasons. In some cases, this meant overturning the religious-based policies of the past. As part of the international settlement in 1648, the king of France annexed Alsace and Lorraine, which had been part of the empire. Suddenly there were several thousand Jews in France, in violation of the 1394 edict that had expelled the Jews in perpetuity. At this point, the French crown chose the potential benefits of revenue from Jews through taxation and gifts, and the stimulation Jews could provide to regional commerce, and allowed the Jews to remain. In retrospect, the decision not to expel the Jews reflected a larger economic-driven toleration of non-Catholics that had allowed thousands of French Huguenots to remain.

In addition, the treaty reaffirmed the political status quo in central Europe, recognizing each of the constituent members of the Holy Roman Empire as sovereign states, a situation that would last until the reign of Napoleon Bonaparte. In an effort to emulate the emperor and other leading rulers, most of the more than 300 sovereigns regarded resourceful Jewish merchants as an indispensable feature of government administration. This led to a proliferation of large-scale Jewish merchants and moneylenders who received an appointment as factor from a royal, ducal, or ecclesiastical court. As a group, these Jews came to be known as court Jews.

Absolutism and the court Jews

The court Jews were a coterie of wealthy, well-connected Jews who were the financial or commercial agents of a powerful sovereign. As a small and atypical but highly significant group, the court Jews can be defined by five general characteristics. First, court Jews were not just wealthy, but also politically well connected. They had direct access to a prince, king, or emperor. Court Jews, also called court factors, supplied the emperor and other sovereigns with cash, and provisioned virtually every army in central Europe. During the 1660s, Samson Wertheimer provisioned the emperor's war efforts against the Turks and enabled Prince Eugene of Savoy, the commander of the imperial army, to provide medical attention to troops. In 1701, Wertheimer replenished the imperial treasury at the outbreak of the War of the Spanish Succession and provisioned troops in Hungary and the Italian states. The same year, Wertheimer obtained 1 million florins for the king of Poland as a dowry for the king's daughter to marry the emperor's brother-in-law Duke Charles Philip.

Second, court Jews formed a separate caste within European Jewry. They were an international community that transcended local and national borders, not unlike the European high nobility. Members of the court Jews' families tended to intermarry among each other.

Third, court Jews and their families lived an exceptional lifestyle. They had virtually no residential restrictions, and had access to the non-Jewish world. Some court Jews lived outside the Jewish quarter, and in cities from which most Jews were banned – even in Vienna. Bernard Lehmann lived in a huge palace, drove a six-horse carriage, and owned several country villas. Samson Wertheimer owned several palaces and gardens in Vienna, and had houses in other cities. His house in Vienna was guarded by ten imperial guards. Court Jews were not forced to conform to restrictions on Jewish dress.

Court Jews, moreover, provided their children with an exceptional education by engaging private tutors, and were thus not confined by the limits of

Jewish communal education. The children of court Jews studied secular in addition to Jewish subjects, and education was provided for girls as well as boys. Some court Jews, such as Samson Wertheimer, were accomplished talmudic scholars. In Wertheimer's case, the combination of scholarship and political stature earned him the dual titles of *Landesrabbiner* from the Jews of Hungary, and *Judenkaiser* from Emperor Charles VI.

Fourth, court Jews' exceptional status was often a source of implicit Jewish toleration. Samson Wertheimer's special permission to reside in Vienna, despite the recent expulsion of Jews in 1670, extended to his entourage. Until 1848, the Jewish community of Vienna consisted largely of an amalgamation of special exemptions to Jews like Wertheimer and their entourages.

Finally, court Jews became the natural leaders of central European Jewry, as patrons of Jewish culture and *shtadlanim*. In 1700, for example, Samson Wertheimer was able to suppress the circulation of Johann Eisenmenger's anti-Jewish tract *Entdecktes Judenthum*, even after Eisenmenger had spent a fortune trying to win the support of the Jesuits. Beyond the small coterie of court Jews, this leadership elite provided a model for smaller-scale Jewish communal leaders, who modeled their tactics and their role in Jewish communal life after the court Jews.

While most of the court Jews were men, their leadership model and paternalistic attitude toward their Jewish constituents provided a model for lesser Jewish leaders, male and female. An instructive example in this regard is Glückel of Hameln. The widow of the leader of the Jewish community, Glückel took over not only her late husband's business but, in no small measure, his role in Jewish communal life. Though partnered by her son and then her second husband, she used the family fortune not only to find acceptable matches for her children, but also for the betterment of the Jewish community. Glückel thus reveals how, in some cases, wealth and political savvy could transcend the boundary between men and women, and allow women to take an active role in public Jewish life.

In a larger sense, the privileged status of the court was symptomatic of the rise of absolutism. As a political philosophy, absolutism emerged out of the exhaustion at the end of the Thirty Years War. In the wake of this costly and destructive war, two attempts to rethink the relationship between state and society appeared in central Europe, by John Calvin and Thomas Hobbes respectively. Calvin regarded the state as the only effective arbiter of religious conflict, and he supported a strong state.

Hobbes expanded this notion in *Leviathan*. People, he argued, are by nature evil and selfish, striving only to avoid pain and maximize pleasure, even at each other's expense. For this reason, the equilibrium state of nature, he argued, was a chaotic and anarchic "war of every man against every man." Life, he concluded, is "solitary, poor, nasty, brutish, and short."

For Hobbes, the solution to this awful situation was a social contract in which individuals cede some of their autonomy and freedom to an absolute monarch who can maintain order and stability. The constitutional monarchs of the past, he argued, were limited by the privileges of the nobility, clergy, and other corporate groups, and thus unable to overcome inherent conflicts like wars of religion. Instead, Hobbes advocated that the state and its absolute monarch be like a leviathan, a great beast that can prevent individuals from devouring one another.

The overriding concern of absolutism was the welfare of the state. Absolutism thus aimed at governing all subjects directly. This did not mean that all subjects had the same rights and obligations; only that all individuals had a direct relationship with the state. In theory, absolutism meant the elimination of the corporate privileges of the nobility and clergy. Early absolutist monarchs put Calvin's and Hobbes's ideas into practice, challenging such privileges and replacing corporate society with royal institutions: bureaucracy, army, the court system. In practice, though, some corporate rights were assailed, but nobles still retained many privileges, including the right to trial by jury, unrestricted residence and mobility, and, often, tax-exempt status.

In addition, absolutism aimed at maximizing the capability of every subject to serve the best interests of the state as effectively and efficiently as possible. This meant something different for different elements of society. For peasants, absolutism meant a way to farm the land more productively. For nobles, it meant participating in the newly created state bureaucracy and courts, and serving as officers in the newly formed standing army.

With regard to Jews, absolutism meant maximizing the revenue that the state collected from Jews by allowing Jews to develop commerce and invest their commercial profit to the benefit of the state. To this end, most German princes chose to protect their Jewish subjects after 1649 rather than expel them. This newfound protection came at a price, as absolutist sovereigns taxed and regulated Jews and interfered in Jewish communal administration to an unprecedented degree. Indicative in this regard was the edict issued by Frederick William I, the king of Brandenburg-Prussia in 1671, *Edict on the Readmission of Fifty Jewish Families of Protected Jews; but They Are Not to Have Synagogues*. This charter, and the expanded version that Frederick II gave the Jews of Prussia in 1750, combined aspects of medieval charters with novel elements. Jews were still subjected to restrictions, seen as pariahs, and still not trusted by the king. On the other hand, Jews were no longer defined as subjects of the king, but of the state, meaning – at least theoretically – not subject to the personal whims of a particular sovereign. In addition, the Prussian charters eroded certain aspects of corporate Jewish autonomy, instructing Jews involved in civil or criminal disputes with other Jews to seek redress in royal rather than Jewish communal courts.

The turn to absolutism was more complex in the Habsburg Monarchy. The reigning Habsburg monarch doubled as Holy Roman Emperor until the empire was dissolved in 1804. The Habsburgs were pious Catholics whose deep immersion in the mentality of the Counter-Reformation was exemplified by their incessant use of Jesuit confessors. In addition, the Habsburgs were also engaged in a protracted war against the Ottoman Turks, and regarded themselves as the defenders of Christendom during the latest crusade against Islam – further intensifying their piety. Their ability to set aside religious disdain for Jews was commendable.

Whereas in Prussia, state-building in the seventeenth and eighteenth centuries meant territorial expansion, for the Habsburgs it meant consolidating a vast and disjointed collection of possessions under a single uniform administration. The Prussian Hohenzollerns, moreover, had subordinated the Prussian nobility into a military caste and the heart of the royal standing army. The Habsburgs had to contend with recalcitrant nobles in Hungary, the Czech Lands and, after 1772, in Galicia.

As in Prussia, the Habsburgs' turn to absolutism began after the Thirty Years War. Typical of Habsburg policy, they flip-flopped regarding the Jews. During the war, Emperor Ferdinand II had employed Jacob Bassevi, whose silver mines in Bohemia helped pay and provision the imperial army. In recognition of Bassevi's service, the emperor gave a new *privilegium* to the Jews of Prague and Bohemia in 1623, which included traditional privileges plus freedom of residence, protection from expulsion, and the right to unimpeded trade and commerce even in royal cities. Four years later, he extended these privileges to the Jews of Moravia. After the war, Ferdinand III changed this policy. In 1650, he attempted to expel Jews from all places where they had not resided legally since 1618, thus reversing the gains Jews had made during the war, and to disqualify Jews from the leasing of tolls and from managing estates. The Moravian nobility delayed implementation of this edict for economic reasons. In 1658, Ferdinand's successor, Leopold I, changed the effective date of the decree from 1618 to 1657, a *de facto* recognition of Jewish expansion during the Thirty Years War.

The situation of Jews in Habsburg lands remained largely unchanged from this point until the reign of Emperor Charles VI (Charles III as king of Hungary). In 1719, he changed tactics. Rather than trying to reduce the Jewish population through expulsion or additional restrictions, he placed a cap on the Jewish population growth through the *Familiantengesetz* (Familiants Law). The intent of this law, the symbol of harsh Habsburg treatment of Jews during the eighteenth century, was to impede Jewish mobility and discourage growth while maintaining a stable tax base.

The Familiants Law was implemented in Bohemia and Silesia in 1726, and in Moravia in 1727. It imposed a limit of 8,541 families in Bohemia, 119 in Silesia, and 5,106 in Moravia. Each head of household was given a residence permit in the form of a familiants number. The permit entitled only one son in the household to marry between the ages of 18 and 24, and to inherit the familiants number after the father's death. Jewish men and women who married illegally were subject to physical punishment and expulsion. Nobles or towns that violated this law were subject to a fine of 1,000 florins, payable to the imperial treasury.

The impact of this law on Jews in the Czech Lands reflected the limits of Habsburg absolutism. Jews in Bohemia and Moravia were able to mollify its harshness. In Bohemia, the law was most easily enforced and regulated in Prague, where most Bohemian Jews lived. In response, Jews in Bohemia who were not firstborn evaded the law by settling in small outlying villages. By 1750, Jews lived in 800 different places in Bohemia, 600 of which had 100 or fewer Jews. In Moravia, the impact of the law was mitigated by magnate owners of private towns, who sheltered their Jewish subjects. By 1754, 29,000 Jews lived in Bohemia and 20,000 Jews in Moravia.

The differences between Bohemia and Moravia with respect to implementing the Familiants Law paralleled the differences between Jewish communal organization in the two states. In Bohemia, the Prague Jewish community was dominant and represented all Jews in Bohemia. As more and more Jews relocated to outlying communities, they attempted to throw off the yoke of Prague Jewry. The focal point of this tension was the authority of the Prague chief rabbi. David Oppenheim was appointed chief rabbi of Prague in 1702 and to provincial rabbinic posts in 1713 and 1715. The state appointed Oppenheim as *Landesrabbiner* for Bohemian Jewry, and *Kreisrabbiner* positions for provincial communities, the *Kreisrabbiner* being subordinate to the chief rabbi in Prague. In Moravia, the lack of a towering center like Prague fostered greater intercommunal cohesion and cooperation. The Moravian Jewish Council (*Va'ad Mehren*) emerged during the seventeenth century as a supracommunal governing body for all Moravian Jews, and was recognized as such by the state.

The rationalist aim of the Familiants Law appears more vividly when seen in connection with Charles's policy in neighboring Hungary. Hungarian Jewry was minuscule at the end of the seventeenth century. Jews lived mainly in a handful of magnate-controlled market towns in western Hungary, where the local authorities governed their Jewish and other non-Catholic subjects with the harshness typical of the Counter-Reformation era. The Jewish community of Buda, which had thrived during the century and a half under Ottoman rule, had been expelled immediately following the Habsburg reconquest of Buda in 1686, although this edict was not enforced until 1749 owing to the intervention of Habsburg military leaders stationed in Buda. In addition, in 1718 Charles gave three Jews in Buda special permits to remain.

During the first half of the eighteenth century, Charles faced the difficult challenge of repopulating central Hungary, which had become an underpopulated wasteland following the Ottoman retreat. In order to repopulate the region, Charles offered loyal magnate families large tracts of land. The magnates, in turn, offered favorable conditions to potential settlers of all kinds, including Jews, in order to rebuild commerce and urban life and create a tax base. This prompted an influx of Moravian and Bohemian Jews into Hungary eager to evade the restrictions of the Familiants Law. As a result, the Jewish population of Hungary doubled between 1720 and 1740 from 20,000 to 40,000. This meant that by 1740, Charles had leveled the Jewish populations of Hungary and the Czech Lands, by capping the Jewish population of the latter and encouraging Jews to emigrate to Hungary.

The situation of Habsburg Jews changed slightly under Maria Theresa, though the basic contours of Habsburg policy remained the same. The moment she assumed the throne, her ascension was assailed by her Hohenzollern cousin, who invaded the empire to start the War of the Austrian Succession. In order to secure troops, Maria Theresa reaffirmed the consitutional rights of the Hungarian nobility, a setback for Habsburg absolutism in Hungary.

In 1744, she suspected the Jews of Prague of siding with her enemies and expelled them. Two years later, she readmitted them for economic reasons, but imposed a new tax, first on the Jews of Prague, then on all Jews in the empire: the Toleration Tax, also called by Jews the *Malke-Geld* (Queen's tax). This tax, originally imposed as a punishment, reflected the two elements of her attitude toward her Jewish subjects. She regarded them as direct subjects of the dynasty, and believed that the only way they could and should serve the state was as a source of tax revenue.

In this light, and in desperate need of money to replenish a chronically bankrupt treasury, she rethought the aim of the Familiants Law. Her father had regarded this law as a way to limit and regulate the size of the Jewish population. Maria Theresa regarded the law as a way to register the Jewish population, in order to raise more tax revenue. To this end, she allowed exceptions to this law, largely to affluent Jewish families. Marriage permits were issued to second-born sons for 700 florins and to third-born sons for 500 florins. Also, in exchange for a considerable "gift," expired familiants status could be transferred to another applicant. During her reign, the Jewish population of the Czech Lands increased by nearly a quarter, and Hungarian Jewry doubled in size.

No less indicative of her Jewish policy was her response to a blood libel accusation against the Jews of Sárospatak, a small town in northeastern Hungary. There, twenty-eight Jews were accused of killing a Christian child and summarily convicted and imprisoned by local authorities. When Maria Theresa received word, she was outraged by the audacity of local officials in usurping jurisdiction over her Jewish subjects. She convened a new trial in a royal court which acquitted the Jews. Twenty-seven of the twenty-eight were released (the other had died in prison).

Non-Reformation Europe: the Jews of Poland

Jews who lived in those parts of Europe that were less affected by the Reformation, Counter-Reformation, Wars of Religion, and the rise of absolutism followed a different course of development from the sixteenth through the eighteenth century. The Ottoman conquest of the Balkans largely insulated southeastern Europe from the ravages of religious wars. Hungary is a case in point. The Jews of Hungary, after a brief revival under Matthias Corvinus during the second half of the fifteenth century, declined steadily under his successors. The Ottoman conquest of the eastern two-thirds of Hungary in 1526 brought a major reprieve for Hungarian Jews. Ottoman rule muted the impact of the Reformation, which had begun less than a decade before the Ottoman conquest, and fostered a sense of ecumenicism between Catholics, Lutherans, and Calvinists – all of whom were equally second-class Christians under Muslim rule. This ecumenical mood extended in part to Jews. In 1623, Gábor Bethlen, the Calvinist prince of Transylvania, gave the Jews of Alba-Iulia a charter that was more generous than most Christian charters. No less indicative of the favorable situation of Hungarian Jews under Ottoman rule was the Jewish community of Buda, where Ashenazic and Sephardic communities coexisted and prospered for much of the sixteenth and seventeenth centuries.

Yet the most vivid measure of the disparate situation of Jews in Reformation and non-Reformation Europe was the rise of Polish Jewry during the sixteenth and the first half of the seventeenth century. Initially invited to Poland from central Europe by the Duke Bolesław the Pious in 1264, Polish Jewry was built primarily by immigration of Jews from Ashkenazic central Europe. (The theory that Polish Jews were the descendants of the Khazars has been summarily refuted.) By 1648, Polish Jewry would emerge as the largest, most prosperous, and most culturally creative Jewry in the world, rivaled only by the Jewish communities of the Ottoman Empire. In fact, parallels between Poland and the Ottoman Empire during this period fostered certain comparisons between the emergence of Polish Jewry and the rise of the Ottoman Jewry. As in the Ottoman Empire, the sixteenth and seventeenth centuries were a period of conquest and expansion for the Kingdom of Poland, which conquered Ukraine and the Baltic Peninsula and expanded eastward into Russia. The union between the Kingdom of Poland and the Duchy of Lithuania in 1569 created the Polish–Lithuanian Commonwealth, the largest European state until 1772. The Polish–Lithuanian Commonwealth, moreover, was the great defender of Catholicism during wars of religion and from the Ottoman invasion. In 1683, the Polish army saved Vienna from a Turkish siege.

The ethnic diversity of the Polish–Lithuanian Commonwealth increasingly paralleled that of the Ottoman Empire. The Ottoman Empire was a Muslim state with substantial non-Muslim minorities. Poland was a Catholic country with substantial enclaves of non-Catholics, including Lutherans, adherents of Eastern Orthodox denominations, and Jews. Like the Ottoman Empire, Poland was a land with multiple religious faiths, ethnicities, languages, and even alphabets. As in the Ottoman Empire, Jews in Poland were one of many ethnic minorities and one of several commercial minorities.

The combination of territorial expansion and ethnic diversity benefited Polish Jews, especially in the newly conquered eastern regions. As early as in 1264, Bolesław the Pious had redefined the status of Jews as "freemen of the chamber," a marked improvement over the "serfs of the chamber." In the newly conquered regions, Jews were needed to help repopulate, stimulate trade, and expand centers of commerce. The Polish magnates who owned and ruled the towns and villages of eastern Poland further expanded the residential and occupational privileges of their Jewish subjects. The majority of Polish Jews lived on the estates of one of the magnates and after 1539 were governed entirely by these magnates.

In western Poland, Polish Jews were largely excluded from major Polish cities by the urban privilege through which cities elsewhere in Christendom had been able to exclude Jews: *de non tolerandis Judaeis*. The lone exceptions were cities such as Kraków, where the power and influence of the royal crown were able to set aside this privilege. Even in Kraków, though, Jewish settlement came late. Until the mid-sixteenth century, Jews were allowed to live in Kazimiersz, a royal-controlled suburb adjacent to Kraków, but not in the city itself. More than 2,000 Jews lived there by 1578. When Kazimiersz was incorporated into Kraków, the Jews of Kazimiersz became residents of Kraków.

The economic and demographic opportunities of Jews in eastern Poland expanded steadily. Elsewhere in Christian Europe, Jews had been confined to the lowest echelons of moneylending and commerce, meaning pawnbroking and peddling secondhand goods. In eastern Poland, as in the Ottoman Empire, the occupational profile of Jews was broader than elsewhere in both vertical and horizontal terms. Polish Jews traded in a wide variety of goods. More important, two areas of the economy were open to Polish Jews that were inaccessible to most of their counterparts elsewhere in Christian Europe. Though excluded from Christian guilds, Jews were allowed to organize their own guilds. In addition, Jews were often employed by their magnate benefactor as arrendator (estate manager). This entitled Jews, in addition to collecting taxes for the magnate, to distill liquor and operate a tavern – a major source of income. To be sure, Jewish guilds and estate management were no less prevalent in Moravia. There, as in Poland, the preeminent position of magnates with respect to the imperial crown provided Moravian Jews with the same added economic opportunities as Polish Jews. Hungarian Jews would attain similar occupational advantages during the resurgence of the Hungarian magnates during the late eighteenth and early nineteenth centuries.

The development of Jewish culture in Poland also mirrored that of Ottoman Jewry. Like Sephardic Jews in the Ottoman Empire, the waves of

Jews who immigrated to Poland from central Europe turned culturally inward, expanding the religious culture they had brought with them rather than fashioning a new one. Just as Ottoman Jews increasingly spoke Ladino, a Jewish language imported from the Iberian Peninsula, the language of Polish Jews was Yiddish, a Jewish dialect of German imported to Poland by Jewish immigrants from central Europe. It is noteworthy that neither Polish nor Ottoman Jews fashioned a Jewish dialect of the local vernacular: there was no Judeo-Polish or Judeo-Turkish. In both cases, the ability of Jewish immigrants to transplant a vernacular across hundreds of miles was made possible by print culture.

Jews in Poland and the Ottoman Empire continued to trade. Illustrative in this regard was the rabbinic career of Ephraim Cohen of Vilna. Born and educated in Vilna, he accepted a rabbinic post as the Ashkenazic rabbi of Buda, Hungary, during the 1660s. Under his guidance, the Ashkenazic Jews of Buda had a close relationship with the Sephardic community. Cohen himself sent his son to study in Salonika, attesting to the interaction between Ashkenazic and Sephardic Jews. In one responsum, Cohen was asked whether an Ashkenazic Jew could fulfill the obligation to pray while in a Sephardic synagogue, and vice versa. Cohen answered emphatically: yes.

Alongside the similarities between Polish and Ottoman Jewry were two important differences: the supracommunal organization of Polish Jewry from the mid-sixteenth century on, and the greater diversity of Ottoman Jewry, which included Sephardic, Ashkenazic, Italian, and Romaniot Jews. Jewish communal organization in Poland developed to a greater degree than anywhere else, epitomized by the emergence of two supracommunal organizations: the Council of Four Lands (Va'ad Arba Arzot) in the Polish part of the commonwealth, and the Council of Lithuania (Va'ad Lita) in Lithuania. The Council of Four Lands grew out of informal meetings of communal elders at the semiannual commercial fairs of Lublin, where they would discuss common problems, challenges, and successes in communal administration. Eventually these meetings were formalized in a supracommunal council, whose centers were in Lublin and Kraków.

The council was made up of leading lay leaders from across Polish Jewry. It was at the top of a supracommunal hierarchy that consisted of individual communities governed by regional councils, each of which was overseen by the high council. The council performed four types of functions: legislative, judicial, administrative, and cultural. It legislated rules for electing communal leaders and for appointing and dismissing communal rabbis, and issued regulations regarding commercial practices between Jews and between Jews and non-Jews.

The council also issued prohibitions, such as a ban on leasing a magnate's estate without the knowledge of the local Jewish community, and injunctions to obey royal edicts, such as the ban on settling illegally where Jews were not permitted. In addition, the council had a coterie of *shtadlanim*, which could be dispatched to Warsaw or Kraków in times of emergency, and took charge of providing royal officials and members of the ruling dynasty with bribes and gifts. More importantly, the council acted as the highest Jewish court of appeals, settling disputes between individual communities. In addition, the council regulated the spiritual and religious life of Polish Jewry, assuring that books were published only with the permission of a noted rabbi, and that the laws of Kashrut and the Sabbath were dutifully enforced and observed. The council imposed safety restrictions, such as a taboo on Jews drinking wine in inns where Christians congregated. The crowning achievement of the Council of Four Lands was the Statues of Kraków (*Takanot Krako*), which were published in 1595. These statutes addressed any and every aspect of Jewish life, on an individual and a communal level.

In a larger sense, the supracommunal organization of Polish Jewry was instrumental in the dissemination and expansion of Jewish culture in Poland. The first major rabbinic figure in Poland, Jacob ben Joseph Polak (1460/70 – after 1522), was born in Bavaria and had studied in a yeshiva in Regensburg. After marrying Esther Fischel, the daughter of a wealthy Jewish tax farmer in Kraków, he founded the first yeshiva in Poland. His student Shalom Shachna (d. 1558) was the first major talmudic scholar in Poland, and became the head of the Lublin yeshiva.

True to its Ashkenazic roots, Polish Jewish culture was primarily religious in nature, but in the broadest sense. The curriculum of Polish Jewish education included biblical commentary, liturgical poetry, rabbinic responsa, non-religious Hebrew poetry such as that of Immanuel of Rome (but never Dante), philosophical works such as those of Maimonides (but never Aristotle), and Kabbala. The leading intellectual of sixteenth-century Polish Jewry, and the embodiment of its cultural development, was Moses Isserles (1530–72), also known as the ReMA. Isserles was a student of Schachna, from whom he received a first-rate training as a talmudic scholar, biblical commentator, and Kabbalist, and was the author of numerous responsa. His major work, the *Mapah*, mentioned earlier, capped a career as a prolific rabbinic scholar. In providing a comprehensive, user-friendly code of law for Polish and other Ashkenazic Jews, Isserles's *Mapah* complemented the Statutes of Kraków in bringing to fruition what the Tosafists had begun centuries earlier: the development of an all-encompassing religious life for Ashkenazic Jews.

A telling measure of the complexity and richness of Polish Jewish culture was the extensive literature written for Jewish women. The most rudimentary part of this literature was made up of handbooks written for women, such as Benjanim Slonik's *Seder Mitzvot Nashim* (The Order of Women's Commandments). This text dealt predominantly with the laws of ritual purity, but began with a series of instructions that reflected the author's idealistic image of the Jewish woman as wife, mother, and homemaker.

More sophisticated were two genres of texts that were written for women to recite in the synagogue or at home. The *Tzeena urena* was a collection of brief summaries of and commentaries on the weekly Torah portion read on Saturday morning in the synagogue. The other was *Tehinos*, an Ashkenazic corruption of the Hebrew *Tehinot* (meditations or supplications). These were special prayers written for women, some as an alternative to the regular liturgy, others for occasions that were unique to the experience of a women: pregnancy, childbirth, nursing, menstruation. Initially these texts were written with the presumption that women lacked the intellectual capacity to comprehend or appreciate fully the prayers and Torah reading recited by men. By the seventeenth century, however, this genre had developed into a sophisticated body of religious literature, comparable to the normative liturgy, and even used in some cases by men in addition to women. In any case, it marked the sophistication, richness, and comprehensiveness of Polish Jewish culture.

The events of 1648

After a century and a half of expansion and development, Polish Jewry suffered a major setback in 1648 with a series of anti-Jewish massacres known as the Chmielnicki uprising. This event, a turning point in Polish, Ukrainian, and Polish-Jewish history, is remembered differently by Jews, Poles, and Ukrainians. Jews remember the uprising as *Gezerot Tach ve-Tat*, the massacres of 1648–9. For Poles, this event marks the beginning of the decline of the Polish–Lithuanian Commonwealth. For Ukrainians, this was a failed attempt at national liberation, led by Bogdan Chmielnicki; to this day, Ukrainians continue to commemorate Chmielnicki, a Ukrainian version of Simón Bolívar, with a huge statue in the central square of Kiev.

The setting for this event was the flat lands of Ukraine. Like other flat areas this terrain was easy to invade but hard to defend. As a result, every country that attempted to rule in Ukraine – Russia, Sweden, the Ottoman Empire, Poland – had to make an alliance with the Ukrainian Cossacks, skilled horsemen who were the most able to defend this region. Since the end of the sixteenth century, Ukraine had been part of Poland. As the landowning class became predominantly Polish, the region was increasingly plagued with social, economic, ethnic, and political tensions between the Polish Catholic nobility and the Ukrainian Orthodox peasantry. Between these two groups was a caste of merchants, moneylenders, and estate managers that was predominantly Jewish. During the sixteenth century, Ukrainians increasingly regarded their Polish landowners as illegitimate foreign rulers, and Jews as their agents of foreign oppression. As many of the Polish landowners ruled *in absentia*, their Jewish estate managers often bore the brunt of Ukrainian discontent. These social and ethnic tensions were superimposed on a political struggle between Poland and Russia for control of Ukraine. In 1637, tensions boiled over in the form of a Cossack attack on Jews in Poltava, in which 200 Jews were killed and several synagogues destroyed.

This was the background to the rise of Bogdan Chmielnicki as the leader of the Cossacks. He was staunchly anti-Polish. According to legend, a Polish noble had pillaged his tent, carried off his wife, and flogged his son to death. By 1648, he had been elected hetman by one of the Cossack clans, and then negotiated alliances with the other clans. In the spring of 1648, he incited the Cossacks to rise against the Poles. Between May 6 and May 15, the first encounter between Cossacks and the Polish army, the Poles were crushed, and the whole region erupted in open rebellion.

The ensuing breakdown of law and order included attacks on Jews throughout the region. As one observer noted, these attacks were brutal:

> Killing was accompanied by barbarous torture; the victims were flayed alive, split asunder, clubbed to death, roasted on coals, or scalded with boiling water. ... The most cruelty, however, was shown the Jews. They were destined for utter annihilation, and the slightest pity shown to them was looked upon as treason. Scrolls of the law were taken out of the synagogues by the Cossacks, who danced on them while drinking whiskey. Jews were butchered without mercy. Thousands of Jewish infants were thrown into wells, or buried alive.

Young Jewish women, when spared, were forcibly baptized and taken as wives. In response, some Jews fled to walled cities, hoping for protection there. This turned out to be even more tragic. In several cases, the attacking Cossacks promised the Poles inside the city walls that the Poles would be spared if they handed over the Jews. By 1650, the worst was over as the Polish army finally managed to restore order. But upheavals continued in Poland. In 1654, Russian and Swedish invasions begin, and continued for nearly a century.

The events of 1648–9 left a permanent impact on Polish Jewry. The number of Jews killed was in the tens of thousands; some estimate the death toll to have been as high as 100,000. Dozens of Jewish communities in southern Poland were devastated, and never fully recovered. Jews learned a valuable political lesson from these events, namely that passivity and total reliance on the authorities for protection were no longer wise. During the Russian invasion of Poland in 1654, Jews played a more active role in defending Poland by helping to build barricades, dig trenches, and provision soldiers. At the same, time, the Catholic Church, particularly its more fanatic elements, reasserted its authority in Poland after 1648. Students at Catholic colleges periodically attacked Jews; in 1657, there was a blood libel accusation in Grodno.

The events of 1648–9, moreover, set in motion a demographic shift within Polish Jewry – specifically, an exodus of Jews from the small towns of southern Poland. Some went westward to Germany, the first stage of a westward movement of Jews that would eventually culminate in the migration of more than 2 million Jews from eastern Europe to America at the end of the nineteenth century. Other Jews headed north to Belorussia and Lithuania, which had not been afflicted with massacres. The center of Jewish life in Poland shifted northward to Lithuania, leading to the emergence of Vilna (today Vilnius) as the center of rabbinic scholarship in Poland during the eighteenth century.

This northward migration would create a cultural and demographic gap between Jews in northern and southern Poland. The former would continue to live in fully functioning Jewish communities; the latter often without the basic institutional infrastructure of Jewish communal life: schools, rabbis, and a full array of voluntary societies. The decline of education and scholarship in southern Poland would encourage Jews in a more superstitious direction – an important element in the rise of Hasidism a century later.

The massacres also left in their wake a certain psychological devastation. In 1650, for example, a Polish Jew named Nathan of Hanover wrote *Yeven Mezula* (Abyss of Despair) as a sort of eulogy of Polish Jewry. In retrospect, such sentiments were premature. Polish Jewry recovered quickly. The Council of Four Lands was still intact, and in 1650 met to restore order in Jewish life. Aside from a few new regulations warning against overly high rates of interest, life went on. In 1661, the king of Poland granted a new charter to the Jews of Kraków bestowing on them the right of free commerce, symbolically reaffirming the privileges of all Polish Jews. A few new restrictions were eventually added, such as a limit of 20 percent on interest rates.

Other developments were no less indicative of Polish Jewry's return to normality. The commercial and managerial role of Jews in eastern Poland continued. According to some historians, it peaked at the end of the seventeenth century, a half-century after the massacres. The commercial and cultural relationship between Polish Jews and Jews in the Ottoman Empire, moreover, continued largely unaffected after 1648.

Shabbetai Zvi

Twenty years after the Chemielnicki massacres, Jews across the Jewish world were shaken by another major episode: the appearance of the messianic pretender Shabbetai Zvi. In 1666, he was proclaimed the Messiah. His was no ordinary messianic movement. Earlier such movements had been localized and short-lived. In 1666, Shabbetai Zvi had a massive following across the Jewish world: rich and poor Jews from the Land of Israel to England; rabbis and laity, educated and ignorant, and even crypto-Jews and *conversos*. Christians, too, were watching to see whether Shabbetai Zvi was Christ returning for the Second Coming.

Historians have adduced three explanations for the unprecedented nature of his following. Some suggested that the Chmielnicki massacres were seen by

Jews as the cataclysmic event that, according to rabbinic tradition, would precede the arrival of the Messiah; thus, the ground was fertile for messianic belief in the aftermath of 1648–9. If this were the case, one would have expected the belief in Shabbetai Zvi to originate, or at least be most intense, in southern Poland, where the events of 1648 had been the most devastating; neither was the case. Other historians suggested the messianic character of the year 1666, noting that Shabbetai Zvi was only one of several messianic pretenders who appeared in or around that year. As with other such "meteorological" explanations (i.e. there was something in the air), there is no evidence of any connection between Shabbetai Zvi's following and the appearance of other messianic figures.

The most compelling explanation was suggested by the historian Gershom Scholem, who rooted Shabbetai Zvi's broad following in the dissemination of Lurianic Kabbala beginning at the end of the sixteenth century; and particularly the Lurianic notion of *Tikkun* (Perfecting the World) through human activity, which had saturated the Jewish world with imminent messianic expectations. Recently, critics of Scholem have questioned how, even if Lurianic Kabbala had been widely disseminated, ordinary Jews could have come to be familiar with and to understand these complex ideas. In response, anthropologist Sylvie-Anne Goldberg suggested a means by which Lurianic Kabbala could have found more grassroots Jewish audience: the emergence of the *hevra kadisha* (Jewish burial society) at the beginning of the sixteenth century as a fixture of virtually every Jewish community in the world.

The Jewish burial society, whose membership was both male and female, attracted the most pious elements within the Jewish community, including pious Jews who were not scholars. The activities of burial societies included not only burial, but also preparing the soul of the deceased for passage from this world to the next. Thus, involvement with a burial society meant encountering the basic rabbinic and kabbalistic vocabulary regarding heaven and earth, and the messianic paradise of the afterlife. This, Goldberg suggested, could have provided a small but distinct constituency in scores of Jewish communities with the necessary vocabulary to grasp at least some of the intricacies of Lurianic Kabbala.

Along with explaining this broad following, historians have also noted a methodological problem in studying Shabbetai Zvi. Like other charismatic figures, he never wrote anything down. We know of him only through the eyes of his believers or detractors. However, historians have gleaned from the various accounts about him and sayings attributed to him, and fashioned a composite image of his life and thought.

Shabbetai Zvi was born in Izmir (Smyrna), in the Ottoman Empire, in 1626. He received a traditional Jewish education. From 1642 to 1648, he lived in isolation and was known as a young man of extremes. By present-day standards, he may have suffered from bipolar manic-depressive disorder. Along with rabbinic literature, he studied the Zohar in Egypt. He married twice, in 1646 and 1650, but was unable to consummate either marriage. In 1658, he made his way to Istanbul, trying to rid himself of demonic obsessions. At that time, he began to engage in antinomian behavior, such as observing three Jewish holidays at once, and declaring the abolition of the commandments.

In 1665, he heard of a man in the Land of Israel named Nathan of Gaza, who had a reputation of being able to help people achieve spiritual perfection and exorcize demons, and he went to see him. Meanwhile, Nathan had a vision of Shabbetai Zvi as the Messiah, and then tried to convince Shabbetai Zvi that this vision was true. On May 31, 1665, Shabbetai Zvi proclaimed himself Messiah (or, according to some accounts, Nathan proclaimed him the Messiah). At this point, Nathan became Shabbetai Zvi's prophet/publicist, and declared the seventeenth day of the Hebrew month of Tammuz – traditionally a fast day commemorating the first stage of the Babylonian conquest of Jerusalem – a day of celebration.

In September 1665, Nathan wrote a letter announcing what would happen next. First, Shabbetai Zvi would dethrone the sultan – a necessary step toward restoring an independent Jewish kingdom in the Ottoman-controlled Land of Israel – and make him his servant. He would then travel to the mythical River Sambatyon, and retrieve the lost ten tribes; and then marry Rebecca, the 13-year-old daughter of the resurrected Moses. These "birth pangs of the messianic age" (*Hevlei ha-Mashiach*), Nathan announced, would take four years.

At this point, a few Jews doubted the veracity of Shabbetai Zvi and Nathan, notably Rabbi Jacob Sassportas. Many, though, began to make arrangements to follow the Messiah back to the Land of Israel, some even selling their property. Most Jews held their breath and awaited the outcome.

Upon his arrival in Istanbul, the sultan presented Shabbetai Zvi with a choice of proving his messiahship to be true or suffering dire consequences. In response, Shabbetai Zvi accepted the sultan's offer to convert to Islam and be spared execution. At this point, most of his believers were severely disillusioned, but found solace in the theological safety net that rabbinic tradition had erected to deal with the false messiahs of the past: the time was right for the Messiah to come, but the Jews were not worthy. This ended the first stage of Shabbetai Zvi's career as Messiah.

A minority of Jews, however, continued to believe that Shabbetai Zvi was the Messiah even after he converted. They called themselves *Ma'aminim* (believers). To be sure, Sabbatean belief was heresy, since the rabbinic establishment had declared Shabbetai Zvi to be a false messiah. These Jews were called Sabbateans by their opponents.

For Sabbateans, the Messiah who converted to Islam posed a quandary, similar to the paradox that early Christians faced in the first century: the Messiah who deviates from the traditional rabbinic notions regarding the Messiah and the messianic age. In the same way that early Christians such as

Paul had to justify believing in a Messiah who died on the cross, Sabbateans had to justify the Messiah who converts to another faith. A solution to this quandary was found by Abraham Cardozo (1626–1706), a Sabbatean and a crypto-Jew living in Italy. If Nathan of Gaza was Shabbetai Zvi's publicist, Cardozo was the architect of Sabbateanism.

Cardozo found the solution in Lurianic Kabbala. Luria had described a version of creation that led eventually to sparks of divine eminence being trapped in this world. Accordingly, the aim of Judaism, and the central task of Jews in the world, was to retrieve and liberate these sparks of the divine, so they could reunite and bring about *Tikkun 'olam* (the perfectivizing of the world). Thus, Lurianic Kabbalists explained events since biblical times in terms of the gathering of divine sparks. For example, the Jews had been enslaved in Egypt to liberate the sparks trapped there; and Jews had been exiled to the four corners of the world to retrieve sparks from all over the world. Cardozo carried this explanation to a logical conclusion: Shabbetai Zvi had converted in order to liberate the divine sparks trapped in the world of Islam. This justification, in one fashion or another, provided the justification for Sabbateans to maintain their belief in Shabbetai Zvi.

Historians distinguish two types of Sabbatean belief: conservative and radical. Conservative Sabbateans were those who believed that Shabbetai Zvi would eventually return to Judaism. In the meantime, they waited for him to reappear, all the while living ostensibly normal Jewish lives. In other words, conservative Sabbateans were secret Sabbateans. Occasionally, secret/conservative Sabbateans would be discovered, precipitating a Sabbatean controversy.

The most notorious secret Sabbatean at the beginning of the eighteenth century was Nehemia Hayyon, a disciple of Abraham Cardozo. Hayyon was an enthusiast and an evangelical who claimed to have had direct contact with the divine. He published esoteric kabbalistic teachings, and was deemed by his opponents to be subversive, dangerous, and a threat to rabbinic authority.

His arch-adversary and pursuer was Moses Hajiz. Hajiz followed him all over Europe trying to apprehend him and prosecute him for heresy. He began a massive letter-writing campaign, trying to expose Hayyon. Hayyon eluded him repeatedly. A similar controversy revolved around Leib of Proznitz, who allegedly conducted secret Sabbatean rituals and recruited a small coterie of followers. He was also forced by his pursuers to flee.

By the mid-eighteenth century, the pursuit of Sabbatean heresy evolved from efforts to eliminate Sabbateanism into a broader suspicion of any deviant or unusual behavior as a possible instance of Sabbatean heresy. This latter suspicion was at the heart of the controversy that erupted in 1751 between Jonathan Eybeschütz and Jacob Emden. Eybeschütz, one of the leading talmudic scholars of his generation, was the rabbi of Altona and Prague before being accused by Emden of being a Sabbatean. He denied it categorically, at which point Emden, with the permission of the Jewish community, pored over Eybeschütz's manuscripts and private correspondence, and even broke open and read the parchments of his amulets. This unprecedented witch hunt and violation of privacy revealed nothing conclusive, although Emden claimed that there were occasional irregularities that suggested that Eybeschütz was indeed Sabbatean.

At this point, Emden and Eybeschütz each rallied support from other communities and rabbis, who began to threaten one another with excommunication. Eventually, the two sides agreed to submit to arbitration, and invited Ezekiel Landau, the up-and-coming rabbi of Yampol, to mediate. Landau initially offered Eybeschütz immunity from prosecution if he admitted to being a Sabbatean; Eybeschütz refused. While Landau agreed with Emden that there was enough circumstantial evidence to validate his suspicion of Eybeschütz, he instead opted for a compromise in the name of Jewish unity. He ordered Emden and his supporters to desist in their persecution of Eybeschütz. He also ordered Eybeschütz to leave his current position. The controversy abated until, several years later, Eybeschütz's son was suspected of being a Sabbatean, at which point Emden went after the son and renewed his pursuit of Eybeschütz himself. This pursuit continued even after Eybeschütz died in 1764.

A similar type of controversy took place in Padua, Italy, during the 1750s, revolving around the enthusiastic religious behavior of a Kabbalist named Moses Hayim Luzzatto (RaMHaL). Luzzatto admitted to having been visited by a *Maggid* – a mystical voice – who revealed secrets to him and to his circle of illuminati. In and of itself, a visitation from a *Maggid* was not cause for suspicion of heresy. Many leading kabbalists, including Joseph Karo and Isaac Luria, had had this type of mystical experience. In this case, however, there were those who suspected that the message Luzzatto had received had led him down the path of Sabbateanism. He was hounded from Padua, and forced to flee to Amsterdam.

In tandem, the controversies involving Jonathan Eybeschütz and Moses Luzzatto reflect the impact of Sabbateanism and the pursuit of Sabbatean heresy. By the end of the eighteenth century, Sabbateanism had become an umbrella term for heresy, and the accusation of Sabbateanism a license for exposing and denouncing any and all deviant behavior. This mentality was galvanized by the emergence of radical Sabbateanism during the eighteenth century.

Radical Sabbateans posed a more radical, utopian, charismatic challenge to rabbinic authority. The earliest manifestation of radical Sabbatean belief was the Donmeh (literally, converts). The Donmeh were believers in Shabbetai Zvi who followed him into the mystical depths of Islam by converting when he converted. They lived ostensibly as Muslims, while continuing to believe secretly that Shabbetai Zvi would eventually reveal himself again and return to Judaism. According to Scholem, the Donmeh numbered around 200 families. They were honored by Nathan of Gaza for their piety and devotion.

The Donmeh first appeared in 1676, and were initially centered in Adrianople. After 1676, they moved to Salonika, where they remained until 1924. The Donmeh's core belief was that the conversion of the Messiah had inverted the world theologically, good becoming evil, piety becoming heresy, and vice versa. To this end, they compiled a list of eighteen precepts to replace the Ten Commandments. They redefined the prohibition on adultery, for example, as optional. They replaced conventional Jewish holidays with new ones, including *Hag ha-Keves* (literally, the Festival of the Lamb), which they celebrated with an orgy a week after Purim; and *Hag ha-Semachot* (literally, the Festival of Happiness), in which they commemorated Shabbetai Zvi's birth on the ninth of Av.

After 1680, the Donmeh began to fragment into subsects. In 1680, Shabbetai Zvi's second wife, Jochebed, also known as Aisha, proclaimed her younger brother Jacob Querido to be the reincarnation of Shabbetai Zvi. This prompted a disagreement between the original Donmeh community and followers of Querido. Initially, this disagreement worked to the benefit of the Donmeh. The propaganda competition that ensued wound up by attracting many new followers and conversions of Jews to Islam, including a growing number of adherents from Poland. When Jacob Querido died around 1695, the Donmeh split into two groups: the original community became known as Izmirim, the followers of Jacob Querido as Ya'akoviim.

During the early eighteenth century, the Izmirim split again when Baruchiah Russo, son of one of the original followers, was proclaimed by his disciples to be the reincarnation of Shabbetai Zvi. In 1716, a third subsect formed around him, known as the Konyosos. This sect was the most radical and zealous among the Donmeh. After Russo died in 1720, his grave became a pilgrimage site. Six hundred followers visited the site in 1774. Among the Konyosos were Jacob Frank and his followers, the radical fringe of the Donmeh.

Frank (1726–91) was a teacher in Czernowitz and initially a conservative Sabbatean. By 1752, his reputation as an inspired Sabbatean attracted the attention of the Konyosos Donmeh, who recruited him, brought him to Salonika, and conferred on him the Sephardic honorific Hakham Ya'akov (Jacob the Sage). When he returned to Poland in 1755, he was referred to as Jacob Frank – Frank being the term that Polish Jews used to describe Sephardic Jews. A year later, while in the community of Lanskroun, he was discovered conducting Sabbatean rituals in a locked house, and forced to flee to back to the Ottoman Empire. He became an icon for secret Sabbateans in Poland and Moravia, who were especially drawn to his theological distinction between *Torat de-azilut* (Torah of emanation) – which he believed contained the truth of Judaism – and *Torat de-beriah* (Torah of creation), which he claimed was the false Torah studied and observed by Jews who were not Sabbateans.

A *herem* (excommunication) issued against Frank in 1756 provoked persecution of members of the Donmeh. At this point, the rabbis who issued the *herem* consulted Jacob Emden, who suggested that they use the Catholic Church to persecute Frank and his followers, on the pretense that new sects were not permitted by church law. This strategy backfired, as Frank found a supporter in Bishop Dembowski of Kamieniec-Podolski. To insure this support, Frank instructed his followers to play up the similarities between Sabbateanism and Catholicism.

Frank and the other Donmeh asked the bishop to convene a disputation between Frank and local rabbis, and prepared a series of arguments against the "Talmudists," including the notions that the Torah and prophets were so obscure that they could be interpreted only with the aid of divine inspiration and not by human intelligence alone; that the rabbis' interpretation of the Torah and the Talmud was nonsense; and that Jews would wait in vain for the Messiah to raise them above the world – instead, God would clothe himself in human form and atone for their sins.

Dembowski decided in favor of Frank and the Donmeh, and ordered the burning of the Talmud. However, he died before the decree could be carried out, and support for the Frank in the church largely died with him. The bishop's death was viewed by communal leaders as a sign of divine intervention, leading to renewed persecution of the Donmeh.

Several years later, Frank declared himself and his followers a separate sect. He announced that he was the third and ultimate incarnation of a messianic trilogy that had begun with Shabbetai Zvi, continued with Baruchiah Russo, and culminated with himself. He and his followers, knows as Frankists, carried Cardozo's notion of a theological inversion to its extreme. They set out to violate as many commandments as possible, conducting orgies and dancing naked with the Torah. In place of the Passover Seder, the Frankists wrote a Haggadah for their Ninth of Av Seder. In 1759, Frank was arrested. Eventually, the Frankists converted en masse to Christianity.

The legacy of the Frankists, and more generally of Sabbateanism, reverberated into the nineteenth century. The association of Sabbatean heresy with Lurianic Kabbala cast a shadow over the latter. During the eighteenth century, Kabbalists would increasingly emphasize the esoteric nature of these teachings and withdraw from mainstream Jewish society and study Kabbalah in a secluded *kloiz* (hermitage) so as not to expose and lead astray rank-and-file Jews. Like crypto-Jews, moreover, Sabbateanism was an instance of Jews living outside the realm of normative rabbinic Judaism, thus posing a second challenge to the premodern notion that the Judaism of the rabbis was the only authentic form of Judaism. Like Karaism, Sabbateanism posed a challenge that the rabbis labored for decades to eradicate.

Moreover, the prolonged fight against Sabbateanism bred among many rabbis a sort of messianic paranoia. From this point on, there would be rabbis like Jacob Sassportas, Moses Hajiz, and Jacob Emden whose first response to any unusual expression of Judaism was to censure and condemn out of a fear that it might be some form of Sabbateanism. This mentality would crystallize at the beginning of the nineteenth century into a novel approach to Judaism called Orthodoxy. The first manifestation of this fear, though, would be the rabbinic opposition to Hasidism at the end of the eighteenth century.

Hasidism and its antagonists

Hasidism, from the Hebrew term *Hasidut* (pietism) was a movement that begin in southeastern Poland in the 1740s, and conquered most of eastern European Jewry by 1810. It remains a major movement to this day. The origins of the movement lie in the aftermath of the Chmielnicki massacres, specifically in developments in southeastern Poland during the first half of the eighteenth century. The scarcity of rabbis and educators in southern Poland created a growing alienation between the scholarship-centered world of Lithuania and the less educated, more isolated Jews of southern Poland. This alienation was exacerbated by the scholarly emphasis on *Pilpul* (casuistry), a method of studying texts that emphasized hypothetical speculation over practical application. Once an effective means of adapting Judaism to the Ashkenazic world, by the eighteenth century *Pilpul* had long outlived its usefulness. Preachers and orators from the north who were sent to the southern communities armed with this scholarly mentality often preached a message that did not resonate among the isolated Jewish communities in the south. The conventional notion that the ideal Jewish life was defined and measured by the study of texts alienated those Jews who had little or no opportunity to engage in such study.

The decline of Jewish communal life in southeastern Poland led to a growing interest among Jews in folkish forms of Jewish observance, such as a belief in demons and spirits. This trend led to the rise of a new type of religious figure: the folk healer known as *Ba'al Shem* (master of the name). These individuals knew how to use roots and flowers to mix elixirs believed to have healing powers, and incantations that would ward off spirits. The best among these figures were known as *Ba'al shem tov* (the good master of the name).

This was the background to the emergence of the founder of Hasidism, Israel ben Eliezer Ba'al Shem Tov, also known as the Besht. Like Shabbetai Zvi, the Besht was a charismatic figure who wrote nothing down. Thus, historians have the same methodological problem in reconstructing his biography and religious worldview. The dearth of first-hand evidence leaves historians to assemble a composite based on the writings of his followers – notably *Shivhei ha-Besht* (In Praise of the Ba'al Shem Tov), a hagiography assembled by disciples – and on the condemnations by his opponents.

Israel Ba'al Shem Tov was born in Miedzyboz, a privately owned town in the Podolia region of southeastern Poland. He received a traditional

Jewish upbringing and education. As a young man he was employed as a schoolteacher, and studied Kabbala secretly at night. At some point, he began to wander and meditate in the forest. Around 1740, he began to preach a new prioritizing of Judaism, tailored to the common folk, that emphasized prayer over study, and melodies over liturgical texts. For rank-and-file Jews, cut off from the centers of Jewish learning but able to pray more independently, this was a powerfully attractive message. He attracted a small circle of followers, mainly from among the Jewish lower clergy – *maggidim* (itinerant preachers) and *mochikhim* (exhorters).

Initially, historians disagreed as to what kind of movement the Besht founded. Some argued that the movement was exclusively religious; other argued that it was a religious movement with a powerful underlying social protest. The most ardent proponents of the latter view were Marxist-Zionist historians such as Ben-Zion Dinur. True to their Marxist orientation, they presumed class struggle to be inherent in all facets of Jewish communal life. For Dinur and other Marxist historians, Hasidism galvanized the protests of the Jewish masses against an oppressive "Kahal regime" made up of rabbis and affluent Jewish families.

During the past three decades, the shortcomings of this view were exposed. Dinur presumed that the Jews of Podolia, the cradle of Hasidism, were largely impoverished, thus fortifying a movement of social protest. Recent scholarship has shown that Podolia, and Mienzboz in particular, was in the midst of a commercial revival for much of the eighteenth century. Dinur's claim that the Besht was leading a social protest against the Kehilla was disproved by Moshe Rosman. Rosman, while studying the role of Jews in the Polish grain trade, examined the records of the Czartoryski family, a Polish magnate family whose estate included thousands of towns and villages, including Miedzyboz – the birthplace of the Besht. Among the records of the Czartoryski family were heretofore unseen tax records of the Miedzyboz Jewish community – a uniquely impartial account of the Besht's relationship with the Kahal. These records showed that the Besht was living in a home provided to him by the Jewish community – belying the argument that he was leading a protest movement against the communal leadership. Thus, there is now a consensus that Hasidism was a movement of religious revival, but not a movement of social protest.

When the Besht died, the Hasidic movement was still minuscule. His two major disciples, Ya'akov Yosef of Polnoie, and Dov Ber, "Maggid of Mezerich," were responsible for the movement's rapid expansion after the Besht's death. Ya'akov Yosef was the movement's major ideologue; he consolidated the teachings of the Besht around three kabbalistic doctrines that became the pillars of Hasidism: *devekut*, *hitlahavut*, and *hitbonnenut*. *Devekut* (clinging to God) refers to the importance of directing all observance and belief toward narrowing the gap between oneself and the divine; *hitlahavut* (ecstasy) refers to using religious acts as a way to elevate oneself into a state of spiritual ecstasy; and *hitbonnenut* (contemplation) means avoiding the rote observance of commandments and performance of religious rituals. The most vivid manifestation of these ideas was the way Hasidic Jews prayed. In contrast to the mundane recitation of prayers by rote in non-Hasidic synagogues, Hasidic Jews sang, danced, and jumped into the air while they prayed.

Dov Ber, "Maggid of Mezerich," was the institutional architect of the movement. More than anything else, he defined the function of the movement's central institution: the *zaddik*. The *zaddik* (literally, righteous man, also referred to as the *rebbe*) was the charismatic leader of a circle of Hasidic followers. He was believed by his followers to have a special connection to the realm of the divine and the resulting special abilities. Thus, Hasidic Jews would ask the *zaddik* to evaluate the prospects of a prosposed marriage or economic endeavor, and to provide aid in times of sickness or danger. As Hasidism spread, each circle of Hasidim clustered around its own *zaddik*. Oddly, the Hasidic notions of *hasid* (pietist) and *zaddik* (righteous man) inverted the conventional rabbinic understandings of these terms. *Zaddik* typically refers to an ordinary observant Jew; *hasid* to the Jew who is uniquely immersed in a world of mystical piety and attains a higher spiritual level than those around him.

By 1772, Hasidism had spread through much of Poland and Ukraine, and was heading northward toward Lithuania. In 1772, the movement encountered opposition from two directions. In Brody, the leaders of the Jewish community objected to the Hasidic refusal to accept the community's ritual slaughterers as legitimate, and their preference for a slaughterer endorsed by their *zaddik*. Initially a conflict over revenue from the meat tax, this conflict soon revealed the real issue of contention: the fear that Hasidism threatened the authority of the *kahal* and the unity of the Jewish community.

The major opposition to Hasidism formed in Lithuania when, in 1772, a circle of Hasidim formed a Hasidic prayer group in Vilna, the center of rabbinic scholarship. In response, Rabbi Elijah of Vilna, also known as the Vilna Gaon (the Sage of Vilna), the leading talmudic scholar of the age and an old-style pietist and mystic, condemned the Hasidic Jews as heretics. Rabbi Elijah thus became the leader of the *mitnagdim* (literally, opponents), as the opponents of Hasidism came to be known.

Rabbi Elijah was by nature a controversialist like Jacob Emden. Previously he had been involved in communal disputes with the chief rabbi of Vilna. He had no official standing in the Vilna Jewish community; rather, he was the head of his own independent yeshiva. Like the Hasidic leaders he was challenging, his leadership was charismatic, deriving in his case from his towering scholarship. Thus, the conflict between Hasidic Jews and the opponents was on an elemental level a contest between two charismatic forms of Jewish leadership.

Rabbi Elijah and his followers accused the Hasidim of three misdeeds: denigration of rabbinic scholars, challenging the authority of the Jewish community, and engaging in practices that appeared Sabbatean. The last included the distinct Hasidic dress (Hasidic Jews all wore white); the wildness of Hasidic prayer, which appeared Frankist; and the widespread use of the prayer book of Isaac Luria, which disseminated kabbalistic ideas, which since Shabbetai Zvi had been regarded by rabbis as dangerous and subversive.

Hasidic Jews, aware of comparisons to Sabbateanism, made sure to refute this damning notion, which they found no less reprehensible than did their critics. In one story told about the Besht:

> Shabbetai Zvi came to the Besht to ask for redemption. ... The Besht began to establish a connection, but he was afraid, as Shabbetai Zvi was a terribly wicked man. Once the Besht was asleep, Shabbetai Zvi, may his name be blotted out [*yimach shemo*], came and attempted to tempt him again, God forbid. With a mighty thrust, the Besht hurled him to the bottom of hell. The Besht peered down and saw that he landed on the same pallet as Jesus.

By 1800, the conflict between Hasidic Jews and the *mitnagdim* abated to a point where the two sides were able to reach a compromise. This compromise was facilitated by five developments. First, Hasidism won, except in Lithuania. Second, real opposition to Hasidism died with Rabbi Elijah in 1799; his disciples continued to combat Hasidism only indirectly, by trying to reinvigorate non-Hasidic Rabbinic Judaism. Third, by 1800 it was clear that Hasidism was well within normative Judaism, that it was a pietistic movement, but not reformist or sectarian, and definitely not Sabbateanism. According to Gershom Scholem, this change of heart was made possible by the way that Hasidism "neutralized" the messianic ideas that had been combustible in the hands of Sabbateans, particularly the Hasidic reorientation of the aim of *tikkun* from a global to a personal form of perfection. Fourth, Shneur Zalman of Lyady, the founder of Lubavicher Hasidism, rehabilitated the study of study under the rubric of Hasidic contemplation, thus curtailing the denigration of talmudic scholars and study by adherents of Hasidism. Finally, during the nineteenth century, Hasidic Jews and their opponents found a new, common threat: the spread of enlightenment.

Hasidism had a major impact on traditional Jewish life in eastern Europe. Hasidism reinvigorated traditional Judaism in Poland, which was in midst of a crisis following the rise of Sabbateanism. This newfound spiritual vitality would fortify the traditional Jewish world to contend with the spread of enlightenment and humanism during the nineteenth century. At the same time, Hasidism was highly disruptive to Jewish family life. The ideal life of a Hasidic man was to spend extensive periods of time in the court and at the table of the *zaddik*, even though this meant leaving his wife alone to raise children, manage the household, and earn a living. This ideal was reinforced by the stories of the Besht's devoted wife supporting him while he wandered around the Carpathian Mountains. Later critics of Hasidism would single out the detrimental effects of Hasidism on the family and the double burden of the wife of the *hasid*, who had to earn a living, manage the household, and raise the children while the *hasid* ate and sat at the table of his *rebbe*.

To some degree, Shneur Zalman of Lyady was able to dampen this disruption to Jewish family life. In his major work, *Tanya*, he defined the concept of the *benoni*, the ordinary Hasidic Jew. This concept emphasized that the ordinary *hasid* need not strive to be a *zaddik*. Rather, the *benoni* could achieve spiritual fulfillment through the conventional life of father, husband, provider, as long as he maintained the proper Hasidic demeanor. The upshot is that Hasidism was the solution to a crisis of rabbinic authority and Jewish identity in eastern Europe. In western and central Europe, this challenge required a radically different solution.

Chapter 7

The age of enlightenment and emancipation, 1750–1880

During the 130 years from 1750 to 1880, world Jewry proceeded along two different tracks. For Jews in western Europe, most of central Europe, and the New World, this was an age defined by the search for and attainment of civic equality, the gradual entry of Jews into mainstream society, and the desacralization of Jewish life through cultural enlightenment. In the Russian and Ottoman Empires, and in the eastern reaches of the Habsburg Empire, traditional Jewish life remained largely intact, buttressed by a surrounding conservative polity and society. Yet even in these regions, Jews were affected in varying degrees during the nineteenth century by internal changes and by the changes emanating from the west. Throughout the Jewish world, disparate political, cultural, and social changes elicited a broad range of Jewish responses that varied between the different states and even within each state. By the second half of the nineteenth century, each Jewry had developed a particular balance between the world of Jewish tradition and the changing world of the nineteenth century, characterized by a distinct spectrum of religious observance and belief, varied forms of Jewish communal organization, and distinct tensions between traditionalists and progressives.

In 1750, the legal status of most Jews remained what it had been for centuries. Whether in the Christian or Islamic world, all but a handful of Jews were defined as second-class citizens, and faced the same residential, occupational, and educational restrictions. In western Europe – England, the Netherlands, France, and the Italian states – as well as in the New World, the situation of Jews had begun to change by 1750, in fact though not yet legally. This change facilitated the return of Jews to western Europe, beginning with the return of semiclandestine enclaves of *conversos* and crypto-Jews to an openly Jewish life in port cities such as Livorno in Italy, Hamburg, Amsterdam, London, and Bordeaux. In Livorno, in 1593 the city fathers issued the *Livornino*, which removed residential and commercial restrictions on Jewish settlers, and protected crypto-Jews from potential persecution by the church:

> No inquisition, visitation, denunciation, or accusation may be made against you or your families. Even though you may have lived outside of

our Dominion dressed as Christians, or were reputed to be Christians ...
and perform all of your ceremonies, rites, laws, and customs according to
Jewish law ... we grant you all of the privileges, rights, and favors which
our merchants ... and Christians enjoy.

Within a few decades, the Jewish community of Livorno grew from a few
hundred *conversos* and crypto-Jews at the end of the sixteenth century to a
community of several thousand Jews by the mid-seventeenth century, and the
city of Livorno, formerly a "paltry fishing village," became a thriving center
of Italian maritime commerce.

A similar course of events took place in Amsterdam following the Dutch
revolt against Spain that began during the 1570s. Although this revolt lasted
until 1648, Spanish rule and the influence of the Inquisition had been drastically curtailed already by the beginning of the seventeenth century. The
Dutch, in effect, replaced the religious persecution and intolerance embodied
by the Spanish Inquisition with a spirit of religious ecumenism between
Dutch Catholics and Protestants. This mood was keenly expressed by the
Dutch jurist Hugo Grotius, who decried the religious coercion embodied in
Spanish Catholicism: "One who is forced to believe does not believe, but only
pretends to believe" (*"Coactus qui credit, non credit, sed credere simulat"*). During
the first half of the seventeenth century, this ecumenism dovetailed with a
powerful economic realism. The Dutch, acknowledging that commercial success had helped them field and provision an army that defeated a seemingly
all-powerful Spain, placed a premium on commerce and subordinated all
impediments, religious and otherwise, to the demands of trade and profit.
The combination of religious ecumenism and economic realism created a
highly favorable situation for Jews. In this atmosphere, *conversos* and crypto-
Jews began returning to Judaism, leading to the growth and transformation
of Dutch Jewry. Alongside immigration from central Europe, the Jewish
community of Amsterdam increased from 400–500 *conversos* and crypto-Jews
in 1570 to 2,000 openly practicing Jews by 1650.

The status of Jews in Amsterdam combined elements of the premodern
with novel elements. The Jewish community still had a measure of communal
autonomy, and was run by Jewish communal leaders – *parnassim* in the case of
the Ashkenazic community, and a *mahmad* for Sephardic Jews – who were
empowered to regulate ritual, though not civic and criminal, matters. More
novel was the fact that Jews in Amsterdam were not saddled with special
Jewish statutes, or a badge or other stigmatizing dress. Jews were not excluded
from honorable activities such as riding horses and carrying swords. They were
allowed to engage in most occupations, and permitted to own property.

This added up to Jews having a limited form of citizenship by the mid-
seventeenth century, implicitly affirmed in 1657 when the Estates General of
the United Provinces demanded that Spain recognize "that those of the afore-
mentioned Jewish nation are truly subjects and residents of the United

Netherlands ... they therefore must enjoy, possess, and profit by the conditions, rights, and advantages provided by the Treaties of Peace and Navigation." This decree placed Jewish and Christian merchants on a nearly equal footing.

For some crypto-Jews, the return to normative Judaism was difficult. Crypto-Jews, while living ostensibly as Catholics, recognized religious rituals as superficial. They and their families had observed them without regard to their meaning, in some cases for multiple generations. The character of crypto-Judaism was based almost entirely on an inner feeling of being Jewish, not on an array of rules and rituals. Having embraced Catholicism only superficially, if at all, they had no desire to replace one set of empty rituals with another. Moreover, they saw no reason to live in an even minimally insular or separate Jewish community.

Not surprisingly, clashes occurred between former crypto-Jews and the Jewish community of Amsterdam, including three well-known cases: Uriel da Costa, Juan de Prado, and Baruch (or Benedict) Spinoza. Uriel da Costa (1585–1640) was born in Oporto, Portugal, into a family that had been converted to Catholicism several generations earlier. As a young man, he was restive in the Christian faith. He persuaded his family to move to Amsterdam, where they returned to Judaism. In 1624, he began to embrace rationalistic, anticlerical doctrines and to criticize Rabbinic Judaism. He was tried by the Jewish community, and then imprisoned and excommunicated. In 1633, he recanted, but soon resumed his heretical behavior and was again excommunicated. In 1640, he recanted for a second time, but this time he was subjected to public humiliation. Rather than endure further trouble, he committed suicide. His inner angst is known to us through an autobiographical sketch that was published posthumously in 1687, *Exemplar humanae vitae*:

> I had not been [in Amsterdam] long before I observed that the customs and ordinances of the modern Jews were quite different from those commanded by Moses. Now if the law was to be observed according to the letter ... the Jewish interpreters are not justified in adding interpretations. Quite the contrary. This provoked me to oppose them openly.

Less dramatic but no less illustrative was the case of Juan de Prado (1615–70). Born into a family of crypto-Jews in Spain, he eventually moved to Amsterdam and returned to Judaism. Soon afterward, though, he embraced deism, denied revelation, and rejected the authority of the Talmud and core Jewish beliefs, such as concepts of chosenness and resurrection during the Messianic Age. In 1656, he was excommunicated, but recanted. In 1657, he was excommunicated again. This time, he moved to Antwerp and converted to Christianity.

Yet the most celebrated case was that of Baruch Spinoza. Spinoza is widely known as one of the leading figures of seventeenth-century European philosophy and an early voice of the European Enlightenment. His parents were crypto-Jews who returned to Judaism. As a young man, he was a lens grinder and eventually studied optics. As a Jewish philosopher, Spinoza broke with the preceding Jewish philosophical tradition, whose primary aim had been to synthesize and reconcile Judaism and Greek philosophy. Spinoza separated these two traditions.

In 1656, his heretical views of Judaism led the Jewish community to excommunicate him. Unlike Da Costa and De Prado, Spinoza left the Jewish community without converting to Christianity or to any other religion. He opted instead to join the community of deist philosophers in Amsterdam. Spinoza's ability to leave the Jewish community without converting was made possible by the mood of religious toleration, and by the emergence in Amsterdam of what historian Jacob Katz termed a neutral society.

In 1670, Spinoza published a philosophical critique of Judaism and religion in general, the *Tractatus Theologico-Politicus*. In this work, he distinguished between two dimensions of western religion: natural law and dogma. Natural law he defined as those aspects of religion that are comprehensible through human reason without revelation. Thus, he argued that human beings did not need God to tell them not to kill each other; human reason could deduce this law simply by noting that without a prohibition on murder, the human species would cease to exist. Spinoza placed Judaism's core belief in monotheism and ethical and moral tradition in this category. The rest of Judaism he defined as dogma, a time-bound collection of rules "ordained in the Old Testament for the Hebrew only ... it is evident they formed no part of the divine law and have nothing to do with blessedness and virtue."

Spinoza claimed that Judaism and other western religions shared the same natural laws and were different only with respect to dogma. Since the latter was non-essential, he concluded, there was no essential difference between Judaism, Catholicism, the various Protestant denominations, or other faiths. In this regard, he rejected normative Judaism as vehemently as he rejected Christianity. Ultimately, Spinoza had little impact during his lifetime. A century after his death in 1685, subsequent generations of Jews living in the late eighteenth, the nineteenth, and even the twentieth century would discover in Spinoza a blueprint, or at least a useful point of departure, in reorienting Judaism to a changing world.

The establishment of Jews in Amsterdam created a foothold for Jews to return to England. In some sense, conditions for Jews in England in the seventeenth century were similar to those in the Netherlands. Expelled in 1290, as late as the 1640s the only Jews in England were a small enclave of crypto-Jews. As in the Netherlands, by the mid-seventeenth century, Catholics and Protestants had largely set aside religious disputes in favor of a pervading religious ecumenism, culminating with the Puritan revolution in 1649. As in the Netherlands, this religious atmosphere was complemented by an overarching sense of economic realism, aptly described by the French philosopher Voltaire in his *Letters on England*:

> Go into the Royal Exchange in London, a place more venerable than many courts of justice, where the representatives of all nations meet for the benefit of mankind. There the Jew, the Mahometan, and the Christian transact together, as though they all professed the same religion, where the only infidel is one who goes bankrupt. There the Presbyterian confides in the Anabaptist, and the Churchman depends on the Quaker's word. If one religion only were allowed in England, the Government would very possibly become arbitrary; if there were but two, the people would cut one another's throats; but as there are such a multitude, they all live happily and in peace.

Currents within English Protestantism and Lockean philosophy (see below) complemented religious ecumenism and economic realism in creating a favorable attitude toward Jews. The break with Rome entailed a break with Catholic dogma, including its harsh view of Jews. There was also a strong interest in the Hebrew language and the Hebrew Bible among Anglicans and other English Christians. Finally, there was the impact of millenarianism among English Christians, sparked by the discovery of the New World. This belief maintained that one of the preconditions of the Second Coming of Christ was Jews inhabiting the four corners of the world, before being converted en masse to Christianity. Along with the break with Rome and the renewed interest in Hebrew, this bred a philo-Semitic view that Jews needed to be admitted to England, although the ultimate aim of this philo-Semitic outlook, ironically, was the disappearance of the Jews through conversion.

The philo-Semitism born of religious currents was complemented by the influence of the philosopher John Locke. Locke's notion of the human mind as a *tabula rasa* set aside the notion that Jews were inherently immoral because of their lack of belief in Christ. In addition, Locke's notion of minimal government interference in the lives of individuals precluded restrictions on Jewish life.

All of these developments provide the context in which the Amsterdam rabbi Menasseh ben Israel lobbied for Oliver Cromwell to readmit the Jews to England. Menasseh ben Israel (1604–57) was born into a crypto-Jewish family in Madeira, and baptized Manoel Dias Soeiro. His father escaped from the Inquisition in Lisbon, resettled the family in Amsterdam, changed his name to Joseph, and renamed his sons Menasseh and Ephraim. Menasseh was a gifted scholar and apologist, and was a friend of Hugo Grotius and the painter Rembrandt. In 1650, after the Puritan revolution, he began to negotiate with English statesmen to readmit Jews to England, using messianic arguments such as the millenarianesque argument *Ketzeh ha-aretz* (literally, the end of the earth, a reference to Jews being scattered throughout the world).

In 1654, Cromwell convened the Whitehall Conference with the aim of readmitting Jews. However, when he saw that the participants were going to readmit Jews, but on unfavorable terms, he dissolved the conference. He then contemplated admitting Jews on his own authority, but did not for fear of a public outcry. Instead, he made a more limited, informal arrangement with London's crypto-Jewish community, which had petitioned for freedom of worship and the right to bury their dead in a Jewish cemetery. Cromwell granted the petition.

In response to these events, Menasseh ben Israel published *Vindiciae Judaeorum* in 1656. This pamphlet, an apology and an argument for the return of Jews to England, defended Jews and Judaism largely in economic and social rather than religious terms:

> Three things ... make a strange nation well-beloved amongst the natives of a land where they dwell: profit they may receive from them; fidelity they hold towards their princes; and the nobleness and purity of their blood. Now when I shall have made good that all these three things are found in the Jewish nation I shall certainly pursuade your highness that ... you shall be pleased to receive the nation of the Jews.

By the beginning of the eighteenth century, the growing presence of Jews, primarily in London, prompted some enlightened Englishmen to call for the naturalization of the Jews as citizens. In 1714, pamphleteer John Toland echoed ben Israel's defense of Jews by contrasting the negative effects of expelling Jews to the benefits of welcoming them: "What a paltry fishertown was Leghorn [Livorno] before the admission of the Jews? What a loser is Lisbon, since they have been lost to it?" By 1740, this attitude crystallized into policy in the English colonies in the New World.

Jewish settlement in the New World was non-existent in Spanish and Portuguese colonies owing to the expulsion edict and – with respect to crypto-Jews – the branches of the Inquisition in South and Central America. It began with the establishment of Dutch and English colonies on Caribbean islands of Curaçao, Jamaica, and Surinam; northeastern Brazil while under Dutch rule; and eventually the eastern seaboard of North America. In 1740, echoing Toland and urged further by the pressing need to attract settlers to British colonies in the New World, the British Parliament passed the Plantation Act in 1740, granting full citizenship to any and all settlers in British colonies who remained for at least seven years. In retrospect, though, the Plantation Act's significance as a legal breakthrough for Anglo-Jewry is overshadowed by the fact that Jews in British colonies had already attained these rights before 1740.

The discrepancy between legal and social emancipation is equally crucial in understanding the conditions for Jews in England itself, which improved gradually along with the broader contours of English society and politics. In 1753, Parliament passed the Jew Bill, named for the legal equality it granted to all English Jews, but repealed it a year later. Despite the apparent legal setback and their official status as second-class subjects, by 1750 English Jews had access to virtually all facets of English society – the lone exceptions being the right to earn a degree from Oxford or Cambridge and to run for Parliament.

The same factors that facilitated Jewish settlement in the English colonies were evident by the brief debacle over Jewish settlement in New Amsterdam (now New York) in 1654 and 1655. When the first Jews arrived in New Amsterdam in 1654 from Recife, following the Portuguese reconquest of Brazil, their settlement was challenged by Peter Stuyvesant, the governor of New Amsterdam. Stuyvesant asked the Dutch government and the Dutch West India Company to authorize his decision to "require them in a friendly way to depart."

Stuyvesant's objections combined economic arguments with older elements of religious disdain. He claimed that "their present indigence might become a charge during the coming winter" and asked that "such hateful enemies and blasphemers of the name of Christ be not allowed to further infect and trouble this new colony." Following protests from leading Dutch Jews, the Dutch West India Company, recognizing "the considerable loss sustained by [the Jewish] nation in the taking of Brazil, as also because of the large amount of capital they have invested in the shares of this company;" denied Stuyvesant's request, with one important caveat, namely that "the poor among them shall not become a burden to the company or the community, but be supported by their own nation." Both the affirmation of Jewish residence and the requirement of supporting their own poor reflected the overriding importance of economics over religious considerations.

The social emancipation of Jews in Western Europe and the New World went hand in hand with their rapid acculturation. By the mid-eighteenth century, these Jews had adopted the vernacular language, dress, manners, and general mores of their home country. In general, acculturating Jews emulated the behavior patterns of non-Jews of comparable economic and social status, with affluent Jews taking on the characteristics of the gentry, and rank-and-file Jews the characteristics of the lower classes.

In England, Bordeaux, and the New World, in particular, this process was aided by the limited authority of the Jewish community, whose jurisdiction did not extend beyond religious matters. The truncation of Jewish communal life to ceremonial and eleemosynary needs reflected the broader compartmentalization of life, which facilitated the emergence of a religiously neutral society in which Jews and non-Jews could interact more freely. By the mideighteenth century, western European Jews had entered mainstream society without fanfare or ideological justification, and the states of western Europe had recognized this situation by treating the ostensibly unemancipated Jews as citizens for all intents and purposes.

France and Germany: *Judenverbesserung*, Haskalah, and legal emancipation

The situation of Jews in central Europe was more complex. There was less economic incentive in central Europe to admit Jews than in England, the Netherlands, southwestern France, and the New World. In central Europe, the impetus for change was war, not property. Moreover, in contrast to the ecumenical moods born of mixed Catholic and Protestant populations in western Europe, adversarial religious camps in central Europe were separated by political boundaries.

As the rulers of central Europe, particularly the leaders of the Hohenzollern and Habsburg dynasties, tempered the harshness of absolute rule under the influence of the ideas of the Enlightenment, they altered the governing strategies and Jewish policies accordingly. In contrast to the gradual and bottom-up process in western Europe, the emergence of a neutral society in central Europe was a top-down process imposed initially by enlightened absolutist sovereigns. Court Jews emerged as living illustrations of Jewish potential and utility if allowed greater felicity and enabled to prosper under a more enlightened regime.

Indicative in this respect was Mayer Amschel Rothschild. The rise of the Rothschild family as the last and greatest of the court Jews began with Mayer Amschel's rags-to-riches ascent from a petty merchant and money changer in Frankfurt to the head of the wealthiest family in Europe – if not the world. Rothschild (1743–1812) was born and grew up in the ghetto of Frankfurt am Main, and worked with his father as a petty merchant and pawnbroker. Originally sent to Furth to train for the rabbinate, he changed careers and took a job in a banking house in Hanover. In 1760, he started his own banking house in Frankfurt and also traded in art and exotica. Eventually he became the financial agent of William IX, landgrave of Hesse-Cassel, who had inherited the largest private fortune in Europe. By 1794, Rothschild was investing 150,000 gold coins for the prince. By 1801, he had became the prince's chief financial agent. Between 1800 and 1806, he invested 1.75 million thalers. From 1798 to 1821, Rothschild's sons became leading financiers in several leading European cities: Nathan Mayer in London, James in Paris, Salomon in Berlin, and Karl in Naples.

Yet Mayer Amschel Rothschild, despite his wealth, was never legally accepted into mainstream society. In this regard, the Enlightenment had particular implications for Jews in central Europe. The primacy of reason over faith, building on Spinoza's distinction between natural law and dogma, downplayed the differences between Jews and Christians in favor of the commonalities between them. Simply put, for many there seemed to be no logical reason to exclude a Rothschild from mainstream society.

This was furthered by the discovery of the non-European world and the recognition that Jews looked less different than had conventionally been assumed. The notion of the perfectibility of humankind suggested that human frailty could be overcome without acceptance of the divinity of Christ or any other religious doctrine. The notion of a universal brotherhood of man belied the conventional notion that Jews were an inherently foreign and unassimilable element.

More specifically, the Enlightenment called into question the conventional assumption that the Jews themselves were responsible for their ostracism from mainstream society and for the general antipathy with which most non-Jews regarded them. It had hitherto been assumed that the alienation of Jews had resulted from a combination of divine retribution for rejecting Christ, hostility from the economic exploitation of Christians by Jewish usurers, and the social barriers between Jews and non-Jews that Judaism itself had imposed on Jews: dietary restrictions, a different day of Sabbath rest, a different cycle of holidays, and taboos on intermarriage.

The solution to this situation was defined differently by enlightened thinkers in France and Germany respectively, owing to a crucial difference between the French Enlightenment and the German Enlightenment or *Aufklarung*. The former regarded religion itself as the source of humanity's shortcomings, and Jews' shortcomings in particular. The German Enlightenment regarded not religion per se, but religious coercion as the source of the problem. These disparate views of religion were reflected in different views of Jews and the ways to improve the condition of Jews.

The French *philosophe* François-Marie Arouet, known as Voltaire, regarded Judaism's lack of a rational or philosophical foundation as the root cause of contemptible Jewish behavior. In response, French Jews such as Isaac de Pinto defended Judaism by conceding that while some Jews are contemptible, there are also Christians who are no less contemptible; and there are other Jews, like himself, who had overcome the ostensible shortcomings of Judaism and embraced French culture. In response, Voltaire pointed to the very existence of contemptible Jews as evidence of how destructive Judaism is. In doing so, Voltaire distinguished Jews from Judaism, criticizing the latter while recognizing the potential of the former. His scathing critique of Judaism, couched in the scientific terminology of the Enlightenment, led some historians to regard him as the first modern anti-Semite. In actuality, his willingness to criticize Judaism but not Jews makes this assertion dubious.

For German enlightened thinkers, the task of *Judenverbesserung*, the civic amelioration of the Jews, meant recognizing that the situation of the Jews was not exclusively their own fault, as Christian dogma claimed, but the combined result of Jewish and Christian attitudes and behavior. This shift in attitude was expressed most vividly in 1781 by Christian Dohm. According to Dohm, a disproportionate number of Jews engaged in moneylending not because they were doing Satan's work, but, more logically, because they were excluded from everything else. He argued further that since Jewish flaws were the result of the moral inferiority of Judaism, Jews could be improved by eliminating or modifying those aspects of Judaism that precipitated moral inferiority, without discarding Judaism entirely. To this end, he favored the retention of rabbinic authority, albeit in truncated form, as the surest means to lead the Jews down the proper moral and civic path. He further argued that improving the condition of Jews would make them better subjects, and help them serve the state more effectively. To be sure, Dohm did not envision the political emancipation of Jews, but rather their civic amelioration; while Jews would not enjoy the same privileges as non-Jews, they would be freed of burdensome restrictions on residence, occupation, and travel.

The most visible and vocal Jewish respondent to Dohm and other advocates of the civic improvement of German Jews was Moses Mendelssohn (1728–86), grandfather of the composer Felix Mendelssohn and the founder of an intellectual movement known as the Berlin Haskalah, or Jewish Enlightenment. Haskalah was once portrayed by historians as a prototypical Jewish response to the changes of the eighteenth century, but recent scholarship has increasingly emphasized the exceptional nature of Mendelssohn and the Berlin Haskalah. In particular, historians have juxtaposed Mendelssohn's program of change with a concurrent and in some places preexisting process of change in western Europe and Italy. The specific changes brought about by the program and process were largely similar: a positive evaluation of secular education; changes in language, manners, and dress; laxity in religious observance; and frequent recourse to non-Jewish courts. Yet the unselfconscious manner in which these changes took place in western Europe and Italy was more representative of European Jewry than Mendelssohn's self-conscious attempt to transform the Jews of Berlin and the German States.

Mendelssohn was, in this regard, more important as a symbol of the possibilities of Jews transforming themselves and being transformed by the state than as an agent of such changes; and the Haskalah was in effect a transitional movement between eighteenth-century traditional Judaism and nineteenth-century progressive Judaism. His initial impact was limited to the immediate environs of Berlin. Further east, in the Habsburg Monarchy and Poland, though, Jews would be inspired by Mendelssohn's writings and life. The celebrated case of Solomon Maimon, a Polish Jew who fled westward from "the world of Talmudic darkness" to study at the feet of Moses Mendelssohn, epitomized Mendelssohn's real impact. Half a century later, Mendelssohn would resonate even more among the adherents of the Galician and Russian Haskalah movements.

Born in Dessau, Mendelssohn received a traditional Jewish upbringing and education. In 1743, he moved to Berlin, where his intellectual gifts won admiration first from Jews and then from the intellectual community. In 1763, he won the Berlin Academy essay contest, thus launching a career as a philosopher. After the publication of his first bestseller, a study of aesthetics called *Phaedon*, he was nicknamed "the German Socrates" and became part of the intellectual elite of Berlin despite his Jewishness.

His friendship with Gotthold Ephraim Lessing, above all, came to symbolize the possibility of a religiously neutral friendship between a Jew and a Christian. Lessing, a leading voice of the German Enlightenment, expressed a sympathetic and favorable attitude toward Jews. In 1754, his play *Die Juden* told of a German aristocrat who, upon being saved from robbers by an anonymous stranger, offers the stranger his daughter's hand in marriage – not realizing that the stranger is a Jew. The daughter, whose youthful spirit represents Lessing's hope for a future enlightened society, is unable to comprehend why the fact that the heroic stranger is a Jew should make any difference.

In 1779, Lessing published *Nathan the Wise*. This play, a take on Boccacio's "Parable of the Three Rings," portrays Judaism, Christianity, and Islam as three siblings who received a ring from their king-father, Saladin. Each son tries to prove that his ring is the only authentic one. Nathan, the spokesman for Judaism and modeled after Mendelssohn, is the voice of enlightenment and religious tolerance. During the course of the play, Nathan takes in a Christian girl and raises her as neither Jew nor Christian but in the religion of reason. Unlike Voltaire, Lessing at no point has Mendelssohn/Nathan abandon Judaism. This stirred Mendelssohn to believe in the possibility of a true rapprochement between Jews and Gentile intellectuals.

Of course, Nathan was a highly idealized version of Mendelssohn. Most Jews were not Mendelssohns, just as most Christians were not Lessings. The disparity between Lessing's idealized vision of what Jews could be and the reality of German Jewry would point to the difficulty of bringing to fruition a program of change aimed at integrating Jews into mainstream society. Integrating Mendelssohn, court Jews, or the handful of atypical acculturated German Jews was no problem; integrating the mass of unacculturated Jews was far more challenging.

Still, his friendship with Lessing convinced him of the possibility of rapprochement between Jews and Christians. This belief was put to the test twice during the 1770s. In 1772, the duke of Mecklenburg-Schwerin, concerned that individuals who only appeared to be dead might mistakenly be thought actually dead, passed a law that required a three-day waiting period between death and burial. For local Jews, this posed a problem, as Jewish law required same-day burial. In response to their protest, the duke agreed to repeal the law if the Jews could demonstrate that same-day burial was an integral part of Judaism. When he was informed that same-day burial did not stem from a fundamental principle of Judaism, he let his new law stand.

The Jews turned for advice and assistance to Mendelssohn and to Jacob Emden. Mendelssohn gave two answers, one to the duke and the other to the

Jews of Mecklenburg-Schwerin. To the duke, he justified same-day burial with a combination of religious justification and reason. He assured the duke that although the literal observance of the Mosaic laws of burial had ceased, the spirit of the law remained binding according to rabbinic law. Moreover, because certainty of death was required according to Jewish law, there was no need to wait.

To the Jews, Mendelssohn sent a letter with a scolding tone that subjected the religious law in question to reasonable arguments. The rabbis, Mendelssohn pointed out, often made exceptions to the same-day burial rule, even for minor reasons such as a close relative of the deceased having to travel a great distance. If they made exceptions for minor reasons, logically they should make an exception for something more pressing, such as a ducal law. Mendelssohn, though, did not know that the Jews had also approached Emden. The latter rebuked Mendelssohn for his response, arguing that medical science was not grounds for changing Jewish law, and that Jews were prohibited from adopting the ways of the Gentiles. Mendelssohn was rebutted, but the two remained friends.

A year later, Mendelssohn was challenged by Johann Kaspar Lavater, a Swiss Calvinist clergyman, who issued a friendly challenge to Mendelssohn that he refute Christianity entirely or become a Calvinist. Mendelssohn refused to enter into a Jewish–Christian polemic, finding such a challenge to be irrelevant. For Mendelssohn, the burial controversy and the Lavater affair represented the lingering notion that Jews and Christians were ultimately separated from one another by outdated Jewish and Christian views. These events also turned Mendelssohn's attention from philosophy to write two Jewish texts: his *Biur*, which was a translation of the Pentateuch into Yiddish-Deutsch, along with his commentary; and *Jerusalem*, a two-part philosophical treatise. In part 1 of *Jerusalem*, Mendelssohn argued for the separation of church and state, that religion was a private matter, and that the Jewish communal right of *herem* be abolished. In part 2, he reconsidered Spinoza's definition of Judaism as an amalgam of natural law and dogma, and instead defined Judaism as being made up of three parts: eternal truths, which coincided with Spinoza's natural law; historical truths, which included the traditional notion of covenant and chosenness; and revealed legislation, which coincided with Spinoza's dogma. Unlike Spinoza, Mendelssohn regarded all three components as equally essential to Judaism.

Ultimately, this definition of Judaism allowed Mendelssohn to respond to enlightened Christians like Lavater, who argued that truly enlightened Jews would abandon Judaism for Christianity. To such claims, Mendelsson retorted that since, historically, Christianity is built on Judaism, if you deride Judaism as irrational and antiquated, you must make the same claim about Christianity; conversely, if you remain Christian, you must accept Mendelssohn as an enlightened Jew. "If it be true," he wrote in *Jerusalem*, "that the cornerstones of my house are dislodged, and the structure threatens to collapse, do I act wisely if I remove my belongings from the lower to the upper floor for safety? ... Christianity ... is built upon Judaism, and if the latter falls, it must necessarily collapse with it into one heap of ruins."

From this ideological point of departure, Mendelssohn forged the *haskalah* program, whose platform consisted of educational, cultural, and political reforms. Education reforms entailed a trilayered curriculum with a Jewish component that included the Bible, Jewish philosophy, Hebrew grammar, and Hebrew poetry in addition to rabbinic texts; a secular component that included practical subjects such as the vernacular language, mathematics, and civics; and the study of an artisanal trade. Cultural reforms meant, in addition to embracing the vernacular language as the lingua franca, adopting the dress, manners, and mores of mainstream society. As to political reforms, Mendelssohn urged the state to remove all restrictions on Jews. In effect, he was proposing that the heretofore exceptional behavior, education, and legal status of the court Jews be extended and applied to all Jews.

Mendelssohn's program of reforms, and, in general, the matter of the condition of Jews in central Europe, remained largely a theoretical question until the ascension of Joseph II as Habsburg monarch in 1780. Unlike his absolutist mother Maria Theresa, Joseph II was an enlightened absolutist. He believed that making Jews happier subjects would make them more productive subjects.

To this end, in 1782 Joseph II issued his edict of toleration. In many ways, this edict translated Mendelssohn's and Dohm's theoretical arguments about Jews into state policy. The edict, a mixture of old and novel regulation, had six essential components and was a mixed blessing for Habsburg Jews. The emperor allowed Jews to engage in crafts, but not to become master craftsmen. He erected a network of state-sponsored dual-curriculum Jewish schools called *Normalschulen*, while pressuring Jews to abandon Hebrew and Yiddish in favor of German. He allowed Jews to engage in agriculture, but not to own land. He allowed Jews to reside in royal free cities, and required them to serve in the military. And he curtailed Jewish communal authority by outlawing the *herem*. Jews responded to this edict with a mixture of optimism and suspicion. They looked to Ezekiel Landau of Prague, the unofficial chief rabbi of the Habsburg Monarchy, for guidance. Landau grudgingly endorsed the reforms.

Despite rabbinic sanction, the creation of the *Normalschulen* set in motion a controversy over Jewish education. One of the instructors in the Prague *Normalschul*, Naftali Herz Weisl (1725–1805), published a treatise on Jewish education called *Divrei shalom ve-emet* (Words of Peace and Truth) in which he argued that general knowledge was more foundational than Jewish learning. In response, Landau and other rabbis severely scolded him. Landau's objection in particular was revealing. He supported the establishment of the *Normalschulen*, partly because the emperor had ordered it, but also because Joseph II had placed Jewish learning ahead of secular study. Thus, Landau and other traditionalists differentiated between Weisl and the *Normalschul*, the

latter falling well within the pale of acceptable Jewish behavior. This difference pointed to the fact that ideological justification of changes such as
Weisl's treatise generally elicited more heated criticism than behavioral
changes such as the curricular changes themselves.

The impact of the *Normalschulen* on Habsburg Jews was far-reaching. These
schools operated in the Czech Lands until 1848, providing a dual education
for several generations of Bohemian and Moravian Jews. The schools also
became a blueprint for subsequent initiatives to reform and improve Jewish
education. During the 1850s, for example, when the Hungarian government
authorized the creation of a network of state-sponsored Jewish schools, these
schools were fashioned for the most part along the lines of the *Normalschulen*.

In contrast to the impact of the *Normalschulen* and, more generally, the
reforms of Joseph II, the immediate impact of the Berlin Haskalah was limited. Its aim of reviving and modernizing the Hebrew language was
overshadowed by increased use of the vernacular. *Ha-me'assef,* a Haskalah literary magazine founded on the principle of developing Hebrew as a literary
language, closed down in 1793. Mendelssohn's *Biur*, intended as a vehicle to
revive interest in Hebrew, became instead a way for young German Jews to
learn German. Moreover, the image of the Berlin Haskalah was tainted as
some of its adherents, including Mendelssohn's children, converted to
Christianity. In the end, the Haskalah failed to provide a meaningful Jewish
ideology for its generation. The notion that Judaism and Christianity were
essentially the same gave way to the reality that there was one essential difference: the religion of the state was Christianity. This reality would be altered
in 1789 during the French Revolution.

The French Revolution in 1789 launched the age of legal emancipation in
Jewish history, which lasted from 1789 to 1917 by way of the late 1860s. The
term "emancipation" typically connotes a transition from slavery to freedom.
For Jews, though, who had always enjoyed certain privileges and had never
been treated as slaves, emancipation meant replacing one set of rights and
obligations by another. Although some Jews had reservations about emancipation – communal leaders, who saw emancipation as a threat to their
communal authority, and religious leaders, who regarded emancipation as a
threat to religious coherence – there was general agreement among Jews that
the material benefits of emancipation outweighed its potential harm.

The debate over Jewish emancipation in France followed on the heels of an
initiative in France to improve the lot of French Jews, which culminated in an
essay contest held by the *Société royale des arts et sciences* in Metz in 1785. The
topic of this contest, "Are there possibilities of making the Jews more useful
and happier in France?", attested to how prevalent the situation of Jews had
become in French Enlightenment thought by the end of the eighteenth century. The three finalists in this contest were Adolph Thiery, a lawyer and
member of the Parlement of Nancy; Zalkind Horowitz, curator of the Royal
Library, who was not totally assimilated but not entirely traditional; and

Abbé Grégoire, a Catholic priest who would later be a member of the national assembly. From these three essays emerged a common set of ideas for transforming French Jewry. First, the acculturated Jews of Bordeaux were esteemed as representing an ideal situation that the Jews of Alsace should aspire to. Second, the clearest ways of improving the situation of French Jewry was a combination of the state removing civic restrictions on Jews, the Jewish community ceding its authority over Jews, and Jews abandoning irrational aspects of Judaism and those that placed social barriers between Jews and non-Jews.

Grégoire, whose essay won this contest, couched these suggestions as political, moral, and physical regeneration. Ultimately, Grégoire called for Jews to abandon those aspects of Judaism that dealt with civic matters such as marriage and divorce; and keep those that dealt with religious matters. Three aspects of the debate over emancipation emerged from Grégoire's essay: an attempt to advocate civic equality for Jews despite Catholic prejudices such as a disdain for Jewish usury; the notion that emancipation would be extended to Jews quid pro quo – that is, in exchange for Jews giving up corporate autonomy and some measure of Jewish observance; and the ultimate aim of improving the lot of the Jews being to entice Jews to convert to Christianity.

The emancipation of the Jews of France, the first great event in the age of legal emancipation, took place in two phases: the debates of the constituent national assembly during the early 1790s, and the policies of Napoleon Bonaparte a decade and a half later. During the initial debates, the question of equality for Jews (and actors) elicited strong support. Jews were offered emancipation conditionally, as stated succinctly and famously by the count of Clermont-Tonnerre: "The Jews should be denied everything as a nation, but granted everything as individuals. ... There cannot be one nation within another nation."

The precise meaning of this statement became clear as Jews were emancipated in two stages, owing to the stark differences between the Jews of Bordeaux and the Jews of Alsace-Lorraine. The former were highly acculturated and lived largely as individual Jews. They were emancipated with little objection. To all intents and purposes, they were emancipated already, and there was no doubt that they did not constitute a nation within a nation.

The Jews of Alsace-Lorraine were largely unacculturated, Yiddish-speaking Jews living in autonomous Jewish communities and disproportionately engaging in petty commerce and moneylending. Nearly two more years of debate passed until these Jews were emancipated. From this delay emerged a clear notion as to the conditions of emancipation: Jews were expected to cede at least some particularistic beliefs and customs, to abandon Yiddish, to cede corporate autonomy, and to move into more productive occupations. This prompted Jews such as Cerf Berr, a leading Jew in Strasbourg, to urge the mass of traditional Jews in Alsace to meet the conditions of emancipation more squarely by "divesting ourselves of that narrow spirit of corporation and congregation in all civil and political matters not directly connected with our spiritual laws." In September 1791, emancipation was extended to all Jews in France, including the Jews of Alsace-Lorraine, with the implicit expectation that the latter would begin to meet the terms of emancipation immediately.

During the 1790s, legal emancipation was extended to Jews in the German and Italian states conquered by the French revolutionary armies. Often the first act of conquering revolutionary armies was to emancipate Jews. In Italy, French armies dramatically tore down the ghetto walls. In countries at war with France, the gradual reforms that had been taking place under the aegis of enlightened sovereigns such as Joseph II were halted by revolutionary paranoia. But when these countries were defeated by the superior populist armies of the revolution and Napoleon, they had to reconsider the benefits of at least some reforms.

The transition from revolutionary government to the reign of Napoleon Bonaparte meant a transition in the nature of political and social reform. Napoleon implemented from above what French Revolution set out to do from below. His policies regarding Jews were in some cases a by-product of his overall policies, in other cases designed especially for Jews. The main example of the former was his consistory system, which placed religious denominations under the supervision of the Ministry of Education and Cults. The Jewish Consistory, led by the Jewish Consistory of Paris, had regulated the religious affairs of French Jewry since 1807. In some cases, the consistory provided a forum for religious experimentation. Israel Jacobson, the head of the Westphalian Consistory, implemented a series of liturgical and ritual changes with state authorization that anticipated some of the early tenets of Reform Judaism a decade later.

The main example of Napoleon's specific Jewish policy began to unfold in January 1806. While returning to Paris from Egypt via Alsace-Lorraine, Napoleon received complaints about the abuses of the Jewish moneylenders. He was outraged by the fact that, fifteen years after emancipation, Jews in Alsace had still not abandoned moneylending in favor of more productive occupations. In response, he convened an assembly of Jewish notables as his agents in transforming the as yet untransformed Jews of Alsace-Lorraine. He addressed a series of questions to this assembly regarding the authority of Judaism over civil matters, intermarriage, and patriotism. In response, the assembly, and subsequently the Parisian Sanhedrin, its more formal incarnation, managed to provide Napoleon with the answers he wanted. Nonetheless, Napoleon imposed a series of restrictions on French Jews, known as *le décret infâme*, aimed at forcing Jewish moneylenders to move into other occupations. While ultimately not transforming Jews into peasants and artisans, this decree did stir emancipated Jews to move into the free professions during the ensuing decades.

In retrospect, the experience of the Jews of Alsace-Lorraine in revolutionary and Napoleonic France anticipated several key aspects of the debate over Jewish emancipation in central Europe. For unacculturated, religiously traditional Jews, legal emancipation would come at a price. Henceforth, these Jews would be expected minimally to give up corporate autonomy and abandon Yiddish in favor of the vernacular; in some places, notably in Prussia and in other German states, the price would be much higher: Jewish assimilation qua conversion as a prerequisite for emancipation.

An exchange in 1831, for example, between the Protestant theologian Heinrich Paulus and the German-Jewish journalist Gabriel Riesser underlines the disparate views of the conditions for emancipation. For Paulus, nothing short of conversion would entitle Jews to citizenship. "As long as Jews believe that continued existence must be in accordance with the Rabbinic–Mosaic spirit, no nation could grant them civil rights." Riesser invoked the separation of religion and state to oppose this claim: "Religion has its creed, the state its laws. ... The confusion of these principles leads to misunderstanding, thoughtlessness, and falsehood." In addition, proponents of emancipation would divide over whether emancipation should be given to Jews as a way to facilitate Jewish acculturation and integration, or whether emancipation should be given to Jews only after they had already met the term of emancipation.

The rise of nationalism after mid-century as an increasingly overarching element of political and social policies added a corollary to the debate over Jewish emancipation: did being worthy of citizenship necessarily qualify Jews to be admitted into the ranks of the nation? This issue apposed the question of Jewish emancipation with the ability of a nascent national movement to absorb a population of unacculturated Jews without undermining itself. This concern was voiced, for example, by the Hungarian statesman István Széchenyi. Though a proponent of eventual Jewish emancipation, as late as the 1840s he was deeply concerned that the newly revived Magyar culture lacked the fortitude of more developed people like, say, the English, to manage the impact of Jews entering the mainstream. "The English lake," he claimed, " could easily absorb a bottle of Jewish ink. Yet the same bottle of ink would ruin the Hungarian soup." By the 1860s, when Magyar culture had begun to challenge Viennese culture, Jewish emancipation was easier to imagine without dire consequences to Magyar culture. Thus, by the 1860s the conditions attached to emancipation had diminished from radical assimilation and religious reform that Széchenyi and Lajos Kossuth demanded during the 1840s to the less demanding embrace of the Hungarian language and literature by the 1860s.

These issues would elicit varied responses from Jewish intellectuals and communal leaders. The more far-reaching the price of emancipation, the more Jewish ideologues were willing to give up in order to be emancipated. Thus, for German Jews the struggle for legal emancipation became singularly linked to the reform of Judaism and Jewish life. Indeed, the line of demarcation in the debate over Jewish emancipation in central Europe and in Jewish responses to this debate was between Jews in the German states, on the one hand, and in the Habsburg Monarchy and the Italian states, on the other.

For German Jews, the defeat of Napoleon in 1814 brought an end to Jewish emancipation in 1815. After 1815, neither German Jews nor Habsburg Jews nor Italian Jews were emancipated, and both lobbied for the next half-century for legal equality and were emancipated within a year or two of each other. There was, however, a crucial difference. German Jews were struggling to overcome the loss of emancipation, a traumatic moment that neither Habsburg Jews nor any other Jews had ever experienced. In addition, German nationalists became increasingly wary of admitting Jews into the ranks of the German nation. Not surprisingly, German Jews were far more self-conscious about the image of Judaism, Jewish identity, and Jewish life than any others. The difference between lobbying to attain emancipation and to reattain it would be at the heart of the difference between German-Jewish efforts to reform Judaism and the efforts of Jews in the Habsburg Monarchy and Italy.

German Jews, non-German Jews, and the reform of Judaism

The loss of emancipation elicited three responses from German Jews. For some, the only recourse to the loss of emancipation was apostasy. These conversions were not out of religious conviction, but for practical reasons, hence they came to be known as "dry baptisms." Among those who opted for dry baptism were Abraham Mendelssohn, the son of Moses Mendelssohn, who converted his children, Fanny and Felix; Heinrich Marx, a successful lawyer who, after being disbarred following disenfranchisement, converted his eight children to Christianity, including most famously his son Karl; and the German-Jewish poet Heinrich Heine, who called his conversion "a ticket of admission to European civilization."

Some German-Jewish intellectuals responded to the loss of emancipation in a project that came to be known as *Wissenschaft des Judenthums* (the scientific study of Judaism). They believed that by subjecting all facets of Judaism to intense academic scrutiny, the rational, ennobling, and citizenship-worthy aspects of Jewish identity could be separated from the irrational, ignoble, citizenship-impeding aspects. This project laid the basis for what eventually came to be known, and is still known, as the academic field of Jewish studies. As a means of gaining emancipation, though, this endeavor had limited impact.

More important, *Wissenschaft des Judenthums* provided the tools for newly emerging religious movements, notably Reform Judaism and Positive-Historical Judaism, to distinguish between the essential and the non-essential elements of Judaism. The endeavor of reforming Judaism had two complementary aims: to make Judaism meaningful to a generation of Jews who, having grown up in the secular age of the French Revolution and Napoleon, were alienated from Jewish tradition; and to make Judaism compatible with modern citizenship, thereby proving Jews worthy of citizenship.

The first reform initiatives in Germany began during the 1810s, led by Israel Friedlander in Berlin, who remodeled the Jewish prayer service so that it took on the decorum of a Protestant church service. In 1812, Friedlander abolished all national Jewish prayers in his Berlin congregation, and added prayers in German. In 1815, Israel Jacobson established a private prayer meeting in his home, where he used an organ and a choir, and had prayers and a sermon in German, and made sure the service was conducted with proper decorum. A second service opened shortly thereafter at the home of Jacob Hertz Beer. In 1817, the Prussian government closed down these "synagogues," partly in response to a request from traditional Jews, but also as a reaction to any and all innovations, which were regarded with suspicion in an age of political reaction.

A year later, Edward Kley, preacher at the Beer synagogue, moved to Hamburg and organized the first lasting Reform congregation, the Hamburg Israelite Temple Association. The very name of this congregation captured much of its religious and social outlook: "Israelite" avoided the stigma attached to the word "Jew"; "Association" because of the connection between "congregation" and corporate autonomy; and "Temple" as a way of dissociating from the traditional Jewish notion of a messianic return to Zion – that is, a permanent replacement for the Temple in Jerusalem. This congregation introduced some of the same innovations as had been introduced in Berlin, such as proper decorum, the use of an organ and choir, and a sermon and prayers in German. Additional innovations included the Sephardic pronunciation of Hebrew; the reading rather than chanting of the Torah portion; and the elimination from the liturgy of prayers that called into question the worthiness of Jews for citizenship such as references to the messianic return to Zion or resurrection of the dead, and the Kol Nidrei, whose ceremonial renunciation of vows seemed to call into question the trustworthiness of Jews in a modern society.

In response to this new congregation, a letter-writing campaign by traditional rabbis in Germany, the Czech Lands, and Hungary culminated in the publication of *Eleh Divrei ha-Brit* (These Are the Words of the Covenant), a concerted denunciation of the innovations by the Hamburg Temple: changing the liturgy, using a choir and organ, and praying in the vernacular. This, as will be seen presently, has been generally marked by historians as the birth of Orthodox Judaism.

During the 1820s and 1830s, Reform Judaism spread to other parts of Germany, and to Vienna, Denmark, and America. Until the 1840s, Reform

Judaism was a loosely connected network of congregations whose rabbis endorsed a varied range of religious innovations. By the mid-1840s, a search for uniformity and a desire to create a movement out of the scattered Reform congregations led to the convening of three conferences where rabbinic adherents to Reform Judaism hammered out the ideological framework of this movement. At the heart of this ideology was an expansion of the basic principles of the Hamburg temple, manifest most vividly in liturgical changes: deleting from the liturgy all references to the messianic return to Zion and resurrection of the dead; replacing Hebrew with German as the language of prayer; and maintaining a general decorum through the use of a professional cantor and choir. In addition, the participants at these conferences redefined the ideal reform rabbi as well versed in rabbinic literature but also with a strong secular education; most Reform rabbis had earned a doctorate from a major European university in addition to rabbinic ordination.

These liturgical changes reflected the larger redefinition of Judaism propounded by the founders of Reform Judaism, in particular Abraham Geiger. Judaism, Geiger believed, had to be purged of its irrational elements, hence the removal of reference to and the belief in the messianic resurrection of the dead, for which there was no scientific foundation. The messianic return to Zion, insofar as it suggested a putative dual allegiance to Germany and the Land of Israel, was eliminated for patriotic reasons.

More broadly, Geiger argued that Judaism, in order to survive as a viable religion, had to adapt to the Zeitgeist. In an age of universal enlightenment and emancipation, he argued, this meant defining the essence of Judaism as its most universal elements: ethical monotheism plus a few key rituals: prayer, the Sabbath and festivals, and circumcision. Other Jewish rituals, such as the dietary restrictions, had ceased to be relevant and thus could be redefined as voluntary or abandoned entirely. In addition, Geiger redefined some particularistic aspects of Judaism in universal terms. Chosenness and messianic redemption, hallmarks of Jewish distinctness and peoplehood, became pillars of a divinely ordained Jewish mission to spread monotheism and morality to all of humanity. This universalist redefinition of Judaism brought Geiger face to face with Spinoza's claim that there was no essential difference between Judaism and other monotheistic religions. To oppose this claim, Geiger arrogated for Judaism a position of moral and theological superiority by arguing that Jesus was a Jew who was the original expositor of Jewish beliefs and values for non-Jews.

As the ideology of Reform Judaism took shape, dissent emerged within the ranks of its adherents, first and foremost over the language of prayer. Zecharias Frankel objected to the elimination of Hebrew from much of the service to the point that in 1845 he walked out of the conference and founded a new movement: Positive-Historical Judaism. In contrast to Reform Judaism, Positive-Historical Judaism maintains that certain aspects of traditional Judaism needed to be retained even if they were neither rational nor out of sync with the Zeitgeist, but simply because they were "positive forms of Judaism deeply rooted within its innermost form." Thus, he defended the use of Hebrew as the language of prayer. In addition, he advocated preserving other core observances such as the dietary laws simply in the name of historical continuity and longevity.

Though they presided over separate movements, Frankel and Geiger shared the challenge of defining the essentials of Judaism, and used the scholarship of the *Wissenschaft* to address this challenge. Both replaced the traditional means of addressing this question – that Jewish law required it – with a novel one: for Geiger, the Zeitgeist; for Frankel, historical continuity. These parallels notwithstanding, though, Frankel's approach to Judaism was more fluid and inclusive, evidenced by the fact that the rabbinical seminary he founded in Breslau during the 1870s – the first of its kind in Europe outside of Italy – attracted students with a broad array of religious outlooks and levels of religious observance.

In this sense, Frankel was a hybrid between the German and the non-German variety of religious reform. "Non-German reform" refers to the character of religious innovation that appeared predominantly in Vienna, Prague, Hungary, and the Italian states. The principal difference between German and non-German reform stems from the fact that Jews in the Habsburg Monarchy and Italy were never as self-conscious as German Jews about proving themselves worthy of emancipation. Jews in the Habsburg Monarchy, though benefiting from the reforms of Joseph II, were never disenfranchised. Italian Jews, while disenfranchised following the defeat of Napoleon, were already deeply acculturated and immersed in mainstream Italian society, thus far less concerned over social acceptance than German Jews. In this sense, Italian Jews were more like the Jews of Bordeaux, England, or the Netherlands than like German Jews. Frankel, born in Prague and educated in Pest, wove elements of this approach to religious innovation into Positive-Historical Judaism.

Non-German reform initiatives were less impelled by an overriding concern lest some aspect of Judaism preclude emancipation. This lesser concern was manifest in several ways. In Vienna, the progressive synagogue adopted the decorum of a Reform temple, but none of the ideological or liturgical changes advocated by German reformers. In Prague, Solomon Judah Rapoport, while insistent that some innovation was necessary, rejected the abrupt and urgent pace advocated by Reform Judaism: "Were there some matter among our customs or laws that stood in need of reform or renewal, it would be renewed or reform with the passing of time. . . . In the meantime, that which remains unchanged will continue to be firmly established."

Similarly, religious reformers in Hungary, while acknowledging the Zeitgeist and historical development as important factors, maintained that all innovations must be justifiable within the corpus of Halacha (Jewish law) – a position that no German Reform rabbi could have maintained. Aron Chorin of Arad, when condemned for ruling that sturgeon was a kosher fish, defended his position in terms neither of the Zeitgeist nor of historical development, but rather as a legitimate rabbinic leniency and because of the widespread custom among Jews to regard sturgeon as a kosher fish. His disciple Leopold Löw, who founded the Neolog Movement, continued to apply this approach into the 1860s to a variety of religious issues, including using mechanized transportation and musical instruments on the Sabbath.

Most interesting perhaps was the attitude of Italian-Jewish scholars such as Samuel David Luzzatto. Luzzatto, a graduate of the rabbinical seminary in Padua – the first such seminary in Europe – and medical school, rejected entirely the notion that Judaism had to be ideologically reconciled with the spirit of the age in order for Jews to be accepted into the mainstream. Rather, he maintained that there was an inherent tension between Atticism – his term for secular culture, derived from a term for Athenian or Greek philosophy – and Judaism, but that Jews could embrace both cultural traditions as long as they were aware of this tension. The upshot is that non-German reformers of Judaism were able to maintain a relatively strong tie to traditional Judaism without reference to the spirit of the age or historical development.

All reformers of Judaism, though, agreed that, regardless of the rationale, Jews could and should embrace the possibilities offered by the changing world of the nineteenth century. This view was reinforced by the wave of emancipation edicts that accompanied the revolutions of 1848. These edicts, though short-lived, demonstrated how deeply Jewish emancipation was woven into the political agenda of liberalism, and that the triumph of liberalism – which mid-nineteenth-century ideologues increasingly regarded as inevitable if not imminent – would emancipate the Jews of central Europe and Italy.

In addition, the emergence of nationalism as a driving force of these revolutions revealed how much the gap between Jews and their non-Jewish neighbors had narrowed in terms of national identity and solidarity, particularly in those revolutions for which Jews fought and died on the battlefield, such as that of Hungary, or led the revolution outright, such as that of Vienna. By the 1860s, the triumph of liberalism, coupled with sufficiently extensive Jewish embrace of the local vernacular and national culture, facilitated the emancipation of all European Jews west of Russia by the end of the 1860s, with little or no fanfare.

Orthodoxy: synthesis, secession, schism

The spread of religious innovation across central Europe prompted a concurrent backlash among religious traditionalists, which crystallized during the nineteenth century into a new religious movement: Orthodox Judaism. Orthodox, though often used interchangeably with traditional or observant, refers to something fundamentally different. While advocating meticulous observance of Jewish laws and customs, Orthodoxy is based on the premise that Judaism mandates a single correct path, and that all deviation from that path connotes transgression. Thus, the emergence of Orthodoxy rested on a paradox: while rejecting deviation from the norm as inherently unacceptable, the mentality and ideology of Orthodoxy itself deviated from a preexisting fluid, diverse, accommodating traditionalism that had been fashioned by centuries of Ashkenazic scholars from the Tosafists through rabbis like Ezekiel Landau at the end of the eighteenth century. In this regard, Orthodoxy was a response to the nineteenth century, no less than Haskalah, Reform, Positive-Historical Judaism, or any other nineteenth-century religious movement. Orthodoxy was born as a backlash to the reform of Judaism.

The long-term origins of Orthodoxy can be rooted in the rabbinic paranoia regarding Sabbateanism. The more immediate origins were exclusively Ashkenazic. In Germany, Orthodoxy was a reaction to the spread of ideologically justified redefinitions of Judaism such as Haskalah, Reform, and Positive-Historical Judaism. Outside of Germany, Orthodoxy rejected halachically justified innovations in Judaism. Until the end of the nineteenth century, when Orthodoxy appeared within Russian Jewry (discussed in the next chapter), the centers of Orthodoxy were Germany and Hungary. Since the character and rationale of religious reform differed in Germany and Hungary, so too did the Orthodox backlash.

Sociologically, it is possible to identify two types of Orthodox Judaism. Rejectionist Orthodoxy rejected wholesale everything innovative, whether religiously, technologically, politically, or culturally motivated. Synthesizing Orthodoxy embraced certain innovations, but then used these innovations to defend an Orthodox position. For example, present-day rejectionist Orthodoxy would ban the use of television, and participation in the political process, as innovations, and hence taboo. Synthesizing Orthodoxy would use television selectively to disseminate a particular message, and the political process to protect Orthodox interests.

In addition, in combating religious innovation, Orthodox Jews generally used one of two strategies or some combination thereof: condemnation and competition. Some Orthodox Jews simply condemned any and all religious innovations and refused to have anything to do with them. Such was the case with the condemnation of the Hamburg temple. The champion of this point of view was the Frankfurt-born Hungarian rabbi Moses Sofer. In condemning the Hamburg temple, he applied a talmudic principle that had originally referred exclusively to the laws of bringing first fruits to the temple in Jerusalem to all facets of Judaism and Jewish life: "All that is new is forbidden by the Torah" (*Kol Davar Hadash Asur me-hatorah hi*).

Other Orthodox Jews believed that some accommodation to contemporary circumstances was inevitable, and that the only way to preserve religious tradition was to create rituals and advocate a way of life that could compete with the allures of reformist movements. The original advocate of this point of view was Samson Raphael Hirsch, who created a form of Orthodoxy called Neo-Orthodoxy. In some sense, Hirsch's Neo-Orthodoxy was a more proactive version of Mendelssohn's Haskalah. Like Mendelssohn, Hirsch advocated changes in Jewish life while leaving the observance of Jewish law intact. Moreover, while defining religious obligations as eternal and immutable, Hirsch, like Mendelssohn, believed that the "externals" of Judaism – language, dress, education – were subject to the spirit of the age. To combat reform, Hirsch advocated a service with greater decorum, and a rabbi who was well versed in rabbinic scholarship but also had a strong secular education and could deliver a sermon in the vernacular on a topic of contemporary interest.

Hirsch's Neo-Orthodoxy had an aim that was similar to that of Reform and Positive-Historical Judaism: to maintain a commitment to Judaism while allowing Jews to prove themselves worthy of emancipation and admission to the ranks of the German nation. Like Reform and Positive-Historical Judaism, Neo-Orthodoxy regarded the balance between tradition and innovation as an either/or proposition. Unlike Geiger and other Reform Jews, Hirsch simply believed that religious observance did not preclude emancipation, and that an acceptable level of acculturation did not preclude complete observance of Jewish law. Like Geiger and Frankel, Hirsch drew a sharp line between the essential and non-essential dimensions of Judaism, regarding the former as immutable and the latter as entirely malleable. Thus, for example, Hirsch regarded changes in language and dress, and a taboo on secular education, as non-essential, and advocated them as wholeheartedly as Geiger and Frankel.

The triumph of Reform Judaism in Germany during the nineteenth century presented Neo-Orthodox Jews with a quandary. Until 1873, Prussia and most other German states allowed only one officially recognized Jewish community in each city or town. This meant that in towns where the majority of Jews embraced Reform, Orthodox Jews found themselves forced to live in a situation where communal institutions such as the synagogue and school operated according to Reform Judaism – which they deemed unacceptable.

Two responses appeared among German Orthodox Jews. Some, led by Hirsch, attempted to secede from the main Jewish community and form a separate Orthodox Jewish community. In 1876, when a new law of secession allowed Jews to form multiple communities, Hirsch and his congregation Adath Jeshurun seceded from the Jewish community of Frankfurt. Some of his Orthodox colleagues, notably Selig Bamberger, rejected this course of action, noting that secession, while ensuring perhaps a more wholesome religious life, threatened Jewish unity – which they regarded as more important. For Bamberger, the proper course of action was to secure the ability to observe properly within a Reform community.

The conflict between Orthodox and progressive Jews in Hungary was far more tempestuous. Sofer, after fleeing from a triumphant Reform in Frankfurt around 1820, settled and founded a new Orthodox yeshiva in Pressburg (Pozsony in Hungarian, today Bratislava, Slovakia), from where he preached his message of complete non-innovation. Following his death in 1839, he was replaced, after a twelve-year vacuum of religious leadership, by Esriel Hildesheimer in 1851. Hildesheimer was a colleague of Hirsch and a proponent of Hirsch's Neo-Orthodoxy. During the 1850s, he won many supporters, partly because his competitive approach – in contrast to his predecessor's condemnation of religious reform – was regarded as a more effective means of containing religious innovation in Hungary.

Circumstances during the 1850s and 1860s in Hungary, however, paved the way for a renewed conflict, and eventually drove Hildesheimer out. In 1851, the Habsburg regime passed the National Education Fund Act, which created a network of state-sponsored dual-curriculum schools for Jews – reminiscent of those of Joseph II, which, in Hungary, had been closed down following Joseph II's death in 1790 – and required all Hungarian Jews to obtain a secular education. In addition, Hungarian Jews were increasingly embracing German or Magyar as their spoken language, and, after 1860, becoming generally more acculturated.

Most important, perhaps, synagogue reforms were becoming more prevalent by the 1860s. To be sure, these innovations were much like those in Vienna: changes in decorum with none of the ideological changes. Hildesheimer, sensing an opportunity to stem the spread of Neolog Judaism, proposed the creation of an Orthodox rabbinical seminary to train Orthodox rabbis who would be as impressive and *au courant* as their Neolog rivals.

The notion of a modern Orthodox rabbinical seminary, however, caused a split within Hungarian Orthodoxy between Hildesheimer and his Modern Orthodox followers, and the disciples of Moses Sofer, who defined themselves as Ultra-Orthodox. Ultra-Orthodox Jews were even more rigid than Sofer himself. Whereas the principal target of Orthodox condemnation had been Reform Judaism, Ultra-Orthodox Jews regarded Hirsch's and Hildesheimer's Modern Orthodoxy as the gravest threat to Judaism. In some sense, this reorientation was not entirely new. Sofer, after all, had been contending with Neolog more than Reform Judaism. Neolog, although advocating a much broader range of religious innovations, shared with Modern Orthodoxy the need to justify innovations in terms of Jewish law. Thus, both Neolog and Modern Orthodoxy were regarded by the Ultra-Orthodox as giving the same false impression that certain innovations were acceptable according to Jewish law.

During the 1860s, the central Ultra-Orthodox organization, *Shomrei Ha-Dat* (Guardians of the Faith), launched a polemical attack on the proponents of all other points of view: Neolog, Modern Orthodox, and traditional rabbis who ascribed to neither of these. In 1863, Ultra-Orthodox Jews issued an injunction against religious innovation. In some sense reminiscent of the condemnation of the Hamburg temple in 1819, this statement went a step further. In 1819, traditionalists had condemned changes in the liturgy, the use of vernacular, and a cantor and choir. This statement condemned these changes but also condemned anyone who even entered a synagogue that had made any of these changes.

The conflict between Ultra-Orthodox, Modern Orthodox, and Neolog came to a head at the end of the 1860s when, following the emancipation of Hungarian Jewry, Baron Joseph Eötvös, enamored with Napoleon's consistory system, asked each religious denomination in Hungary to form a synod and to submit a list of statutes through which the government could administer and regulate religious affairs. To this end, he instructed Hungarian Jewry to convene a congress in 1869. Orthodox Jews, and especially the Ultra-Orthodox, seeing that 60 percent of Hungarian Jews were Neolog and the statutes would reflect the views of a Neolog majority, refused to participate. The statutes submitted by the congress to Eötvös, therefore, were those of Neolog communities; thus, Neolog Judaism became known as Congress Judaism.

In response, Orthodox Jews petitioned the baron to recognize Orthodox Judaism as a separate religious denomination, which he did in 1869. Eötvös then instructed every community to affiliate with either Orthodox or Neolog; most did. However, there were a number of communities who did not feel comfortable with either Orthodox or Neolog. In 1870, they petitioned the baron to exempt them from having to choose between Orthodox or Neolog, and instead to allow them to continue to practice according to the pre-congress status quo. The baron acceded, and these Jewish communities were recognized as Status Quo communities. By 1870, then, there were three state-recognized Jewish denominations in Hungary.

Seen together, the conflicts between Orthodox and progressive Jews in Germany and Hungary underscored the complexities of religious life in nineteenth-century central Europe. To be sure, secession and schism were possible only insofar as the state allowed it; otherwise, Jews had to work out a way to coexist. Even where there was a schism, moreover, it was never total schism. Marriage between Orthodox and Neolog Jews, although it was often regarded as scandalous, was not considered as marrying outside the faith. More important, in smaller communities, Jews of various denominations shared institutions such as the local cemetery. Nowhere other than central Europe, moreover, did religious conflicts play out with such intensity prior to the 1880s. Reform and Orthodoxy found little following in Russia or western Europe, and even less in the Ottoman Empire.

The emancipation of Jews in Europe, whether by a legislative act or gradual social evolution, was accompanied by larger processes of social transformation.

During the nineteenth century, Jews of all denominations became increasingly urbanized, as rapidly growing Jewish communities appeared in virtually every major European city. By mid-century, there were large Jewish communities in Paris and London. Once emancipated, the Jews of central Europe began to settle in large numbers in Vienna, Budapest, and Warsaw. By the end of the nineteenth century, the Jewish communities of these communities would exceed 100,000. Warsaw Jewry would increase from around 5,000 in 1800 to more than 400,000 by the end of the century. The Jewish population of Óbuda and Pest – which were later amalgamated with Buda to form Budapest – numbered less than 2,000 in 1800 but exceeded 200,000 by 1900.

At the same time, the removal of restrictions precipitated a shift in the Jews' occupational profile. This shift was not in the direction that proponents of emancipation had envisioned. Few emancipated Jews became farmers or artisans, for the simple reason that agriculture and crafts were in sharp decline during the nineteenth century. Instead, Jews moved vertically up the ladder of commerce from petty merchants and pawnbrokers to shopkeepers, insurance brokers, and small-scale industrialists; and horizontally from commerce into now accessible free professions such as medicine, law, and teaching. All of this added up to the embourgeoisement of central European Jewry.

Ironically, the transformation that led to the entry of Jews into the European middle class preserved certain elements of an earlier traditional Jewish way of life, especially with respect to division between public and private. In traditional Jewish life, communal life was the domain of men; women were largely excluded from synagogue and school. In bourgeois society, while most Jewish women received a first-rate general education, they were still confined to the home, by bourgeois domesticity rather than a traditional division of labor. Similarly, weddings in traditional Jewish society were often arranged by the parents or a professional *shadchan* (matchmaker); love and compatibility were seldom taken into consideration. Although bourgeois society regarded love and compatibility as important features of marriage, nonetheless marriages were still arranged, in this case between members of wealthy Jewish families for commercial rather than personal reasons. The upshot is that the processes of change that transformed European Jewry during the nineteenth century were, at least initially, a lateral step for Jewish women, who still found themselves living in a male-dominated society and Jewish community.

These demographic and occupational shifts were elements of the embourgeoisement of Jews in western and central Europe. By 1880, Jews were increasingly an urban, educated, politically liberal, increasingly secularized commercial and professional caste. These changes, moreover, cut across denominational lines. Even the Jews who were ardently and ideologically opposed to acculturation embraced some measure of acculturation, as evidenced by the Hungarian- rather than Yiddish-speaking Ultra-Orthodox Jews of Hungary.

American Jewry to 1881

The American Jewish experience was unique in certain respects, but also combined elements of the Dutch, English, and French, and German Jewish experiences. The United States was the first country born of the principles of the European Enlightenment, and free from a medieval legacy: royalty, aristocracy, an established church, or any tradition of hereditary privilege. Because it was a frontier, all available human resources were needed to build a new world; thus, there was less room for discrimination against minorities such as Jews.

By the eve of the Revolutionary War, approximately 3,000 Jews lived in North America, mostly of Sephardic descent. They generally lived inconspicuously. Occasionally they played a prominent role in public life, such as Hayim Solomon, who financed the Revolutionary War.

Legally, American Jews were never emancipated. Owing to legal acts such as the Virginia Act of 1785 and then the First Amendment to the U.S. Constitution, they enjoyed legal equality as Americans from the beginning of the republic. There were exceptions. Some states maintained religious restrictions. In New Hampshire, no non-Protestants could hold office until 1877. In Maryland, a Jew Bill in 1819 reflected the fact that equal rights for Jews were still not a foregone conclusion.

Most Jews in early America lived on the eastern seaboard; the largest Jewish communities were in Philadelphia, New York, and Charleston. In general, there was little in the way of organized Jewish life. There were no rabbis, and only a few cantors and ritual slaughterers. The Jews were highly acculturated and religiously lax. There were isolated attempts toward communal organization, notably by Rebecca Gratz. By 1820, most synagogues were Sephardic, but the majority of Jews were Ashkenazic Jews from central Europe pretending to be Sephardic.

In retrospect, America Jewry probably would have disappeared through assimilation and intermarriage if a second, larger wave of around 250,000 Jewish immigrants had not arrived between the 1820s and the 1880s. These Jews arrived as part of a larger wave of nearly 3 million Europeans who arrived in America during the mid-nineteenth century. Most of the Jews came from Bohemia, Moravia, and the German states to escape the renewed restrictions on Jews after the defeat of Napoleon, or in search of economic opportunity. Generally these Jews were poorer than those who had come before 1820. Most were engaged in petty commerce, and were moderately traditional but acculturated. Most were German speaking with some secular education, particularly the Jews from Bohemia and Moravia, many of whom had studied in one of the *Normalschulen* set up by Joseph II.

Whereas the earlier wave of Jews settled on the eastern seaboard, those belonging to this wave moved west with the general westward movement, founding Jewish communities west of the Appalachians such as those of Albany and Pittsburgh, and many Midwestern communities such as Detroit, Cleveland, Milwaukee, St. Louis, and Chicago. Typically, these Jews started out as peddlers and improved their position, becoming shopkeepers. A handful of them prospered, becoming major commercial magnates, such as Levi Strauss.

During the first half of the nineteenth century, there was a growing sense that the openness of life in America was not conducive to the preservation of traditional Judaism. In response, there were Jews who attempted to create some sort of organizational framework to maintain a sense of solidarity among Jews, notably Isaac Leeser (1806–68). Leeser tried to adapt traditional Judaism in such a way that it could survive in America.

Born in Germany, Leeser moved to the United States in 1824, and served as the *hazzan* (cantor) for Congregation Mikveh Israel in Philadelphia. In lieu of a rabbi, he delivered the weekly sermon, and was the first to first to introduce an English-language sermon. In 1838, he wrote the first Hebrew primer for Jewish children in the New World. In 1843 he founded the first Jewish newspaper, the *Occident*. In 1848, he published the first English translation of the Sephardic prayer book. In 1849, he founded the first Hebrew high school. Despite these successes, Leeser was unable to create any sort of umbrella organization for American Jewry.

Two other organizations had greater success in this regard: Bnai Brith and the American branch of Reform Judaism. Bnai Brith was a Jewish fraternal organization founded on November 5, 1843, by twelve men who had concluded that the synagogue could not provide a meaningful Jewish life. Instead, they founded the Independent Order of Bnai Brith, modeled after other fraternal orders such as the Masons, to foster some sense of Jewish solidarity outside the synagogue. Like the Masonic orders, they blended their religious beliefs and the educational philosophy that their German forebears had known as *Bildung* with the civic religion of America: monotheism, rationality, active charity, exemplary morality, dedication to self-improvement, and "moral elevation that comprised the education of heart and mind." They stressed group identity, defined the Jewish community as a "distinct moral community," and adopted the mission theory that Geiger espoused for Reform Judaism. One had to be Jewish to join, but Jewishness was interpreted very liberally.

In 1868, Bnai Brith issued a manifesto comprising five principles: (1) all men are brothers, sons of one God, vested with the same inalienable rights; (2) social relations should be dictated by love, and not only by law; (3) charity and enlightenment are the choicest gifts of love, and sons of the covenant (i.e. Bnai Brith) are specifically charged with the practice of the former and the diffusion of the latter; (4) the best interests of humanity are promoted by combined efforts of associated philanthropists; and (5) divine and everlasting doctrines of Judaism are the basis of all civilization and enlightenment, of universal charity and fraternity. Until 1873, Bnai Brith was the only nationwide Jewish organization in America. By the end of the 1870s, it would be joined and complemented by the spread of Reform Judaism.

Reform Judaism found fertile ground in America, although not for the same reason it had succeeded in Germany. American Jews had no angst over the loss of emancipation – which had never been an issue in America. Instead, Reform Judaism naturally fitted the openness and individualism of American society. In Germany, reform had been a means to prove Jews worthy of emancipation; in America, reform was a natural outcome of civic equality.

The first Reform congregation was founded in Charleston in 1819. A second was founded shortly thereafter in Manhattan. By the 1840s, though, the majority of Reform congregations, and the largest, were in the Midwest, particularly in Albany and Cincinnati. Like Bnai Brith, Reform Judaism was well suited to the conditions of the frontier. The growing influence of these Reform congregations by the end of the 1840s allowed newer communities in the Midwest to challenge the older eastern seaboard communities for national leadership.

The end of the 1840s was a point of inflection for Reform Judaism in America, and for America Jewry as a whole. The collapse of the revolutions of 1848 coupled with the discovery of gold in California accelerated the migration of Jews from central Europe. Moreover, after 1848 a number of Jewish intellectuals and Reform rabbis who had supported one or another revolution were forced to flee to the New World to evade arrest. Among them were the Hungarian Jewish revolutionary Michael (Mihaly) Heilprin, who after fleeing from Hungary in 1849 emigrated to the United States and became an active abolitionist.

By the end of the 1840s, two tensions emerged within the ranks of Reform Judaism in the United States. The influx of German-Jewish émigré intellectuals after 1848 created a tension within American Jewry regarding the cultural orientation of American Reform Judaism. The newly arrived rabbis and intellectuals wanted the language of prayer and cultural orientation of Reform Judaism to be German. Jews born and raised in America preferred English, and American culture. At the same time, some Reform Jews believed the Reform movement should be a vehicle for supracommunal organization; others believed that any supracommunal organization would be contrary to the core American notion of individualism.

At the center of these tensions was Isaac Meyer Wise, who emerged during the 1850s as the undisputed leader of Reform Judaism, and the highest-profile Jew in America. He favored American over German culture, and English as the language of prayer. He believed that the religious organization provided by Reform was superior to the cultural organization provided by Bnai Brith, and hence advocated that the Reform movement form a supracommunal organization uniting all of its constituent congregations. As the rabbi of a leading Reform congregation in Cincinnati, he believed the Midwest had replaced the eastern seaboard as the center of American Jewish life. Wise published the first prayer book designed for American Jews, called *Minhag America* (American Custom), which quickly overshadowed the European imports. He also believed that the civic and open quality of American society precluded the necessity of Jewish particularism. Thus, he advocated jettisoning the dietary laws, and most Jewish rituals not directly associated with prayer, which he collectively called "kitchen Judaism."

During the1870s, Wise created the first two successful supracommunal religious organizations in the United States. In 1872, he founded the Union of American Hebrew Congregations (UAHC), which began with thirty-four member congregations. Under his guidance, this congregational union founded the Hebrew Union College in Cincinnati in 1874. The choice of location – off the eastern seaboard, in the geographical center of the United States – reflected how the center of American Jewry had followed the westward movement; more important, it reflected Wise's belief that Jews would participate in American manifest destiny, creating Jewish communities from coast to coast.

Within the UAHC, however, tensions emerged between more traditional and more radical reformers. Kaufman Kohler, a German-born and -trained radical reformer, emerged as the leader of the radical wing of Reform Judaism. Through his personal dynamism and scholarship, the movement moved steadily to the left, culminating in 1882 with an event known as the Trefa Banquet. This sobriquet referred to an annual dinner of Reform rabbis that took place in Cincinnati. Despite the fact that some of those attending the dinner were moderate reformers who still observed the dietary laws, the menu of this dinner included shellfish, which rabbinic tradition defines as *trefa* (unfit to eat). In response, the moderate reformers stormed out in protest and seceded from the movement.

In order to counterbalance Kohler's prominence, the moderates took advantage of the arrival of Alexander Kohut from Hungary in 1885. Kohut was a towering scholar who was one of Zacharias Frankel's prized students. Kohut had been a leader of the moderately traditional Status Quo Movement in Hungary from 1868 to 1885. In 1885, he moved his family to America, and was hired as the rabbi of Ahavas Chesed in New York, less than a mile from Kohler's congregation. During the spring of 1885, Kohut delivered a series of Saturday afternoon sermons on the rabbinic text *Ethics of the Fathers*, in which he criticized Kohler and the radical reformers. He described Kohler's Reform as "a deformity, a skeleton without flesh and nerves, spirit and soul." In 1885, he joined several moderate reformers and moderate traditionalists in founding a new rabbinical seminary to rival the Hebrew Union College, the Jewish Theological Seminary.

In response, Kohler convened a conference of radical reformers in Pittsburgh in 1886, at which they issued what would be the official position of American Reform for half a century: the Pittsburgh Platform. This eight-point platform carried the universalist trend in Reform Judaism to its extreme, recognizing monotheism and the moral and ethical tradition of the Hebrew Bible as the only binding aspects of Judaism, and the remainder of

Judaism as "a system of training the Jewish people for its mission during its national life in Palestine" that had long since ceased to have any validity or meaning. The platform rejected dietary laws and much of Judaism as "foreign to our present moral and spiritual state." The Pittsburgh Platform defined what would come to be known as "classical Reform Judaism" in America, and would outstrip virtually all Reform currents in Europe in terms of its reduction of Judaism to a religion of ethical monotheism.

The triumph of Reform in the United States between 1820 and 1880 reflected the fact that, more than anything else, Jews in America were becoming Americans. The degree to which Jews were part of American society was made plain during the Civil War. Like Americans in general, Northern Jews opposed slavery and defended the Union; Southern Jews defended slavery and states' rights. Jews fought and died on both sides of this conflict.

Equally indicative of the situation of American Jewry was a brief incident of anti-Semitism that took place during the Civil War. General Ulysses S. Grant, suspecting that Jews in border states were smuggling war materials to the South and selling Southern cotton illegally in the North, issued General Order 11 on December 17, 1862 , expelling Jews from Mississippi. When several Jewish friends of Abraham Lincoln informed the president, he immediately ordered General Grant to rescind the order. The rights of Jews in America were never at issue, even when challenged by someone as prominent as General Grant.

The Ottoman and Russian Empires: tradition in an imperial world

The absence of emancipation and enlightenment, and the survival of Jewish tradition, in Russia and the Ottoman Empire give the impression of Jewish stasis or even stagnation. In fact, despite the stark differences between Europe and America on the one hand, and Russia and the Ottoman Empire on the other, Jewish life in the latter states underwent significant changes during the nineteenth century. The efforts by the Ottoman and tsarist regimes to create more homogeneous and centralized states began to affect Jews there by the beginning of the nineteenth century. The arrival of European and European Jewish ideas in these parts of the Jewish world accelerated changes that had already begun to take shape under the aegis of these autocratic regimes.

In the Ottoman Empire, the status of Jews was largely a function of general political stability. The expansion and resurgence of the Ottoman Empire under Suleiman during the sixteenth century had vastly stabilized and improved the situation of Jews. From the seventeenth century on, the situation of Jews destabilized as the Ottoman Empire entered a period of decline. By the beginning of the nineteenth century, Jewish inhabitants of the "sick man of Europe" faced an increasingly precarious situation.

Until the mid-nineteenth century, two aspects of traditional Jewish life in the Ottoman Empire remained largely unchanged. Culturally, the Jews in the Ottoman Empire, and in the Islamic world generally, had never been as isolated from the outside world as their counterparts under Christendom. Traditional Jewish life in the Islamic world was much like that in the Christian world: the same laws, the same yearning for Zion, the same notion of the Messiah, and the experience with Shabbetai Zvi. On the other hand, there was less rabbinic backlash to Sabbateanism in the Islamic world than in the Ashkenazic world. To repeat, Jews in the Islamic world were never as isolated from the outside world as Jews in Christendom, and Jewish scholars never as alienated from the rest of the Jewish community. There was no internal Haskalah or reform movement, and thus no anti-reform Orthodox backlash. Such innovations would arrive eventually, but largely as a result of the growing presence of European Jewry in the Ottoman Empire.

In general, Jews in the Ottoman Empire had a non-confrontational attitude toward social, political, and technological changes. Even those rabbis who were disturbed by the potential consequences of western cultural influences did not reject modern civilization per se. In this sense, the prevailing mentality was akin to non-German Reform: innovations were seen as a logical continuation of the halachic process and a naturally evolving Jewish law.

This mentality prevailed in virtually all facets of Jewish life. For example, traditional Jews studied foreign languages largely for material gain through access to European commerce, rather than as part of a program of enlightenment. Rabbis in the Ottoman Empire tended to be less stringent regarding contacts between Jews and non-Jews. For example, Rabbi Joseph Hayyim ben Elijah of Baghdad (Ben Ish Hay) allowed Jews to go to Gentile coffeehouses, even on the Sabbath, as long as they consumed only that which was prepared prior to their arrival, in accordance with Jewish law. He also allowed Jewish pharmacists to remove their *talit katan* (a prayer shawl with fringes) before going to work, for reasons of hygiene. The Hakham abd allah Somekh, a supreme Iraqi rabbinic authority, allowed Jews to ride trains on the Sabbath, although not to travel between cities. The positive attitude of rabbis toward changes was in contrast to the negative response of Muslim leaders. The upshot is that a movement like Haskalah was largely unnecessary because Ottoman Jews did not need one; dual education and minimal social isolation were the rule.

The Jewish courtier class in the Ottoman world remained perched atop Jewish communal life well into the nineteenth century. The courtiers had the most extensive contacts with the European world through international business ventures; like the court Jews, they were the most worldly, providing their children with the highest-quality education and the most strongly secular education. They were also the most politically and socially conservative, and the most resistant to the new ideas emanating from the West. Until 1839,

Jews, along with other non-Muslims in the Ottoman Empire, were defined as a millet (recognized minority), as mentioned earlier in the book, and were largely autonomous as long as they paid their taxes. On the whole, Jews tended to be more open to westernization of the Ottoman Empire than Muslims.

By the mid-nineteenth century, the Jewish population of the Ottoman Empire was estimated at around 150,000. Developments after mid-century would cause it to rise to 250,000 by 1912. Two changes transformed the Jews of the Ottoman Empire and, more generally, much of the Islamic world. First, from the end of the eighteenth century on, European powers established consulates in the empire, initially out of a desire to protect their co-religionists and citizens living under Ottoman rule. This led to increasing intrusion into internal Ottoman affairs and an expanding influence of European culture in the Ottoman Empire.

At the same time, in an effort to shore up government administration and the economy, in 1839 the sultan, motivated by a desire to join and compete with the European community, issued the Tanzimat, a program of social and political reforms. More than anything else, this was an attempt to centralize the empire by trying to eliminate or curtail corporate entities – not unlike initiatives by European enlightened absolutists a century earlier. The Tanzimat granted equal rights to non-Muslims, eliminated the *jizya* and other humiliating taxes, subjected non-Muslims to military service (although it allowed them to buy out of it), put non-Muslim millets on an equal footing with Muslim millets, while eroding the communal autonomy of the millet. In actuality, these reforms did not eliminate the millet system, but merely added to it. By the mid-nineteenth century, there were four competing legal and judicial systems: secular courts, Islamic courts, millet courts, and consular courts.

The impact of the Tanzimat was limited to countries ruled directly by the Ottoman Empire. It had little impact in Morocco, Yemen, Algeria, and Egypt. Nonetheless, the situation of Jews in those parts of the Islamic world would also be a function of local administration and European influence. Following the French conquest of Algeria in 1830, for example, the Colonial Office invited Jews and other non-Muslims to be treated as French subjects, *indigènes*. This would be the first step toward the full emancipation of non-Muslims in Algeria in 1870.

Yet perhaps the most telling indicator of the change of Jewish life in the Ottoman Empire was the series of events that took place in Egypt in 1839–40, particularly the events surrounding a Damascus blood libel that occurred at the time. This event unfolded amid a campaign by Muhammad 'Ali, an Egyptian leader, to break away from the sultan; and English and French intrigues to reap the benefits of this conflict.

In February 1840, a Capuchin monk in Damascus, which was part of the Ottoman province of Egypt, disappeared around Passover time. An ensuing investigation led to the arrest and torture of several Jews. The French consulate in Damascus, eager to win 'Ali as an ally, supported this investigation.

European liberals – Jews and non-Jews – were outraged, regarding the event as an affront to western values. At this point, a coterie of European Jews decided to intervene, and dispatched a delegation to the sultan that consisted of the English Jew Moses Montefiore, the French Jew and statesman Adolphe Crémieux, and the German Jews Solomon Monk and Louis Loewe.

For Monk and Loewe, in particular, this decision to intervene seemed to run contrary to the terms of emancipation – that is, maintaining an extranational sense of solidarity. They justified their actions in two ways. First, they claimed that their solidarity was exclusively religious, like Catholics helping Catholics across national borders. In addition, they regarded their actions as integral to the values of their country. Freedom from religious persecution and civil rights were European and not simply Jewish values.

In retrospect, despite such claims, this event marked the emergence of a transnational sense of solidarity that was not only religious but quasi-national in nature. This new mentality found expression during the 1840s in Jewish newspapers such as the German-Jewish *Allegemeine Zeitung des Judenthums* and the Anglo-Jewish *Jewish Chronicle*. It found full expression two decades later with the founding the first modern Jewish philanthropic organization, the Alliance Israélite Universelle, in 1860.

The immediate origin of the Alliance was the Mortara affair, an incident that took place in Bologna, Italy, in 1858. A Jewish child named Edgardo Mortara was kidnapped from his parents by a papal guard on the pretext that his nanny had already had him baptized secretly. In response, Adolphe Crémieux and other French-Jewish leaders formed the Alliance to protect all Jews who faced such persecution.

From the vantage point of these French Jews, the Jews who were in the most obvious need of assistance were the politically second-class, relatively powerless, and culturally backward (i.e. non-European) Jews in the Ottoman Empire. The creation of the Alliance thus reflected a broader trend of European intervention, and had the classically liberal aim of helping those less fortunate by turning them into Europeans – in this case, European Jews. To this end, the Alliance set up a network of dual-curriculum Jewish schools in various parts of the Ottoman Empire. These schools were funded by the Alliance and protected by French consulates.

For Jews in the Ottoman Empire, these schools offered a new alternative to a centuries-old traditional Jewish existence: westernization. Unbeknownst to the Alliance, this alternative would be the cutting edge of a wedge between Jews in the Ottoman Empire and their Muslim neighbors. For centuries, they had lived as neighbors as parts of the same world. As Jews became increasingly westernized, they were seen by their neighbors as foreigners and, for some, as agents of European imperialism. Later, such nascent sentiments would be exacerbated, though not created, by the emergence of Zionism.

Thus, the Alliance extended the program of Haskala and the debate over Jewish emancipation to the Ottoman Empire. The crowning achievement of the Alliance came in 1878 at the Congress of Berlin, as the Great Powers prepared to recognize the independence of Romania and other Balkan states from Ottoman rule. At the urging of the Alliance, the Great Powers required these states to grant civil rights to Jews as a condition of political recognition. This moved the eastern edge of emancipated Jewry eastward into the Ottoman Empire, leaving Russian Jewry as the only Jewish population untouched by emancipation and enlightenment.

The Pale of Settlement

Russian society and politics, though Christian, differed from those found in the rest of Christian Europe. In Europe, a tradition of individuals other than the king having rights had emerged as early as the thirteenth century with the granting of the Magna Carta in 1215 to the English nobility and the (only slightly lesser known) Aurea Bulla to the Hungarian nobility in 1222 – pivotal moments in the development of feudalism. Henceforth, other social castes would apply for and be granted rights, including Jews. Jewish emancipation in Europe culminated centuries of extending rights to a broader segment of the general population.

By contrast, there was no tradition of rights in tsarist Russia. Until the 1860s, the notion of Jewish emancipation in Russia made no sense in a country where only a tiny minority of the population had any rights. In general, historians point to the fact that, prior to 1881, there was no coherent or consistent Jewish policy aimed specifically at persecuting Jews, with one notable exception (to be discussed presently). Rather, laws regarding Jews reflected other overriding tsarist concerns.

Russian Jewry, moreover, came into existence almost overnight. Prior to 1772, there were virtually no Jews in the tsarist empire, owing to a pervading Judeophobia on the part of the tsars and the Russian Orthodox Church. The three partitions of Poland between 1772 and 1795 abruptly brought tens of thousands of Jews under tsarist rule. Rather than expel the Jews or admit them into the Russian interior, Catherine the Great confined them to the provinces that had been annexed by Russia, which became known as the Pale of Settlement. This would be the defining tsarist policy regarding Jews from 1772 until the abolition of the Pale of Settlement in 1917.

Historians disagree as to the impact of this policy on Russian Jewry. Some argue that because the Pale of Settlement was roughly the size of France, confining Jews to the Pale was not a particularly harsh restriction. Moreover, since Jews had virtually unimpeded mobility within the Pale, they had greater mobility than 85 percent of the Russian population, who were confined to their own village or town. During the reign of Alexander I, the Pale was expanded to include Novorussia, a newly conquered and underpopulated region. Alexander, in a brief foray into European Enlightenment, encouraged Jews to settle there by allowing them to acquire land and live tax-free in exchange for a commitment to stay for ten years.

Other historians point to a rapid increase in the Jewish population of the Pale, which quadrupled during the nineteenth century. Without the ability to expand in response to population increase, the towns and villages of the Pale became increasingly crowded and impoverished, especially after Alexander I evicted Jews from local villages in 1804. In any case, other than the 20,000 Jews who became farmers in Novorussia, little changed for Jews until the reign of Nicholas I.

Nicholas I, raised to be a general, became tsar in 1825 following the premature death of his brother Constantine. For Nicholas, all solutions were military solutions. Thus, he believed that the most effective ways of helping non-productive subjects serve the state more efficiently was conscription. Similarly, he regarded conscription as the surest method of Russifying the non-Russian population, including the Jews.

In 1827, he ordered the conscription of Russian Jews. Jews were not the only group conscripted for the first time; Polish nobles, for example, were also conscripted. Yet Jews were conscripted into special units known as Cantonist units. Jewish conscripts were conscripted from the age of 12 and required to serve for twenty-five years. Moreover, they were subject to intense missionary pressure during their term of service.

The harshness of this imperial order was exacerbated by the fact that, like peasant communes and towns, the leadership of the Jewish community, the kahal, was responsible for supplying the annual quota of Jewish recruits. Given the nature of cantonist military service, this was tantamount to sending Jewish boys away possibly never to return. Once the most obvious suspects had been tapped to fill the quota – miscreants, the religiously lax, children of the poor, orphans, and the weak-minded – the kahal had to choose among less obvious candidates. The difficulty of finding volunteers forced the kahal to hire *khappers* (literally, grabbers) – thugs who would locate and drag off the remaining children. The participation of the kahal in supplying recruits undermined the confidence of rank-and-file Jews in their leaders. No longer was it clear that the kahal, traditionally the protector of its constituency from outside threats, had their best interests in mind.

During the 1840s, Nicholas went a step further in his attempt to Russify the Jews. Convinced that the main impediment to Russification was the leadership of the Jews itself – which was ironic, given its assistance in delivering recruits – Nicholas attempted to eliminate the kahal, without success. He then attempted to transform rabbinic leadership into a government agency by synthesizing his own rabbinate. In 1849, he created government-sponsored rabbinical training academies in Vilna and Zhitomir. The graduates of these schools would be assigned to individual Jewish communities as government rabbis. In addition to performing the standard rabbinic functions, these rabbis would provide a detailed registry of birth, marriages, and deaths, and would be the official liaison between the Jewish community and the state. This initiative also failed, as most Jewish communities had a government rabbi and an unofficial actual rabbi.

Apart from the harsh impact of the cantonist system, Russian Jewry by and large remained minimally affected by Russian rule prior to the 1850s. The two main religious currents within Russian Jewry were those that had crystallized at the end of the eighteenth century: Hasidic and Mitnagedic Judaism. Mitnagedic Judaism, which had begun largely as a movement opposed to Hasidism, developed during the first half of the nineteenth century into a religious movement of its own. Instrumental in its development were Hayyim of Volozhin and Israel Salanter. Hayyim of Volozhin, a disciple of Elijah of Vilna, recognized Hasidism as not only a legitimate but also a permanent feature of Jewish life in Russia.

Accordingly, in an effort not to lose young people to Hasidism, he reinvigorated non-Hasidic traditionalism by revamping its education system. Drawing on the educational innovations of his mentor, Hayyim of Volozhin introduced a modicum of secular subjects into the traditional curriculum – to be sure, only the minimum necessary to enhance and improve the study of rabbinic texts. He also created a new kind of yeshiva. In contrast to the community yeshiva, which was funded by the local community, run by the community rabbi, and often attended by local youth, the Volozhin yeshiva was privately funded and thus operated independently of the local community. This new kind of yeshiva offered superior facilities, teachers, and provisions, and attracted a higher caliber of student. The heads of these yeshivas were not only accomplished rabbinic scholars, but also highly charismatic – akin to the Hasidic *rebbe*. These changes narrowed the gap between the world of rabbinic learning in Lithuania and the world of Hasidism.

Yet non-Hasidic traditionalism still lacked the spiritual allure of Hasidism. This lacuna was filled by Israel Salanter, a product of the schools and of Hayyim of Volozhin. Salanter introduced into his yeshiva a new emphasis on Jewish ethics, known as *mussar* – the essence of what came to be known as the Mussar Movement. Whereas Hasidic Jews sought spiritual fulfillment through prayer, song, and dance, the Mussar Movement promised spiritual fulfillment through the contemplation of an ethically superior life. Though largely an intellectual movement, at times Salanter applied his emphasis on ethics to everyday situations. For example, he refused to approve the Passover matzoth made in a factory where the women workers were mistreated.

During the second half of the nineteenth century, Hasidic and Mitnagedic Judaism were challenged by the emergence of a third religious current: the Russian Haskalah. Until the 1850s, this was less a movement than a few isolated individuals, often barely distinguishable from Mitnagedic Jews. Alienated from the rest of the Jewish population, these individuals found employment as government rabbis. During the 1860s, though, the Russian Haskalah would take a major step forward, buttressed by the policies of Tsar Alexander II.

Alexander II, the "liberal" tsar ascended to the throne following Nicholas's death in 1855. His reign is known as "the great thaw" in Russian history, owing to a sweeping array of reforms that he implemented during the 1860s. Regarding Jews, he eliminated the cantonist units and relaxed the regulations governing the Pale of Settlement, allowing certain types of Jews to live outside the Pale: soldiers, first-rank merchants, and university graduates. He also relaxed censorship, allowing the emergence of a Jewish press.

Most important, perhaps, was his emancipation of the Russian peasantry in 1861. For the first time, the notion of Jewish emancipation seemed plausible, at the moment when it seemed that the tsar was transforming Russia into a European-style country. This attracted a small but growing number of Russian Jews to the Russian Haskalah.

Like the Berlin Haskalah, the Russian Haskalah called for political emancipation while advocating the transformation of Jewish life to make Jews more productive and more involved in mainstream society. The Russian Haskalah echoed Mendelssohn's notion of a making Judaism private and voluntary. As the maskil Judah Lieb Gordon put it, "Be a Jew in your tent and a man in the street." This allowed the Haskalah to embrace the tsarist aim of Russification. Writing in 1861, Osip Rabinovich called on Russian Jews to abandon Yiddish, "these old rags, a heritage of the Middle Ages," concluding that "our homeland is Russia – just as its air is ours, so its language must become ours." Others, such as Judah Lieb Gordon, used the pages of the nascent Jewish press to urge Jews to embrace the new possibilities dawning in Russia: "This land of Eden – Russia – now opens its gates to you, her sons call you brother. How long will you dwell among them as a guest?" Such optimism was epitomized by an obituary for Tsarina Maria Alexandrova, the deceased wife of Alexander II, that appeared in the Jewish weekly *Ha-meliz* on June 8, 1880: "Even if we tried, we could not enumerate all the good that the deceased has done for us from the time she ascended the throne until the time she met her maker."

At the same time, there were stark differences between the Russian and Berlin Haskalah. The adherents of the Russian Haskalah were drawn from a constituency that differed quantitatively and qualitatively from its central European counterpart. Russian Jewry numbered in the hundreds of thousands, German Jewry in the tens of thousands; Russian Jews often lived in small towns where they were the local majority. Russian Jews tended to be more traditional, thus the Russian Haskalah had stronger ties to Jewish tradition.

In addition, Russian maskilim were never drawn to Russian culture in the way maskilim in central Europe were drawn to German or Viennese culture. Whereas the Berlin Haskalah, after a brief foray into Hebrew, turned largely to the vernacular as its language of expression, the Russian Haskalah was multilingual, its adherents producing works in Russian, Hebrew, and Yiddish. At the heart of the Russian Haskalah, in fact, was a literary renaissance of the Hebrew language. Previously a language of prayer and rabbinic discourse, by the 1860s, Hebrew emerged as a modern literary language. The appearance of Hebrew newspapers such as *Ha-Maggid* (The Preacher), *Ha-Shachar* (The Dawn) and Ha-Melitz (The Intercessor) created fora for the dissemination of Hebrew poems and short stories to a vast Jewish audience.

Given that they were situated in a sea of Hasidic and Mitnagedic Jews, it is not surprising that Russian maskilim were severe critics of traditional Jewish life. The maskilic critique of traditional Jewish life was reflected in derogatory depictions of the shtetl, the literary sobriquet of a typical small town, illustrated by the names of the fictional shtetls in maskilic literature: Tonyadevka-Betalon (Donothingville), Kaptunsk-Kaptsiel (Beggartown), Glupsk-Kesalon (Stupidville), and Lohayapolie (No Such Place)

Similarly, in a seminal narrative poem called *Kozo Shel Yud* (Tip of the [Hebrew letter] Yud), Gordon delivering a scathing critique of traditional Jewish society while simultaneously advocating for the liberation of Jewish women from the tyranny of the rabbis. This poem, whose title alludes to Akiva's second-century C.E. maxim concerning the limitless possibility of rabbinic interpretation, tells of the plight of the *'aguna* (literally, anchored women), the tragic situation of Jewish women who were trapped by a rabbinic law that allowed only the husband to initiate a divorce.

In this story, the husband of an *'aguna* is missing. Thus, she could never remarry. Fortunately, her husband had had the foresight to add a clause to the wedding contract stipulating that if he should be missing for a year, his wife could have a divorce. The adjudicating rabbi, however, notes that the tip of the letter yud in this last clause is missing – nullifying the missing husband's special provision and rendering his wife an *'aguna*. As part of his critique of traditional Judaism, Gordon called for the elimination of this and other similarly oppressive laws and customs, and the rigid rabbinic mentality. Interestingly, recent research in archives of the former Soviet Union has revealed that what Gordon was demanding in theoretical and idealistic terms, *'agunot* themselves were pursuing in actuality by going over the head of the Jewish tribunals and getting their marriages annulled by state courts.

No less impressive than the revival of Hebrew was the revival of Yiddish as a literary language. Previously a street dialect of German that had been rejected even by other Russian maskilim, Yiddish, too, was transformed into a modern literary language. Spearheading this effort was Shalom Jacob Abramowitsch, more commonly known by his pen name and the name of his most famous literary character Mendele Mokher Seforim (Mendele the Bookseller). After starting out writing in Hebrew, Abramowitsch switched to Yiddish and defended Yiddish as the true Jewish language: "Here I am ... attempting to write for our people in the holy tongue, yet most of them do not even know this tongue. Their language is Yiddish."

The simultaneous revival of Hebrew and Yiddish, remarkable in and of itself, fostered by the end of the 1860s the first stirrings of a Jewish national ethos in the nineteenth-century sense of the term. This national ethos would not fully mature until after 1881, but its earliest expression is detectable within the Russian Haskalah. Writing in 1868, Peretz Smolenskin, the editor of *Ha-Shachar*, captured this ethos:

> When people ask what the renewal of the Hebrew language will give us I shall answer· it will give us self-respect and courage. . . . Other peoples may erect stone monuments ... and spill their blood like water in order to perpetuate their own name and language. . . . We have no monument, country, or name, and the only memory remaining to us from the destruction of the Temple is the Hebrew language. ... Our language is our national fortress.

The spread of Haskalah in Russia during the 1860s and 1870s culminated the transformation of world Jewry during the eighteenth and nineteenth centuries. In 1750, Judaism was overwhelmingly synonymous with Rabbinic Judaism, non-rabbinic forms of the religion being deemed odd and heretical. By 1880, traditional Judaism still predominated in Russia, the Ottoman Empire, and the eastern parts of the Habsburg Monarchy, but non-rabbinic forms of Judaism such as Reform had conquered Germany and America, while progressive forms of Judaism had made inroads everywhere. This change called into question the very nature of Jewish identity. In 1750, the litmus test for inclusion within the Jewish community was adherence to rabbinic laws and customs, and acknowledgment of rabbinic authority. While Jewish identity was still defined in 1880 in religious terms, was this still as pervasive a litmus test? Moreover, in 1750 the existence of a neutral ground between Jews and non-Jews was more the exception than the rule. By 1880, world Jewry appeared to be well on the way toward complete political equality and acceptance by mainstream society. But was it?

Chapter 8

Anti-Semitism and Jewish responses, 1870–1914

The rise of anti-Semitism during the second half of the nineteenth century challenged the gains that Jews had made during that century. Initially a central and western European phenomenon, anti-Semitism differed fundamentally from the earlier expression of anti-Judaism. The latter was primarily religious – the Jew as guilty of deicide and in league with Satan – with an economic component: the Jew as usurer. By contrast, anti-Semitism condemned Jews in racial and political terms. Like anti-Jewish sentiments, though, anti-Semitism appealed to a varied and broad audience. It could be tailored to win believers among the uneducated masses, but also appealed to an educated audience.

Historians distinguish three overlapping periods in the history of European anti-Semitism. From 1870 to 1918, anti-Semitism was largely polemical in nature, expressed in word and text. From the end of the First World War until 1938, systemic forms of anti-Semitism – anti-Jewish legislation – were adjoined to polemical anti-Semitism. After 1938, as anti-Semitism was subsumed by Nazi anti-Semitism, it turned predominantly violent until 1945. In this regard, it is important to distinguish anti-Semitism from Nazism. Not all anti-Semites were Nazis, nor is it possible to draw a straight line from the rise of anti-Semitism to the rise of Nazi anti-Semitism.

Anti-Semitism began as a critique of the changes of the nineteenth century: capitalism, industrialization, secularization, urbanization, and civic equality. For some, these changes were essential elements of the path to a perfect world. They saw the years leading up to 1914 as an age of progress in which crime, disease, poverty, war, and intolerance were disappearing. They explained away evidence to the contrary as vestiges of the Middle Ages, and assumed that the evils of society existed only in backward parts of the world, and among the reactionary and ignorant elements of the population such as the clergy and nobility. The spread of enlightenment, coupled with scientific and technological advances, they assumed, would eventually rid the world of anti-Semitism and other evils. They viewed emancipation and the acceptance of Jews into the mainstream as a measure of the perfectibility of humanity.

Others, however, regarded themselves as the victims of the changes of the nineteenth century, specifically the clergy, nobility, peasantry, and craftsmen. The influence of the church had been eroded by the rise of secular culture. The nobility had been diminished in stature by the liberal politics that eliminated corporate privileges. Craftsmen had been competed out of existence by industrialization. Peasants had been uprooted by capitalistic and industrialized agriculture. These groups regarded Jews not only as the embodiment of all of these changes, but also as the principal beneficiaries and the agents of these changes. Jews, especially in western and central Europe, they noted, had been transformed from a predominantly poor, marginal, despised population at the beginning of the nineteenth century into an upwardly mobile, well-educated, urban population perched atop the triumphant world of capitalism.

Three developments fed this general discontent with the changes of the nineteenth century. In 1864, Pope Pius IX issued a papal bull in which he denounced the changes of the nineteenth century, especially secular culture. This fortified socially conservative elements to reject these changes. In addition, the economic recessions of 1873, 1884, and 1895 revealed a dark side of capitalism and industrialization, as laissez-faire economic policies did little or nothing to aid the thousands who were unemployed. In an earlier age, such individuals would have turned to the church or their lord for charity, but neither had sufficient means to care for the poor as effectively, while the welfare state was still a generation away.

Finally, anti-Semitism emerged out of a disjunction between the rhetoric of emancipation and the social reality of emancipated Jews – that is, out of a growing sense that political emancipation was, at best, an incomplete means of Jewish assimilation. By the end of the nineteenth century, there was a sense that neither Jews nor the state had met their part of the bargain. The state, while removing legal disabilities from Jews, was unable to eliminate social discrimination against Jews. Thus, while Jews had the legal right to reside anywhere and pursue any occupation, there were neighborhoods that continued to exclude Jews and occupations that were still closed to Jews.

Moreover, Jews had not met two conditions of emancipation. They had not abandoned commerce for more productive occupations such as farming and crafts. To be sure, this expectation had become ludicrous, as agriculture and crafts were in sharp decline by the end of the nineteenth century. What is more, while Jews in western and central Europe had enthusiastically embraced the language and culture of the country where they lived, they had preserved a strong sense of ethnic cohesiveness and thus were far from integrated. Vienna Jewry was a case in point. The highly acculturated Jews of Vienna lived predominantly in the Leopoldstadt district, sent their children to the same gymnasia, and attended the theater and the opera on the same nights. Even Jews who converted to Christianity continued to socialize almost exclusively with their Jewish friends or with other Jews who had converted.

Anti-Semitism galvanized all of this criticism and discontent. The term, coined by the German sociologist Wilhelm Marr in 1879, had a racial and political dimension. The racial dimension combined the modern nationalist division of humanity into groups based on language and culture with the social Darwinist notion that, like species, races and nations are in a constant state of competing for survival – some surviving only at the expense of others. Thus, Friedrich List had argued that the survival of the German people was threatened by the cultural superiority of peoples to the west and by the numerical superiority of the Slavic people.

In a similar vein, anti-Semites claimed that the presence and prosperity of Jews were antithetical to German national development. Jews, they argued, corrupted German culture. This was ironic, given that Jews tended to be the most loyal, ardent German patriots. The notion of Jews corrupting German culture had been pioneered by the composer Richard Wagner. In an essay entitled "Jews in Music," Wagner attributed the inability of enlightened individuals such as himself not to detest Jews to the "be-Jewing of modern art." Interestingly, Wagner originally published his essay anonymously in 1850. As his daughter Cosima recalled in her diary, he was initially afraid to publish it openly because the music publishing industry was run by Jews, and most music critics were Jews, not to mention that such sentiments were politically incorrect in 1850 – the high point of liberalism in central Europe. By 1869, the climate had changed to the point where Wagner could publish his essay openly.

The political dimension of anti-Semitism was rooted in a paradoxical conclusion drawn from the revolutions of 1848. Jews figured prominently among the liberal revolutionaries, particularly in Vienna, where the revolution was led by two Jews, Adolf Fischhof and Joseph Goldmark. After 1848, Jews were stereotyped as the ultimate liberal revolutionary. At the same time, the defeat of these revolutions by revamped royal and imperial forces was made possible by the financial assistance of the Rothschilds; thus, the image emerged of Jews as the ultimate conservative counter-revolutionaries. By the end of the nineteenth century, therefore, it was possible to stigmatize Jews from either the left or the right wing of the political spectrum. For socialists, Jews were Rothschilds; for conservatives, Jews were Fischhofs.

Right-wing anti-Semitism was easier to comprehend. Conservatives were at the forefront of the discontent with the changes of the nineteenth century. Their politics tended to be crude and parochial, and appealed to ignorance, prejudice, and fear. Conservative anti-Semites defended Christian values and tradition, and denounced anything novel. They blamed all social problems on Jews, a strategy that bore results at the end of the nineteenth century. In the German election of 1893, anti-Semitic parties received 293,000 votes. More dramatic was the election of Carl Lueger, who campaigned on an anti-Semitic platform, as mayor of Vienna from 1895 to 1910.

Left-wing anti-Semitism was more subtle and more sophisticated, dating back to an essay by Karl Marx on the question of Jewish emancipation. Marx had argued that since "the worldly basis of Judaism was practical necessity and selfishness," and that "the worldly culture of the Jew is commerce," therefore "the emancipation of the Jews is the emancipation of humanity from Judaism." Thus, for Marx, Judaism personified and perpetuated the evils of capitalism.

The other element of political anti-Semitism was the myth of Jewish power and the notion of a world Jewish conspiracy. The myth of Jewish power was woven into the fabric of anti-Semitic discourse as early as the 1870s. Marr, for example, claimed that the Jews "fought against the western world for 1,800 years and finally conquered and subjugated it. German culture proved itself ineffective and powerless against this foreign power."

The notion of a Jewish conspiracy was expressed most vividly in the *Protocols of the Elders of Zion*, a forgery authored by the Russian secret police that purported to be the minutes of the Elders of Zion, a secret coterie of powerful Jews who ruled the world. The Protocols explained major world events in terms of this secret Jewish conspiracy. Accordingly, the French Revolution was a conspiracy by Jewish merchants to destroy the European nobility; and socialism was a conspiracy by Jewish capitalists to dupe Christian workers into destroying Christian capitalists. At the heart of this conspiracy theory was the claim that Jews controlled all forms of media and the conclusion that all perceptions of reality were the result of Jewish manipulation.

These elements of anti-Semitism crystallized in the Dreyfus Affair. The Dreyfus Affair refers to the trial and conviction of a French-Jewish officer, Alfred Dreyfus, for treason, his subsequent exile to Devil's Island, and the upheaval this caused in France. The roots of this episode date back to the defeat of France by Germany in 1871, a defeat that shattered the myth of French military superiority, and the ceding of Alsace-Lorraine to Germany. Humiliated by this defeat, the French military began a witch hunt for spies. Individuals from Alsace-Lorraine tended to be suspected of espionage, as is often the case with people in border territories. In addition, the French military and other conservative elements blamed the republican principles of the French Revolution for weakening France. They claimed, for example, that the French Commune in 1871 had divided and weakened France in the face of a German attack.

Against this background, the Dreyfus Affair was the third part in a trilogy of turn-of-the-century French politics. In 1888, General Georges Boulanger, a hero in defeat in 1871, attempted to overthrow the French Republic, supported by a conservative coalition of army officers, church officials, and former nobility. He was defeated, further humiliating the military's conservative old guard. In 1892, several Jewish entrepreneurs, after botching an attempt to build a canal across Panama, absconded with millions of francs from French investors. This incident resonated with the anti-Semitic and conspiratorial claims of *La France juive*, a popular book that had been published by Eduard Drumont in 1886. By 1894, the disillusionment of the military and conservatives after the Boulanger fiasco, combined with claims of Jewish swindlers ruining France after the Panama scandal, set the stage for the arrest of Albert Dreyfus.

In 1894, Dreyfus was accused of selling military secrets to Germany. In retrospect, we know he was framed and that the dossier "of evidence" used against him was forged. Circumstances, however, acted against him. He was an acculturated Jewish republican – the embodiment of republican France and Jewish emancipation at a time when anti-Semitism in France was peaking. He was also Alsatian at a time when the military suspected Alsatians of disloyalty and needed to find a scapegoat.

Dreyfus was tried by a military tribunal, convicted, and publicly stripped of his rank. When he was convicted and sentenced in a public square, the assembled crowd began to shout, "Death to the Jews!" Dreyfus responded with the mantra of an acculturated Frenchman of the Jewish persuasion – "Vive la France!" – before being sent to Devil's Island. (Theodore Herzl and Max Nordau, Budapest-born assimilated Jewish journalists covering this event, would later recall this moment as integral in their embrace of Zionism.) During the days that followed, anti-Semitic riots broke out all over France. The French military and police quashed the riots and limited the destructiveness, a tribute to the strength of the republic. Yet the incidents themselves revealed a deep fissure within French society between republicans and conservatives.

This fissure would widen in a struggle over the fate of Dreyfus. Following his conviction, there was an outcry against this travesty of justice among supporters of the republic. Emile Zola, the leading French writer of the time, published a letter in a leading newspaper, *L'Aurore*, in which he accused the French military and government of betraying the principles of the revolution and the republic to bigotry and reaction. France divided into two camps: Dreyfusards, who supported Dreyfus and the republic; and anti-Dreyfusards, who defended Dreyfus's conviction and opposed the republic. Dreyfus became a *cause célèbre* and the central issue in the national election of 1898. The Dreyfusards won, and in 1904 Dreyfus was retried, acquitted, and promoted to major. The same year, the separation of church and state that had begun decades earlier was consummated, a final blow to French conservatives and a fitting end to the trial of a Jew that became a referendum on republican politics and values in France.

The vindication of Dreyfus meant a victory for the changes of the nineteenth century in France. It also underscored the way that, in pre-First World War western and central Europe, anti-Semitism was seemingly ever-present but often not victorious. Moreover, the riots in France notwithstanding, anti-Semitism tended to be minimally violent in western and central Europe, even during the height of the Dreyfus Affair. For example, an anti-Semitic French general had designed and marketed special canes to be used when beating Jews. During the riots, virtually no incidents of its use were reported. The state maintained order, and protected Jews as French citizens. The lack of violent anti-Semitism in western and central Europe explains Jewish responses to anti-Semitism prior to the First World War.

The question of Jewish responses became a matter of historical debate during the 1960s. Following the Eichmann trial in 1962, the German-Jewish émigré and political scientist Hannah Arendt accused European Jewish leaders of political passivity in the face of anti-Semitism. Emancipated Jews, she argued, had a pathological dependence on the state and its laws for protection. Disciples of Arendt looked for earlier examples of passivity, concluding that there was a lack of any Jewish response to anti-Semitism at the end of the nineteenth century, except in the case of the few Jews who presciently embraced Zionism.

In response to this claim of passivity, a closer examination of Jewish responses subsequently revealed that Zionism was one of three Jewish responses to anti-Semitism. In addition to Zionism, which attracted only a tiny minority of central European Jews prior to 1914, some Jews became socialists, on the assumption that social revolution would eliminate anti-Semitism. Jewish socialists tended by and large toward moderate forms of socialism, such as the trade unionism advocated by Edward Bernstein, or Viktor Adler's Austro-Marxism.

The most common response by far, however, was to combat anti-Semitism by actively working within the system. This meant suing anti-Semitic orators and journalists for libel and malice, responding to anti-Semitic statements by publishing letters and editorials in the press, and disseminating positive propaganda about Jews and their contributions to European society and culture. Spearheading such efforts in France was the *Alliance*. Elsewhere, new organizations such as the German-Jewish *Centralverein deutscher Staatsbürger judischen Glaubens* (the Central Organization of German Citizens of the Jewish Faith) performed similar tasks. Comparable organizations appeared in Vienna, Budapest, London, and eventually in the United States, with the formation of the Anti-Defamation League.

The outlook of these organization reflected the mentality of the Jews who joined. They regarded anti-Semitism as a secularized version of antiquated religious bigotry. Moreover, they regarded themselves as citizens of their country, and combated anti-Semitism as not only an affront to Jews but also to liberal or republican values. This mentality was vindicated by the decline of anti-Semitism in western and central Europe before the First World War. Anti-Semitic political parties won fewer votes and seats, and anti-Semitic newspapers such as Drumont's *La Libre Parole* went bankrupt for lack of subscribers.

1881

In contrast to the non-violent nature of anti-Semitism in western and central Europe was the outbreak of pogroms in the Russian Empire, beginning in the spring of 1881 – a turning point in modern Jewish history. In March 1881, Tsar Alexander II was assassinated by anarchists, bringing his son Alexander III to the imperial throne. The new tsar was among those who blamed his father's liberalizing policies for unleashing the forces that led to his premature death, leading the young tsar in a reactionary direction. His chief influence was Constantin Pobedonostsev, the principal spokesman of political conservatism, who regarded democracy as "the falsehood of our time." Pobedenostsev also believed that the peasantry should be suppressed and denied education, and that freedom of the press should be severely limited. As a solution to the Jewish problem, he believed that one-third of the Jews should be baptized, one-third should be forced to emigrate, and one-third should perish.

By April (Easter)1881, generally a time when religious fervor and anti-Jewish sentiment were on the rise, pogroms broke out all over the Pale of Settlement. Two hundred Jewish communities were attacked. Until recently, historians debated whether these outbursts were spontaneous or organized by the government and, if the latter, whether they were organized by the central government or locally. Those who claimed that the violence was organized by the tsar claim that he authorized the pogroms to deflect attention from more pressing issues. However, recent scholarship has shown that, as a rule, the tsar would never have encouraged the lawlessness associated with pogroms, lest it escalate into attacks on other elements of Russian society (some historians refer to this attitude as "Pugachevaphobia" in reference to an overriding tsarist fear of a general peasant uprising like the one led by Pugachev in 1773). The upshot is that the pogroms were supported by local police, who erroneously believed that the tsar had authorized them to support and participate in the violence.

For Jews in this part of the world, this was the most traumatic experience for Jews since 1648. It was especially traumatic for maskilim and other Jews who had begun during the reign of Alexander II to believe that Russia was becoming a western country, and had started to participate in Russian life and culture. For traditional Jews, the pogroms were just another episode that characterized the ephemeral nature of Jewish life in exile. For maskilim, the pogroms caused major disillusionment.

The physical devastation of the pogroms was aggravated by subsequent anti-Jewish legislation. In May 1881, the new Minister of the Interior, Count Ignatiev, blamed the pogroms on the Jews' economic exploitation of the peasantry. Jews, he claimed, had sold the peasants the very liquor that made them drunk and violent. The count set up sixteen commissions to investigate the causes of the pogroms more rigorously, one in each province of the Pale. Five out of sixteen suggested abolishing the Pale of Settlement and letting Jews settle in the Russian interior.

Instead, the count imposed a series of "temporary" laws in May 1882, which came to be known as the May Laws. According to the May Laws, there was to be no new Jewish settlement in the villages of the Pale, and no Jewish leasing or managing estates in the Pale. In addition, Jews were prohibited from conducting business on Sundays or Christian holidays. Though officially temporary, the May Laws remained in effect until 1917, leading to sporadic expulsions from villages (like the one described at the end of *Fiddler on the Roof*). These laws were demographically and economically devastating. The curtailment on Jewish settlement in villages without the admission of Jews to larger cities meant further overcrowding in the small and medium-sized towns of the Pale. Overcrowding meant increased economic competition and impoverishment. The ban on Jews leasing estates deprived many Jews of a vital source of income. Most devastating, perhaps, was the prohibition of working on Sundays and Christian holidays. Coupled with the Jewish prohibition of working on Saturday and Jewish holidays, this meant that Jews in the Pale were prohibited from working for more than one-third of the year.

Outside the Pale, moreover, the tsarist regime imposed a severe *numerus clausus*. From 1889 to 1895, no Jewish lawyers were admitted to the Russian bar, and the number of Jewish students admitted to Russian universities was significantly curtailed. In 1891, Jews were expelled from Moscow and St. Petersburg. Along with the May Laws, these policies marked a reversal of the Russification policy that had been followed since Nicholas I.

Jewish responses to the pogroms and the May Laws reflected a growing sense that, barring any radical changes in Russian politics or society, there was little or no future for Jews in Russia. The most widespread response was emigration, primarily to America. More than 2 million Jews emigrated from the Pale to the United States between 1881 and 1924. As a worldview, emigration reflected a sense that, though Jewish life in Russia was over, Jews could still make a good life elsewhere in the diaspora.

The westward exodus of Jews from Russia made Jews in western and especially central Europe very nervous. Fearing that an influx of unacculturated *Ostjuden* would undermine their recent acceptance into mainstream society, Jews in western and central Europe moved quickly to shuffle the newly arriving *Ostjuden* off to America as quickly as possible, and to acculturate those who remained with even greater alacrity. Such concerns were justified. In Hungary, the possibility of an influx of *Ostjuden* after 1881 became a central plank of Viktor Istóczy, Hungary's most outspoken anti-Semite. A blood libel in 1882 against the largely unacculturated Jews of Tiszaeszlár, a small village in northeastern Hungary, fed this xenophobic concern about the *Ostjuden*, part of the reason why this incident escalated into a national crisis and trial.

Among those Jews who chose to remain in Russia, many joined the Russian Socialist Party, on the assumption that social revolution would eliminate anti-Semitism. To be sure, Jewish labor organization had preceded 1881. A Jewish working class had emerged in the Pale by the 1870s, and some Jewish workers had joined the socialist movement even before 1881. For others, the decision to join seemed obvious. Russian socialists, after all, had condemned the pogroms as counterrevolutionary. By 1897, Russian-Jewish socialists had organized a separate Jewish wing of the general Socialist Party, which came to be known as the Bund. Initially, the aim of the Bund was to bring socialism to the Jewish street – that is, teaching Jews in Yiddish about the benefits of social revolution.

Zionism

The most dramatic Jewish response to the pogroms was a renewed sense of Jewish nationalism among disillusioned Russian maskilim, which resulted in the birth of Zionism. Zionism refers to an ideology and political movement that aimed at creating a Jewish homeland in the Land of Israel. As such, Zionism was fundamentally different from the messianic return to Zion, though referring perhaps to a spatially similar movement. The return to Zion was a divinely driven movement; Zionism was primarily a secular (with the lone exception of religious Zionism) and humanistic endeavor. Furthermore, Zionism emerged as a movement in the context of the age of nationalism. The beginnings of Zionism coincided with Italian unification, Germany unification, and – as some Europeans termed the Civil War – the American war of national unification. Moses Hess, a German-Jewish socialist turned Jewish nationalist, regarded nationalism as a natural development, and noted in *Rome and Jerusalem* how Italians and Jews rediscovered an ancient national heritage and recast it in nineteenth-century terms. Like other national movements, the realization of Zionist aims was a tortuous process. Though Zionism wound up as the great success story of modern Jewish history, its success was by no means inevitable.

In retrospect, Zionism solved different problems for different groups of Jews. For Jews in western and central Europe and America, Zionism created a new sense of honor, improved their image, and combated negative stereotypes such as Jews being weak, bookish, unproductive, racially inferior. For Jews in eastern Europe, Zionism provided a refuge from persecution, pogroms, anti-Jewish legislation, and poverty.

The impact of Zionism was not only in creating a new center of Jewish life, but creating for Jews a secular alternative to various religious identities. By the beginning of the twentieth century, Zionists began to take over Jewish communal leadership. Zionism introduced new possibilities, especially for heretofore marginal elements in the Jewish community, such as women.

As a movement and an ideology, Zionism began in earnest after 1881 with a renewed sense of Jewish nationalism, articulated most vividly by Moses Lieb Lilienblum and Lev Pinsker. Lilienblum wrote in response to Judah Lieb Gordon, who was among the few maskilim whose view of the future was largely unaffected by the events of 1881. When Gordon reiterated his call for political emancipation and internal Jewish reform as the solution to the problems of the Jews even after 1881, Lilienblum responded with an essay "Let Us Not Confuse the Issues," in which he rejected Gordon's aims in favor of a nationalist revival. Even more powerful was Pinsker's essay "Auto-emancipation," in which he attributed the travails of the Jews to an exaggerated reliance on the state to improve their lot. Only by emancipating themselves, Pinsker argued, could Jews escape persecution. The ideas articulated by Lilienblum and Pinkser laid a cornerstone for political Zionism.

Alongside these political ideas was the emergence of practical Zionist initiatives in the form of two settlement movements: Hovevei Zion (Lovers of Zion) and BILU, an acronym for *Bet Ya'akov Lechu ve-Nelcha* (House of Jacob Come Let Us Depart, from Isaiah 2:5). Like Pinsker and Lilienblum, these were secular Jews who were disillusioned by the pogroms of 1881. These organizations advocated resettling Russian and Romanian Jews in the Land of Israel, and formed local organizations in dozens of Jewish communities in the Pale and in Romania to this end. In addition, they founded several dozen settlements in the Land of Israel after 1881.

These new settlements transformed the Yishuv, the collective term for Jewish settlements in the Land of Israel. The Old Yishuv, the term for Jewish settlements in the Land of Israel prior to 1881, was demographically skewed, consisting mainly of yeshiva students and older men who had opted to die in the Land of Israel with the hope of being buried on the Mount of Olives, and thereby to be among the first to be resurrected with the advent of the Messianic Age. Most Jews in the Old Yishuv, moreover, were traditionalists who lived in Jaffa, the Old City of Jerusalem, and two or three other towns. Most did not work, but were supported by the Haluka, a system of annual charitable donation sent by diaspora Jewish communities to support the Jews in the Land of Israel. The language of the Old Yishuv was a diverse collection of Jewish languages and European and Middle Eastern vernaculars.

The Zionist settlers who arrived after 1881 were secular young men and women who founded agricultural settlements. Though secular, they borrowed from the language of the Bible and rabbinic tradition in defining their secular Zionist aims. They came to be known as *halutzim* (pioneers) engaged in a process of Aliyah (ascent) to the Land of Israel. Implicit in the nascent political and practical Zionism were a critique of traditional Judaism and the limitations it imposed on Jewish productivity by prohibiting work on the Sabbath and festivals; a frustration with Jewish passivity, particularly the traditional Jewish notion of passively awaiting the Messiah for redemption;

and a rejection of *shtadlanut* (advocacy for the Jewish community), the predominant Jewish political strategy, which resorted to backdoor tactics by well-connected individuals.

Conditions for Jewish settlement at the end of the nineteenth century were difficult, to say the least. Centuries of Turkish mismanagement had left the land untamed and the infrastructure in tatters. Bands of Bedouin robber bands harassed settlers. Trade was minimal, often impeded by drought and swarms of locusts. Nonetheless, during the First Aliyah (1882–1903), 25,600 Jews settled in Palestine. Most went there as refugees with little ideological motivation. Ninety-five percent settled in towns, and only 5 percent on the land. But those who did settle on the land established a few key settlements such as Petah Tikva and Rosh Pina. By 1900, there were 50,000 Jews in the Land of Israel, including 5,000 in twenty villages.

Among these early *halutzim* was Eliezer ben-Yehuda (1858–1922, born Eliezer Perlman). Ben-Yehuda was born in Lithuania into a Hasidic family. In 1871, he was sent to a modern yeshiva in Polotsk to study with his uncle. The head of the yeshiva was secretly a maskil, and introduced young Eliezer to Haskalah literature. In 1877, he graduated from Dvinsk Gymnasium. In 1878, amid the Russo-Turkish war and the struggle by Balkan peoples for national liberation, ben-Yehuda began thinking about a Jewish national revival, in terms of land and language, and planned to move to the Land of Israel. The same year, he went to Paris to study medicine, so he would have an income in Israel. In 1879, he published his first essay in Smolenskin's *Hashacar* called "*She'ela lohata*", (The Burning Question), in which he began to articulate his nationalist vision.

While in Paris, he met George Selikovitch, a Jewish traveler who had spoken Hebrew with Jews in North Africa and Central Asia. From Selikovitch, Ben-Yehuda realized that Hebrew might not be an entirely dead language. Later in 1879, he contracted tuberculosis, quit medical school, and prepared to relocate to a more favorable climate in the Land of Israel. To this end, he attended an Alliance school in order to obtain a teaching post in Israel. There he attended lectures by Joseph Halevy, an Assyriologist who had already advocated the coining of new Hebrew words. In 1880, ben-Yehuda entered Rothschild Hospital in Paris for treatment, where he met A. M. Luncz, who spoke to him in Sephardic Hebrew and told him that in Jerusalem, Jews from different communities spoke Sephardic Hebrew to one another. This further reinforced Ben Yehudah's belief that Hebrew was a living language and a means of reunifying the Jewish people.

In 1881, he arrived in Palestine, and married his childhood sweetheart. Beginning in October of that year, they decided to speak only in Hebrew, thus becoming perhaps the first Hebrew-speaking household since biblical times. They even posed as Orthodox Jews to be around the more Hebrew-literate Orthodox community. In 1881, Ben Yehuda founded Tehiyat Yisrael (The Revival of Israel), which had five aims: working the land, creating a modern nationalist Hebrew literature, providing national and universal education for young people, actively opposing the Halukah system, in addition to reviving Hebrew as a spoken language.

The practical Zionists convened conferences in 1882 and 1884, the first in Focşani and the second in Kattowitz. The first was significant in that the local traditional rabbi presided; despite its secular aims, Zionism had not yet alienated the traditional Jewish world of eastern Europe. At Kattowitz, representatives of local settlement chapters, while discussing their goals, agreed that they needed western European leadership to enhance their prestige and improve their political connections. Ideally they hoped to attract the leadership of a Rothschild or Moses Montefiore. Instead, they found their leadership at the end of the 1890s in Theodore Herzl.

Theodore Herzl's arrival on the Zionist scene in 1897 is often regarded as the conventional birth of Zionism, despite nearly two decades of Russian Zionist activity. His leadership is a textbook case of "leadership from the periphery." Born in Budapest, Herzl was raised in a bilingual, bicultural environment speaking German and Hungarian, and embraced Viennese and Magyar culture. It is useful in this regard to compare Herzl with the early Prague Zionists. Like Herzl, the Prague Zionists lived between two cultures and languages: German and Czech. Each gravitated away from the dominant culture, Herzl toward Viennese and the Prague Zionists toward Czech culture.

Herzl was largely assimilated. He had a bar mitzvah but had to have the blessings transliterated into Latin characters. He considered himself Viennese first and Hungarian second; his Jewish identity came a distant third. Until the age of 17, he lived in Budapest at a time when the city was largely devoid of anti-Semitism. He then moved with his family to Vienna, where he had his first anti-Semitic encounters. He was called *"Sau-Jud"* (Jew-pig) by a passerby. More importantly, when he entered university he was denied entry into a fraternity on the grounds that Jews lacked honor, precluding him from participating in the central fraternity activity: dueling.

His alleged lack of honor spurred him to overcome the limits imposed by his Jewishness by helping all Jews achieve honor. Eventually, his search for honor would lead him to Zionism. Prior to Zionism, though, he contemplated the mass conversion of the Jews of Vienna in a dramatic, public midday ceremony in front of Saint Stephen's Cathedral. He then proposed having a dozen Jews challenge and best a dozen Christians in a series of duels. After discarding these ideas, he noted that the distinguishing feature between honorable and non-honorable peoples was having a national homeland, and concluded that the acquisition of a homeland would restore honor to the Jews.

His anti-Semitic encounters, moreover, were galvanized by witnessing the Dreyfus Affair, which convinced him that anti-Semitism and the Jewish Question were endemic to Jewish life in the diaspora. "The Jewish question," he wrote in 1896, "still exists. It would be foolish to deny it. It exists wherever Jews live in perceptible numbers. Where it does not yet exist, it will be brought by Jews in the course of their migrations." He thus concluded that the creation of a Jewish homeland was the only means through which Jews could escape anti-Semitism.

To this end, he decided to convene the First Zionist Congress in 1897 as a grand ceremony with himself presiding. The problem was that no Jewish community in western or central Europe was willing to host the congress. The idea of creating a Jewish state in the Middle East and expecting European Jews to relocate to a area that was largely swampland and deserts seemed ludicrous and was embarrassing to emancipated Jews. Thus, the Jews of Paris, Vienna, Berlin, London, Geneva, and Budapest refused to host the conference. In addition, none of the leaders of western or central European Jewry agreed to attend or even endorse the congress. As a result, the first Zionist Congress took place in Basle, Switzerland. Other than Herzl and Max Nordau, all of those in attendance were members of Hovevei Zion or BILU from Russia, Galicia, or Romania.

Herzl's Zionism was almost exclusively political Zionism. His chief goal was to obtain a charter from the sultan; he also wanted to create a refuge for less fortunate, persecuted Jews. He did not expect western or central European Jews to move to Israel, and had little interest in founding a settlement or transforming the Jews.

He presented his Zionist vision principally in two works: a treatise called *Der Judenstaat* and a utopian novel called *Altneuland*. *Der Judenstaat* (mistranslated as *The Jewish State*; "The Jews' State" would be a more apt translation – "The Jewish State" is a translation of "Der jüdische Staat") was Herzl's Zionist manifesto. *Altneuland* (Old-New Land) was a utopian novel written in 1902 but set "far in the future" in 1923. In it, the main character leaves civilization for twenty years. On his return home, he stops in Palestine and notes the changes that have taken place.

Thus, his novel and manifesto expressed the same vision using two different genres. In each work, his vision of the Jewish state differs from the eventual State of Israel in four respects. First, Herzl did not envision the language of the Jewish state as Hebrew, but rather "German, French, or some other civilized language." In addition, he did not envision a major presence of religious Jews; rabbis in the Jewish state would be like soldiers, living apart from the general population, just as soldiers are housed in barracks and summoned when needed to perform specific functions. Third, Herzl regarded socialism as too radical and extremist. Thus, his Jewish state has no socialist presence; rather, he envisioned the economic organization of the Jewish state as a network of Saint-Simonian agricultural cooperatives: shared labor with private ownership. Finally, Herzl never envisioned a conflict with the indigenous Arab population. He imagined himself wearing a suit with tails and attending the opera – just as he would do in Vienna or Paris. His image of the flag of the Jewish state – seven stars in a circle – exemplified its lack of Jewishness: seven stars symbolized the seven-hour work week.

Herzl presented much of this vision in the Basle Program that he issued at the First Zionist Congress. This program elicited strong criticism from five directions, three from outside the Zionist movement and two from within it. Socialist Jews regarded Zionism as capitalist and as an imperialist ploy. Orthodox Jews, disturbed by its secular character, condemned Zionism as religious heresy. Zadok ha-Cohen Rabinowitz of Lublin, the principal Orthodox critic of Zionism, regarded Zionism as a ruse by Reform Jews:

> For me the matter is perfectly plain. The enlightened ones and the Reformers who imperil the existence of our people have discovered that through blatant unbelief they will not succeed in driving Israel from its faith and religion. Therefore, they have thrown off the garment of assimilation and put on a cloak of zeal so that they appear to be zealous on behalf of Israel.

Reform rabbis were equally critical, regarding Zionism as pure folly and contrary to the natural course of history:

> What more can one say if people are so naïve as to believe that European Jews will hand over their money to purchase Palestine from the Turks to create a Jewish organization that will reverse the entire development of the Jewish nation. Eighteen hundred years ago history made its decision regarding Jewish nationhood with the dissolution of the Jewish state."

Within the Zionist movement itself, two critiques of the Basle Program emerged. Some Zionists believed that the pressing need for a refuge superseded the need to secure the Land of Israel as the Jewish homeland. These Jews came to be known as Territorialists, and broke with the Zionist movement in 1903 when the movement rejected the British government offer of Uganda as a Jewish homeland. In addition, there were Russian Zionists, most notably Ahad Ha'am, who regarded Herzl's Zionism as too narrow, not attuned to the needs and lifestyle of eastern European Jews, and lacking a plan to transform the Jews themselves.

The notion of transformation was incorporated into Zionism soon after the First Zionist Congress by Max Nordau. In an essay called "Muscular Jews," Nordau envisioned Zionism as a way to transform Jews into physically stronger people, thus alleviating what he regarded as the central malady of diaspora Jews: "In the narrow Jewish street our limbs soon forgot their gay movements ... the fear of persecution turned our powerful voices into frightened whispers." With this aim in mind, Nordau helped Zionists found sports clubs. The names of these clubs – Bar Kochba, Samson, and of course Maccabee – harkened back to the physically powerful Jewish warriors of a heroic Jewish past.

Subsequently, other Zionist leaders added alternative notions of Zionism as a way of transforming Jews. Each of the varieties of Zionism that had appeared by the First World War – Cultural, Spiritual, Labor, and Religious Zionism – offered a distinct means of transformation. Cultural Zionism was the brainchild of Asher Ginsberg, commonly known by his pen name, Ahad Ha'am (literally, One of the People). Born in Skvira near Kiev in Ukraine, Ginsberg was the son of a wealthy Hasidic lumber merchant. He was given a traditional Jewish upbringing and education, and taught himself Russian, German, English, Latin, French, and German. He was deeply influenced by Maimonides' *Guide to the Perplexed* and read Haskalah literature. As a young man, he abandoned his Hasidic upbringing in favor of a rationalist outlook. In 1884, he moved to Odessa, and joined the local Hovevei Zion chapter. Lev Pinkser was his mentor.

In 1889, he published a critique of Hovevei Zion's settlement policy, claiming that without proper education, the settlers would lack the dedication to succeed. In 1897, he founded a secret society called Bnai Moshe (Sons of Moses) to realize his aim of improving the settlers' education and disseminating Hebrew literature. In 1896, he became the editor of *Ha-Shiloach*, the leading Zionist newspaper. Following the First Zionist Congress, he criticized Herzl's plan as premature and ineffective without a strategy for cultural transformation.

Ginsberg's emphasis on transforming the Jews stemmed from the fact that he regarded assimilation rather than anti-Semitism as the greatest threat to Jews. He believed that Jews in western and central Europe had paid far too great a price for emancipation, as he noted in one of his most important and oft-quoted essays, *"Avdut be-Toch Herut"* (Slavery within Freedom): "Do I envy the rights enjoyed by my brothers in the West? Absolutely not – not them and not their reward. Even if I have no rights, I did not sacrifice my soul in order to get them." Ginsberg proposed the creation of secular Jewish culture as a buttress against cultural assimilation, comprising Hebrew as a spoken and literary language, Jewish history and literature, and a general revaluation of Judaism in all its complexity from religious into cultural-historical terms. Thus, he was nicknamed Zionism's "agnostic rabbi." Ginsberg also believed that the creation of a Jewish state did not mean the immediate end of diaspora Jewish life. Rather, he saw the proposed Jewish state as the center of world Jewry, radiating cultural influence via secular Jewish culture to Jews throughout the world.

Spiritual Zionism was the creation of Aaron David Gordon (1856-1922). Like Ginsberg, Gordon was raised in a traditional Jewish home, which he rejected in favor of Haskalah. After 1881, he became a Zionist. An avowed secularist, he went to Palestine in 1904 imbued with the pioneering spirit of the Halutz movement. Although much older than most Zionist pioneers, he nonetheless joined an agricultural settlement. Within a short time, he became a guru and the spiritual mentor of the younger members of his settlement. He preached a message of transformation through labor and, more specifically, through working the soil of the Land of Israel. His mantra became the slogan for generations of Zionist pioneers: We have come to the land to build it, and to be transformed by it (*Anu Banu Artza Livnot u-lehibanot ba*). If Ginsberg was Zionism's agnostic rabbi, Gordon was the movement's secular mystic.

Alongside the emergence of spiritual and cultural Zionism was the rise of Labor or Marxist Zionism. This brand of Zionism emerged following a second wave of Russian pogroms in 1903–6. Compared to the pogroms of 1881, these pogroms resulted in far more loss of life. Moreover, whereas the Russian Socialists had condemned the pogroms of 1881 as counterrevolutionary, they endorsed the second wave of pogroms as a revolutionary blow against Jewish capitalists. This set off a wave of disillusionment among Jews who had joined the Russian Socialist Party after 1881. Many of these, recognizing that social revolution in Russia would not eliminate the inherent presence of anti-Semitism, but unwilling to abandon socialism entirely, created a hybrid of socialism and Zionism: Marxist Zionism.

As the name connotes, Marxist Zionists advocated creating a Jewish state, but also believed that class struggle would be an inherent feature within that state – that the Jewish state would be shaped by social revolution just like any other state. The immigration of Marxist Zionists to Palestine after 1903 delineated a new stage of immigration and settlement, the Second Aliyah. Prior to 1903, most Jewish settlements were small and teetering on the brink of collapse. Marxist Zionism, when combined with cultural and spiritual Zionism, forged a new, more vigorous type of agricultural settlement: the kibbutz. The kibbutz was a collective settlement whose members pooled all resources, and shared all goods and labor. In addition, the kibbutz movement was infused with the socialist notion of active armed self-defense, teaching its members to use weapons and defend the kibbutz from vagabounds and other threats. In this way, the kibbutz movement accomplished two tasks that were crucial to the development of Zionism and the expansion of the Yishuv: transforming city Jews into farmers, and civilian Jews into soldiers.

Among the early success stories of the kibbutz movement was a young Russian Jew named David Green. After moving to Palestine and joining a kibbutz, he replaced Green, his "diaspora" name, with a more heroic one: David ben-Gurion (literally, son of a lion). Ben-Gurion, who would later become the first prime minister of the State of Israel, added two components to the Zionist endeavor that reflected a seamless synthesis of Marxist and spiritual Zionism. First, he argued that it was not enough for all Jews to engage in labor; all labor on the Yishuv had to be performed by Jews, menial as well as romantic. Second, he advocated settling the entire Land of Israel – not only the most fertile areas of Galilee, but also the Negev Desert. For this reason, the university named for him is called Ben-Gurion University of the Negev.

All told, 30,000 Jews came to the Land of Israel during the Second Aliyah, many if not most consciously motivated by labor Zionism. Although 70 percent eventually returned to Europe, those who remained created the institutions that shaped settlement and the state: the kibbutz and the Sachnut (Jewish agency). The key year during the Second Aliyah was 1909, which witnessed the creation of a kibbutz movement that united the individual collective settlements; and the founding of a new city on the outskirts of Jaffa: Tel Aviv.

The common thread between the varieties of Zionism was their secular demeanor. Yet there was one brand of Zionism, religious Zionism, that found a way to synthesize religious practice with Zionist aims. Religious Zionism originated in a controversy that took place in 1888 between secular Zionist settlers and the rabbinate of the Old Yishuv. That year was the first sabbatical year – when, according to biblical tradition, the land of Israel was to lie fallow – but there were secularists farming the land. When the rabbis asked the settlers to refrain from agriculture for a year, the secular settlers refused, on the grounds that to cease expansion on a brand new settlement was tantamount to total collapse; in addition, the settlers refused the rabbis' offer of sharing for the year in the Haluka system.

In response, with no authority over the secular Zionist settlers, the rabbis began writing to rabbis in the diaspora asking them to appeal to the settlers or to their supporters abroad. The rabbis in the diaspora divided over whether or not the settlers should observe the sabbatical year. For those who condemned the religious indifference and intransigence of the settlers, this event crystallized their religious worldview, leading to the emergence of a form of religious orthodoxy within Russian Jewry. From this point on, an increasingly politicized Orthodoxy would engage Zionism and other secular Jewish currents at their own game, publishing an Orthodox Jewish newspaper and forming an Orthodox political party: Agudat Israel (the Party of Israel).

By contrast, those rabbis who supported the settlers were among the first to reconcile the seemingly irreconcilable dictates of Jewish tradition with secular Zionist aims. In 1902, this mentality crystallized in the creation of Mizrachi, the religious Zionist movement. This name was chosen as a *double entendre*. Mizrachi (literally, eastern or eastward) is an allusion to the advent of the Messiah, who traditionally is said to arrive from the east. In addition, Mizrachi was a contraction of *merkaz ruhani* (spiritual center). Not to be confused with Gordon's secular spirituality through labor, Mizrachi believed that the rebuilt Land of Israel, even if rebuilt by secularists as a secular state, was an indispensable element of Jewish rejuvenation.

The most eloquent spokesman of this position was Abraham Isaac Kook, also known simply as Rav Kook. Kook, a mystic in addition to being an accomplished rabbinic scholar, believed that secular Zionists were performing a religious act without realizing it. Kook was able to bridge the gaps between the various Zionist camps and foster a sense of solidarity across seemingly irreconcilable positions.

In a sense, Gordon's call for the amelioration of the status of Jewish women in matters of marriage and divorce paralleled similar efforts by Jewish women themselves. Unable to find recourse within the framework of a male-dominated Jewish community, Jewish women appealed to Russian courts to intervene. Periodically the latter did intervene and helped liberate Jewish women from recalcitrant husbands.

Each of the varieties of Zionism embraced some practical strategy and program for settling the land, building a state, and transforming the Jews. There were limits as to how far this transformation progressed during the early years of the movement. The experiences of women in the Zionist movement, and especially in the settlements of the Yishuv, attest to these limits. Some women, for example, were dismayed by the contrast between the utopian egalitarianism that pervaded Zionist activities in Russia and the sexist division of labor on the settlements in the Land of Israel. Often, women who had been inculcated with a romantic notion of reclaiming the land and making the desert bloom were assigned instead to the kitchen and the kindergarten – the very gender roles they had hoped to evade by becoming Zionists in the first place. A generation would pass before traditional gender roles would be eviscerated on the New Yishuv.

Diaspora nationalism: Autonomism and the Bund

Zionism was not the only form of Jewish nationalism that appeared after 1881. There were also two forms of diaspora nationalism: Autonomism and the Bund. In retrospect, diaspora Jewish nationalism may seem silly and short-sighted in light of the destruction of European Jewry during the Holocaust, and the eventual triumph of Zionism. Until the end of the 1930s, though, these political movements were extremely popular.

Autonomism was a political ideology propounded by Simon Dubnow (1860-1941). Born into a traditional Jewish family in Mstsislavl, Belorussia, Dubnow received a traditional Jewish upbringing before rebelling as a young man. From 1880 to 1906, he traveled between his hometown, St. Petersburg (where he lived illegally), Vilna, and Odessa, where he joined Asher Ginsberg's circle of intellectuals. Odessa was especially important in his intellectual and political development. Since the early nineteenth century, Odessa had been the great Russian exception, and a city of contradictory experiences for Russian Jews. Odessa was part of Novorussia, but not part of the Pale of Settlement. It was a port city that was open, multiethnic, and multinational.

It was administered separately, and exceptionally western. In Odessa, civic equality for Jews was realized *de facto* by the mid-nineteenth century.

For Jews like Dubnow, long before any other Russian Jews, Odessa instilled a sense that emancipation was possible in Russia. The multiethnic populace of Odessa, moreover, gave Dubnow a sense that Jews could remain Jews even as citizens. This view was evident in his understanding of Jewish history. In the diaspora, he argued, Jews had lost certain normal attributes such as territory and political sovereignty, but had been compensated by a special social system and communal ideology embedded in the autonomous Jewish community.

This view reflected his overall understanding of Jewish national development. Dubnow believed that every nation went through three stages of national development: a tribal stage; a political-territorial stage, in which most nations were situated at the end of the nineteenth century; and a post-territorial cultural stage, in which territory was no longer necessary for nationhod. Jews, he argued, had moved beyond the political-territorial stage in 70 C.E., and were the only nation to have reached the third and ultimate stage of national development. Hence, he regarded Zionism as retrograde nationalism, trying to revert atavistically back to the second stage. In this context of national development, Dubnow conceptualized the future of world Jewry: Autonomism.

The basic concept of Autonomism was cultural autonomy for Jews in the diaspora. Inspired by the Austro-Marxist notion of a community of nationalities enjoying equal rights in a single state, Autonomism recast the premodern notion of corporate autonomy in a new political garb. Dubnow believed that the corporate Jewish community organized around religious laws had held the Jews together as a people for centuries, but its usefulness had expired in age of modern politics. As such, Autonomism had two components: political emancipation and cultural autonomy in the form of a national language, schools, literature, and theater. In contrast to Asher Ginsberg, who regarded the language of the Jews as Hebrew, Dubnow defined the Jewish national language as the language of the center of world Jewry: Yiddish. Several decades later, the aims of Autonomism would be realized in interwar Poland and, in some ways, in twentieth-century America.

The other diaspora Jewish national movement was the Bund, shorthand for *Algemeyner Yidisher Arbeter Bund in Lite, Poyln, un Rusland* (General Jewish Workers' Party in Lithuania, Poland, and Russia). Originally organized in 1897 as a Jewish wing of the Russian Socialist Party in the wake of the Kishinev pogrom, the Bund broke with its mother organization in 1905. Initially it had 25,000–30,000 members. The Bund had three main aims: socialist revolution, national cultural autonomy for Jews, and the creation of socialist secular Jewish culture in preparation for Jewish life in the postrevolutionary world. Like Autonomism, the Bund advocated Yiddish as the national language of the Jews.

Bundists were in conflict with virtually all other groups of Jews. To traditionalists and the politicized Orthodox, Bundism was even more
antireligious than Zionism. Zionists at least spoke Hebrew and were trying
to rebuild the ancestral homeland; there was no such mystical rationalization
for the Bund. Liberal, assimilationist Jews regarded the Bund as a radical
Jewish fringe. Zionists regarded Bundists as assimilationists; Bundists
regarded Zionists as capitalist imperialists, and totally unrealistic in their
aims. Labor Zionists and Bundists, while sharing some aims in common and
periodically cooperating to work toward them, generally regarded each other
as a corruption of authentic Jewish socialism which was dangerously mis-
leading its followers.

The most challenging aspect of Autonomism and Bundism was impugning traditional Jewish culture without impugning diaspora itself, epitomized
by their endorsement of Yiddish as a viable secular national language.
Previously, Yiddish had been assailed by every progressive movement (Reform,
Modern Orthodox, Zionism) as outdated and the epitome of diaspora decay.
The challenge of reviving Yiddish and creating a secular Yiddish culture was
eased by the literary revival of Yiddish literature during the 1870s. Initially
an offshoot of the revival of Hebrew that began in the Russian Haskalah,
Yiddish, too, became a language of social criticism. In general, Yiddish writers presented alternatives to the difficulties of Jewish life that did not entail
leaving the diaspora.

The leading Yiddish writers in this respect were Shalom Rabinowitz
(also known as Shalom Aleichem) and Isaac Leib Peretz. Rabinowitz was
born in Ukraine and received an upbringing that was a mishmash of tradition and change. He studied in a *heder* and a gymnasium; his father, though
traditional, loved Haskalah Hebrew literature. Rabinowitz wrote in Hebrew,
yet he regarded his most serious works as those in Yiddish. His first Yiddish
work was a dictionary of curses used by stepmothers. He used the pseudonym Shalom Aleichem for the first time in 1883. In 1905, he emigrated to
the United States. Through his most famous literary character, Tevye the
Dairyman, he expressed a sharp criticism of traditional Jewish life. The stories of Tevye and his family illustrated that traditional Judaism could no
longer sustain the complex fabric of Jewish family life, and that Jews were
politically weak and completely vulnerable to tsarist decrees. In one especially poignant exchange, Tevye attempts to explain his daughter Chava's
devastating and scandalous marriage to a Russian Christian peasant by
quoting (or misquoting) a rabbinic aphorism. In response, his wife scolds
him for spending too much time quoting the rabbis and not enough time
being a good father. Tradition could unwittingly unravel the fabric of
Jewish family life.

No less critical was Isaac Leib Peretz (1851–1915). Born in Zamość, he
was raised as a traditional Jew but acquired a secular education independently. He was married by arrangement at 18, but rebelled, divorced his wife,

and married his sweetheart. During the 1870s, he wrote Hebrew and Polish poems and stories. He regarded Yiddish, at best, as a temporary vehicle through which to reach the Jewish masses. In 1876, he completed law school and was admitted to the Russian bar.

The events of 1881 transformed him, and he came to regard Yiddish as a way of identifying with less fortunate Jews, though he continued to write in Hebrew. In 1886, his license to practice law was revoked on false pretenses, at which point he moved to Warsaw and was employed by the Jewish community. He was critical of anti-Semites, but also of Jewish intolerance of other Jews. His most famous story and sharpest critique of traditional Jewish life was *"Bontsche Schweig"* (Bontsche the Silent). This story tells of an oppressed, impoverished Jew who, despite an unrelentingly difficult life, remains silent and never wavers in his faith in God. After his death, he stands trial before a heavenly tribunal. The prosecuting angel, who ordinarily lists the misdeeds of the deceased, merely says, "All his life he was silent; now I, too, shall be silent." At this point, with no misdeeds arrayed against him, Bontsche is offered anything in paradise. He asks only for a fresh roll and butter every morning, at which point the prosecuting angel laughs. Bontsche's faith, Peretz shows, had reduced him to the point where, offered all of paradise, he could aspire to nothing more than a roll with butter.

American Jewry and the melting pot, 1881–1914

Amid the explosion of Jewish politics in Russia and the Land of Israel, a less ideological though equally dramatic transformation of Jewish life was taking place in America. After 1881, several million Jewish immigrants arrived on the shores of the New World. These Jews were part of a larger wave of 20 million people who emigrated to the United States from eastern and southern Europe.

Like the previous wave of Jewish immigrants, these Jews tended to be neither the richest nor the poorest, but lower-middle or working-class. Moreover, the most religious Jews tended not to go to America, where, it was believed, "religion went to die." The Jews who went there were moderately traditional or moderately progressive. In contrast to other groups, Jews arrived largely as families. By contrast, most Italian immigrants were single men who traveled to the United States to make money; more than a third returned to Italy. Jews went to America to stay.

Whereas the previous wave of Jewish immigration had taken place during the westward movement, this wave arrived as America was entering its industrial age. Most of these Jews followed the general pattern of settlement and settled in industrial centers, primarily in New York but also in other industrial cities. Most found employment as industrial workers in the harsh condition of small-scale sweatshops. As in Russia, Jewish workers were skilled or semi-skilled and tended toward light industry.

From the beginning of this immigration movement, there were attempts to counter the demographic and economic trends of this immigration movement by settling Jews outside of industrial cities and finding them other jobs. Jacob Schiff, a wealthy Jewish financier, funded the Galveston Project, a settlement initiative that created an absorption center in Galveston, Texas, as a way of diverting Jewish settlers from New York City and the east coast to the Southwest. Many of the present-day Jewish communities along the Mississippi were founded by Jewish immigrants who landed at Galveston. The Am Olam Movement, which started in Odessa in 1881, aimed at settling Jews on agrarian settlements, but ultimately managed to establish only four such settlements: two in South Dakota, one in Louisiana, and one in Oregon.

In contrast to the previous wave, who maintained strong ties to German culture for several generations, Jewish immigrants from eastern Europe arrived as American culture was coming into its own. They were greeted with a powerful appeal to embrace American culture. This impulse was intensified by the mentality within American society: the melting pot.

The native-born Jews (called uptown Jews in reference to New York City) regarded the immigrants (downtown Jews) with a certain ambivalence. On the one hand, they distanced themselves from new immigrants, insisting, in the words of Kaufman Kohler, that "Judaism in America not be ghettoized." On the other, they attempted to Americanize them as quickly as possible. Education Alliance, for example, was founded by uptown Jews to teach Jewish immigrants English, and prepare them for their citizenship exam.

Within the immigrant community, there was a substantial generational difference in the attitudes toward American culture. Within the first generation, some Jews tried desperately to hold on to Old World traditions, while others were determined to make it in America and become Americans. Jews in the latter group, in particular, often sacrificed themselves and their own happiness for the sake of their children's advancement and education. The crowning achievement of these Jews was a child who graduated from high school and was admitted to college. The second generation, schooled in American public schools, immersed itself into American culture.

Prior to 1914, there were several attempts at organizing this large immigrant Jewish community. First, there was the Jewish labor movement. Starting as a series of local neighborhood organizations, Jewish workers eventually organized several of the largest and most powerful labor unions, notably the International Ladies' Garment Workers' Union. There were also attempts to organize an American branch of the Bund, led by Chaim Zhitlowski. The Jewish labor movement did not last for more than a generation. As second-generation immigrants left the workforce and became self-employed or professionals, the labor movement lost much of its constituency.

The American Zionist Movement had the opposite experience. Until 1913, it had few members. Most Jewish immigrants, after all, had opted for America over Israel. The pressure of the melting pot, moreover, dissuaded

immigrants from undermining their status as Americans by joining a movement that was oriented around a different part of the world. This changed
when Louis Brandeis joined the movement. Brandeis, an assimilated lawyer
and an uptown Jew, came into contact with Jewish immigrants as the legal
advocate for the labor movement. Perhaps the most successful and high-
profile American Jew of his time, Brandeis belied any claim that affiliating
with Zionism somehow conflicted with loyalty to America. "Let no American
imagine," he wrote in 1915,

> that Zionism is inconsistent with patriotism. ... Every Irish American
> who contributed toward home rule was a better man and a better
> American for the sacrifice he made. Every American Jew who aids in
> advancing Jewish settlement in Palestine ... will likewise be a better
> man and a better American. ... The Jewish spirit ... is essentially mod-
> ern and essentially American. ... Indeed, loyalty to America demands
> rather that each American Jew become a Zionist.

When he joined the American Zionist Movement in 1913, more than
300,000 Jews followed suit within a few months.

The influx of eastern European Jews transformed the religious landscape of
American Jewry. For the first time, there was a large constituency of traditional, and at least semiobservant, Jews. This prompted Orthodox rabbis,
themselves from eastern Europe, to found in New York in 1898 the Orthodox
Jewish Congregational Union, an umbrella organization for Orthodox congregations. They soon discovered, however, that even observant Jews in
America had no interest in a European-style supracongregational organization. While many congregations joined the Orthodox Union, it took decades
before it emerged as the voice of Orthodox Judaism in America.

Most Jews from eastern Europe regarded classical Reform Judaism as more
akin to Protestantism than to anything Jewish. In order to attract constituents from among these immigrants, progressive rabbis such as Stephen
Wise and Benjamin Szold began to step away from the dictates of the
Pittsburgh Platform. The most significant change was to embrace Zionism,
even before Brandeis validated such a move. Interestingly, these rabbis tended
not to be of German-Jewish origin, but rather were advocates of non-German
Reform. Wise and Szold were Hungarian rabbis whose families in Hungary
had been Neolog and not Reform Jews.

The movement that benefited most from the influx of immigrants was
the nascent Conservative Movement. Founded in the mid-1880s, this movement was minuscule until 1902, when a new leader was imported from
England: the Romanian-born, eastern- and central-European-trained
Genizah scholar Solomon Schechter. Like the other founders of Conservative
Judaism – the Hungarian Alexander Kohut, the Pole Marcus Jastrow, and
the Italian Sabato Morais – Schechter had embraced the moderate non-

German variety of religious innovation. Under his leadership, and owing largely to his overarching notion of religious inclusiveness, Conservative Judaism began to appeal to the traditional but accommodating religious outlook of eastern European Jews. The outlook of Conservative Judaism was also similar to that of the Russian Haskalah, further helping eastern European Jews to find Conservative Judaism highly appealing and familiar.

Schechter, moreover, understood the challenge posed to Jewish survival by the openness of American society. Thus, while he saw that Yiddish had no future in America, he regarded the Hebrew language as essential to Jewish survival in America. He urged American Jews to embrace English and Hebrew as their languages. Not surprisingly, he advocated Zionism as a natural element of American Jewish identity.

The emergence of the United States as one of the largest centers of Jewish life by 1914 – second only to Russia – reflected how world Jewry had been dramatically altered between 1880 and 1914. In addition to a demographic shift, by 1914 there were multiple forms of Jewish identity that were not only non-rabbinic but independent of Judaism and religion entirely. It was entirely possible by 1914 to be a fully committed and even passionate Jew without believing in God or observing a single Jewish law or custom. Of course, secular Judaism itself made profound demands on its adherents, whether a commitment to building a Jewish state or a desire to bring social revolution to the Jewish street. This unprecedentedly diverse constellation of Jewish identities, dispersed more broadly around the world than ever before, would face another set of challenges with the outbreak of the First World War. By 1920, the foundations of social and especially legal emancipation would face a new challenge in the age of ultra-nationalism, fascism, and Nazism.

Chapter 9

From renewal to devastation, 1914–45

The First World War was as much a turning point in Jewish history as in world history. The war brought a triumph of national self-determination and popular sovereignty, epitomized by the collapse of multinational empires in Europe and the rise of ethnically more homogeneous states out of the ashes of the Habsburg, Ottoman, Russian, and German Empires. The interwar years were marked by the triumph of democracy and nationalism, but also by rising xenophobia and fear of communism, which were exacerbated by economic depression. Jews benefited from the benign manifestations of these political impulses – inclusive democratic political definitions of nationalism that included Jews and other minorities, and states that allowed Jews rights and participation – but languished under the darker sides of nationalism and popular sovereignty – right-wing nationalist impulses, and totalitarian regimes. As Europe was redrawn geographically, politically, and ethnically, Jews who, prior to the war, had been one of several religious and ethnic minorities – and, in the Habsburg or Ottoman Empire, often the most favored – found themselves after the war the only minority in an otherwise ethnically and religiously homogeneous successor state.

The war marked the beginning of the end of European imperialism, amid the rise of Arab nationalism and anti-European impulses in the Muslim world. For Jews, the diminishing western presence in the Islamic world accelerated the decline and collapse of Jewish life there. In addition, the war brought Palestine under British control; British imperialist interests, especially in India, undermined attempts to mediate the growing conflict between Jews and Muslims in Palestine. Finally, the war brought an end to unimpeded westward immigration, particularly to America. Henceforth, growing xenophobia would result in a series of quotas on Jewish immigration. The end of Jewish immigration facilitated the rapid Americanization of second-generation American Jews and American Judaism.

The triumph of national self-determination as the dominant political consideration of the age redrew the map of Europe and the Ottoman Empire along national and ethnic lines in the name of national self-determination – the right of every nation to govern itself and not be subject to foreign rule.

This created new possibilities and new difficulties for Jews. Smaller, ethnically more homogeneous states replaced the multinational Habsburg, Ottoman, and Russian Empires. Many thousands of Jews in central and eastern Europe and the Middle East found themselves living in a different country. Poland, which was reunited in 1918 after 123 years, had a population of 3 million Jews who prior to the war had lived in the Russian, Austro-Hungarian, and German Empires. The 900,000 Jews who lived in the Kingdom of Hungary in 1914 found themselves living in six newly created states by 1920: Austria, Czechoslovakia, Yugoslavia, Poland, Romania, and truncated Hungary.

The situation of Jews in these new states depended on a combination of political and economic factors, principally whether the new state regarded itself as a beneficiary or a victim of national self-determination. Jews generally fared better in the former, at least until the end of the 1920s. Some Iraqi nationalists, for example, including King Faisal, lauded the creation of an independent Iraqi state out of the dismembered Ottoman Empire, and reached out to Iraqi Jews and other non-Muslims "because we all belong to one stock, the stock of our noble ancestor Shem; we all belong to that noble race, and there is no distinction between Muslim, Christian, and Jew." In some cases, nationalists were willing to forget the prewar Jewish loyalties to a rival national cause. Czech nationalists, for example regarded their Jewish neighbors as Czechs, although prior to 1914 most had been culturally oriented toward German culture. Jews fared less favorably in states that felt victimized by the post-war settlement, notably German and Hungary, where anti-Semitism reached new heights.

The war also marked the end of the age of progress, and thus fed a growing disillusionment with science, technology, reason, and bourgeois lifestyles and values. This critique had begun to simmer even before the war among urban intellectual elites in a cultural movement called *fin de siècle*. Centered in Paris and Vienna, this movement provided a forum for criticism of a variety of widely accepted cultural norms and scientific conventions. Such criticisms included Freud's challenge to the notion that the human mind was knowable and a reflection of divine or natural beneficence, Albert Einstein's upending of the pillars of Newtonian physics with relativity theory, Arnold Schoenberg's dissent from the rule of musical tonality, Arthur Schnitzler's insertion of interior dialogue in a modern novel, and Franz Kafka's sweeping critique of everything modern.

Kafka's angst, in particular, exemplified the general angst and discontent of the immediate prewar years. His critique of the age paralleled a critique of the pervading Jewish identity of the age. He rejected and was highly critical of his father's liberal, progressive Jewish identity, which, according to Kafka, had been watered down by his entrance into mainstream society. "As a young man, I could not understand how, with the insignificant scrap of Judaism you yourself possessed, you could reproach me for not making an effort to cling to a similar insignificant scrap."

For Jews, the sense of prewar angst was at once mitigated and animated by the ebb and flow of anti-Semitism, illustrated by the trials of two Jews during the early 1910s: Mendel Beilis and Leo Frank. Mendel Beilis was a Jew in Kiev who was accused in a blood libel in 1911. Though the local authorities, judge, and jury were slanted against him, he was eventually acquitted. Leo Frank was a Jewish factory manager in Atlanta, Georgia, who was accused of raping and killing Mary Phagan, a teenage girl who worked in the factory. Frank was arrested, tried and convicted of murder, and sentenced to death. The governor commuted his sentence, but before he was released, a lynch mob hanged him. Seen side by side, the acquittal of Beilis in Russia and the killing of Frank in America, albeit in the American South, underlined an element of unpredictability in the spread of anti-Semitism prior to the war.

The *fin de siècle* was not a Jewish movement, but Jewish intellectuals and literati were conspicuously and disproportionately represented in it – mainly because a disproportionate number of Jews were urban and educated. As these embryonic feelings of discontent matured and expanded during and after the war, there was a sense that the Jewish critique of prewar civilization had contributed to the demise of this world after the war. This was ironic given that the bourgeoisie, the main target of this critique, was also seen as being largely Jewish. Like the apposition of Fischhof and Rothschild into a single Jewish target for all forms of political anti-Semitism, the juxtaposition of the Jewish bourgeoisie and the Jewish cultural critique of the bourgeoisie would become an important foundation stone for the postwar surge of anti-Semitism.

The Great War

The course of the war was surprising almost from the outset. Most military and political leaders presumed that the war would end with quick victories and minimal casualties – hence the waves of excitement when the war began. There was also a misconception that technological advancements would make war faster with less harm to human life; such notions did not anticipate the defensive power of new weapons such as the machine gun, and underestimated the amount of punishment an ordinary foot soldier could withstand, even in the trenches of the Western Front. Most socialist leaders had opposed the war as a capitalist nationalist venture and had promised neutrality. When push came to shove, though, the socialists joined right in. In 1914, Frederick Ebert, the leader of the German Social Democrats, voted for war credits; the power of nationalism overwhelmed international socialism.

Jews were equally swept up by this tide of nationalism. Jews defended their own country even when this meant fighting against other Jews, thus fulfilling a central condition of emancipation. At the same time, Jews who fought for the Central Powers regarded the struggle against Russia as a way of liberating Russian Jews from tsarist tyranny. Zionists, too, shared this perception of the war.

Thousands of Jewish soldiers and officers fought, on both sides of the war. In Italy, there were fifty Jewish generals – one Jewish general for every thousand Italian Jews. In Austria-Hungary, most Jewish officers were reserve officers at the start of the war, mainly in the medical, communications, and transportation corps. During the first year of war, however, the decimation of the front-line and combat officer corps brought most of these Jewish officers to the front, further validating the emancipation of the Jews.

Russian Jews bore the brunt of the war. Much of the Pale of Settlement was located in the heart of the Eastern Front. Jewish civilians were ravaged by both sides, particularly during the chaotic slash-and-burn retreat of the tsar's army. Hundreds of thousands of Russian Jews became refugees. Nearly half fled to the interior of Russia. In recognition of this changing demographic reality, in 1915 the tsar abolished the Pale of Settlement. The demographic shift continued unabated into the 1930s, particularly toward the two Russian capitals. In 1915, the combined Jewish population of Moscow and St. Petersburg was 15,000. By the early 1930s, this number exceeded 300,000. In addition, traditional Jews in Galicia and the Pale of Settlement came into contact with more progressive, assimilated Jews, which helps explain the rapid growth of secular Jewish movements after the war.

Diplomatic initiatives by the Central Powers and the Allied forces worked to the advantage of the Jews. Because there was no clear-cut villain like Hitler or Mussolini, until 1916 it was unclear whether the United States would enter the war, and on which side. A primary diplomatic aim during the first two years of the war was to win the support of the United States. A widely circulated myth contended that the best way to win the support of the US government was to win the support of the American Jewish elite. To this end, German and British officials approached the leaders of the World Zionist Organization with a promise of a Jewish homeland if the United States entered on their side and helped them take Palestine from the Turks.

This is the background to the Balfour Declaration, issued by the British government following the capture of Palestine. In this declaration, the British committed to the "establishment in Palestine of a national home for the Jewish people." The last-minute change in the language of this text from "the national home" to "a national home" would lay the basis for subsequent disputes as to the specifications of this homeland. In any case, this was a major triumph for Zionism. In retrospect, the Balfour Declaration turned out to be a paper tiger, a sweeping statement infused with idealism that was later set aside in the face of more urgent problems.

Communist revolutions, 1917–19

In the aftermath of the war, the situation of Jews throughout Europe and the Middle East was transformed either by the triumph of communism, nationalism, or the triumph of nationalism over communism. The devastation of the war was instrumental in the outbreak of communist revolutions in Russia, Hungary, and Germany. The Russian Revolution, in particular, transformed a still largely traditional Russian Jewry into a highly secularized and Russianized Jewish population in less than a decade. In 1917, Russian Jews felt as though it was still 1772, but they were wrong. In 1917, most Russian Jews were largely traditional, living with one foot in the world of tradition and the other in the changing world of the twentieth century. Though only a minority of Russian Jews had affiliated with Zionism, Autonomism, or Bundism by 1917, most had embraced as least some elements of one or more of these movements. Clearly, though, traditional Judaism was in decline and being replaced by either ideologies of national and social liberation or a self-conscious Orthodoxy. Most communal elections were won by Orthodox, Zionist, or Bundist candidates.

The fall of the tsarist regime in March 1917 brought to power a western-style provisional government. One of its first acts was to abolish national and religious restrictions, including restrictions affecting Jews. In July 1917, in preparation for the first democratic election in Russia, Russian Jews convened a congress to elect delegates to the new government. Such preparations never came to fruition. In October 1917, a second coup brought the Bolshevik Party to power.

From the outset, the pervading perception that the Bolsheviks were a Jewish party stemmed from the fact that six out of the twenty-one members of its central committee were of Jewish origin, including Leon Trotsky, Lenin's right-hand man. In fact, the Bolsheviks were unique among Russian parties in the rejection of Jewish nationalism; and most Jews opposed the Bolsheviks and preferred the more moderate provisional government. During the ensuing civil war, this preference was irrelevant. The anti-Bolshevik, reactionary, right-wing, anti-Semitic White Army equated Jews with Bolsheviks, and sponsored pogroms against Jews qua Bolsheviks. In response, Lenin saw an opportunity to win the support of Jews. In 1918, he called on his supporters to combat anti-Semitism. The Red Army stopped anti-Semitism systematically, winning Lenin the support of Russian Jewry.

The anti-anti-Semitic posture of the Red Army took several years to take hold. In the interim, Jews suffered major losses, especially in Ukraine, the major battleground of the civil war. During this three-year conflict, Ukrainian leaders oscillated between support for and antagonism toward Jews. In the summer of 1917, the Russian Provisional Government recognized Ukrainian autonomy; Ukraine recognized the rights of its Polish and Jewish minorities. In January 1918, Ukraine concluded a separate peace with Germany, prompting the Red Army to attack. Initially, the Red Army was repelled by German troops, who set up a right-wing Ukrainian regime under Cossack leadership. This regime rescinded minority rights and instigated pogroms against Jews.

Every side in this conflict attacked Jews and associated Jews with the enemy. The Ukrainian populace associated Jews with the Soviet regime, which was confiscating grain and closing churches. Anti-Jewish riots and vandalism increased in frequency and intensity, reaching a high point in 1919. In 1918, there were 30 pogroms and 50 riots in Ukraine; in 1919, there were 685 pogroms and 249 riots.

In December 1920, the Treaty of Brest-Litovsk ended fighting between Poland and Ukraine, and brought Ukraine into the newly forming Soviet Union, thus ending the civil war. By the end of the civil war, Ukraine was full of homeless Jews and Jewish self-defense units. Moreover, the civil war brought the collapse of traditional Jewry in Ukraine, and prompted a steady migration of Jews, initially into the Russian interior and eventually from small Ukrainian villages to larger cities such as Kiev and Lvov.

By 1920, most Russian and Ukrainian Jews supported the new Soviet regime. This regime had no specific Jewish policy until the end of the 1930s. Until then, Jewish policies grew out of overall policies, much as in pre-1881 Russia. The broader Soviet antagonism to all vestiges of the old regime, and the new regime's overall aim of revolutionizing social and economic structures, resulted in a brutal campaign against pre- and counterrevolutionary society, such as attacks on Ukrainian churches, culture, and language. Regarding Jews, this meant a frontal attack on Judaism and Jewish communal organization, and all Jewish political movements: Zionism, Bundism, and Autonomism. It also meant the seizure of synagogues, the arrest or deportation of rabbis and ritual slaughterers, confiscation of religious items, and a massive antireligion campaign – putting holidays and rituals on trial.

At the same time, the regime honestly opposed and persecuted all manifestations of anti-Semitism. In addition, Stalin revolutionized Jewish economic organization, transforming some Jews into agriculturists, but, more important, incorporating Jews into the Soviet industrial proletariat. This meant new opportunities for Jews, even as other ethnic minorities such as the Ukrainians languished under Stalin. Most important, thousands of Soviet Jews became bureaucrats and managers; by the end of the 1920s, one-third of Jews were managers, one-fifth of university students were Jews, and half of the Jewish population was in the upper economic stratum. This upward mobility was available to Jewish women as well as men, and Jewish women reached managerial positions at a greater pace than non-Jewish women.

In contrast to the Russian Revolution, the communist revolutions in Germany and Hungary were short-lived enterprises that were defeated by anticommunist reaction. Revolution in Germany broke out during the final days of the war. Until January 1919, this revolution proceeded along socialist lines. In January, the Spartacus League, a German communist party, attempted a coup. Prominent among the Spartacist communists was Rosa Luxemburg (1870–1919). Born in Russian Poland near Lublin, she was the daughter of a timber merchant. As a teenager, she moved to Warsaw and attended a gymnasium. In 1886, she joined a local communist party, and later the Spartacus League. She was eventually executed by anticommunist forces.

In Hungary, the revolution was led by Béla Kun (1886–1938). Born in Transylvania to an assimilated Jewish father and a disinterested Protestant mother, Kun was first indifferent and later hostile to religion. In 1906 he Magyarized his name from Kohn to Kun. Prior to the First World War, he was a journalist for the Hungarian Social Democratic Party. Like other socialists, he fought for Austria-Hungary during the war. He was captured by the Russians in 1916 and sent to a prisoner-of-war camp in the Ural Mountains. In 1917, he was swept up by the romance of the Russian Revolution. In 1918, he founded the Hungarian group of the Russian Communist Party, the forerunner of the Hungarian Communist Party.

In November 1918, Kun returned to Hungary with several hundred Hungarian communists. Supported and funded by Lenin, he deposed the provisional government, which had been unable to deal with inflation, unemployment, and shortages of housing, food, and coal. By February 1919, the Hungarian Communist Party had 40,000 members. The Social Democratic Party, still the largest and most dominant party, invited Kun to join a coalition socialist government. In March 1919, Kun and the communists took over government and founded the Hungarian Soviet Republic. Kun was appointed Commissar for Foreign Affairs, but was the *de facto* leader.

From March to August 1919, the communist government undertook a series of drastic reforms, most notably the elimination of noble titles and privileges. The government also nationalized industry, commerce, transportation, financial institutions, and medicine. The regime also nationalized private property but, contrary to Lenin's advice, refused to redistribute land, opting instead to nationalize farms. The management of farms defaulted to preexisting estate managers, which alienated the peasantry.

In June 1919, a failed anticommunist coup prompted a Red terror in which the communist secret police convened tribunals and executed 500–600 people who were suspected dissidents. In response, opponents of the regime, led by Admiral Miklós Horthy, formed a National Army to fight the communists. Before this civil war could break out, Romania invaded and defeated the Hungarian Red Army, captured Budapest, and forced Kun and the Hungarian Soviet Republic to cede authority to the Social Democrats. On November 14, the Romanians withdrew from Budapest, leaving the city to Horthy's National Army. This prompted an anti-communist White terror.

The perception that these were Jewish revolutions galvanized and exacerbated preexisting anti-Semitism, an important element in the sharp rise of anti-Semitism during the interwar years. The prominent role of Jewish communists such as Luxemburg and Kun animated a perception that Judaism and communism/Bolshevism were largely indistinguishable. From this point on, anti-Semitism and anticommunism would dovetail in a single virulent xenophobic strain that would find a growing audience during the interwar years.

The deleterious effect of the postwar settlement was especially evident in Hungary, where the truncation of the Kingdom of Hungary into "rump" Hungary inverted the relationship between the Hungarian nobility and Hungarian Jewry. Prior to the war, the nobility and Jewry in Hungary coexisted in a mutually advantageous symbiosis. Until 1920, the Magyars were an ethnic minority in their own country, comprising only 45 percent of the total population. Jews made up 8 percent of the total population, and thus the Magyarization of the Jews was seen as an integral element of Magyar nationalism in the face of rival nationalist aspirations. In the overwhelmingly Magyar rump Hungary, Jews were no longer needed to produce a Magyar majority. Moreover, the concentration of Jews in commerce and the professions complemented the concentration of nobles in the state bureaucracy. The truncation of Hungary to a third of its prewar size substantially reduced the number of government and civil service positions, driving the nobles into commercial and professional careers, and thus into competition with Jews. In addition, prior to the war the nobility had regarded Jews as a loyal ally against the Habsburg dynasty and local urban elites. The perception of the communist revolution of 1919 as a Jewish revolution and Béla Kun as a would-be destroyer of the nobility recast Jews as the mortal enemies of the nobility's privileges and property.

Within the space of a few years, the situation of Hungarian and German Jewry deteriorated rapidly from exceptionally good to exceptionally bad. In contrast to the decline of mainstream anti-Semitism in Germany prior 1914, and the lack of anti-Semitism in pre-war Hungary, by the early 1920s Hungarian and German society and politics were rife with anti-Semitic polemics and even systemic limitations. This was the background to the rise of the troubled Weimar Republic.

Born out of the ashes of the second German Reich, the Weimar Republic was caught from the outset in the contradiction between losing the peace after not definitively losing the war. The German surrender in 1918 took place when German troops were not in retreat, but rather were still situated in France and Belgium. The surrender was signed by civilian, not military, leaders. Some among the latter would regard the surrender as a premature and cowardly act by politicians. At the peace negotiations, Germany was forced to cede territory, including Alsace-Lorraine to France. Germany was also blamed for the war and forced to pay reparations. The treaty also limited the size of the German military, a devastating blow to a society that prized military service.

In retrospect, the survival of the Weimar Republic for more than a decade was remarkable, given that the Weimar government faced four problems that it was ultimately unable to solve, and that would eventually be solved by Hitler: national humiliation, political polarization, paramilitary chaos, and economic turmoil. The need to explain defeat led Germans to the *Dolchstosslegende*, the legend of the stab in the back. This was an image from German folklore: Siegfried was stabbed in the back by his supposed friend Hagen von Tronje.

Such notions had appeared already during the war. There were those who believed that German Jews were not doing their share to contribute to the war effort. This prompted the Jewish census of November 1916, an attempt to confirm accusations of a lack of Jewish patriotism; in fact, the census proved the exact opposite. In addition, there were accusations that Jewish industrialists were engaging in war profiteering.

Those who bought into the claim that a world Jewish conspiracy had brought Germany down and erected Weimar as a Jewish quisling regime regarded Walter Rathenau (1867–1922) as proof. Rathenau was a member of a German-Jewish family who converted to Christianity – the embodiment of the assimilated Jew who was undermining the strength of the German *Volk*. He was appointed Finance Minister of the Weimar regime.

National humiliation was aggravated by the polarization of German politics during and after the war. During the war, labor strikes undermined the war effort. By 1917, there had been 500 strikes and 2 million man-hours lost, alienating the German left from the rest of the German population. The ensuing communist revolution convinced propertied Germans that there was no reconciling the aims of the left and German nationalism. By 1920, therefore, the German population was sharply divided between those who favored all but the most moderate forms of social democracy, and those who vehemently opposed any manifestation of the political left, including trade unions and social welfare. The initial coalition government of the Weimar Republic, a hodgepodge of centrist parties such as the moderate Social Democrats and the Catholic Center Party, barely represented a majority of German voters. The weak political center, coupled with the decline of the left, would facilitate the growth of small right-wing parties, including Hitler's National Socialists.

The Weimar government, weakened by national humiliation and a polarized electorate, faced the tasks of restoring and maintaining order after the failed revolution, and resuscitating a once-vibrant economy that had been devastated by defeat and the postwar settlement. Maintaining order meant reining in the plethora of paramilitary bands of decommissioned soldiers who were traumatized by defeat, wary of revolution, and unemployable after the military was downsized. These bands questioned the legitimacy of the Weimar government, owing to rumors that its civilian leaders had sold Germany out by surrendering at a moment of strategic advantage. Their victims were often Jews, communists, and anyone else they regarded as enemies of the German *Volk*.

This paramilitary chaos aggravated and was aggravated by the deteriorating economic situation. Runaway inflation and widespread unemployment were endemic until 1933. In 1914, one US dollar was worth 4.2 marks; in 1923, the dollar was worth more than 1 million marks. Horror stories abounded about unemployment, impoverishment, and the worthless paper currency that the Weimar government continued to print. To make matters worse, in 1923 Germany defaulted on a war reparations payment, prompting French and

Belgian troops to occupy the economically crucial Ruhr region – further adding to the national humiliation and economic hardship.

Remarkably, there was a period of recovery at the end of the 1920s. The government issued a new currency, the rentenmark (security mark), which, though valued at 1 trillion papiermarks, was also valued at 4.2 rentenmarks to the dollar. In addition, in 1925, the Locarno Treaty restored the diplomatic status of Germany, thus allowing the country to obtain foreign loans more easily. The same year, the Dawes Plan ordered French and Belgian troops out of the Ruhr region, regulated reparations payments, reorganized the failing German Reichsbank under Allied supervision, and allowed the Weimar government to use tax revenue to defer the cost of reparations payments.

Ultimately, however, recovery was temporary. The rentenmark and the Dawes plan alleviated but did not solve economic problems, and the Great Depression torpedoed the German economy amid a worldwide economic collapse. By 1930, it was clear that the Weimar government was on the verge of collapse.

Despite precipitous economic and political decline, German Jews in particular continued to be culturally and intellectually innovative and creative. Indeed, the 1920s and even the early 1930s were a period of cultural renaissance for German Jewry. The revival of Jewish culture stemmed from a combination of four factors: a romantic reaction to secularism; a generational revolt against the prewar faith in liberalism and progress; rising anti-Semitism, which belied the belief in a German–Jewish symbiosis; and encounters with eastern European Jews.

In particular, German-Jewish intellectuals challenged the preexisting paradigm of religious reformism wed to political liberalism, and produced new expressions of Jewish identity. Hermann Cohen, the most renowned of German–Jewish intellectuals prior to the war, rediscovered a sense of Jewishness and spirituality during the 1920s. Leo Baeck, Cohen's disciple and the chief rabbi of German Jewry during the interwar years, recast the essence of Judaism, moving it from the ethical monotheism that had predominated prior to the war to include what his academic mentor Rudolf Otto described as the "spiritual experience of holy fascination and fear." In this vein, Baeck distinguished between mystery and commandment. Mystery he defined as that which is real; commandment as that which is yet to be realized. Thus, he concluded, Jews experience the mystery of the world by observing the ethical and moral commandments of the biblical prophets.

Even more innovative in this regard was Martin Buber. Through his own critique of German idealism, combined with an encounter with Hasidic *Ostjuden* who migrated to Germany during the war, Buber shifted the focus of Judaism from its legal tradition to the experience of being Jewish. He redefined revelation at Sinai from the transmission of laws into a pure encounter with God. This pure encounter, he suggested, became the model for the ideal, I–Thou relationship between human beings, as opposed to the I–It relationship in which one person objectified another. With the aim of helping Jews achieve an I–Thou approach to life, Buber distinguished laws from commandments. Laws he defined as those aspects of Judaism that were arbitrary, that Jews observed because they were ordered to by God or by a rabbinic interpreter of divination. A commandment was an act that arose out of an I–Thou relationship with God, an act that a Jew performed because it had profound meaning. Buber advocated observing commandments while disregarding laws. In the end, the only expression of Jewishness that he thought meaningful was Zionism. He eventually emigrated to Palestine and joined the ranks of secular Jews building the Jewish State.

Similar to those of Buber were the life and outlook of Franz Rosenzweig (1886–1929). Born into an assimilated Jewish family, he eventually decided to convert to Christianity. However, he wanted his conversion to be authentic, by which he meant becoming Christian in the same way as the original Christians – by first being a Jew and abandoning Judaism for Christianity. Thus, he decided to have an authentic Jewish experience before converting. To this end, he attended the Kol Nidrei service held on the evening of Yom Kippur at a local synagogue. He was so moved by the service that he put off his planned conversion to explore Judaism further, and soon discarded the idea of conversion entirely. His return to Judaism culminated with the publication of *Star of Redemption*, in which he conceptualized Judaism as two interlocking triangles, like a Jewish star: the points of one triangle were creation, revelation, and messianic redemption; the points of the other triangle were God, the Jewish people, and the Torah. In his conception of Judaism, Rosenzweig agreed with Buber's distinction between laws and commandments. Unlike Buber, he did not advocate jettisoning laws, but rather trying to discover the meaning – that is, the commandment – even in arbitrary aspects of Judaism.

Another revival of Jewish culture took place in interwar Poland. The reuniting of Poland after the war under the aegis of national self-determination brought the Jews of Prussian Poland, Russian Poland, and Galicia together in a single state for the first time in more than a century. From the outset, two competing visions of reunited Poland, those of Marshal Józef Piłsudski and Roman Dmowski respectively, would determine the situation of Polish Jewry. Piłsudski, the leader of the Polish legions during the war, was instrumental in securing Allied support during the war for Polish independence. After the war, he expanded the territory of reconstituted Poland through successful military expeditions in Lithuania, Russia, and Ukraine. The greater Poland he established through military victory mirrored his romantic, eighteenth-century conception of Poland as an expansive multinational and multiconfessional kingdom, which included Jews as an important and loyal minority. Dmowski, by contrast, envisioned Poland as ethnically Polish; his Poland had little or no room for Jews. Until Piłsudski's death in 1935, Piłsudski's vision dominated Polish politics;

thereafter, Dmowski's ascendance to leadership marked a sharp decline for Polish Jewry. In all, the experience of Jews in interwar Poland was the inverse of that of Jews in the Soviet Union. The latter was good for Jews but bad for Judaism. Interwar Poland was better for Judaism than for Jews.

Initially, the situation of Polish Jewry was defined by the National Minorities Treaty, signed by Poland and the Allies in 1922. In accordance with this treaty, the newly reconstituted Polish Republic promised to guarantee the political and cultural rights of national minorities, which during the interwar period meant Ukrainians and Jews. In practice, this meant that Jews were allowed to organize political parties and elect representatives from each Jewish community to the Polish Sejm (parliament), and to establish a network of state-funded Jewish schools. By 1922, there were thirty-five Jewish delegates to the Sejm. By the mid-1920s, the three leading Jewish political parties were Zionists, Bundists, and religious parties such as Agudat Israel. The last won a plurality of Jewish communal elections; thus representatives of religious-dominated communities had the largest portion of the Jewish bloc in the Sejm. The Gerer *rebbe*, the leader of the Gur Hasidim, was the head of the Jewish bloc.

The three leading networks of Jewish schools paralleled the three parties. Zionists set up Tarbut schools, secular Jewish schools conducted in Hebrew whose curriculum derived from Asher Ginsberg's notion of secular Jewish culture. Bundists set up Tsisho schools, a Yiddish acronym for Socialist Jewish School Organization, which taught secular Yiddish culture. Religious parties expanded the network of traditional Jewish schools in size and scope. To be sure, state sponsorship of these schools did not last through the 1920s. Nonetheless, the sanctioning of these schools by the state, seen together with the emergence of Jewish political parties, realized the vision of Simon Dubnow's Autonomism, albeit in a more politically and religiously diverse form.

These political and cultural successes were mitigated by the growing economic difficulties of the 1920s and 1930s. In 1926, Piłsudski instituted a series of statist economic policies that, among other things, nationalized commerce and industry. While not aimed at harming Jews economically, these policies forced many Jewish merchants and industrialists out of this sector of the economy, precipitating a period of economic decline. Dmowski's ascendance after 1935 brought a sharp rightward shift in Polish politics, including the introduction of a massive boycott of Jewish-owned businesses and industries. It is important to note that, despite this decline, the situation of Polish Jews in 1939 was still qualitatively different from the situation in Nazi-occupied Poland. Nonetheless, by the end of the 1930s the situation of Polish Jewry had deteriorated. Thousands of young Polish Zionists were preparing to emigrate to Palestine. That they remained in Poland was due to the inaccessibility of Palestine by the late 1930s, which resulted from the policies of the British Mandate and the growing conflict between the Yishuv and the Arab population of Palestine and the Middle East.

The rise of the Arab–Israeli conflict

In studying the conflict between Jews and Arabs in Palestine, it is important to note several scholarly problems, given that the basic elements of this conflict are still playing themselves out. Most pertinent sources are biased in one direction or another. In addition, it is essential to distinguish the views of rank-and-file Jews and Arabs from those of leaders and ideologues on both sides; the latter have tended to be more radical and contentious.

From the outset, moreover, there were three sides to this conflict. The Jewish/Zionist side included Jewish settlers in Palestine, and "third-person" Zionists. The Muslim/Arab side of the conflict included Arabs in Palestine and neighboring Arab and Muslim states. Finally, the British Mandatory government in Palestine's role as mediator of the conflict played a key role in its expansion and intensification.

In locating the beginnings of this conflict, historians generally agree that it began after the First World War. Prior to the war, Arabs and Jews had a long tradition of peaceful coexistence in Palestine that dated back to the Middle Ages. The initial Zionist settlers, moreover, brought improved technology, making the land more livable by draining swamps and "making the desert bloom." They traded with Arabs and improved the local economy, which had deteriorated under Ottoman rule.

Moreover, prewar Zionists did not see Arabs as an obstacle to settlement. Before 1908, violence between Arabs and Jews was sporadic, and consisted mainly of unorganized Arab banditry. There were occasional clashes over livestock and water, but without any nationalist component. Palestine was sparsely populated, with only 500,000–600,000 people, and had vast tracts of unpopulated land. There was every reason to believe that there was plenty of room for Jewish settlements. This explains the willingness of Arab landowners to sell land to Zionist settlers. Until the 1930s, Arabs offered Jews more land than the latter could buy. However, the Arabs who owned and sold the land were not those who lived on and worked the land.

In addition, there was no organized Palestinian national movement prior to the First World War. Palestine was not a well-defined entity, but part of Syria. Few Arabs in Palestine were politically mobilized or literate. A small circle of Muslim landowners dominated Arab society in Palestine. By 1914, Arabs in Palestine began to resent Turkish domination, prompting a more pan-Arab outlook and the beginnings of the notion of an Arab nation. Yet such sentiments were minimal before the First World War.

Early Zionist leaders had little concern regarding a conflict with the indigenous Arab population. Some Zionist leaders regarded Palestine as an ideal refuge for Jews because it was largely uninhabited or, at least, underpopulated. Theodore Herzl had little to say about Arabs in *Altneuland* or *Der Judenstaat*; neither did Asher Ginsberg envision any clash. An extreme example in this regard was Israel Zangwill, who described the Land of Israel as "a land without people for people without land." A few Zionists did raise the concern, notably Baruch Epstein. In a 1907 essay entitled *Sheela Ne'elma* (Hidden Question), Epstein argued that the economic advantages brought by the Zionist settlers would be outweighed by the complexities of competing Jewish and Arab nationalist visions. In retrospect, he was exactly right.

The first signs of conflict appeared during the early 1920s, the result of three developments: the emergence of Arab nationalism, the growth of the Yishuv, and British policy in Palestine. The spread of modern nationalism in the Arab world engendered a sense that the entire region should be ruled by Arabs and carved into separate states out of the defunct Ottoman Empire. In general, the underlying source of hostility was not economic but political. Arab agitators were more alarmed by the sale of land than by the wages of Arab workers; less concerned with Jewish immigration per se than with who would be the majority; not disturbed by Zionist settlement, but by who would ultimately replace the British.

These sentiments crystallized into periodic Arab attacks on Jews in Palestine. In 1920, during the Nebi Musa festival, Arab rioters attacked and wounded 160 Jews in the Old City of Jerusalem. In May 1921, Jewish social-ists in Jaffa were attacked. The rioters, denouncing Zionism as Bolshevism, killed 44 Jews (48 Arabs were also killed by the Arab rioters) These riots set the tone. Until the 1950s, Zionism was denounced as Bolshevism. Thereafter, Arabs denounced Zionism as fascism.

Although the violence of 1920–1 shocked Zionists out of complacency regarding Arab nationalism, the situation remained relatively quiet until 1929, leading most Zionists to conclude that the problem either did not exist or was fleeting. Mainstream Zionist leaders such as Chaim Weizmann and David ben-Gurion believed that a rising standard of living would prevent a repeat of 1920–1. In August 1929, a second, more deadly wave of riots broke out in Hebron and Safed. Though these were the last major Arab riots until the Arab revolt of 1936–9, they precluded Zionist leaders from dismissing the violence as ephemeral.

Arab nationalism and the accompanying violence was driven by the the growth and development of the Yishuv by the end of the 1920s, particu-larly by the maturing of the three major Jewish/Zionist political institutions in Palestine: the National Council, which managed social, reli-gious, and educational affairs; the Zionist executive, which managed the Jewish National Fund; and the Jewish Agency (Histadrut), the major arm for economic development and settlements. Together, these institutions increasingly resembled the nucleus of a state, creating a growing sense among Arabs that this settlement movement was permanent and would keep growing. In other words, what the British had promised in the form of the Balfour Declaration appeared to be coming to fruition, startling and frightening Arab leaders.

Ironically, British policy in Palestine was heading the opposite direction. British policy in Palestine was inconsistent, except that it was consistently two-faced. This lack of integrity stemmed from the fact that the primary concern of British colonial policy was not the Middle East, but India. Thus, British policy in Palestine often reflected an overarching concern to placate Muslims in the Middle East in order to appease Muslims in India. Moreover, Gandhi also supported the Arabs in Palestine, whom he regarded as non-Europeans ostensibly oppressed by Europeans; he, too, wanted to placate Muslims in India. As the British became more desperate during the 1920s to hold on to India as the sun set on the British Empire, they offered more and more concessions to the Muslims in Palestine.

The upshot is that the British government reneged on the Balfour Declaration almost immediately, largely in response to complaints from Arab leaders, and imposed a series of quotas on Jewish immigration to Palestine during the interwar period. This shift in policy was articulated in several White Papers, which emphasized that a Jewish national home in Palestine did not necessarily mean a sovereign Jewish state there. On the contrary, White Papers and other policies restricted immigration and areas of Jewish settlement.

British policy and Arab violence, coupled with the deteriorating situation of Jews in east-central Europe, led to the emergence of Revisionist Zionism under the leadership of the Polish Jew Vladimir Ze'ev Jabotinsky. Jabotinsky disagreed with many existing Zionist views and tactics. In contrast to those Zionists who believed that the Jewish state would be a cultural center for Jews in the diaspora, he called for an immediate mass transfer of Jews from Poland and Romania. He also disagreed with ben-Gurion regarding the use of military action. Ben-Gurion believed that Jewish military action should be exclusively defensive. Jabotinsky advocated violence against Arab and British military personnel as an acceptable response to anti-Jewish violence. The escalation of Arab violence at the end of the 1930s convinced him that his assessment and tactics were correct.

By the end of the 1930s, Britain began to recognize that a major change was necessary. In 1937, the Peel Commission recommended partitioning Palestine into an Arab and a Jewish state. The Zionists accepted the recommendation; Arab leaders rejected it. For the moment, the British left the status quo intact, allowing only 12,800 Jewish immigrants to enter Palestine in 1938, despite the rapidly deteriorating situation of the Jews in Poland and Nazi-occupied central Europe. These restrictions would remain in effect throughout the Second World War.

Interwar America

The end of Jewish immigration from eastern Europe accelerated the already rapid acculturation of American Jews. Even before the curtailment of immigration, the grown-up children of immigrants, once they achieved a measure of financial success and stability, relocated out of the Lower East Side and immigrant neighborhoods of other cities to new neighborhoods. The migration of Jews away from immigrant neighborhoods, among other things, meant that synagogues and other aspects of communal life were no longer organized according to eastern European origins.

The children of the immigrants were almost universally fluent English speakers. The sons of peddling and working-class immigrants often fulfilled their parents' aspirations by becoming self-employed businessmen or factory owners; or, better yet, becoming doctors, lawyers, or members of some other profession. The tendency was buttressed by the rising levels of education among second-generation Jews. For their parents, the ultimate goals were English literacy for themselves and a high school diploma for their children. Second-generation Jews looked higher: a college degree. Thousands entered urban colleges such as City College in New York or Wayne State University in Detroit.

The vertical rise of Jews within the ranks of commerce and industry, alongside a horizontal shift into the professions, recalled a similar occupational shift a century earlier by western and central European Jews. Moreover, the entry of Jews into middle-class professions reduced the Jewish labor movement to a small, marginal movement within American Jewry. In addition, universal English literacy and high school education meant that Yiddish was no longer a major language for American Jews.

To be sure, Jews continued to face impediments to their entry into mainstream American society, in the form of social discrimination. Elite professions such as engineering and architecture remained closed to Jews, as did elite neighborhoods in and around every major American city. Moreover, while the percentage of college-educated Jews soared during the 1920s and 1930s, elite colleges and universities excluded Jews, often through a quota system that circumvented claims of First Amendment violations by accepting applicants on the basis of geographic location. By limiting the number of incoming students from Brooklyn or Manhattan, and accepting students from the American hinterland, these institutions hoped to minimize the number of Jewish students. In fact, because often the lone applicants from hinterland cities and towns were Jews, the number of Jewish students in most Ivy League schools increased. This upward mobility and rising education of American Jews bred not only a sense of belonging and rootedness, but also a sense of self-confidence. The latter manifested itself in American Jewry's willingness to take on Henry Ford, the most powerful man in America during the 1920s. Ford was a rabid anti-Semite who disseminated his disdain for Jews and published an English translation of *The Protocols of the Elders of Zion* in his weekly newspaper, *The Dearborn Independent*.

Ford's outspoken anti-Semitism prompted a response, the Anti-Defamation League (ADL), a Jewish organization originally formed in 1913 in response to the Leo Frank Affair. The ADL's mission was to combat anti-Semitism and other forms of racism by working within the system, much like the Centralverein in Germany. Henry Ford was thus its greatest challenge. By appealing to American liberal values, the ADL mustered support from leading American politicians and intellectuals, including former president Woodrow Wilson, and forced Ford to issue a public apology.

The upward mobility and enhanced self-confidence of second-generation American Jews was paralleled by the Americanization of Judaism in America. Each of the three major American Jewish religious movements – Orthodox, Conservative, and Reform Judaism – adapted themselves to the two realities of American Jewry: that the vast majority of American Jews were of eastern European and not central European origin, and that they were rapidly entering the mainstream of American culture. Within the Reform movement, this process of adaptation was led by Rabbi Stephen Wise. By 1930, more than half of Reform Jews and most Reform rabbis were of eastern European origin. Under Wise's leadership, the Reform movement embraced Zionism, echoing Brandeis's notion that Zionism and American patriotism were entirely compatible, but also the stronger sense of ethnicity even among the non-traditional second-generation immigrants from eastern Europe. This new mentality crystallized in the Columbus Platform of 1937, which stepped away from some of the radical reforms that had been entrenched by the Pittsburgh Platform half a century earlier.

Within American Orthodoxy, the 1920s and 1930s witnessed the emergence of Yeshiva College as its leading institution and Bernard Revel as its leading spokesman. Yeshiva College, an extension of Yeshiva High School that had been formed in 1915, combined an advanced Jewish education with a first-rate college education. Revel championed this dual education as a key element in the survival and expansion of Orthodox Judaism in America. Until the 1950s, American Orthodoxy was moderate in temperment, evidenced by the fact that the boundary between Orthodox and Conservative Judaism remained decidedly blurred.

Yet the most interesting example of the Americanization of Judaism emanated from within the Conservative movement in the writings and efforts of Mordechai Kaplan. A maverick and an innovator, Kaplan flirted with Orthodox and Conservative Judaism before breaking with the latter and forming a new Jewish movement: Reconstructionist Judaism. At the heart of this new movement was Kaplan's conceptualization of Judaism as an evolving civilization that naturally adapted to context and circumstance. Kaplan believed that the openness of American society presented challenges that Reform and American Orthodoxy, in particular, were simply incapable of managing. Because Judaism in America was entirely voluntary, Kaplan argued, the practice of Judaism had to be recast as voluntary. Thus, he replaced the notion of commandments with what he called folkways, ritual and religious behavior that Jews embraced voluntarily. He also believed that Jewish communal institutions had to adapt to American society. Hence, he advocated transforming the synagogue into a synagogue-center, where Jews would not only pray and study but engage together in all forms of activity, religious and non-religious. In effect, he invented the now ubiquitous institutions of the Jewish community center.

Kaplan also believed that Jewish education had to expand the decrepit Jewish schoolhouse to less formal surroundings such as summer camps and college campuses. He also advocated an egalitarian relationship between men and women, advocating the introduction of a bat mitzvah ceremony for girls that was comparable to the bar mitzvah, mixed seating in synagogues, and the admission of women to the rabbinate. Finally, he believed, like Brandeis, that Zionism was integral to the survival of Judaism in America. Ultimately, the movement that Kaplan founded never attracted very many members. More important, though, many of the changes he advocated – notably Jewish summer camping and the synagogue center – would eventually be embraced across the spectrum of Jewish religious practice.

By the end of the 1930s, Judaism in America had been transformed across the board to suit the changing religious needs of second-generation American Jews. The Americanization of Judaism paralleled a growing sense of confidence on the part of American Jews, even in the face of economic depression and the rising anti-Semitism of the 1930s.

Hitler and the Final Solution

The rise of Hitler and the destruction of European Jewry was the single watershed event for world Jewry during the twentieth century, with the exception of the founding of the State of Israel. Given the importance of this event, it is not surprising that there is considerable debate as to its origins and to the relationship between Nazism, German nationalism, and anti-Semitism. There are two schools of thought regarding the role of Hitler and Nazi ideology in the Holocaust. Intentionalist historians believed that the annihilation of the Jews was the primary aim of Hitler and Nazism as early as the 1920s. Representative of this point of view is Lucy Davidowicz's *War against the Jews*. In contrast, functionalist historians believe that Nazi policy, including the Final Solution, was a function of circumstance and of competing bureaucracies and government officials, whose primary concern often lay elsewhere. An extreme example of this point of view is Arno Mayer's *Why Did the Heavens Not Darken?*, in which he claims that the war against the Jews was a by-product of the primary concern of Nazi policy: the defeat of Bolshevism. Recently, historians Christopher Browning argued for a modified functionalist position that wove together the strengths of both positions.

Historians have also debated the inherent Germanness of the Holocaust. Some, such as Daniel Goldhagen, rooted Nazism in "eliminationist" expressions of anti-Semitism that appeared at the end of the nineteenth century, claiming that the willingness of even ordinary Germans to kill Jews was rooted in the unique circumstances of German history. That Germans were situated at the heart of every major European war, the argument goes, not only enhanced the prestige of the Prussian, and later German, military, but also desensitized Germans to violence. This *"Sonderweg"* (special path) approach has been challenged, not least by Holocaust historians, who have noted that there were people in every European country who embraced Nazism – some with even greater enthusiasm than German Nazis themselves.

At the heart of both of these debates is the role of Adolf Hitler in perpetrating the atrocity of the Holocaust. In some sense, Hitler's life embodied the frustration and disillusion of German nationalism. He was born in Austria and later emigrated to Bavaria – two focal points of German nationalist activity. Thus, he was especially sensitive to the impact of the First World War on German nationalism. The Treaty of Versailles and other treaties, while recognizing the right of many people to national self-determination, denied Germans the right to create a *Grossdeutchland* by amalgamating Germany and Austria. In addition, in 1919–20 he fought against communism and communist revolution in Bavaria.

In 1923, Hitler joined the local branch of the National Socialist German Workers' Party (NSDAP), or Nazi Party, in Munich, and soon became one its most important leaders. Later that year, he led a failed attempt to take over the city, and was imprisoned. While in prison, he wrote *Mein Kampf*, his manifesto, in which he described his pathological hatred of Jews, and internalized and systematized racist ideas and his belief in theories concerning Jewish conspiracy. Some historians see this as a sort of conversion experience, in which he reevaluated his prewar life as a time of ignorance and naïveté. Upon his release from prison, he began to reorganize the Nazi Party, making use of his personal charisma and oratorial skills, and his quick denunciation of Jews and communists as the enemies of the German people.

The rise of Hitler and the Nazi Party to power coincided with and was facilitated by the collapse of the Weimar Republic. By 1930, the Weimar government was on the verge of collapse, with no viable alternatives. Its immediate replacement was a right-wing coalition led by Hindenburg. In 1928, the Nazi Party entered the national elections, but its showing at the polls was weak. Through a campaign of propaganda and brutality, the Nazis won more votes in the elections of 1930 and 1932. In 1932, after the Nazi Party received nearly 40 percent of the popular vote, a coalition of conservative parties under the leadership of Franz von Papen invited Hitler to join the cabinet. Von Papen and others assumed that they could use him to enhance the tenuous coalition's narrow majority. In January 1933, Hitler was named chancellor by Hindenburg. Following Hindenburg's death in August 1934, he assumed the title of führer.

With respect to Jews, Hitler's regime is best divided into three periods:1933 to November 1938; November 1938 to June 1941; and June 1941 to 1945. From 1933 to 1935, Hitler enacted a series of anti-Semitic laws that in effect de-emancipated German Jewry. Jews were excluded from most professions, the civil service, and the universities. A state-wide boycott of Jewish businesses was implemented. In 1935, the Nuremberg Laws de-Germanized the Jews and separated them from the rest of the population by requiring them to wear a yellow badge and outlawing most intimate relationships between Jews and non-Jews. In addition, the Nuremberg Laws defined which *Mischlinge*, or persons of mixed blood, were legally Jews.

Jews responded to these policies in two ways. First, many German Jews embraced Zionism. For the first time, Zionism became more than a small minority movement within German Jewry. Second, more than half of German Jewry emigrated between 1933 and 1938, most to neighboring countries: France, the Netherlands, Czechoslovakia, and Austria.

By 1938, the situation of German Jewry had deteriorated enough for the Great Powers to convene the Evian Conference from July 6 to 15 of that year to discuss the problem of Jewish refugees. Little came of this meeting. Indicative of the conference's inability to take serious action was the absence of any high-level American official. Indeed, President Roosevelt sent Myron C. Taylor, a personal friend and businessman, to represent the United States. After Evian, Zionist leader Chaim Weizmann noted despairingly, "The world seems to be divided into two parts – those places where the Jews cannot live and those where they cannot enter." The one tangible result of the conference was the organization of the International Committee on Refugees, which would come to the assistance of Jews during the waning days of the Second World War.

Nazi policy turned more aggressive after November 9, 1938 following *Kristallnacht*, the night of shattered glass, a massive state-sponsored attack on Jewish synagogues and stores. More than one hundred synagogues and thousands of Jewish shops were destroyed. During the days that followed, the Nazi regime blamed the Jews for inciting the attacks, and fined them more than 1 million marks. In addition, hundreds of Jews were deported or sent to concentration camps such as Dachau or Matthausen that had been built several years earlier to incarcerate political dissidents.

The immediate impetus for this event was the assassination of a Nazi official in Paris by Hershel Grynszpan, a Polish Jew whose parents had been deported to Poland. In the longer term, this attack on Jews reflected the growing confidence of the Nazi regime following the occupation of the Sudetenland and Austria with little real resistance by the Great Powers. In addition, historian Saul Friedlander suggested that this event grew out of tension between two ministries, those for war and propaganda; that Propaganda Minister Goebbels orchestrated *Kristallnacht* to make up for his propaganda failure over the Sudentenland. In any case, from this point on, Nazi policy toward Jews would turn increasingly violent.

The Nazi conquest of Poland at the end of the 1939 marked the next turning point in its Jewish policy. This invasion brought an additional 2 million Jews under Nazi occupation (the remaining 1 million had fled eastward into the Soviet Union). This was far more than the combined Jewish populations of Nazi Germany and Nazi-occupied Czechoslovakia and Austria, significantly altering the scope of the Nazi policies regarding Jews.

Other than the western provinces of Poland, which were incorporated directly into the German Reich, Nazi-occupied Poland was renamed the General Government. Jews there were forcibly concentrated in the newly created ghettos that were set up in every major Polish city. The largest ghettos were in Warsaw, Łódź, Lublin, and Kraców. The initial purpose of ghettoization was to concentrate Jews and separate them from the general population. The ghettos were horribly overcrowded, and rife with starvation and disease. A Jewish council (*Judenrat*) was appointed – usually from the existing Jewish leadership – to administer each ghetto and implement Nazi policies. There is no evidence at this point that a mass genocide was intended. On the contrary, the abortive Madagascar Plan, in which the Nazi regime planned to relocate Polish Jews to the island of Madagascar, indicates that the main strategy was separation and enslavement, not annihilation.

The Nazi invasion of the Soviet Union in June 1941 marked the next shift in Nazi policy. The rapid conquest of the western part of the Soviet Union brought millions more Jews under Nazi occupation, including the 1 million who had fled Poland in 1939. It was at this point that mass killing became the main Nazi strategy for dealing with Jews. Special units known as *Einsatzgruppen* trailed the advancing German army and executed the Jews from each newly conquered town and village. From June 1941 through July 1942, the *Einsatzgruppen* killed more than 1 million Jews, including more than 300,000 Ukrainian Jews in a few weeks at Babi Yar, a stream near Kiev. This mass execution raised the possibility of removing the Jews through genocide. In January 1942, Hitler, his closest advisers, and a team of scientists and engineers met at Wannsee to discuss "the Final Solution of the Jewish problem."

Following the Wannsee Conference, construction began on a series of death camps. In contrast to concentration camps and labor camps, death camps were built primarily for the mass killing of Jews. All of the death camps were located in Poland, and most were built adjacent to an existing concentration camp; Birkenau, for example, was built next to Auschwitz. The death camps were set up near one of the ghettos. Majdanek was located on the outskirts of Lublin. Treblinka was less than an hour's drive from Warsaw. Between 1941 and 1944, all Jewish ghettos were "liquidated" and the Jews deported to one of the death camps. Jews from all over Nazi-occupied Europe, from the Netherlands to Greece, were deported to the death camps.

The death-camp experience was one of indescribable horror. Although there is some variation among the slew of death-camp memoirs, the basic elements were largely homogeneous. At the same time, the experience of Jews under Nazi occupation varied from state to state. One of the striking ironies of the Jews' wartime experience is that Jews in Nazi-allied states – Italy, Hungary, Romania, and Bulgaria – had a far greater rate of survival than Jews in states at war with the Hitler – Poland, France, and the Soviet Union. In each Nazi-allied state, the treatment of Jews depended largely on a combination of local self-interest and the preexisting relationship between Jews and their non-Jewish neighbors.

In Hungary, the situation of the Jews had deteriorated precipitously since the early 1930s as the Horthy government and public opinion shifted to the right. While himself a rabid anti-Semite and fascist, however, Horthy held the Arrow Cross, the Hungarian Nazi Party, at bay into the 1940s. While implementing a series of anti-Jewish laws in 1938 and 1939, which placed strict limits on the number of Jews in business, industry, and the professions, and imposed a racial separation between Jews and non-Jews, Horthy refused to allow Hungarian Jewry to come under Nazi policies toward Jews.

This is not to suggest that Horthy did not treat Hungarian Jews with much cruelty. On the contrary, by 1940 he had conscripted thousands of them into forced labor. At the same time, he refused to allow Hungarian Jews to be deported to the death camps; few were deported until Horthy was forced to resign in the fall of 1944. For Hungarian Jews, this would prove decisive. Upon Horthy's departure, Adolf Eichmann set in motion a two-stage plan for the annihilation of Hungarian Jews. Stage 1, the deportation of Jews from the Hungarian countryside, was largely completed between June and September 1944. These Jews, while having been protected from Nazi occupation for most of the war, had the misfortune to be deported when Auschwitz-Birkenau and other death camps were operating at maximum efficiency; few of these Jews survived. Stage 2 of Eichmann's plan, the deportation of more than 100,000 Jews in Budapest, was never put into effect; Budapest was liberated first by the Soviet Army. In retrospect, these Jews were spared the horrors of the death camps by Horthy's refusal to comply with Nazi demands that Hungarian Jews be deported.

Romanian Jews had a higher rate of survival. In this case, the opportunism of Romanian statesmen determined the fate of Romanian Jews. Until 1943, when Romania was allied with Hitler, more than 300,000 Romanian Jews were systematically killed by the Romanian government. After Romania changed sides, however, the killing of Jews was halted, allowing nearly 100,000 Romanian Jews to survive the war. As in Hungary, Romanian Jews were aided by state leaders who were themselves rabidly anti-Semitic.

In contrast to Hungary and Romania, the high rates of Jewish survival in Italy and Bulgaria were the results of a powerful humanitarian tradition and a highly loyal and acculturated Jewish population. The deportation of Bulgaria's 50,000 Jews was averted almost single-handedly by Prime Minister Dimitar Peshev and King Boris III, who regarded Bulgarian Jews as citizens and as Bulgarians. Jews in Italy were largely protected by Mussolini until his overthrow in 1943. Only thereafter were Italian Jews deported by the newly installed Nazi regime. In the end, more than 80 percent of Italian and Bulgarian Jews survived.

Resistance, collaboration, response

In retrospect, any Jewish resistance is remarkable, given the situation. Jews under Nazi occupation were an unarmed, depleted, starving civilian population facing a highly trained, well-armed military and the SS. Jews received little or no assistance, not even from other resistance movements. Nonetheless, virtually every ghetto and internment camp had some kind of Jewish uprising. At the same time, it is important to maintain a sense of proportion. The postwar notion of *Shoah u-Gevura* (Holocaust and heroism) does not belie the fact that all of the remarkable acts of resistance saved only a minuscule number of Jews compared to the millions who were murdered. As Leon Wieseltier noted, "the Nazis did not win their war against the Jews; but they did not lose it either."

Historians' definitions of resistance have varied from Raul Hilberg's definition, which included only active and armed resistance – that is, partisans and ghetto fighters – to a broader, all-inclusive definition that includes less obvious forms such as passive and spiritual resistance, and "keeping body and soul together under extreme misery." A median and more usable definition was provided by Michael Marrus, who defined resistance as "organized activity consciously taken to damage the persecutors of Jews or seriously impede their objectives."

Yet even in the context of these definitions, there were cases that are not easily definable. In 1943, for example, a group of Jews escaped from the Vilna ghetto, obtained weapons, and fought with local Nazi units. In response, the Nazis killed the families of the fighters who were still in the ghetto and thereafter killed the entire work detail of any Jew who escaped from the ghetto. The ghetto newspaper called the original escapees traitors and condemned them for "endangering the existence of our entire ghetto and the lives of their loved ones ... they are responsible for the spilt blood." Jacob Gens, head of the Vilna *Judenrat*, called fleeing to fight an act of cowardice, and staying and enduring an act of heroism. In 1943, the Vilna *Judenrat* wanted the Jewish underground to surrender its leader to the Nazis.

In general, active armed Jewish resistance never broke out until Jews decided their situation was hopeless. Until the end of 1941, Jewish tactics consisted largely of evading Nazi rules. In the ghettos, for example, this meant procuring and providing food above the allocation from Nazis. This points to the controversial actions of the Jewish councils in the various ghettos. Some have condemned the members of the *Judenrat* as collaborators, willing or unwilling, who facilitated the Nazi efforts by registering the Jews and maintaining a sense of order in the ghettos that made it easier for the Nazis to round up and deport Jews. Most notorious in this regard were the decisions by the *Judenrat* as to which Jews should be deported. In 1942, for example, the Łódź *Judenrat* selected 20,000 Jews for deportation and certain death.

Others, however, have defended the actions of the *Judenrat*, citing three arguments. First, it seems clear that if the *Judenrat* had done nothing, Jews would not have lasted very long. Second, the members of the *Judenrat* were operating under the perfectly sensible supposition that the demands of the war effort would preclude the Nazis from killing a large potential labor force. Chaim Rumkowski, the head of the Łódź ghetto, carried this assumption to its extreme, putting thousands of Jews to work in the name of a strategy called "survival through work." Finally, armed resistance in the ghettos, though heroic, left most or all Jews dead. Virtually all Jews in Warsaw who were still alive when the Warsaw Ghetto Uprising broke out in April 1943 were killed during the revolt. By contrast, when the Łódź ghetto was liquidated, in the summer of 1944, more than 68,000 Jews were still alive, a tribute to the effectiveness of Rumkowski's "survival through work" strategy. The choice between heroism and survival was a trade-off.

Armed resistance generally reflected the mentality and political ideology of a younger Jewish leadership. The older, prewar, conservative leadership tended to rely on the traditional Jewish political tactic of *shtadlanut*, relying on the state for protection. By 1941, much of the older leadership had either fled or been deported. The younger leadership that took over was reared by a different Jewish political tradition that drew on late-nineteenth-century notions such as auto-emancipation, and the activist elements of Zionism and Bundism. In July 1942, Polish Zionists formed the ZOB (United Combat Organization).

No less ambiguous were cases where individual Jews worked with Nazi officials to save Jews. Miklós Nyiszli, a "doctor-prisoner" in Auschwitz, aided Josef Mengele in his cruel experiments on Jewish inmates. On the other hand, the privileged status that Nyiszli gained through working with Mengele allowed him to save many Jewish inmates from certain death.

At the heart of the problem of evaluating the actions of Jewish leaders during the war is understanding how well they understood their situation – that is, what information was known, and when? By early 1942, some information was readily available and disseminated in numerous ways: the Polish underground; refugees in Switzerland and Turkey; German soldiers who witnessed atrocities; newspaper correspondents stationed in Germany; visitors from allied states and neutral countries; diplomats such as Giuseppe Burzio, papal nuncio in Bratislava, who reported the deportation of 80,000 Jews in March 1942; and the Bund, whose report of deportations and the death of 700,000 Jews at Chelmno was broadcast by the BBC on June 2, 1942. Information was also transmitted by the Jewish Telegraphic Agency and by Jewish newspapers such as the *Jewish Chronicle* and the *Zionist Review*.

Yet these were all localized reports The first report of European-wide genocide came in August 1942 with the Riegner telegram, in which Gerhardt
Riegner, World Jewish Congress representative in Switzerland, reported that
Jews were being deported, concentrated in the east, and "exterminated at one
blow to resolve once and for all the Jewish Question in Europe." Riegner also
mentioned prussic acid (the gas used at Auschwitz). By December 1942, the
United Nations confirmed news about mass killings

Even at this point, however, it was difficult to make the leap from the facts
to the scope and significance of the events. Available information left certain
things unexplained. The World Jewish Congress believed that starvation, not
mechanized killing, was the major cause of death. The assembly-line process
that made it possible to kill so many Jews so quickly was unknown until mid-
1944, when four Auschwitz inmates escaped. Hitherto, the full extent of
killing at Auschwitz-Birkenau had largely been concealed.

In addition, the overall skepticism of the American press made it more difficult to believe reports of Jews being killed. Such skepticism was augmented
by the lingering experience of exaggerated reports of atrocities during the First
World War. Thus, reports in 1942 and 1943 were often buried in the back
pages. Moreover, Japan, not Germany, was seen as the great barbaric threat to
humanity. This was true until December 1944, when, at the Battle of the
Bulge, SS officers shot a group of unarmed American prisoners in Belgium.

The tortuous dissemination and slow understanding of information is
important in assessing the responses of Jews (especially in the United States),
non-Jews, and state governments. The ability of American Jews to offer aid was
limited by a lack of political influence and diplomatic leverage. American
Jewry made up only 3.6 percent of a population whose popular anti-Semitism
peaked during the war. American Jewish leaders, moreover, lacked the diplomatic leverage they had had during the First World War, since there was no
doubt as to which side in the war would have the support of the American government. Most important, perhaps, American Jews shared in the belief that an
Allied victory in Europe was the most effective and expedient way to save Jews.

By contrast, it is clear that the US government could have acted to save at
least some Jews, particularly the hundreds of thousands of Hungarian Jews,
who were not deported until 1944. By May 1943, the U.S. Fifteenth Air
Force division, operating at full strength, had begun to bomb Nazi industrial
complexes in Nazi-occupied Europe. This attests to the Allied capacity to
bomb the death camps, or the railroad lines transporting Jews there. Some
historians have argued that simply destroying key railway lines such as the
Kassa–Presov line could have halted the killing process, or at least slowed it
long enough for more inmates to have survived. By June 1944, moreover, the
allies had received the Vrba–Wetzler Report, a detailed report by eyewit-
nesses of the geographical layout of Auschwitz, the killing process, and
internal conditions in the camp.

That the US government took no action has been explained in terms of both existing anti-Semitism and practical military matters. Some historians, such as Deborah Lipstadt, have noted the high level of American anti-Semitism during the war. According to a July 1942 census, 44 percent of Americans thought Jews had too much power and influence; a July 1944 census reported that 44 percent of Americans regarded Jews as a threat to America. Other historians, such as David Wyman, noted the presence and influence of anti-Semitic State Department officials. Raised in neighborhoods and schooled in institutions that excluded Jews, these men, while not countenancing genocide, de-prioritized the need to save Jews in their recommendations to President Roosevelt.

Other historians have noted the difficulty of aiding Jews through military action. In order to incapacitate a railroad line, it would have been necessary to bomb and destroy it repeatedly. In addition, bombing the camps might well have killed or wounded thousands of Jews. In the end, like American Jews, government officials from President Roosevelt down through the ranks of the State Department believed that defeating Hitler took priority, and was also the best way to help Jews under Nazi rule.

Non-Jewish bystanders in Europe, too, could, in retrospect, have aided Jews far more than they did, to say the least. There is no question that the Nazis could not have carried out this plan without the support of local collaborators, whom they found in every country, without exception. Most non-Jews, however, neither resisted nor collaborated with the Nazis, but remained bystanders. In some cases, this inaction was due to a preexisting animosity or indifference toward Jews. More frequent was a fear of reprisal and the possibility of material gain by expropriating Jewish property and homes; the latter was especially true in Poland and Hungary.

These were powerful considerations for ordinary people. Thus, it is remarkable that, despite dire consequences, there were non-Jews who helped Jews. Most famous among these righteous Gentiles was Raoul Wallenberg (1912–?). Born into a famous Swedish family of bankers, industrialists, and diplomats, Wallenberg studied architecture at the University of Michigan (where a plaque in front of a local preschool still honors him) and graduated in 1931 with honors, winning an award for outstanding academic achievement. After graduating, he visited Haifa, in 1935–6, where he met Jewish refugees from Nazi Germany. Upon returning to Sweden, he became an importer and exporter, working closely with a Hungarian Jew, Koloman Lauer. While running their joint venture, the Mid-European Trading Company, Wallenberg traveled through Nazi-occupied Europe, in the process learning how to handle German bureaucrats.

During the war, he entered the Swedish diplomatic corps, and was assigned as a Swedish emissary to Budapest. There, in 1944, he used his connections and diplomatic skills to save 30,000 Hungarian Jews. At the close of the war, he was captured by the Soviet army, arrested as a collaborator, and never heard from again. As late as 1975, he was rumored to be alive in a

Soviet prison camp. Individuals such as Wallenberg and other well-known rescuers such as Oskar Schindler were rare exceptions. Yet it is tragically tantalizing to ponder how many Jews even a few more Schindlers and Wallenbergs could have rescued.

The individual who was in the best position to help Jews was undoubtedly Pope Pius XII. For more than half a century, there has been an ongoing debate as to the actions of the pope on behalf of the Jews, beginning with two contradictory versions that appeared during the 1950s. One, articulated by Israeli historian Pinchas Lapides, contended that "the Catholic Church under the Pontificate of Pius XII was instrumental in saving at least 700,000 Jews, but probably as many as 860,000." Every defender of Pius XII has cited this figure, most recently Pat Buchanan. The problem is, there is no factual basis for this claim. A more negative appraisal of the pope appeared in a play written by Rolf Hochhuth during the 1950s, *The Deputy*. This play described how Eugenio Pacelli, the future Pius XII, while serving as papal nuncio to Germany during the 1930s, had come to love German culture and was thus unwilling to oppose Hitler.

More recently, historians have looked beyond these two charged claims and set the actions of the pope in the context of the war and the decline of the papacy. Since the 1860s, the Vatican has been largely powerless, and dependent on political authorities even for basic necessities such as water and electricity. During the war, the pope's fear of Stalin led him to turn to Hitler as the only guarantor of the survival of the church in the face of the communist threat to destroy Catholicism. On the other hand, the heroic support of Catholic clergy on behalf of Jews suggests that if the pope had given even the slightest indication of opposition, there might have been a wellspring of Catholic resistance to Nazism. In the absence of a clear policy from the Vatican, the actions of Catholic clergy were mixed. Numerous German, Hungarian, and Italian clergy, notably the Hungarians Angelo Rotta and Sister Margit Schlachta, helped Jews. Croatian priests helped round up and deport Jews. Most notoriously, Pius XII himself did nothing when the Jews of Rome were deported literally under the window of the Vatican.

In the end, the impact of the Holocaust, as the destruction of European Jewry came to be known at the end of the 1950s, left a profound imprint on world Jewry. The killing of between 5 and 6 million Jews, and over a million Jewish children, destroyed multiple generations, inflicting a demographic blow from which world Jewry has still not recovered. Beyond physical destruction, the destruction of the Jews of central and eastern Europe brought an end to a Jewish civilization and culture that was on the verge of a cultural explosion. Until the Second World War, the best rabbinic scholars came from Poland, Germany, and Hungary, as did the best Jewish writers and political thinkers.

This event, moreover, had a profound impact on the understanding of Jewish history. The Holocaust promoted a preexisting "lachrymose view" of Jewish history that regarded the history of the Jews as a history of unending suffering and persecution. This view, though a highly oversimplified view of Jewish history, was harder to critique in the wake of Auschwitz. At the same time, the Holocaust affirmed the Zionist view of Jewish history, that Jewish life in the diaspora is ultimately pointless. Finally, the Holocaust set in motion a critique of Jews' political behavior and elicited a prevailing notion of the passivity and political impotence of Jews in the diaspora.

In addition, the Holocaust had a decisive impact on Jewish theology, specifically Jewish theodicy. The conventional rabbinic notions of chosenness and that God rewards the just and punishes the wicked, and even the belief that such rewards and punishments would be divinely meted out in the after-life, were harder to swallow after the murder of more than a million Jewish children. To be sure, some rabbis continued to refer to conventional Jewish theology. Joel Teitelbaum, the Szatmar *Rebbe*, interpreted the Holocaust as divine retribution for the evils of the Jews themselves, particularly assimilation and secularism. The Reform rabbi Ignaz Maybaum interpreted the Holocaust in terms of Isaiah 53, in which Israel is described as God's suffering servant. Needless to say, both explanations sounded hollow after the war.

Other scholars looked for new theological explanations. The most compelling was offered by the Jewish philosopher Emil Fackenheim. Rather than trying to explain how the Holocaust could have happened, which he believed was beyond the capability of human understanding, Fackenheim instead defined what he believed was the proper Jewish response to it. In this vein, he defined the 614th commandment as "Thou shalt not give Hitler a posthumous victory." In the aftermath of Auschwitz, he argued, Jewish survival became a divine commandment.

Finally, the destruction of the Jews of eastern and central Europe led to an abrupt shift in the center of world Jewry, and the rise of three new centers of world Jewry: Israel, the United States, and the Soviet Union. These three Jewish communities would define the parameters of world Jewry in the post-war world.

Chapter 10

Jews in the postwar world

At the end of the Second World War, the Zionists were more militant than ever. Zionist leaders such as Chaim Weizmann and David Ben-Gurion expected an "open gate" immigration policy after the Holocaust and in light of the Jewish support for the British and Allied war effort. This expectation was belied by the British Labour Party's shift from a pro- to an anti-Zionist stance. The Zionists' disappointment was aggravated by the plight of Jewish displaced persons (DPs), 100,000 of whom the British denied entry into Palestine. The growing sense of urgency, prompted by the clear intent of the British government not to allow these Jews into Palestine, led militant Zionists such as Jabotinsky in a more radical, proactive direction.

As before the war, these British policies aimed at maintaining close ties with Arab leaders, but for different reasons. Britain was largely bankrupt at the end of the war and needed to secure its oil reserves. From a geopolitical standpoint, France was eliminated from Middle Eastern politics by 1947, and the Soviet Union was rapidly moving in to fill the void left by France; Britain needed alliances to stay the growing Soviet presence in the region. No longer able to maintain a dominant military establishment in the Middle East, Britain supported Arab nationalist aspirations to eliminate anti-British feeling; to this end, it entered into joint military maneuvers and defense agreements with Arab leaders.

In response, the Jewish Agency launched an illegal immigration movement called Aliyah Bet. This movement was supported by the French and Italians as a way of getting back at the British. In turn, the British blockaded Palestine from 1945 to 1948. All but five immigrant ships were intercepted, and the immigrants interned in detention camps on Cyprus. From 1945 to 1948, only 18,000 Jews per year entered Palestine.

These British actions elicited staunch criticism as the British were portrayed as cold-hearted villains. It is true that the British detention centers were a world removed from the Nazi camps. Jews there were properly housed and fed, and received more than adequate medical treatment. Yet the image of Jews recently liberated from the Nazi camps now interned behind the barbed-wire detention camps made headline news, as did the the image of the

British accosting shiploads of Jewish refugees and denying them entry into Palestine. The most celebrated case was the *Exodus*, a battered American ferry boat that sailed from Chesapeake Bay to France, where it collected a shipload of DPs. When the British tried to halt the ship, the DPs on board fought back, surrendering only when the British started to ram the ship. The British sent them back to Marseilles.

Zionists were outraged. In 1945, ben-Gurion and the Jewish Agency approved measures of violence. The Haganah, the mainstream Zionist defense organization, began operations against the British, as did the Irgun and its radical fringe, Lechi (*Lochamei Herut Yisrael*, Freedom Fighters of Israel), a radical right fringe group under the leadership of Abraham Stern, also called the Stern Gang. On October 31, 1945, the Palestine railway was blown up in 153 places.

In November 1945, the Irgun, Haganah, and Lechi agreed to coordinate efforts against the British. In February 1946, they conducted raids on three airfields, destroying three planes. On July 17, 1946, the Haganah blew up ten out of eleven bridges in Palestine.

To be sure, there was a difference between the Haganah, on the one hand, and the Irgun and the Stern Gang on the other. The Haganah attacked only military installations. The Irgun and the Stern Gang attacked British personnel. Most notoriously, on July 22, 1946, the Irgun blew up the King David Hotel, British military headquarters in Palestine, killing ninety-one Britons, Jews, and Arabs. Subsequently, Irgun leaders claimed they gave a warning to vacate the hotel. British leaders denied ever receiving such a warning.

By 1947, it was clear that security under the British Mandate had collapsed. From May 1945 to October 1947, 127 British nationals were killed. Eighty-thousand British troops and 16,000 British policemen were stationed in Palestine by 1947, meaning one-tenth of the British army, and one police officer for every eight people in Palestine.

There was also growing pressure on Britain to abandon the Mandate. In Britain, this pressure stemmed from the loss of lives and the escalating cost: £50,000,000 had been spent on Palestine by the end of 1947. In the United States, there was growing pressure to admit the Jewish DPs. Truman wanted 100,000 admitted.

By the end of 1947, it was clear that Britain could no longer hold on to Palestine, or many other colonial possessions. In addition, Indian independence in 1947 made Palestine strategically less important. In February 1947, Ernest Bevin, the British foreign secretary, suggested partitioning Palestine as a new solution. The matter was referred to the United Nations, which began to deliberate the prospect of an independent Jewish state in Palestine.

Support for Jewish statehood within the US government came primarily from President Truman, who supported the creation of a Jewish state mainly for reasons of conscience, but also to win Jewish votes. Truman repeatedly overruled the State Department, which was leaning in a more pro-Arab direction, and ignored the lobbying efforts of the oil industry, which was staunchly pro-Arab.

The Soviet Union also supported the creation of a Jewish state. Stalin preferred Jewish nationalism, with its socialist component, to Arab nationalism, which appeared more backward. In addition, an alliance with a Jewish state whose founders had a strong anti-British attitude seemed like a good way to oust the British from the region.

In May 1947, the United Nations formed a special committee on Palestine (UNSCOP). On August 31, 1947, UNSCOP recommended the creation of a Jewish and an Arab state, with the Jews receiving 62 percent of Palestine and the Arabs receiving 38 percent. On November 29, 1947, the UN approved partition of Palestine, with 34 votes in favor, 13 against (11 Arab countries, Greece, and Cuba), and 10 abstentions. The UN partition deviated from the recommendation by UNSCOP, allotting 55 percent of Palestine to the Jews and 45 percent to the Arabs, and placing Jerusalem and Bethlehem under UN administration. The Zionist executive accepted this resolution immediately. Arabs in Palestine and elsewhere in neighboring states rejected it outright, claiming that "Jews had no legitimate right to any territory."

The UN partition marked the end of the diplomatic struggle for Jewish statehood, and the beginning of a military struggle. All the surrounding Arab states participated in this military conflict, as the British involved other Arab states in discussions about the fate of Palestine. The British, moreover, refused to facilitate an orderly transfer of power, largely retreating into their bunkers after November 1947.

Hostilities between Jews and Arabs began in the winter of 1947–8, with the Haganah, Irgun, and Lechi engaging Palestinian Arab guerrillas and military units from other Arab countries. By May, 1948, included regular troops from Egypt, Jordan, Syria, Iraq, and Lebanon. The majority of Arab troops were not from Palestine. King Abdullah of Transjordan sent legions, even though he did not favor the creation of a Palestinian state. On May 14, 1948, the British departure was followed by a declaration of the State of Israel as an independent state.

Arab military forces invaded the next day, beginning what came to be known to Israelis as the War of Independence. Arab forces had certain clear advantages, including superior military strength. Unofficially, Britain had aided the Arab military effort since late 1947, maintaining an embargo on Jewish immigration and military supplies for Jews. The British also continued to sell weapons to Iraq and Transjordan, and made no attempt to prevent infiltration by Arab guerrillas. Finally, the British handed over virtually complete military installations to the Arabs.

At the same time, the Arabs had certain disadvantages. Their soldiers lacked real commitment. Many of their troops were peasants who had been forcibly recruited to fight a war in another country. Some Iraqi troops were chained to their machine guns to make sure they did not desert. The Arab forces also had a decided lack of military experience. By contrast, many Israeli soldiers had served in the British army and had fought in North Africa. In addition, the Israelis had superior military leaders, most of whom had been trained as officers of the Palmach, a British unit of Jewish strike forces (*Plugot Mahatz*, whence the name Palmach). In addition, the Israelis recruited Mickey Marcus, a decorated American army officer, to lead their military campaign.

The war lasted until January 1949; during the subsequent six months, Israel signed cease-fire agreements with Egypt, Lebanon, Jordan, and Syria, based on the front lines at the cessation of military hostilities. Israel wound up with 80 percent of Mandatory Palestine: 25 percent and 2,500 square miles more than partition had allotted them. The West Bank, including East Jerusalem, was annexed by King Abdullah of Jordan. The Gaza Strip was annexed by Egypt.

The most controversial aspect of the War of Independence was the fate of the civilian Arab population of what had been Palestine. Jews were a minority in Mandatory Palestine in 1947; by the end of 1948, they were a majority. All in all, there were 600,000 fewer Arabs in 1949 than there had been in 1947, prompting the still controversial and debated question: Why did they leave?

Arab leaders and intellectuals claimed that these Arabs had been driven out; Israelis claimed that they had fled at the instruction of Arab leaders, who promised that they would be able to return once the Israelis had been vanquished and driven out. In fact, there are a few documented instances of Arabs being driven out, but no evidence of a mass effort by the Israelis to pursue a policy of expulsion.

Moreover, many Arabs fled before Israeli forces reached their town or village, and more than 30,000 had fled before Israeli independence was declared on May 14. Many among the first to flee were Arab professionals and leaders, who left for Egypt and Lebanon. Their departure by May 1948 led to a collapse of Arab social services. As the Jews gained the upper hand in the war, a further exodus of traditional Arab leaders and communal leaders followed, along with thousands of town dwellers. Most thought they would return in the wake of Arab victory. As more Arabs fled, more Arab social services collapsed.

Haifa is a useful case in point. Prior to 1948, Haifa had 70,000 Arab residents. From November 1947, Arab businessmen began to leave. A total of 25,000 Arabs had left by March 1948, and 20,000 more left in April, especially after the British left the city on April 21.

Most controversial perhaps was the tragic fate of Deir Yassin. On April 9, 1948, this Arab village was captured by the Irgun and the Stern Gang, which, in the process of securing the village, executed more than 200 men, women, and children. This incident, some historians have claimed, subsequently prompted entire Arab communities to flee in terror.

In fact, the extremist behavior of the Zionist/Israeli right quickly abated after 1948. As the leaders of the Irgun and Lechi were absorbed into Israeli politics and society, they largely abandoned their military activities and became the core of the Israeli political opposition. Menachem Begin, the principal disciple of Jabotinsky and the leader of the Irgun, led the opposition party until his election as prime minister in 1977.

The establishment of the State of Israel marked the fulfillment of Zionism and its multifaceted nationalist aims. Israel became a refuge for Jews around the world. The 100,000 Jews interned on Cyprus were welcomed immediately. During the five years after independence, thousands of Jews from Arab countries immigrated to Israel.

This "ingathering of the exiled" was a cause of great celebration and triumph, but also posed the first domestic challenges to the fledgling state, first and foremost over the question of Jewish identity in the Jewish state. The Law of Return, enacted by the Israeli parliament in 1950, granted automatic citizenship to any Jew who immigrated to Israel; non-Jewish immigrants had to follow a more conventional path to citizenship. An early test of this law, and one of the first decisive judicial cases that came before the Israeli High Court, involved a Carmelite monk named Brother Daniel, born a Polish Jew named Oswald Rufeisen. Rufeisen was raised a Jew and embraced Zionism before being forced to go into hiding during the Nazi occupation of Poland. Rufeisen was hidden by a Polish Catholic family and eventually converted to Catholicism. He remained a Catholic even after the end of the war, and eventually entered the priesthood. He became a monk and was renamed Brother Daniel.

During the 1950s, he was assigned to a monastery near Haifa. At this point, Brother Daniel claimed Israeli citizenship under the Law of Return, explaining that he was Jewish by nationality and Catholic by religion. The case came before the Supreme Court in 1958. The court denied Brother Daniel's petition, defining Jews as people whom most Jews regard as Jewish. In other words, because most Jews, whether secular or religiously observant, regarded a Jew who converted to Christianity as non-Jewish, Brother Daniel could not claim to be Jewish.

Although an apparent setback to the early Zionist secular understanding of Jewish identity, this case underscored the blurring of the lines between secular Zionism and traditional Judaism. This reflected a subtle but crucial element of Israeli society. Between the ranks of the avowedly secular and fervently religious were many Israelis whose Jewishness was a composite of religious and secular elements.

In some sense, this blurring of the lines was furthered by the influx of non-Ashkenazic Jews from the Arab states. Zionism, after all, was an Ashkenazic invention, and the response of Ashkanzic Jews to the particular circumstances of the late nineteenth century. Jews in Arab lands had always lived comfortably between the religious and non-religious dimensions of Jewish life; thus, incorporating secular Zionist views into their Jewish outlook was less of a disjunctive experience than it was for many Ashkenazic Jews, for whom accepting Zionism meant rejecting Jewish tradition.

The influx of Jews from Arab lands, moreover, introduced a social tension within Israeli society. The Zionist enterprise and the creation of the state was an Ashkenazic endeavor, and the leadership of the new state was composed almost exclusively of Ashkenazic Jews. Amid the highly syndicated nature of Israeli society, this meant that Jews from Arab lands had far less access to the best goods and services that the state had to offer; they lacked the *protektsia* (connections) that most Ashkenazic Jews had. Thus, Jews from Arab lands increasingly became a social underclass, submerged beneath a system dominated by an Ashkenazic elite. This was ironic, given the utopian egalitarian aims shared by the Israeli left and right.

By the same token, Israeli society offered ways around this disparity, particularly for second-generation immigrants. Army service, for example, had a distinct leveling effect, in that it provided similar benefits to all those who served. In addition, connections with one's regiment and officers often translated into professional and social connections after military service was completed. To a lesser extent, affiliation with a kibbutz offered similar opportunities. In any case, by the 1960s there had emerged a distinct Israeli identity that, among other things, allowed Israelis to see themselves as distinct from – and often superior to – their fellow Jews in the diaspora.

The postwar Diaspora

The creation of the State of Israel had an impact that reverberated throughout the Jewish world. In the Soviet Union, the creation of the state dovetailed with a subtle change in the situation of Soviet Jewry that followed on the heels of Soviet Jewry's great moment of solidarity with Soviet society during the Second World War. Jews participated in the great Soviet struggle against fascism, embodied by the creation of the Jewish Anti-Fascist Committee.

Developments during and after the war altered this situation. The addition to Soviet Jewry of the several hundred thousand Polish Jews – those among the 1 million Polish Jews who fled to the Soviet Union in 1939–40 – reinfused Soviet Jewry with some form of Jewish identity. After the war, Stalin became increasingly suspicious of Jews. As the Cold War took hold, he suspected Jews of being sympathetic to the West.

The creation of the State of Israel accentuated both of these developments. In 1948, Golda Meir's visit to the Soviet Union as an emissary of the State of Israel revealed an unexpected extent and depth of Jewish solidarity and passion for Zionism among Soviet Jews. Initially, this fed into Stalin's support for the Jewish state. By the end of the 1940s, as it became clear that the State of Israel had allied more with the United States than with the Soviet Union, Stalin recast Zionism as anticommunist, and Jews qua Zionists as the enemies of the state. This was a key element in Stalin's anti-Jewish purges of the late 1940s. By the time of his death in 1953, Stalin had driven a wedge between Soviet Jewry and the Soviet Union.

In the United States, the creation of Israel would have its most visible impact only after 1967. Between 1945 and 1967, American Jewry would follow the larger trends of American society and culture – the central characteristic of American-Jewish history. Demographically, Jews joined the movement to suburbia, typically concentrating in one or two suburbs of each major urban center. The political outlook of American Jews gravitated toward the political center during the late 1940s and the 1950s. Until the end of the 1940s, there was considerable support among American Jews for the left, a continuation of the prewar support for the left among immigrants, Bundists, and other working-class Jews. During the war, the popularity of the American Communist Party was buttressed by the Soviet Union's struggle against Hitler. Bundist and Labor Zionist summer camps were sources of support for the left.

This trend continued through the 1940s. In 1946, the Communist candidates for the New York state comptroller and attorney general received more votes from Jews than from anyone else, although their votes represented only a minority of the total Jewish vote. In the 1948 presidential election, Henry Wallace, nominee of the Progressive Party, was endorsed by the American Communist Party. Half of his 1.1 million votes were from Jews. In short, although most Jews were not leftists, much of the left was Jewish.

By the 1950s, this support had waned with the disappearance of immigrant and working-class Jewish neighborhoods, whose limited privacy, street life, and stoops were amenable for political action. In contrast, the increased privacy and individualism of suburban middle-class neighborhoods was more amenable to a liberal rather than a socialist outlook. In addition, the upward mobility made possibility by the GI Bill, coupled with the souring of communism during the McCarthy era, drove Jews from the left to left of center. Yet Jews remained liberal. Jewish support for the radical left waned, but Jews remained supporters of labor unions.

The upward mobility of American Jewry bred a growing self-confidence that was evidenced, among other things, in the emergence of massive synagogues and temples in many American cities. Like the Dohány Street Temple in Budapest and other large European synagogues built during the heyday of European liberalism, these new American synagogues signaled a coming of age of American Jewry.

At the same time, suburbanization and prosperity also introduced certain uncertainties and tensions within postwar American Jewry. The flight to the suburbs and the decline of immigrant neighborhoods eliminated the built-in ethnic and religious flavor that had hitherto been a pervasive component of Jewish life in America. This shift was manifest in the controversy over driving to the synagogue on the Sabbath – which traditionally was taboo. During the 1950s, the Conservative Movement, sensing that few of its members could attend Saturday morning services without riding in a car, allowed its members to drive. This drove a rift between Conservative and Orthodox Judaism, which previously had been divided by a line that was, at best, blurred.

The generation of American Jews that came of age during the 1950s, moreover, lacked not only a widespread commitment to traditional observance but also any direct connection to the traditional world of the shtetl. Their parents, raised by immigrants, maintained a strong sense of ethnicity even in the absence of a traditional lifestyle. This was reflected in the final decline of Yiddish as a lingua franca of American Jews during the 1950s. The decline of Old World ethnicity stirred a sense of nostalgic loss among American Jews. Such nostalgia became manifest in the romantic views of immigration Jewish life on the Lower East Side, as evidenced by the popularity of the *The Goldbergs* television program, and in the growing interest in stories about life in the shtetls of eastern Europe.

1967 and beyond

A singularly influential event for postwar world Jewry was the Six Day War. In retrospect, the rapid victory of the State of Israel over its Arab assailants from June 4 to June 10 set in motion several key developments for Jews in Israel and the United States. The territorial expansion of Israel through the capture of the West Bank, the Gaza Strip, the Golan Heights, and the Sinai Peninsula shone immense prestige on what had hitherto been a fledgling state amid a host of larger, antagonistic neighbors. The Six Day War changed the perception of the State of Israel from a tenuous invention that Jews hoped would survive the birth pangs of statehood and the ever-present threat of military destruction into a state whose permanence was no longer in doubt. For some Jews, territorial expansion not only marked a military victory but had messianic overtones, particularly the capture of East Jerusalem and the unification of Jerusalem under Israeli rule.

In a sense, the timing of this great victory was crucial. Only five years earlier, the attention of Israelis and Jews throughout the world had turned to the trial of Adolf Eichmann, Hitler's right-hand man, who had been captured by the Mossad, Israel's secret intelligence service, and taken from Argentina to Israel. The Eichmann trial was a litmus test of the Jewish state in certain ways. That a Jewish state was insistent on giving the most evil of Nazis other than Hitler a fair trial attested to its democratic character – a realization of one of the core aims of most early Zionist thinkers. In addition, the trial included extensive testimony by Holocaust survivors, called to the stand to attest that the defendant was indeed Eichmann and that he had committed the atrocities of which he stood accused. This marked the first extensive public airing of survivors' testimony, opening the doors for more than a generation of such testimony in the subsequent collection and publication of memoirs and video histories.

Moreover, among those who testified was Hannah Arendt, a German-Jewish émigré who accused wartime European Jewish leaders of passivity in the face of persecution. For an Israeli audience, such an accusation underlined the difference between the alleged weakness of diaspora Jews and the power and vigor of Israelis. In this sense, the Six Day War affirmed what had been suggested at the Eichmann trial: Israel and Israelis as warrior heroes, latter-day incarnations of King David and the Maccabees. That the Israeli high command consisted mainly of men who were archeologists and scholars when not in battle further recalled David, the great biblical warrior-poet. This heroic image would reach its apogee during the next decade and a half, first in 1976 during the heroic rescue of Jewish hostages in a raid on the airport in Entebbe, Uganda; and then in 1981, when the Israeli air force destroyed a nuclear plant in Iraq (the implications of which have loomed ever larger since that time).

Most important, perhaps, the outcome of the Six Day War fundamentally altered the relationship between Israel and its Arab neighbors, for better and for worse. The war demonstrated not only the ability of Israel to survive a full-scale Arab invasion but also left little doubt that Israel was the military power in the region. A similar conflict six years later, the Yom Kippur War, while inflicting many more casualties, left this impression intact. It is not surprising that less than a decade after 1967, Egypt abandoned its aim of driving the Jews into the sea, and chose instead to seek peace.

On the other hand, the extension of Israel sovereignty over a large Arab population in the West Bank, Gaza, and East Jerusalem introduced the problem of dealing with a large ethnic minority. Israelis and their leaders disagreed as to how to resolve this quandary. Some raised anew an older argument for a binational state; others regarded the best solution as extensive Jewish settlement so as to Israeli-ize these territories as quickly as possible. In retrospect, the defeat of the Arab neighbors in 1967 came at the cost of galvanizing the discontent of Arabs in Israel, thus transforming a conflict between Israelis and Arabs into a conflict between Israelis and Palestinians.

Yet it was not only the events of June 1967 that strained relations between Israelis and Palestinians. Religious leaders and religious fundamentalists on both sides of the conflict have exerted increasing influence over their respective leadership and popular opinion. In addition, Palestinians living abroad, many of whom had been displaced in 1948, have become more vocal and politically organized. This means that since 1967, the multifarious support that world Jewry has provided to the Israeli cause through diplomatic, economic, and political support is gradually being rivaled and challenged by the support of Palestinians for the Palestinian cause. The parallels notwithstanding, there is still a key difference between Israeli and Palestinian tactics. One-time Zionist military organizations such as Begin's Irgun, almost immediately upon becoming part of a conventional political leadership, largely abandoned their use of violence and militarism in favor of diplomacy and economic development. Begin, after all, negotiated the most lasting peace treaty in Israel's short history. By contrast, Palestinian military organizations such as Hamas and Hezbollah have yet to renounce their violent tactics, even though they, too, are now part of a conventional political structure.

Outside of Israel, too, the Six Day War had a significant impact on Jewish life, particularly in the United States. As in Israel, the Six Day War accelerated certain developments in American Jewish life that had been unfolding for several years prior to 1967. For many young American Jews, the cultural revival of the 1960s led, often tortuously, to a reconnecting with Jewish roots, not unlike that experienced by other Americanized ethnic groups such as African-Americans, Native Americans, and Latino Americans. For Jews, this reconnecting was often facilitated by neo-Hasidic spiritual revival movements led by rabbis such as Shlomo Carlebach and Zalman Schacter-Shalomi, who fused the Hasidic upbringing that had eventually alienated them with the bohemian culture and eastern religion that they had embraced during the 1960s. The resurgence of messianic fervor after 1967 spurred the popularity of these spiritual movements.

More important, perhaps, Israel's victory over its seemingly unconquerable adversaries instilled American Jews with the confidence and willingness to speak out with more proactively on behalf of Jewish causes such as the plight of Soviet Jewry, and to defend themselves actively when necessary. The generation of American Jews that came of age after 1967 combined the self-confidence born of economic prosperity with a new-found sense of pride and courage that emanated from Israel after 1967.

This sense of comfort and confidence ironically did not always result in a stronger sense of Jewishness. On the contrary, the mainstreaming of Judaism and Jews in American culture often reflected the extent to which American Jews opted for American over Jewish identity. Indicative in this respect is the rapid increase in the intermarriage rate after 1967. Beyond the quantitative increase in intermarriage, for Jews and non-Jews alike intermarriage seemed commonplace and unremarkable. To cite an example from the world of American popular culture: during the early 1970s, a short-lived television comedy series called *Bridget Loves Bernie* centered around an intermarried couple. Their intermarriage, though treated in comic style, was nonetheless the subject of tension and angst over questions such as "how will we raise the children?" A generation later, intermarried couples abound on television shows, often with no mention that they are intermarried.

In the end, the growing complexity of Israeli and American Jewish society has provided world Jewry with a tension between its two postwar demographic and cultural centers. As in generations past, this tension is at times a source of disagreement and conflict between Jewish constituencies, but more often than not a source of dynamism.

Conclusion: world Jewry faces the twenty-first century

The mass exodus of Jews from the lands of the recently defunct Soviet Union set the stage for world Jewry to face the twenty-first century. This migration of more than 1 million Jews, coupled with the capitalist tendencies of the State of Israel since the 1980s, underscored the decline of socialism as a leading Jewish political ideology. As the twentieth century ended, America and Israel were the only major centers of world Jewry. Indeed, although smaller numbers of Russian Jewish émigrés settled in Germany, Austria, and Hungary, the choice essentially came down to Israel or America.

That choice involved more than choosing a new address. As with previous migration movements, it reflected a larger decision between two fundamentally different situations, political strategies, and ranges of possibilities. The State of Israel embodied Jewish sovereignty – life as part of the ethnic and religious majority; the United States offered Jews the latest installment of living as an ethnic and religious minority.

In a sense, this was not a new decision for Jews, but echoed a centuries-old dichotomy in Jewish history between homeland and diaspora that dated back to the sixth century B.C.E. From the moment that the majority of Jews in ancient Babylonia opted to remain in the diaspora under foreign rule rather than returning to rebuild the Land of Israel, Jewish life in the diaspora became a viable option for many (and for long stretches of time, most) Jews in the world. At the beginning of the twenty-first century, this dichotomy is as much a part of Jewish life as it was more than two millennia ago.

The decision represented not simply a difference in address, but a decisive element in the formation and development of Jewish identity. Israeli identity is defined in terms of residence and citizenship in a Jewish state, and in living immersed in the only mainstream culture in the world that is Jewish culture. In America and elsewhere in the diaspora, Jewishness is often peculiarly defined officially in religious terms – peculiarly because only a minority of diaspora Jews are religiously observant. In fact, most diaspora Jews define themselves ethnically, not religiously.

The ongoing choice between homeland and diaspora, moreover, reflects a broader understanding of the Jewish past and its implication for the future of

world Jewry. For those who see the Jewish past as a lachrymose trail of persecution and adversity, the State of Israel represents liberation and redemption
from history. From this vantage point, the successes and failures of Jews in the
diaspora either reflected the inherently finite character of diaspora Jewish life
or were taken to be provisional measures to preserve the Jews until statehood,
sovereignty, and agency could be regained – rabbinic law and custom, and
Jewish communal organization.

For those who regard the heart of Jewish history as the history of the diaspora, the situation of Jews in the diaspora at the end of the twentieth century,
even in the aftermath of the Holocaust, marks the triumphant culmination
and resilience of centuries of diaspora life. From this point of view, life in the
diaspora was always possible – if not everywhere, then at least in many places.
More important, life in the diaspora made it possible and necessary for Jews
to refashion the limited institutional and territorial practices of ancient Israel
into a multifarious way of life: Judaism. Those who laud the centrality of the
diaspora note that the survival and coexistence of disparate forms of Judaism
at the end of the twentieth century in America and elsewhere in the diaspora
celebrate the vibrance that the diaspora experience has infused into Judaism
and Jewish life.

Each of these seemingly contradictory appraisals of contemporary world
Jewry has its merits and deficiencies. The important question is not which is
right or which is better, but how the tension between the two maintains a
certain dynamism within world Jewry. For millennia, Jewish life has benefited from the tension between competing Jewish groups and worldviews:
prophets and priests, Hellenizers and Hasideans, Pharisees and Sadducees,
Hillelites and Shammaites, exilarch and gaon, philosphers and mystics,
Hassidim and Mitnagdim, Reform and Orthodoxy, Zionists and assimilationists. The sum total of these tensions, as Gershom Scholem and other
historians have duly noted, was the dynamic tapestry of Jewish life that managed to adapt and even flourish in the diaspora and in a Jewish state. It took
hundreds of years for Rabbinic Judaism to become Judaism. During the past
two hundred years, Rabbinic Judaism has lost some ground in all directions:
to Reform Judaism, Orthodoxy, and Zionism.

Yet the notion of what is normatively Jewish still refers at least to some
aspects of Rabbinic Judaism as a point of departure, in Israel and in the diaspora. Despite the vast diversity in Jewish life that has taken shape, especially
but not exclusively during the past two hundred years, there is a pervading
unity and arguably some measure of uniformity that binds world Jewry
together. To date, a Jew who is familiar with the synagogue service can enter
any synagogue in the world and have some notion as to what is happening.
Even Jews who are not religiouly observant in any respect will generally be
greeted with some measure of kinship upon entering even the most remotely
located Jewish community.

There are, of course, limits to this sense of unity. Consider the contentious disagreement over whether or not the *Beta Yisrael*, the Jews of Ethiopia, could be accepted as Jews when they immigrated to Israel. Largely cut off from the authority and development of Rabbinic Judaism, the Jewishness of Ethiopian Jews, though they were bearers of a tradition that was as old as Rabbinic Judaism, was seen as problematic. In a sense, the Ethiopian dilemma was a more complex incarnation of the Brother Daniel case. The latter claimed that Jewishness could be defined in non-religious – that is, national – terms; Brother Daniel's request to be defined as Jewish was denied on the grounds that he belonged to another religious faith. The Ethiopian Jews, though, regarded themselves as part of the people of Israel, in religious and not only national or ethnic terms. Thus, the controversy over the identity of Ethiopian Jews reflected the centrality of Rabbinic Judaism in defining Jewishness, even at a time and in a place where most Jews regarded the practice of Judaism with indifference or outright disdain.

Equally problematic and more far-reaching, perhaps, is the recent divergence from a uniform definition of who is a Jew. I refer to the Reform Movement's redefinition of this standard according to patrilineal descent – that is, it defines as a Jew a child of a non-Jewish mother and a Jewish father. This decision immensely complicated what had been hitherto a largely unselfconscious definition of a Jew as the child of a Jewish mother or of one who had been properly converted.

More typical, even today, is the ability of Jewish individuals, families, or entire communities to transplant themselves to a radically new location and join the existing Jewish community. An interesting example in this regard is the recent immigration of Persian Jews from Iran to America, mainly to the Greater New York and Los Angeles areas. Persian Jews who arrived in America prior to 1979, meaning those who arrived willingly rather than fleeing from Islamic fundamentalism, were generally willing to acculturate themselves and their children. Though still firmly attached to their language and culture, these earlier Persian immigrants embraced much of American culture. Persian Jews who arrived after 1979 resisted Americanization beyond a certain point more vehemently. Regardless of when they arrived, though, many still maintain a powerful sense of ethnic, cultural insularity, exerting powerful social pressure to marry within the Persian Jewish community.

Despite the cultural separation that many Persian Jews strive to maintain, though, their sense of kinship with non-Persian Jews is far greater and qualitatively different than any sense of kinship with non-Jews. This is true even – or perhaps especially – with those from their own homeland. They regard Jews from Iran as Persian, and Muslims from Iran as Iranian. The arrival of Persian and Russian Jewish immigrants to America is but the latest example of world Jewry, transformed yet again through migration, finding new ways to exist as a minority in the diaspora.

Further reading

Historical atlases

Eli Barnavi, *A Historical Atlas of the Jewish People: From the Time of the Patriarchs to the Present* (Schocken Press: 2003)
Haim Beinart, *Atlas of Medieval Jewish History* (Abm Komers, 1992)
Evyatar Friesel, *Atlas of Modern Jewish History* (Oxford University Press, 1990)
Martin Gilbert, *The Routledge Atlas of Jewish History*, 8th ed. (Routledge, 2009)

Anthologies of primary sources

Robert Chazan (ed.), *Church, State, and Jew in the Middle Ages* (Behrman House, 1980)
William W. Hallo, David B. Ruderman, and Michael Stanislawski, *Heritage: Civilization and the Jews: Source Reader* (Praeger Publishers, 1984)
Paul Mendes-Flohr and Judah Reinharz, *The Jew in the Modern World*, 2nd ed. (Oxford University Press, 1995)
——, *The Jews in Arab Lands in Modern Times* (Jewish Publication Society, 1991)
Norman Stillman, *The Jews of Arab Lands: A History and Source Book*

General works

Judith Baskin (ed.), *Jewish Women in Historical Perspective*, 2nd ed. (Wayne State University Press, 1999)
——, *Power and Powerlessness in Jewish History* (Schocken, 1986)
David Biale (ed.), *Cultures of the Jews: A New History* (3 volumes, Schocken, 2002)
Gershon David Hundert (ed.), *The YIVO Encyclopedia of Jews in Eastern Europe* (2 volumes, Yale University Press, 2008)
Antony Polonsky, *The Jews in Poland and Russia* (3 volumes, Littman Library, 2009)
Moshe Rosman, *How Jewish is Jewish History?* (Littman Library, 2008)
Yosef Hayim Yerushalmi, *Zakhor: Jewish History and Jewish Memory* (University of Washington Press, 1996)

Essential papers on Jewish studies (New York University Press)

Individual volumes:

Michael Chernick, *The Talmud* (1994)

Jeremy Cohen (ed.) *Judaism and Christianity in Conflict* (1991)

Naomi Cohen, *Jewish–Christian Relations in the United States* (1991)

Lawrence Fine, *Kabbalah* (2000)

Frederick E. Greenspahn, *Israel and the Ancient Near East* (1991)

Gershon Hundert, *Hasidism* (1991)

Ezra Mendelsohn, *Jews and the Left* (1997)

Jehuda Reinharz and Anita Shapira, *Zionism* (1995)

David Ruderman, *Jewish Culture in Renaissance and Baroque Italy* (1992)

Marc Saperstein (ed.), *Messianic Movements and Personalities in Jewish History* (1992)

The ancient world

Shaye J. D. Cohen, *The Beginnings of Jewishness: Boundaries, Varieties, Uncertainties* (University of California Press, 1991)

David Weiss Halivni, *Revelation Restored: Divine Writ And Critical Responses* (Westview, 1998)

——, *Peshat and Derash: Plain and Applied Meaning in Rabbinic Exegesis* (Oxford University Press, 1998)

W. Lee Humphreys, *Crisis and Story: Introduction to the Old Testament* (McGraw-Hill, 1990)

Lee Levine, *The Ancient Synagogue: The First Thousand Years* (Yale University Press, 2005)

Alan Segal, *Rebecca's Children: Judaism and Christianity in the Roman World* (Harvard University Press, 1986)

Lawrence Shiffman, *From Text to Tradition: A History of Judaism in Second Temple and Rabbinic Times* (Ktav, 1991)

Islam and Medieval Christendom

Elisheva Baumgarten, *Mothers and Children: Jewish Family Life in Medieval Europe* (Princeton University Press, 2007)

Marc Cohen, *Under Crescent and Cross: The Jews in the Middle Ages* (Princeton University Press, 2008)

Kenneth Stow, *Alienated Minority: The Jews of Medieval Latin Europe* (Harvard University Press, 1998)

The early modern period

Dean Bell, *Jews in the Early Modern World* (Rowman & Littlefield, 2007)

Elisheva Carlebach, *The Pursuit of Heresy: Rabbi Moses Hagiz and the Sabbatian Controversies* (Columbia University Press, 1990)

J. H. Chajes, *Between Worlds: Dybbuks, Exorcists, and Early Modern Judaism* (University of Pennsylvania Press, 2003)

Jacob Katz, *Tradition and Crisis: Jewish Society at the End of the Middle Ages* (Syracuse University Press, 2000)

David Ruderman, *Jewish Thought and Scientific Discovery in Early Modern Europe* (Wayne State University Press, 2001)

Stefanie Siegmund, *The Medici State and the Ghetto of Florence: The Construction of an Early Modern Jewish Community* (Stanford University Press, 2005)

The modern period

Shlomo Avineri, *The Making of Modern Zionism: Intellectual Origins of the Jewish State* (Basic Books, 1981)

Israel Bartal, *The Jews of Eastern Europe, 1772-1881* (University of Pennsylvania Press, 2006)

Yehuda Bauer, *The Holocaust in Historical Perspective* (University of Washington Press, 1978)

Esther Benbassa and Aron Rodrigue, *Sephardi Jewry* (University of California, 2000)

Pierre Birnbaum and Ira Katznelson (eds.), *Paths of Emancipation: Jews, States, and Citizenship* (Princeton University Press, 1995)

David Cesarani and Gemma Romain (eds.), *Jews and Port Cities, 1590-1990: Commerce, Community and Cosmopolitanism* (Vallentine-Mitchell, 2006)

Deborah Dash Moore, *American Jewish Identity Politics* (University of Michigan, 2008)

Deborah Dash Moore and Paula Hyman (eds.), *Jewish Women in America: An Historical Encyclopedia* (Routledge, 1997)

István Deák, *Essays on Hitler's Europe* (University of Nebraska Press, 2001)

Hasia R. Diner, *The Jews of the United States, 1654-2000* (University of California Press, 2004)

Lois C. Dubin, *The Port Jews of Habsburg Trieste: Absolutist Politics and Enlightenment Culture* (Stanford University Press, 1999)

Glenn Dynner, *Men of Silk: The Hasidic Conquest of Polish Jewish Society* (Oxford University Press, 2006)

Arnold Eisen, *Rethinking Modern Judaism: Ritual, Commandment, Community* (University of Chicago Press, 1999)

David Ellenson, *After Emancipation: Jewish Religious Responses to Modernity* (Hebrew Union College Press, 2004)

Todd M. Endelman, *The Jews of Britain, 1655-2000* (University of California Press, 2002)

Shmuel Feiner and David Sorkin (eds.), *New Perspectives on the Haskalah* (Littman Library, 2004)

ChaeRan Freeze, *Jewish Marriage and Divorce in Imperial Russia* (Brandeis University Press, 2001)

Harvey E. Goldberg, *Jewish Life in Muslim Libya: Rivals and Relatives* (University of Chicago Press, 1990)

Jeffrey S. Gurock, *Orthodox Jews in America* (Indiana University Press, 2009)

Gershon Hundert, *Jews in Poland-Lithuania in the Eighteenth Century: A Genealogy of Modernity* (University of California Press, 2004)

——, *Gender and Assimilation in Modern Jewish History: The Roles and Representation of Women* (University of Washington Press, 1995)

Paula E. Hyman, *The Jews of Modern France* (University of California Press, 1998)

Jacob Katz, *A House Divided: Orthodoxy and Schism in Nineteenth-Century Central European Jewry* (Brandeis University Press, 2005)

Steven T. Katz (ed.), *The Shtetl: New Evaluations* (New York University Press, 2007)

Hillel Kieval, *Languages of Community: The Jewish Experience in the Czech Lands* (University of California Press, 2000)

Eli Lederhendler, *The Road to Modern Jewish Politics: Political Tradition and Political Reconstruction in the Jewish Community of Tsarist Russia* (Oxford University Press, 1989)

Michael R. Marrus, *The Holocaust in History* (Brandeis University Press, 1987)

——, *The Jews of East Central Europe between the Two World Wars* (Indiana University Press, 1987)

Ezra Mendelsohn, *On Modern Jewish Politics* (Oxford University Press, 1993)

——, *Jewish Identity in the Modern World* (University of Washington Press, 1991)

Michael Meyer, *Response to Modernity: A History of the Reform Movement in Judaism* (Wayne State University Press, 1995)

Benjamin Nathans, *Beyond the Pale: The Jewish Encounter with Late Imperial Russia* (University of California Press, 2002)

Aron Rodrigue, *Jews and Muslims: Images of Sephardi and Eastern Jewries in Modern Times* (University of Washington Press, 2003)

Marsha L. Rozenblit, *The Jews of Vienna, 1867-1914: Assimilation and Identity* (SUNY Press, 1984)

Jonathan Sarna, *American Judaism: A History* (Yale University Press, 2005)

Shaul Stampfer, *Families, Rabbis and Education: Essays on Traditional Jewish Society in Nineteenth-Century Eastern Europe* (Littman Library, 2009)

Michael Stanislawski, *Tsar Nicholas I and the Jews: The Transformation of Jewish Society in Russia, 1825-1855* (Jewish Publication Society of America, 1983)

Sarah Abrevaya Stein, *Making Jews Modern: The Yiddish and Ladino Press in the Russian and Ottoman Empires* (Indiana University Press, 2006)

Adam Sutcliffe, *Judaism and Enlightenment* (Cambridge University Press, 2005)

Daniel Tsadik, *Between Foreigners and Shi'is: Nineteenth-Century Iran and Its Jewish Minority* (Stanford University Press, 2007)

Ruth R. Wisse, *I. L. Peretz and the Making of Modern Jewish Culture* (University of Washington Press, 1990)

Index